T0369523

Angela Thompson

Blackout

A Woman's Struggle for Survival in Twentieth Century Germany

iUniverse, Inc.
Bloomington

Blackout: A Woman's Struggle for Survival in Twentieth Century Germany

Translated from the German by Angela Thompson

Revised 2nd Edition

Author web address: www.angela-thompson.com

Previously published in Germany as:
Bleib immer neben mir – Ein deutsches Frauenleben By Angela Thompson

Photos on front cover and all photos inside book owned by Angela Thompson
Photo of author: Bruce Bisenz

iUniverse books may be ordered through booksellers or by contacting:

iUniverse
1663 Liberty Drive
Bloomington, IN 47403
www.iuniverse.com
1-800-Authors (1-800-288-4677)

ISBN: 978-1-4697-4652-4 (sc)
ISBN: 978-1-4697-4653-1 (e)
ISBN: 978-1-4697-4654-8 (dj)

Printed in the United States of America

iUniverse rev. date: 4/10/2012

Contents

List of Illustrations

List of Illustrations

Search for Truth

It is not the truth that we possess, or believe to have, but the earnest effort we make to reach the truth that constitutes our worth. For it is not the possession, but the pursuit of truth that enlarges our power, wherein alone lies our ever-increasing perfection. Possession makes us tranquil, lazy, and proud.

If God were to hold all truth concealed in his right hand, and in his left only the promise of a never-ending diligent drive for truth, albeit with the proviso that we would forever err in the process, and say to me: "Choose!" I would in all humility take the left hand and say: "Father, give! The pure truth is after all for you alone!"

Gotthold Ephraim Lessing from: *Eine Duplik*, 1778
Translation by Angela Thompson

Acknowledgement

I would like to thank my son Alexander for his technical support and encouragement over the many years it took me to write this book, for his patient advice, as well as his editorial skills, both in German and English.

My sincere thanks go to the German-American sculptor, Manfred Müller, whose studios are in Düsseldorf and Santa Monica, for his genuine interest, his inspiration and continued motivation while I was working on this project.

And finally my gratitude goes out to all my German readers and American friends who have never tired to ask me for an English edition so the story can find a worldwide readership.

For Elfriede Hildegard,
Martha Magdalena,
Alexander, Andreas and Kevin Michael

Preface

For as long as I can remember, my mother talked to me about the way she grew up in Germany, relating the earthshaking political events she witnessed, and describing how they affected her very private life. She was born in Dresden because her mother, my grandmother, had run away from home after WW I to escape the exhausting physical work on my great-grandfather Valentin's farm in Upper Silesia. Both women instilled in me their deep love for the city of Dresden that is still with me today.

Particularly prominent in my mother's stories were her descriptions of how her beloved father experienced the rise of Hitler, his warnings to family members and friends of an impending disaster, and her annual summer trips to her grandfather's farm near Zülkowitz in Upper Silesia. She also spoke of how she came to embark on her last journey to Königsberg in East Prussia, the city of the philosopher Immanuel Kant, in the late fall of 1944 to visit her husband, who was stationed there with the Regiment Großdeutschland, that had been set up in 1938, and later became the Division Großdeutschland, a special teaching and fire-fighting unit.

My mother was a passionate woman and very good at storytelling. She would frequently gather us around her in the living room on a Saturday or Sunday evening. When I was small, I listened spellbound, but as I grew up and began collecting my own memories of the bombing of Dresden in February 1945, the ensuing downfall of Germany, and our flight from the approaching Soviet army, I was no longer willing to listen to her obediently and faithfully, which upset her greatly. Today I understand that talking about those horrific events was the only therapy available to her. Her husband also survived the war. He was lucky, because his commanding officer made the decision to defy Hitler's orders, and marched their unit west instead of continuing to fight the Soviet army. Somewhere west of Berlin they became American prisoners of war, and were released by the middle of July 1945.

By 1948, my parents realized that life in communist-controlled East Germany, where we felt imprisoned, wasn't much better than life had been under Hitler, and so we gathered all of our courage and fled to West Germany in the fall of 1951. It was a rough new beginning for us. We were poorer than ever before. Freedom on an empty stomach was suddenly much less appealing. Even so, undaunted by political events and economic problems, my mother continued telling her stories of past hardships, above all the destruction of Dresden, with renewed zeal. Our new life, however, was not only overshadowed by the past and the difficulties of adjusting to life in West Germany, but much more so by her husband's extremely irrational and violent behavior, especially toward her.

After moving to Los Angeles, California in 1968, where I attended university, I soon realized that my new American friends, the other students, and even my professors knew little or nothing of daily life in a divided Germany. I continued to hear my mother's voice speak about her life, and after reading Kurt Vonnegut's version of the bombing of Dresden in his book *Slaughterhouse-Five or The Children's Crusade,* I began to write down her stories and researched the great historical and political events that had led to the division of Europe and Germany, and to the Cold War. When my mother died in 1999, the time had come for me to write about her life in earnest, which stands as an example of the lives of millions of German women of her generation.

At first I thought it would be easy; after all, hadn't I memorized everything? I was convinced that all I had to do was sit down at the computer and start typing. Originally I decided to write the book in English because I thought we already had enough such accounts available in Germany. As I quickly discovered, however, I wasn't able to readily put my mother's vivid narratives on paper with all of those colorful German adjectives, nouns, verbs, and idioms she used, for which I couldn't always easily find an English equivalent. As a result I changed my plans, and started writing in German, hoping to translate everything once I was done. As I progressed, I realized that I had failed to consider many other difficulties inherent in such a huge project. I couldn't simply write down all the stories I had heard repeatedly all of my life, but had to do elaborate research first to find out what had really happened so my mother's accounts would make sense to the reader. Since I could no longer ask my mother for clarification, I not only felt compelled to read countless history books, but also took endless notes, and sometimes I came close to despair over the sheer dimension of the task. I also researched the years from the end of WW I to the mid sixties in the Bundesarchiv (Federal Archive) in Koblenz and the Stadtarchiv (City Archive) in Dresden, and spent hours hunched over maps of Germany, Central and Eastern Europe, and the city of Dresden that I had spread out on my grand piano.

The book is written from the points of view of two women, a mother and her eldest daughter. For easier reading, and so the flow isn't interrupted, I inserted a blank line and began the next paragraph flush left whenever there is a change of narrator.

It took me five years to write the book in German, and three more to translate it into American English after its German publication. It is my sincere hope that reading about this dark chapter in history will have an impact on the readers and contribute to their ability to understand those harsh years a little better. With this book I would also like to thank my American friends, because writing it for them helped me ultimately to better understand my own background and European history.

Angela Thompson, Ph.D.
Los Angeles, January 2012

Prolog
The Hidden Crabs

I am flying to Germany to visit my mother for the sixth time since I've known she has cancer. After the diagnosis twenty months ago, she visited us once more in California. Between visits I made countless telephone calls, wrote her letters and talked with my sons, relatives and friends about her illness and impending death, but I could never have imagined how difficult these last few months would be, and how hard she would fight for her life.

This visit will be my last one, and I wonder if she knows it too. When I left in April 1999 I had promised her that I would return soon. In the meantime, my son Alexander, her first grandson, was with her. It had become increasingly difficult for her to hold the telephone receiver close enough to her ear. Alexander helped her, but even then it didn't go well. She wanted to know when I would come back.

"Soon," I said, "I'll come as soon as I can."

"That is good. I need you now," she whispered.

She spoke slowly. At this late stage of her illness it was hard for her to pronounce so many words distinctly, but her voice sounded as it always did, clear and very young, and not a bit broken, though a little disheartened. Judging from the sound of her voice she ought to get well again, and for a moment it was tempting to give in to this deception and imagine that she wasn't that sick after all.

After we said good-bye, I was plagued by a slight dizziness, and I held on to the kitchen counter. I must pull myself together and remain calm, I told myself, and took a deep breath.

The following evening Alexander called unexpectedly. "The time has come," was all he said.

"Time for what?" I asked, although I sensed what he was trying to tell me. My heart began to race.

"Well, Omi won't get up anymore."

"She won't get up anymore? What are you saying? Not even to go to the bathroom?"

"No. Last night she said that it was enough. Can you come?"

I didn't need to think about it. "Of course I'll come. I'll call my travel agent first thing tomorrow morning and book a flight." Never before had I made up my mind so quickly to fly to Frankfurt.

I was haunted by a desire to know more about my mother, but my image of her remained incomplete in spite of all my efforts to understand her better. No matter how hard I tried, I couldn't uncover the secret of who she really was and why she gave up so early in life. My perception of her changed during my search, but it did not become any clearer. There are things she locked away so deeply inside of her that they remained forever beyond my reach, even though I knew so much about her. Then again I wondered if I wasn't complicating things too much or whether I was simply looking in all the wrong places. Perhaps everything is right out in the open, only I cannot see it?

And suddenly I realized that the death of this woman coincided with the end of the 20th century, through which she lived for nearly eighty years. I pondered this thought, the juxtaposition of the century and this woman, and wondered what they had given each other? After countless struggles it reluctantly brought women the right to vote, the right to attend university, own land and open a bank account in their own name. Daily housework and cooking became easier with various innovative gadgets. And yet, in spite of these achievements, I felt compelled to ask, what did this century withhold from women? Women were finally allowed to work in factories and offices, performing endless, mindless, repetitive tasks, but they continued to be excluded from attending university in greater numbers. They were rarely given access to the fields of medicine, physics, chemistry, mathematics, architecture, economics and law. And I wondered how my mother dealt with National Socialism and fascism, which not only radically changed everyone's political and economic life, but also interfered in every aspect of peoples' private lives?

It was then that I understood that this past century had made life hard for her. There were few rays of hope, meager successes in the shadow of men, no fulfillment of deep longings, nothing to show for the endless drudgery, hardly ever a little rest and even less peace. Nevertheless I wanted to know what prevented her from enduring and asserting herself and maintaining her joy of living. I wanted to meet this woman who lived in the 20th century, and as I thought about her, I realized that for her the 20th century was no more a good century than any of the preceding ones had been for the women that came before her. In her roles as wife, housewife, mother and daughter, she had to fight her way through her century – the last one of the second millennium after the birth of Christ.

She was ill equipped for the battle. The tools and weapons of the men of her generation were not at her disposal. She was aware of them and without a doubt would have known how to use them well in spite of her mere eight years of public school education, because she could apply her mind better and with greater agility than many of her male contemporaries, even those with graduate degrees. Why then did she shy away from using these more suitable and efficient male tools, which would have required less energy and would have allowed her to work faster and become more independent in her journey through life? Was it because she lacked women as role models who could have encouraged her to reach out for what she needed and what should have rightfully been hers, or did she fear to incense men through her independent actions to the point that they might revenge themselves by depriving her of their love and support? Did she hope instead that if she stayed within her prescribed boundaries that men would behave decently and respectfully and give her her fair share? She knew that they led more powerful, interesting, successful and, as far as appearances went, more responsible public lives. She talked about it and often mentioned the injustice of it all.

To be made dependent because she belonged to the so-called weaker sex, but not be protected by the stronger one, that was a woman's lot. No one paid attention to the warping and mutilation of the strong female psyche that resulted from such unfair treatment, although it was just as eager and capable of accomplishing heroic deeds as was the overbearing male psyche, which had become hard and spoiled by centuries of success.

And so women fought an unfair fight. Their tools were made for little tasks, and therefore achieved little. My mother was more likely to injure herself than complete her task with the small, dull kitchen knives or the awkward can opener that required every bit of her strength to cut the lids out of thick cans, or the small hammer, with which she couldn't even pound a nail straight into the brick wall, or a weak pair of pliers with short handles that didn't allow her a tight grip, so objects would often slip away. Her hands grew weary, and eventually she went to her husband saying, "here, you do it," and then he brought out his larger tools and had it done in a flash.

She struggled with the tiny seam ripper that was her constant sewing companion through decades of permanent shortages during the depression and after World War II, because it had a mere three and a quarter inch long round wooden handle that was no thicker than a pencil, and therefore difficult to hold. Work progressed slowly, her hands became sweaty, cramped and ached, and were constantly red and swollen from having to keep a tight grip as she almost broke her fingers while ripping apart the seams of stiff, heavy coats and jackets to create new articles of clothing for us. Sometimes the ripper would slip and prick her causing a drop of blood to run from her fingertip onto the material, and if its color was light she would have to get up immediately to wash out the blood with cold water.

Such flimsy utensils were hardly fit to clear even the most narrow path through the thicket of centuries of old undergrowth surrounding women like the hedge that had grown around Sleeping Beauty's castle, and kept them from stepping out into the open, where the air is easier to breath, eyes could see farther, and arms could be stretched out wider to make work more effortless and inspire the mind! She could have made it, considering her numerous talents and intellectual abilities, her great courage, happy nature, radiant beauty, and the immense amount of work she accomplished as a matter of course every single day. Hardly a man ever worked harder.

Now that my mother had arrived at the end of her life, I felt an urgency to rethink things and include her illness and death in the plans for my life because I realized that time was rapidly running out, and the two of us were not yet done with each other. There was still so much to talk about and work through. Countless questions I've always hesitated to ask were still waiting for answers. She couldn't simply go away, not just yet anyway. I wanted to hear her speak once more of her childhood, about the long summers in Upper Silesia at her grandfather's farm, her life in Dresden and the many evenings at the theater and opera, and how they drank a glass of wine in the Italienische Dörfchen afterward, a restaurant that got its name from the Italian bricklayers and artisans who had come to Dresden to help build the Frauenkirche from 1727 to 1743. I wanted to hear the stories of the zoological garden one last time, where she had spent so many afternoons as a young girl because her father was the head cashier, employed by the city as she had always stressed. His workplace was safe, which was incredibly fortunate during the inflation of the 1920s when millions were out of work. I wanted her to talk once more about how she met her husband during the family gathering of her confirmation, how they got to know each other and stayed together, although they were not well suited to each other, as she frequently pointed out and I often witnessed. And, for one last time, I longed to hear about my parents' wedding on the 20th of April 1940 in the Sophienkirche in Dresden. This time I would be prepared to listen without interrupting her. I also wanted to know how she experienced the beginnings of National Socialism and the war years. I must hear her talk once more about the firebombing of her city on the 13th, 14th and 15th of February 1945, and ask her about our flight from the Soviet army a few months later. And then there was this sudden need to speak with her about our life after the war, first in the Soviet-occupied Zone and then in a small town on the Mosel river after our escape to West Germany. For the first time I was determined to really pay attention to the stories she had offered so willingly over the past five decades, the stories I couldn't bear to hear anymore as I was growing up, and therefore would often get up and walk away. At last I was ready to sit still and embark with her once more into the past, now that she was leaving.

Did she have to become sick unto death before I finally understood that all this concerned me too? No, it wasn't quite that simple. I just needed a long time to absorb her stories and come to grips with them, because the events went far beyond Dresden, and the guilt that had come over Germany weighed heavily on me. When I was young I blamed my parents for having allowed things to just happen until the war was upon us. In those early days I had to deal with it all on my own, and it took years before I was able to talk about it, because as a child I lacked the words, while horrible pictures of death and destruction pursued me in my day dreams and haunted me at night, whose true meaning escaped me for a long time.

While pacing distractedly through my house, gathering up my things for my last visit with her, I suddenly knew that I would have to tell my mother's story. I would write about the unique life of this woman the way she had described it to me, and the way I had witnessed parts of it.

Then came the call from Yvonne at the travel agency. I'd be leaving in two days.

That evening I followed a sudden impulse and drove the five miles to my favorite place on the beach so I could calm down. It was seven-thirty when I backed my car out of the garage. The sun was still high in the sky, but I knew it would be setting very soon.

I walked along the shore, stopping now and then, lost in thought. The waves rolled in forcefully up the sandy beach during high tide before breaking in wide foaming half circles, while the water disappeared quickly into the sand. I took off my shoes, held one in each hand and felt the cool and very fine sand beneath my feet. As the water rushed back out, pulled by an eternal force, thousands of tiny air bubbles came up, bursting immediately as they reached the surface, and left as many tiny holes for a few seconds, surrounded by barely visible rings, no larger than a fingertip. If I were to dig into these circles, I would find the tiniest sand crabs beneath them. Every now and then I ran up the shore to escape an especially large wave. Swarms of sandpipers fled from every incoming wave as if running for their lives, lifting a few inches into the air when one rolled in faster and higher, threatening to overtake them, only to set down again moments later as the water receded to continue their tireless search for food. As one particularly high wave forcefully churned up the sand, I lifted my eyes and looked west, far over the dark evening water to the point where the curvature of the earth held my eyes.

In the twilight, the black gray of the water and the distant, slightly lighter blue-gray of the sky merged so effortlessly that I had to look long and hard for the line where sea and sky meet at the distant horizon. Toward the west it was still deceptively light as I walked quickly into the sunset to reach the end of the breakers that extend far out into the water on both sides of the mouth of the harbor to watch the sun disappear behind the rugged mountain tops that form the wide semi-circle of the Santa Monica Bay. I kept my eyes on the setting sun, which had turned into a large glowing ball. It was a race into the yellow-orange evening light. The outer rim of the sun glowed almost purple. Along the beach the sunlight reflected off the huge windows of the houses of Venice and Marina del Rey, glistening like silver.

Behind me toward the east everything was already immersed in a deep blue gray. The color reminded me of the slate of the mountains along the Mosel river valley that had been spread in small cube-like stones between the grapevines to retain the warmth of the sun through the night. The slate was also used for the supporting dry walls in the vineyards, transforming the steep hills into countless terraces, where on the smallest ones only five or six vines grew, neatly tied to wooden poles. The century-old houses and churches were all built entirely of slate, including the roofs. In my mind I was already on my way to Germany.

By then, the distant mountains around Los Angeles, the shore, the ocean and the high sky were hardly distinguishable anymore. Only directly above me drifted a few clouds that the sun had colored bright pink to medium purple. The contrast between the light from the evening sun in the west and darkness toward the east couldn't have been greater in this vast coast and seascape as it presented itself in ever new and exciting ways.

At last I reached my destination. I had won the race against the setting sun, and breathed easier. A few sea gulls followed me idly, others overtook me in a sudden burst of energy, flying quickly ahead toward the open sea, only to glide back in a wide, sleepy circles moments later, landing on one of the huge rocks. Lonely anglers stood or sat motionless on either side of the breaker, staring silently at the spots where their fishing lines disappeared into the dark, clear water.

I was all alone out here as I sat on a rock facing west. It was calm and peaceful. The last few sail- and motorboats were returning, surrounded by screaming seagulls catching the scraps of fish in midair that were thrown overboard by the fishermen. Hardly a sound from the metropolis reached me. The sun was dangerously low in the western sky, oversized and round, approaching the mountains. My eyes wanted to stop the sun in its course, but at that very moment it touched the highest of the wild, jagged peaks, disappearing behind it with incredible speed, a brief nightly spectacle that never fails to captivate me.

During these moments when day turned into night, I was always overcome by a slight melancholy. I wanted to stay in the light, but I couldn't alter the course of nature. Suddenly, I understood that in her fight against her illness, my mother had reached that state where she just simply slipped away, and not even the most ardent desire to hold her back could change her fate.

There is no twilight in Southern California; night descends fast over the city. The most brilliant stars become visible almost immediately, and the light escaping from the large windows of the houses around the bay shines more brightly. My thoughts overwhelmed me, and, unsure of what to do, I stayed a little longer. On that particular evening it was harder to let go of the day because it reminded me of the fact that my mother would leave me soon. She had been out here with me many times. I couldn't imagine having to say good-bye to her. I couldn't imagine what life would be like without her.

"Things are getting serious," she would often say when something with an uncertain outcome was imminent. It could be something wonderful and ardently longed for. A certain irony was in her voice on such occasions, and she smiled mischievously as her eyes sparkled with anticipation.

Suddenly the heavy thunder of a Boeing 747 shattered my thoughts during its steep ascent over the ocean as it took off from LAX just to the south and began its non-stop flight to Europe or Asia. Out here the airplanes were already quite high, and I couldn't make out the logo on its tail in the dark light.

Finally I got up and walked back. My eyes took in the city, then I looked at the sky above me, where, toward the east, the last rays of the sun were still glowing on the edges of the few clouds, and I watched as one cloud after the other lost its brightness, sinking into the night. I took the shorter way along the street back to my car and turned on the radio. Beethoven's 5th piano concerto had just begun.

The following afternoon on the airplane I thought of my mother and slowly began to understand that it was unkind not to have tried to resolve the estrangement between us in years past. I was barely aware of the people around me as I drank a glass of red wine and carbonated mineral water while I embarked on a trip that took me back to the important places of my life. My family had been torn apart by two opposing political systems and the Iron Curtain, and not only lived in two German states until the fall of the Berlin wall, but also on two continents, and I asked myself why things had to turn out so badly for us.

When I arrived in Koblenz, situated in the loveliest countryside where the Mosel river flows into the Rhein, I walked the few steps from the apartment door through the entry area and dining room into the living room where my mother was lying on a high hospital bed that dominated the room. She'd been on this sickbed for weeks already, which was accessible from all sides and would become her deathbed. How horrible, I remember thinking. I kissed her while I slightly touched her cheeks and stroked her hands.

Her eyes smiled quietly as she whispered almost inaudibly, "You are here already?"

Everything seemed strange in the apartment that I had known for decades. I looked around, embarrassed by how she lay there helpless and pathetic in the middle of the room. There was no sheltering wall next to her toward which she could turn, and nothing in front of the bed to protect her from the views of strangers at the door. Defenselessly, she was exposed to everyone, and there was nothing she could do about it. It hurt to see her like that. Her dying took place right before our eyes in a repulsively public way. Her bedroom, where she retreated when she could no longer stand it anywhere else, felt empty, and I entered it only occasionally to get something for her. As time passed, she asked less and less frequently for any of her personal things.

Her husband and my sister Bettine were present as I greeted my mother. Alexander carried my luggage into the house. I didn't embrace her enough, and I didn't say all the loving words I had prepared during the long flight. I couldn't say them in front of these witnesses, and told myself that I'd go back to her when the others have left. We were not accustomed to showing our feelings when family members were present.

I said to my mother, "I'll freshen up quickly and come right back."

She nodded. "Yes, go freshen up, I'll wait for you."

As I walked up the steps toward the bathroom I knew that I was on my own, that I would have to find the way to her without her help. We wouldn't be able to talk much with each other anymore. I'd waited too long and missed the last opportunity to speak with her and ask her important questions, because I must have thought that life goes on forever.

When I came back I pulled up a chair and sat down next to her. Dying so hard is unnatural. Didn't she deserve an easier, kinder, more humane death after all of the endless hardships and lifelong disappointments, after the lack of love and consolation? Besides, wasn't death supposed to mark the natural end of our lives, coming to us swiftly in our sleep? Was life worth so little that death could come in such an insidiously cruel and underhanded way, and so mercilessly slowly? Life cannot be meant to end this way, neither by humans nor any higher being. Her dying was not the fulfillment of her existence on earth; it held no salvation for her. It was nothing but suffering and torment for body and soul. This illness took away her dignity. Forsaken and defenseless, her naked, sick body covered only by a white sheet, we became witnesses to a terrible battle as her life slipped away while she was unable to die. In my horror and disappointment over such betrayal, I wanted to scream and hurl these accusations at someone, demanding something better, but there was no one. People entered the room and left again, they looked at her, sat on chairs next to her, bent over her, searched for signs that might tell them what to do, but there was nothing anyone could do, there was no help for her anymore, and no hope.

Her body was being consumed from within, and she had to let it happen, and we had to watch as her heart continued to beat, strong and steadfast.

I felt ill as I watched her suffering and how she stopped being human. In an attempt to find some sense in this physical and mental destruction before death, I wondered whether her wasting away didn't signify more than just the end of her life, but that it was a mirror of our society? Quietly I sat next to her for a long time.

At last I said, "Mutti, I love you," and stroked her right hand while looking into her blue eyes.

She returned the gaze. Then she lifted her hand slowly, stroked my left hand and forearm, saying, "I love you, too, Anne."

She was so weak that her hand sank back onto the mattress almost immediately, but her eyes continued to look at me lovingly. Her face seemed like a mask. There was no movement, no visible expression, only her eyes were still alive.

Then she turned her head ever so slightly away from me that I sensed it more than I actually saw it. Her eyes seemed to look into the distance, beyond the walls of the room. I tried to follow her glance, but all I saw was the wall about three feet from her, and I understood that I couldn't follow her where she had gone.

I was still aware of the touch of her hand. Why haven't we shown each other such small signs of love more often? How had it become so hard one day long ago to touch each other? When did we stop and why?

All of a sudden her right hand twitched and moved restlessly over her sheet, like a seismograph needle. The day was hot. The afternoon sun shone against the west side of the building and heated up the apartment. There wasn't the slightest breeze although the balcony door and the window stood wide open. While I was wondering how I could help her cool off, her hand flew up as if to ward something off. I reached for it and held it lightly in my hand, then I put it slowly back on the sheet, but I did not let go of it.

"Fire," she whispered hoarsely, "fire!"

"Mutti, there is no fire, what are you saying? Is it too hot for you?"

"But it's burning all around us."

"Where do you see fire, Mutti?"

"Everywhere, can't you see it?"

I stroked her face. "Don't be afraid, Mutti, there is no fire."

"Go get some ice cubes in a damp facecloth," I said to her husband who was entering the room at that moment. "For her forehead and temples, to cool her off."

"But the fire, the house, can't you see?" she insisted, and once more her hands twitched, lifting a few inches into the air.

Suddenly I realized what she was seeing. "Mutti, calm down, please, there is no fire. I am with you." My words didn't convince her, and her body seemed to quake.

"Mutti," I whispered as I placed the cooling facecloth tenderly on her forehead and temples. "It's all right. The fire, that was long ago. Everything turned out well in the end. Life was good again, Mutti, wasn't life good again, after the fire?"

"Oh, Anne," was all she said as she lay there completely motionless. The nightmare was over, and disappointment resonated in her voice.

She was thinking of Dresden, even after all these years. My mouth was dry. I looked away because I didn't want her to see my wet eyes.

"Everything is all right," I repeated, "we are all here with you."

"Yes," she said, but this yes did not sound very happy, and I thought, nothing is all right, nothing at all.

I wanted to tell her we had survived, that she had led us out of the flames. But she was dying now, and perhaps she was asking herself why she had survived and whether it had been worth it. I felt so unsure. Should I talk to her about Dresden?

"You rescued us from the flames," I heard myself say before I had decided what to do. "Without you we would all have burned to death."

She said nothing.

"And now we are here with you."

"Yes," she said softly. That was all.

Her eyes wandered into the distance again. They were large and blue. Never before had I seen her eyes so large and blue. Her skin was stretched tightly over her nose and cheekbones. It appeared transparent. Her white hair framed her face in soft waves. The only jewelry she still wore were her diamond earrings. She took long calm breaths. Her heart beat unperturbed in a regular rhythm.

What was it like back then, I asked myself, and heard her voice as she was talking about that one night, again and again, throughout her entire life, always about that one night.

1. A Wedding in the Baroque City

My mother loved to talk about her wedding. There was always a joyous excitement in her voice, as if the past became the present once again. At times it even seemed as though the wedding festivities still lay ahead, and she could change the future by virtue of the power of her words and start all over again, and forget all the terrible experiences that followed.

It all began with a telegram from France that came on a Monday morning, my mother began her story. At first I was terribly frightened because in those days a telegram hardly ever brought good news. The envelope was addressed to Elfriede Richter, and I tore it open hastily and read the words again and again: "Arrival Thursday. Wedding Saturday. Kurt."

The sheet of paper trembled in my hands as the words danced before my eyes. I only understood little by little what I was reading. In a dreamlike state I walked into the kitchen and took the calendar off the wall. It was the 15th of April 1940. Kurt would arrive on Thursday the 18th and our wedding would be on Saturday the 20th. My legs felt weak, I sank onto a kitchen chair and put the telegram down on the table in front of me.

That only gives me five days to sew my bridal gown and prepare for the wedding, I thought, that's impossible, that's not nearly enough time! My heart began to pound hard, but suddenly great joy came over me, and I calmed down. It was war and the telegram sounded so romantic. Besides, I wouldn't be able to reach Kurt anyway to tell him that Saturday was too early, so there was nothing else to do but begin with the preparations immediately. After all, we had spoken about the wedding often enough. I put the telegram aside, which later burned with everything we owned, and looked at the kitchen clock. It was around ten, time enough to run over to the palace to order the Saxon court carriage with the two golden lions, one on each side, and the golden crown on top and four horses that would pull it. This carriage, the most beautiful and elegant of the three Saxon court carriages, was draped inside in gold colored silk, and I had wanted it for my wedding as long as I could remember. The caretaker had promised Papa before the war that I would get it. Unfortunately he could only offer me the second best carriage, which was padded with pink silk inside, because the other one had been reserved for that day already months ago, and he could give me only two horses instead of four, the way it should have been. "We are at war, Fräulein Richter," he whispered, when he noticed my disappointment. "The carriage and two horses is all we can do. What a pity that your father is no longer with us to celebrate the day with you!"

I had taken enough money along and paid for everything right away so no one else would be able to snatch the carriage away. Then I ran to the photographer to arrange the time for our formal wedding pictures. After that I hurried to the pastor to discuss the ceremony in the Sophienkirche at one o'clock in the afternoon. I was already on my way home when I remembered that I had forgotten to give notice of our intent to get married. I rushed home, grabbed the documents and records and hastened to the town hall where I arrived just in time before closing. For war marriages, the bride and groom were not required to give notice an entire week ahead of time, as was customary. I had already completed the genealogical research required under Hitler to prove our Aryan decent. In Silesia, I was able to trace our family back to the middle of the 17th century. That's how long Grandfather's farm had been in our possession. It had taken me over a year to gather all the information, it was actually much more than I needed, but because it was so interesting and the church registries were at my disposal, and because I was finding more and more records and details, I had simply continued with my research and copied everything. Those documents also burned with everything else. I'll never be able to duplicate them.

When I finally entered our street, the Fürstenstraße, late that afternoon, I was relieved that I had been able to take care of everything in one day. I had neither eaten nor had anything to drink all day. With just one cup of coffee and a slice of pound cake for breakfast I had run off, and suddenly I felt sick from hunger. Omi was waiting for me. She was irritated because I wasn't home when she came back from the factory and supper wasn't ready.

Because we children called my mother's mother "Omi", my mother called her "Omi", too.

"I'll get supper ready right away. Come along into the kitchen with me," I said, and showed her the telegram. She was neither thrilled by the thought of the wedding nor that everything would have to be ready at such short notice, but then she took two days off to help with the cooking and baking. I had put together the guest list months ago, and Omi addressed the invitations after supper so they could go out the following morning.

The patterns for the wedding dress and the dark blue lace overcoat for the evening I had bought months ago when Kurt had sent the lace from France. I spread the lace out on the kitchen table, pinned on the pattern and cut it out. The next morning I awoke before daybreak from all the excitement and began to sew my wedding dress by the light of the kitchen lamp. I completed it just before midnight. The following day, I finished the last stitches by hand, made the loops for the buttons all the way down the back to the waist, and then I took enough lace to Herr Zeisig, so he could cover the buttons for me in his workshop. Next, I sewed an elegant light overcoat of delicate royal blue lace so I would be able to wear the dress to the opera. The coat was done faster, it was only held together at the waist with a long lace band. I steamed and pressed both garments and hung them up. The coat I wore over the wedding dress in the evening, after the big wedding feast, and then once more to the opera and a third time for your christening, Anne. Both the wedding dress and the blue coat burned during the night of February 13th.

After I had finished the sewing, I could concentrate on the preparation for the wedding. Kurt arrived on Thursday, shortly after noon. He brought two cases of Bordeaux, several pounds of cheese and his dirty laundry, which had to be washed in the midst of all the hectic preparations, and all of a sudden he sat down on a chair in the middle of the kitchen and began to shine his shoes. He was always in our way. Unnerved, Omi told him to go out on the balcony, and later I sent him with his uniform to Herr Oppau, Papa's tailor, who brushed and steamed it for the wedding.

Most of the guests came for the traditional party on the eve of the wedding, and Omi cooked and fried tirelessly for us all. She and Lieselotte, my brother Rolf's fiancée, washed and dried the dishes until long after midnight, cleaned the kitchen and set the table for breakfast in the dining room before they also went to bed.

A few hours later the festivities resumed. Everyone arrived on time for a generous breakfast, consisting of two eggs each, fried sunny side up, ham, bread and butter as well as big platters piled high with cake and large pots of coffee.

While the guests were eating, the hairdresser came. She also helped me with the wedding dress and fastened the veil in my hair. Suddenly things moved very quickly. Lieselotte and Rolf, who were standing on the balcony, announced the arrival of the coach, and when Kurt and I walked toward it arm in arm from the front door across the wide sidewalk, Aunt Gertrud's two little girls held the long veil. I asked Kurt who would be taking the wedding pictures, because I wanted photos of us and the royal carriage in front of our house. He had promised me that he would take photos and that I should not engage a photographer. To my horror he said, "You can't be serious, Effi, and expect me to take photos at the wedding! Who gave you that idea?"

I thought I hadn't hear right, and reminded him that he had suggested it to save the money for the photographer. "Why didn't you say anything last night, Kurt, when I gave you the rolls of film? I could have asked Rolf to take pictures." I felt sick at the thought of not having any photos of the wedding and the church ceremony.

"I took it for granted that someone else would take photos at my wedding," Kurt replied tersely. His voice sounded strangely cold.

"At *your* wedding?" I asked. "When did you change your mind? And where is your camera anyway?" I wanted to know, because I suddenly realized that I hadn't seen it.

"I did not bring it," he said.

I was quiet when I heard that because I didn't want to start a fight, but I felt like running back into the house and canceling the wedding. Omi and I had labored for days to have everything as perfect as possible, and now there would be no photos of us and the carriage, none of the celebration at home, no pictures of the beautifully set dinner table with my Meißen porcelain, there would be no pictures of the cakes, the lovely flowers and our wedding guests!

Two pages in livery were waiting. They opened the carriage door for us and we climbed in. One of them helped the two little girls with my veil. The people in the street stopped in surprise and marveled at us. On the 20th of April, the Fürstenstraße was a sea of flags, the entire city was decorated with garlands, flags were flying from all public buildings, apartment houses and flagpoles, and even the city palace of the former kings of Saxony looked festive.

When my mother told us how they rode in a horse drawn carriage through the decorated old town of Dresden, she always laughed happily, like a young girl. Her voice sounded warm and high-spirited, and she enjoyed it greatly when our eyes grew wide with surprise. Why were there flags all over town, I always wondered, but I never dared to ask her, because I didn't want to appear completely stupid. It took years before it dawned on me that the city had been decorated in celebration of Hitler's birthday on the 20th of April. After the church ceremony, my parents drove to the photographer, who took the only wedding photos of them. These photographs also burned during the bombings. Everything burned. Later, relatives gave us the few pictures we have today.

"Everything burned." These words sounded like an ill-fated formula in my mother's life. Nothing ever gained such importance again as the things that burned in Dresden during that night and shattered her life.

As a child I couldn't imagine my parents' wedding because I only knew postwar misery, but the way my mother described the festivities and the ride in the royal coach, it must have been a fairytale wedding despite the fiasco with the camera.

Elfriede Richter's Wedding in Dresden on the 20th of April 1940

I took the three wedding photos that my mother had given me and looked at my parents' young faces and gazed at my mother's wedding dress, of which she was so proud. Then I reached for the magnifying glass because I want to see the lace pattern more clearly.

My mother has beautiful, even features and high cheekbones. Her sensuous mouth is barely open, spreading a faint, almost reluctant and slightly discouraged smile across her face. Although they are looking at me, her eyes glow quietly, as if gazing inwardly. The splendor of her brown, wavy hair frames her face. The curls are artfully held together underneath the veil, which flows in lovely, soft waves over her shoulders, framing her slender figure tenderly, until it spreads out around her in a soft, wide, transparent circle on the floor. The veil lets her figure appear fragile. The expensive lace of her dress falls in heavy, round, elegant pleats, covering her feet and shoes, but it does not touch the floor. I like to look at my mother; she appears so graceful, light and gentle next to the dark figure of her husband in uniform.

The man stands proudly beside his wife, and yet he doesn't seem to belong in the same picture. His face is young and handsome, but his eyes are like those of a stranger under the visor of his military hat that covers his forehead almost completely. As a child I ran away from these eyes. It is a face I still cannot look at for long.

2. Life in the Thirties

Months after my mother's death I found the family book among her things, but I have no idea how it survived the bombing. To my surprise, the book contained the original photo of my young maternal grandparents with their two small children. The soft gold-brown tones of the photo let them appear even lovelier. Stamped on the back are the name and address of the photographer, Curt Kroh, who photographed them in 1924.

The picture is of a middle-class family dressed for the occasion. Mother and father are sitting to the left and the right of their two small children. They are beautiful people, with finely cut even features, who are facing me in this classical arrangement. The girl is nestling up to her mother, the little boy is sitting on his father's right leg. Mother, daughter and son are looking slightly toward the left, past the photographer, while the father smiles faintly into the camera, the left corner of his mouth barely pulled up. But it is more than an almost hidden smile for the photographer, recorded for posterity. Something amuses him. Is he perhaps remembering the elaborate procedure of getting dressed to look good for the occasion, a secret delight in the moment that I only discover bit by bit?

The woman bears the trace of an enigmatic smile on her smooth, young face. She was thirty years old when the photo was taken. I remember Grandmother as a beautiful woman. Her calm expression and her loving bright brown eyes have been imprinted on my memory forever. Both children are sitting very still, as if they are looking at something that captures their attention, perhaps some object that the photographer is showing them. The father holds his son's tiny left hand as he embraces him. The little boy's eyes are large and round with his tiny mouth just barely open. The girl looks up skeptically. I noticed this quiet skepsis in her glance only after gazing at the photo for a long time. Because this girl is my mother, I never tire of looking at her as I explore her face in the hope of finding something I might have missed until now. It is as though I am waiting for the people in the picture to reveal a family secret, and thus unravel for me the meaning of life and of things to come, of the horrors that are lying ahead in a distant future.

Martha and Paul Richter with their children Elfriede and Rolf in Dresden, 1924

My grandmother was the eldest of eleven siblings, and after the early death of her mother, my Polish great-grandmother Pauline, she had to take care of the smaller children and household. She only finished four years of grade school because she had to work like a man on the farm, in the stables, the mill and the greenhouses. At seventeen she ran away from her father's farm and went to Breslau, where she took care of the household of a wealthy family. She knew the town, which became Polish after the end of World War II, because her father used to deliver tomatoes and cucumbers from his greenhouses to the rich families. But life in that household was hardly any easier, and she often told us indignantly how hard she had to work for that family from early morning until late at night, how she could hardly stand up straight anymore after hours of drudgery, and that her feet hurt so badly she was no longer able to think clearly. Her room was no bigger than a broom closet, her bed very narrow and the mattress hard as a rock. So early one morning, while everyone was still asleep, she resolutely packed her few belongings and took the first train to Dresden.

There she got lucky and quickly found easier work in a cigarette factory. Not long thereafter my grandmother met her future husband during one of her visits to the zoological garden. They fell in love, and my mother came along soon enough. Unfortunately my grandparents couldn't get married because my grandfather was married at the time. The divorce was not granted until three years later, which caused the three of them a great deal of unhappiness, as my mother often stressed.

Right after Hitler's election as Reichskanzler in January 1933 and his first radio addresses, proclamations and citywide parades, my grandfather predicted even before the Act of Enablement, which gave Hitler broad plenary powers, and the ensuing decrees he issued, that things would not go well for Germany with this Mr. Hitler. Hitler means war, everything points to it, mark my words, my grandfather prophesied long before anyone in his circle of friends talked about it, and by autumn of 1938 he said that his colleagues, most of them city employees, considered Dresden to be extremely vulnerable should a war break out, as they discussed the situation during their weekly billiard nights. As we know today, there were never any serious attempts made to protect the city against air raids. Perhaps it was lucky for my grandfather that he didn't live to see the destruction of Dresden.

In the mid-thirties, when they were still living on the Schmalwiesenstraße, my mother told us how Grandfather often brought home men who were out of work. Sometimes he approached them in the street. He had a knack for knowing whom he could trust. They would work in the house and in the garden, and in return they received food, they could take a bath, do their laundry and spend the night. Some stayed for weeks. Herr Pollack lived with them in the room in the basement for over two years, until he found work again. He was a gentleman, and soon became part of the family, ate all meals with them and even helped my mother with her homework. Later on Herr Pollack married and visited them often with his wife and little boy, and always said that Grandfather had given him a second chance in life.

Throughout her life, my mother nurtured a strong connection to her father, and the closer she came to her own death, the more she looked back to her beloved Papa, seeking comfort in her memory of him. She praised him as the ideal man: patient, kindhearted, understanding, and a caring and loving husband and father who always thought well of others, and for whom every unpleasant word and quarrel was painful. He was the kind of man she had been looking for all of her life, but there was not another one like him anywhere.

Because her Papa had led such an exemplary life, my mother relied on his advice and judgement as if he were still alive. I remember the soft, longing sound in her voice when she spoke of her father, and how she livened up at such moments. She often mentioned how quickly her mother grew loud when things didn't go her way, and how her father suffered under her scolding and eventually capitulated in the face of her Upper Silesian catholic stubbornness. Even so he loved his wife's beautiful sensuality and wanted her to be elegantly dressed and happy, and never could do enough for her.

Omi had such a good life with Papa, my mother emphasized repeatedly, but she didn't know it until it was too late. Over the years the silly quarrels of Omi's equally noisy catholic sisters, with their demagogy and intolerance, got to him. Papa was Lutheran, and therefore they predicted he would take them all to hell with him. When Papa entered the kitchen one afternoon, they attacked him, wailing loudly that God would punish them because he had closed himself off to the only true faith. That day he'd finally had enough, and instead of just walking away he calmly told them to get out of his house. They were so perplexed that they obeyed without protest.

Omi was desperate. She sat at the kitchen table with her head propped up in her hands lamenting that she had just lost her sisters. Papa stroked her and kissed her, saying calmly, "Now we have peace at last, my darling Martha. Prepare supper for us, my angel, and set a beautiful table in the dining room. I'll be right back."

Then my father took my hand and we walked straight to the Lutheran parish, where he settled everything on the spot with the pastor so that I could be christened on one of the following Sundays. We were indeed back home very quickly. Papa had taken a stand at last. No one ever dared to accuse him of apostasy again in his presence. Omi went to see her sisters for a few weeks until everything was smoothed over and they were allowed to visit again, for they had little to eat during those years. However, Papa forbade any further discussion of religion and the Catholic church in our house. Those topics were taboo from then on when Papa was home.

What a pity that you didn't get to know your grandfather, Anne, my mother would say wistfully at such moments. He would have loved to have grandchildren. Unfortunately he died two years before you were born.

The drastic political changes soon caused upheavals at his workplace, and Papa perceived this beginning of moral decline as threatening to daily life. As he watched the events around him break down the old order, he felt helpless and looked for peace and relaxation more than ever within his family. An evening of billiards once a week after work with long-time friends was his sole diversion. I did not begrudge him this pleasure, but I couldn't sleep until I heard him enter the house late at night. After Hitler's seizure of power, his sensitivity and sensibility had further weakened his already irritated stomach, causing him to suffer greatly from ulcers, to the point that his doctor urged him to undergo surgery.

I had stayed at the hospital during his surgery, which had gone well, and when my father was wheeled out of the operating room I sat next to his bed until he woke from the anesthesia. He smiled at me, and although he hadn't completely come to, he said I should go home and rest, adding that he was feeling fine. I didn't want to leave him, but he assured me that he would be sleeping most of the time anyway, and he could ring for the nurse should he need anything. At that moment a nurse entered the room with a glass of water, which she put on his nightstand saying, "Herr Richter, please listen carefully, you must not drink the water under any circumstances, you mustn't drink anything at all until the doctor will allow it, no matter how thirsty you are. But you can moisten your lips with some drops of water when they become too dry and begin to burn."

The nurse also admonished me to go home and promised that she would stay with my father until he was fully awake, and sat down on a chair near the window. Papa was so drowsy and exhausted that it was hard for him to keep his eyes open. Thinking he was in good hands I left after a while with a heavy heart. I promised him that I would return early in the evening and kissed him goodbye. The nurse probably walked out of the room soon thereafter, leaving him alone. Papa must have woken up during her absence, and when he saw the glass of water, he took it and drank it. As a result his stomach began to contract causing the stitches to tear and hemorrhage, and he bled to death internally.

I returned unsuspectingly several hours later to find Papa already dead. Omi was alone at home when someone from the hospital came to bring her the news of his death, and the neighbors said that she screamed like a crazy woman. It was gross negligence on the nurse's part to leave a newly operated patient alone with a glass of water. The nurse was transferred to a different ward. That's all I know. If only I had stayed with him!

Perhaps it was suicide, my mother speculated at times. He no longer understood the world and suffered greatly under the worsening political conditions. Given the way my mother talked about the history of his illness and the surgery, such an interpretation is possible.

Omi was inconsolable over Papa's untimely death. She tore her hair, screamed and wailed for days, or she just sat in the living room drinking coffee while staring into a void for hours, caring about nothing. I had to buy the mourning dress for her, select the coffin, arrange the funeral ceremony, order the flowers, choose the Bible verse and the music, and go to the town hall for the death certificate.

Two days after the funeral I happened to see Omi with a man as they were getting on a streetcar at the Pirnaische Platz while I was running around town, taking care of formalities. I'll never forget the sight of her, how she climbed aboard the streetcar with that man. It was as if someone had stabbed me in the chest. How could she do that so soon after Papa's death? She came home very late that night.

My grandmother's behavior upset my mother so much that she never forgave her. I know today that this, too, is part of life, but when I was young, I wanted to hear nothing about it and changed the subject by saying, "Why don't you tell me something about Great-grandfather Valentin?"

3. The Last Trip to Grandfather

That's all over now, my mother said, those days will never return. Long ago, before the war and during the first years of the war, when I would take the train to visit Grandfather in Upper Silesia, I saw large herds of cows grazing in the meadows everywhere. In the villages, on the country roads and paths through the fields, people were walking with their animals and going about their business. Oxen were pulling plows, horse-drawn carriages filled the highways, horsemen galloped along country roads, rabbits hopped across harvested fields, the summer sky was full of birds, deer and occasional bucks stood at the edge of the forests at nightfall. Seen from the train, an idyllic way of life presented itself. During summer, when the windows of our compartments were open, you could hear the deep mooing of the cows or sheep bleating, and now and then the barking of sheepdogs. Automobiles drove alongside of us on the roads, and at times were so close you could make out the faces of the passengers, then the next moment they sped up ahead of the train or a bend in the road took them in a different direction.

Whenever I traveled to Grandfather, I could hardly wait to arrive at the station in Leobschütz, where he would meet me with his carriage. Once he had come all the way to Ratibor because he had to take care of some business there. My heart and my senses were filled with happiness and the anticipation of a long summer on his farm with the whole extended family, the aunts, uncles and cousins, male and female farmhands for the harvest, the stable boy and the local craftsmen, the forester and the villagers. I long for the endless hot, lazy summer afternoons, which I spent lying in the lush grass under an apple tree at the shady banks of the Zinna river where I loved to swim. To this day, I miss the hikes in the nearby Riesengebirge, with its tall black pine trees, the vast open landscapes, deep dark forests, the brooks that flowed through our property toward the Oder river, or the duck pond with the water lilies, and of course our watch dog, named Kuno. And then there were the trips to Breslau, Ratibor, Krakau and Kattowitz.

In the summer of 1944, I traveled to Grandfather's as always while Omi stayed home with you and your sister Bettine. Little did I know that it would be for the last time. When we sat together at the kitchen table after supper on the first evening of my arrival, he asked me all of a sudden, "What do you think, Elfriedchen, things are not looking good. We are going to lose this war, too, only this time it will turn out much worse."

I didn't dare answer as Grandfather continued to talk about the eventful history of Upper Silesia, which inevitably turned into an extraordinary tale of people and places and times long past that stirred up my imagination, taking on a legendary character for me. "For centuries our family has lived here, first under the Austrians, then under the Prussians, but we never concerned ourselves with politics because it was our land and nothing else mattered. I never paid much attention to the secular authorities, as long as they left me alone, and up to now our family fared well with this attitude. I couldn't have changed things anyway. Napoleon marched his army across Europe not far from here, but my father, your great-grandfather, took little notice of it. We were farmers, and the news of such upheavals often didn't reach us until much later when everything was long over. Bismarck built a new Reich without Austria, then came the great war and finally the Weimar Republic, but again it did not touch us, and that is how it remains until today. We labor, sow the fields, take care of the animals, bring in the harvest, prepare for winter, just like it's always been, until ..." he hesitated, searching for fitting words,"... until these scoundrels, who brought us this war, came to Berlin."

Thus spoke Grandfather, but it wasn't true that he didn't care. I could tell from the tone of his voice, which betrayed his agitation and deep anger. During World War I he had given a war loan of 100,000 gold marks. He never got his money back and worked even harder after the war to make up for the loss. When the Nazis came and also asked him for money, he gave them nothing, and when they came a second time, he chased them off his property. They were furious. Many village dwellers had been watching his success with malevolence, but they had to leave him alone because he continued to take care of the people in the area. Grandfather was not only a good farmer, he was also a clever businessman who went with the times. He had a sense for new things, and knew instinctively what the people in the cities were looking for and what they would buy from him.

"Come along, Elfriede Hildegard, that is your complete beautiful name, isn't it?" he said the following morning in high spirits, laughing loudly. "You and I, we are going to take a coach ride all the way around our land so that you will see the whole estate. We'll take along the baskets with the tomatoes and stop at the market place in Zülkowitz, and afterwards we'll drive over to Leobschütz to pick up my pocket watch from the watchmaker. I want Rolf to have it some day, remember that."

In celebration of the day, Grandfather had four horses harnessed to the coach and put on his best clothes. He never bought a car. In the winter he wore his fur coat, his Cossack boots and the Russian cap made of Persian lambskin.

Valentin Kallabis during the wheat harvest in Upper Silesia, circa 1920

He looked very distinguished, like a big-landed property owner from one of Tolstoy's novels, as he sat on the coach box, reins in hand. I climbed up next to him. It was always an adventure to ride to town with Grandfather. I saw the swaying bodies of the well-groomed horses in front of me, and along straight stretches of road I was allowed to hold the reins, and Grandfather was pleased to see how the horses obeyed me.

"This here is our land," he explained during our ride. "Remember everything well, my young woman, this will all belong to you one day, and to your children, and then you will come back and live here. You should have a son after the two girls," he admonished me. "You already know how to herd geese, what a goosegirl you were," he smiled mischievously as he reminded me once again of the incident. "If I had counted on you we would no longer have any geese, you would have scared them all away. Take a look down there, that's my mill, and the glass houses over there, see them sparkle in the sun? That's my greenhouse nursery. We deliver tomatoes and cucumbers all the way to Kattowitz and Breslau in winter. These greenhouses were one of my best ideas. The rich people always want exactly what's not available, and they pay well."

"But Grandfather, I know all that," I interrupted. He was very proud of the products from his greenhouses.

"I am showing and telling you today what you need to know, so listen to me and pay attention and don't forget anything," he repeated as if he hadn't heard me. "Who knows how soon we'll have another chance. This once I want you to hear it all from me so that no one can tell you anything different some day. And finally there are my horses, the carriages, coaches and the farmhouse, and I am never leaving from here."

After that, Grandfather remained silent for a long time and I lost myself in my daydreams. At last he went on, "Franz will continue to manage the farm when I can't do it anymore, you can trust him. He is the most faithful human being, you'll never find anyone like him again. When he is old, he will stay on, and you'll leave him his room and whatever else he may need. He'll still be useful and advise you even then, so just go to him every day and talk everything over with him before you make your decisions."

Franz had arrived on Grandfather's farm one day after World War I asking for work, my mother explained. There was little work in Upper Silesia in those days, and many men worked as day laborers. Franz must have made a good impression on Grandfather. He was young and strong and worked hard and fast. When Grandfather saw that he wasn't afraid of any kind of work and took care of everything in an exemplary way, he let him stay, and soon he became his trusted partner.

When we arrived back home, grandfather stopped in front of his chapel and said, "Step down, Elfriede, let's go inside and pray together."

It was cool in the chapel, and my skin began to tingle pleasantly after so many hours in the sun. I couldn't take my eyes off of Grandfather as we both kneeled in front of Mary and the child. Never had I been alone in the chapel with him, which he had built for himself, his family and his farm workers. He was a deeply devout Catholic. In the summer everyone had to go to the chapel at four in the morning before beginning with their daily chores. In the deep of winter he made allowances and would read from the Bible in the kitchen. Omi often complained about his strict regiment.

From the chapel, the women went to the stables to milk the cows, then the animals were cared for while a large breakfast was being prepared in the kitchen in huge frying pans. Fried potatoes, eggs, bacon, large, thick slices of bread, pitchers full of fresh foaming milk, buttermilk with chunks of real butter swimming on top, as well as sheets of freshly baked cake were daily staples. The people on his farm were fed well and their bedrooms were heated in winter, but they had to work hard.

"Don't forget what I've told you today," Grandfather reminded me, when we left the chapel.

"Yes, Grandfather, but you'll be with us for many more years," I said quickly so this blissful moment wouldn't be spoiled. The war had passed by this remote area up until then, and in those days Grandfather seemed fit and vigorous. His inner peace and confidence were contagious. His energy was catching, even though I had doubts about my competence and was unable to comprehend his plans fully, because I understood little about farming. Our ride on that summer day in 1944 was the most beautiful experience we ever shared. I was twenty-four at the time, and he treated me as his heiress and was proud of everything that would belong to me someday, because Rolf didn't want the farm. It was an extraordinary experience to drive around with Grandfather and feel his deep contentment. After our return we walked through the stables with Franz while the old stable hand took care of the horses.

When I departed three weeks later, it was a farewell forever, but we didn't know that when I boarded the train in Ratibor! Dear Grandfather, my mother sighed, looking at me. How differently things turned out. Everything changed so much faster than we could have imagined.

I have three small black and white photos of Great-grandfather. One of them shows him with his people during the wheat harvest, on another one he is standing in front of his hothouses, and on the third one he is sitting on a bench in his garden reading a letter. Those are the only photos that survived the war and postwar confusion. But there is another photograph from those years of my mother as she is sitting in a meadow in front of a proud two-story farmhouse with a tall roof and a wooden fence around it. She is wearing a light summer dress with a tiny floral design on barely transparent, softly falling muslin that flatters her body. She once told me that the dress was dark blue. The puffed sleeves held together by narrow cuffs accentuate her sensual arms. The skirt is spread in a wide circle around her, covering her legs completely. Her left hand lies weightlessly on her left knee as her right hand, with slightly curled fingertips, gently touches the material of the dress on the grass, but doesn't support her. Her medium brown hair frames her face in long soft waves, as she looks from below up into the camera with an open smile. Her eyes sparkle. Life lies ahead of her, as we would say, and while we speak these words, we hope that it is going to be a grand, interesting and long life. In short: a full life. It must have been in the summer of 1938 or 1939. The picture shows no trace of the approaching war, nothing of the calamity that is to come. It is just a sunny summer afternoon in an idyllic setting. The trees are full in leaf and cast short shadows on the meadow, the fence and the house, and in the midst of it all she is sitting happily and full of confidence. More than any other, this photograph has always fascinated me. My mother seems so carefree and her posture looks so natural that I tried it and noticed that it was anything but easy to sit like that, and I envied her for her grace and beauty. I would like to ask her about that summer day when she was sitting on that meadow, which lives on in her tales. Was she in love, perhaps with the man who took her photo, and whom she later grew to hate?

In the winter of 1945/46, almost a year after the end of the war, Russians arrived on his estate one morning before daybreak, my mother ended the story of Grandfather, the way he had related it to her. When he heard the noise in the farmyard, he stepped out of the house. The soldiers conveyed to him that he and his people were to leave the farm immediately because Poles were to settle there and take over like everywhere in Silesia. The Russians had driven these Polish farmers from their farms in the eastern part of their country, but Grandfather paid no attention to them and was about to go back into the house when they blocked the door and ordered him bluntly to get a few things and leave. Grandfather spoke fluent Polish, and insisted that he would not abandon his farm, after all, this was his property. The soldiers lifted their rifles, pointing them at him. When he realized that they were deadly serious, he repeated that he would not leave voluntarily, but that they would have to shoot him, and then he positioned himself protectively in front of his people, who had been chased out of the house and the stables into the open courtyard, while calling the intruders a pack of robbers.

Polish neighbors had come along with whom he had lived in peace all the days of his life. They had helped each other out whenever necessary and had worked side by side in the fields. But now they didn't help him. They looked at him grimly, and would no longer tolerate his presence. The Russian commanded him one last time to leave. At that moment Franz approached from the horse stable and tried to pull Grandfather aside, but he would not move. The intruders gave a warning shot; Grandfather remained steadfast. So they pushed him aside with their rifle butts and shot his faithful people right before his eyes. Then they dragged him into the stables, where they made him watch as they cut the pigs' throats. The horses and other animals they divided up amongst themselves. More and more neighbors came, and together they looted the house. After he had been forced to watch everything they chased Grandfather off his property. They refused to shoot him, even though he begged them. Him they did not shoot, my mother repeated. Like a tramp they drove him off his own farm and even took away his fur-lined winter coat, fur cap and leather boots in that bitter cold winter.

Weeks later, Grandfather arrived in Dresden with rags wrapped around his feet and wearing one of those Russian coats made of cellulose wadding that didn't keep you warm. To this very day I am surprised that this stately man didn't freeze to death on his long foot-march. One day, in icy cold weather, he stood in front of Aunt Lene's apartment, Omi's younger sister, who lived on the Bergmannstraße. They hadn't been bombed and he found their house after having looked for ours in vain, because there were only ruins left on the Fürstenstraße.

Valentin Kallabis reading a letter in his garden in Upper Silesia, circa 1920

In spite of it all, Grandfather never lost his faith in God. Every day he sat at the kitchen table and read his big black Bible. And when he was done with the apocalypse he began again with the Book of Genesis. He wanted nothing to do with the new men in power; he didn't even want to read the newspapers anymore. When we offered him one, he simply shook his head. It took Omi a long time to persuade him to register for food stamps and his small pension, because he simply couldn't imagine asking for money. To him it seemed like begging. He lived the years after his expulsion in complete confidence in God and bore his fate with equanimity until his death in 1954, just like Job, who had become his example.

At this point, my mother took a deep breath and wiped her eyes dry. I consoled her while wondering aloud how one could go on living after such an ordeal without losing one's mind.

"Well, Anne, your great-grandfather was a strong, deeply religious man," she answered. "The heart doesn't stop beating that easily, and neither do we lose our mind that fast. And who knows whether his servants and workers had survived the flight, and how, may I ask you, how should they have lived in the destroyed city of Dresden? They only knew their life on the farm and only spoke broken German; Grandfather spoke mostly Polish with them."

I remember Great-grandfather Valentin well. I can still picture him today sitting at Aunt Lene's kitchen table, as if it had been only yesterday, a sight that has etched itself indelibly on my mind. Whenever I came to visit him with Omi he was sitting at the table with the open Bible lying in front of him. I was supposed to walk over to him, curtsey and talk to him, but I hesitated to take the few steps through the gloomy kitchen, whose window opened into a sunless courtyard. I cannot recall what he asked me, and I never knew what to answer.

Omi coaxed me, saying, "Come on, Anne, talk to him, you aren't afraid of Great-grandfather, are you? Tell him what we did today."

Even so, I felt strangely intimidated and remained at a certain distance from him. I cannot say whether it was the long white beard, the big black Bible or his personality. Finally Omi gave me a plate of cake, which I was supposed to give to him, and pushed me toward him. "Don't be so silly," she whispered, "go to Great-grandfather, he's been waiting for you, shake his hand and curtsy."

When I stood beside him at last, he smiled at me with his blue eyes and encouraged me to choose a story from the Bible that I would like to hear. He was sitting very straight, hardly touching the back of the chair. His hands were resting on the table next to the Bible while he was reading to me as I looked at him intently.

4. Preparing to Survive

On a hot weekend in the autumn of 1944, after my return from Grandfather's, I decided to arrange things in our cellar in such a way to be better prepared in case of emergency, my mother continued. I can still recall the pleasant coolness in the cellar. "In case of emergency," that's what we used to say in those days, without having any clear idea of what we would really need during a bombing attack. Over the months Omi and I took many things to the cellar, and the more time went by, the greater our fear grew and the more we hoarded.

It wasn't easy to organize and store everything inside our narrow wooden partition. I moved the things that I didn't consider to be absolutely necessary onto the higher shelves or put it into boxes, which I set on top of the old wardrobe. Some items I stacked on the balcony to gain more storage space in the cellar. Then I placed jars with preserved fruit, vegetables and jam within easy reach on the lower shelves, put a camping stove, matches and candles on a small table as well as a large old pot to boil water for coffee and tea. Next to it I placed a stack of soup plates, smaller bowls for compote and oatmeal and two baby bottles with extra nipples. Flatware and dishes I wrapped in dishtowels, and I hung a large soup ladle and other utensils on hooks on the wooden board behind the shelves. Underneath the table I stored a second pot for soup, a frying pan and a deep brown enamel bowl. Then I filled paper bags with noodles, rice and oatmeal and stored sugar, salt, tea, barley malt coffee and milk powder in tin cans. Sacks of potatoes, baskets of red and white cabbage and beets we kept in the cellar anyway. Smoked sausages, meat and bacon from Grandfather were hanging from a hook in the ceiling. Finally, I secured a blanket to the inside of the lath wood door so no one could look inside, and attached a stronger lock, because many strangers came into the basement during air raids. I checked perishable provisions frequently and exchanged them every few months.

The most important item was my small suitcase made of the finest red saffiano leather, which Papa had given me for my tenth birthday after I had learned to sew. Although I felt sad about it, I emptied its contents into a box and set it on the foot pedal of the sewing machine. As I removed the many items Papa had selected so lovingly, I was glad he didn't have to live through these trying times. The small suitcase was exactly the right size for all papers, documents, certificates, savings books, insurance policies, identity cards and letters from Papa and Rolf, as well as other valuables like my jewelry, my mother's and father's gold watches, Papa's rings, tiepins, cuff links, some cash and an envelope with family photos.

After I had put everything inside, I had to press the lid down in order to lock it. I always kept the red suitcase in the same place on the floor in the right hand corner of the wardrobe where I could reach for it in the dark in the event of an electric power failure. The key I wore on a silver chain around my neck.

My mother described everything so graphically as though it had happened just hours ago. With incredible accuracy she painted a picture of our daily life, weaving her own feelings and thoughts into it when she spoke about Dresden, the river, its meadows and bridges, the lovely Elbe river valley with its vineyards, villas and palaces, as well as the famous sandstone mountains. My mother and grandmother loved this city, and both women passed this special love on to me as they spoke endlessly about it.

Dresden was a baroque city of singular beauty, an architectural dream, music turned into stone, playful, virtuous and alive. Seen from the other side of the Elbe, the silhouette of the city, with the spires of churches and worldly buildings reaching high into the sky, appeared graceful and delicate, like the finest lace from Plauen. Among the most famous buildings were the Katholische Hofkirche, the Kreuzkirche and the Sophienkirche, the steeple of the new town hall, the Brühlsche Terrasse, the Royal Palace with the Hausmannsturm, the Semper Opera, George Bähr's Frauenkirche (which was rebuilt after the reunification of Germany and dedicated in October 2005) with the Silbermann organ, the glass dome of the Art Academy and Daniel Pöppelmann's Zwinger, which houses the Meißen porcelain collection, the Armory and the Gallery of Old Masters. She passed her delight in the sensuous Meißen porcelain on to me, and of all the paintings in the Gallery of Old Masters she singled out Raphael's "Sistine Madonna", which Graf von Brühl had bought for the king of Saxony, Augustus the Strong. The way my mother talked about this painting, it became the most beautiful one in the whole world to me. I admired the lovely face of the Madonna, and was astounded by the way she carried her beautiful child with his pouting mouth and tousled hair so weightlessly in her arms as she is walking on clouds toward us, surrounded by a host of angels. She is holding the child close to her body, and at the same time appears to offer him to a person opposite her, or to the world, and it always seemed to me that Raphael's angels were hovering over us, guarding our lives.

As she narrated her story, my mother never left out even one building, and her voice was filled with both pride and pain when she called each one by its name. Thus they came together for me in a grand *gesamtkunstwerk*, which can be best expressed as "synthesis of the arts". I never tired of gazing at prints of paintings by Canaletto of Dresden and the black and white postcard-sized photographs by Walter Hahn, which he took in the 1930s. Her reminiscences touched me and ensnared me with a certain magic as I grew up with the image of a city that no longer existed by the time I heard of it. Especially when we had guests that had never been to Dresden, she praised the town and its treasures with ever-new words, and never forgot to mention that Johann Gottfried Herder had called it the "German Florence on the Elbe", the embodiment of baroque splendor. This city was to be preserved for posterity despite the war. There were international plans and agreements to ensure the safety of Dresden. And so we secretly hoped until the end that there would be no large-scale attack on the city, or that the war would be over before the unthinkable could occur.

In the fall of 1944, I moved the sewing machine and an old floor lamp into the kitchen so I could sew in a warm place after you were in bed, my mother continued her never-ending story. The other rooms had to remain unheated because we used the coal rations, that we had saved up in our cellar, extremely sparingly in the large stove in the kitchen, where our life took place exclusively ever since. Even then, the only time I put on enough coal was to cook our meals. We had stopped heating the living room months ago because our apartment had large rooms and high ceilings. When occasional visitors were invited on Sunday afternoons, I fired the big tile stove for a few hours, which then gave off a comforting heat long into the evening. After supper, you, Anne, and I would sit on the sofa wrapped in a blanket as I read stories to you. After I put you to bed I would read one of my own books. There remained so little time for reading at the end of each day; there were so few good books, and hardly any other pleasant entertainment or diversions.

In the winter of 1944/45 I read the novel *Effi Briest* by Theodor Fontane (1819-1898) whenever I had an hour to spare, and when Kurt came home on furlough we'd read from it together. Kurt raved about the novel and called me Effi from then on instead of Elfi, short for Elfriede, like everyone else did. The other novels and plays from Kurt's high school years I found hard to read. They didn't really fit into those times, and I needed something lighter and more beautiful, something romantic for the heart.

I seldom went to bed before two in the morning, because I wasn't tired. Besides I couldn't sleep well during the war anyway, and so I sewed and knitted clothes for all of us or mended sheets and towels, darned socks and repaired Omi's work clothes.

In later years, my mother proudly showed us on photos the pullovers, cardigans, colorful shawls and warm caps she had knitted and the dresses, jackets and coats she had sewn. She described the quality, design and color of the material, she remembered where she had gotten it, how it felt to the touch and how much others admired her talent. And she always added: I listened to the radio while I worked, which I had turned on very low, as I tried to find out how things were going for Germany and how close the enemy was on the eastern front.

Even though the kitchen was big, it had become crowded because of all of the activities that suddenly took place there. We had always eaten our meals in the dining room. Omi was an excellent cook, my mother reminisced, and Papa wanted to eat in beautiful surroundings with good dishes and silverware and sit comfortably together with his family after supper. On the weekends, he allowed himself a cigar and cognac with his coffee. As a child, I often sat on his lap after the meal, and to this day I remember the scent of the cigars. After Papa had died and Rolf had been drafted, Omi and I began to eat our meals in the kitchen. It just happened that way. It was less work, even clearing the table went faster and we didn't feel so alone in the smaller room. Soon enough our whole life became centered in the kitchen during the winter. I used the kitchen table for cutting out my sewing patterns and to do the ironing, and you also played on it, Anne. I had put your toys and books into a large wicker basket that I pushed under the table at night. These cramped quarters gradually got on my nerves, however, especially after we had to take in an older couple from East Prussia in October 1944.

"Anne, you must remember these resettlers," my mother said while turning demonstratively to me when others were present, as if she were looking for confirmation for her stories. Her immaculate German sounded even more refined during such moments. She aimed to distinguish herself in her speech from those intruders from the east, and sat up straighter to lend the proper dignity to her narration. She looked like an aristocrat, as her well-manicured slender hands lay in her lap, like the hands of women in Dutch oil paintings. She held her head high, but her proud facial expression nevertheless betrayed years of suffering and deprivation.

Dresden was one of the few large cities that hadn't sustained any damage from large-scale bombings, and hope lived on that we would be spared, my mother continued without interruption. Therefore, we had to take in an increasing number of bombing victims from the Rheinland. By the fall of 1944, refugees from East Prussia and the Warthegau began crowding into town as well. In the beginning, these refugees were called resettlers so as not to give the impression that they were fleeing from the approaching Soviet armies. I had gone to the registration office to prevent having to take in refugees, and was successful because we were living with Omi in her apartment. But as the months passed, the stream of refugees increased dramatically, and our apartment was considered too large for only four people. We were lucky they sent us an elderly couple and not a whole family with children and grandparents. These two people, who were good-natured, joined us in the kitchen every evening, until they went to bed around nine thirty. This continued on with no end in sigh and soon became very stressful. Omi was at work all day and said nothing, although it was her apartment. The old woman muttered to herself all day long, wailing about the loss of their farm, their horses and livestock, and wondered what was to become of them. Their daughter worked in Berlin and their two sons were in the war, so they were expecting to be treated as part of the family.

Because I baked two or three times a week and I had to cook twice every day, once for you children at noon and then again for all of us in the evening, I had made a schedule for the use of the kitchen stove, which she ignored. Instead, she began cooking at the same time I was using the stove, saying that as long as it was hot anyway, and since it was big enough, she might as well make use of it, too. She often cooked the most awful stuff, like marinated lungs, kidneys and other tripe. The penetrating smell alone made me feel ill. The pots stood on top of the range for hours uncovered, simmering slowly, so that I had to open the window to let in fresh air, even though it was bitter cold outside. Even if I asked kindly for some consideration, it didn't help any. They both pretended everything was just fine, but maybe they just didn't understand. Who knows what they were used to at home?

When her husband came home from the factory after six at night, he sat down on a chair in the middle of the kitchen, took off his shirt, shoes and socks, which stank terribly because they changed their underwear and socks only once a week, rolled up the legs of his pants, took a footbath, and smoked a dirty pipe filled with cheap, horrid-smelling tobacco, while reading the paper out loud, commenting on the news. He sat there for an hour while we had to walk around him. Just the sight of him made my stomach feel queasy. His wife had to add hot water to the enamel tub every so often, after having scooped out some of the cooler water first. They had received their ration of coal, but they wanted to save it for harder times instead of heating the small stove in their room, where they could have heated water for the footbaths as well as for coffee and tea.

Omi was glad about the extra coal and said, "You never know, Elfriedchen, just let them be!" Finally I couldn't take it any longer and locked them out of the kitchen, and only let the woman cook during the agreed upon times. Even so it was very hard; I would never want to have to go through anything like that again.

My mother shuddered, moved her fingers through her hair and smoothed out her pullover and skirt as if to drive the cooking smell out of her hair and clothes once more.

Since she had prepared the cellar for an emergency and the war raged on mercilessly, the idea of another great trip began to take shape in her mind. The older I became and the more I understood about the severity of the combat at the eastern front, the more importance my mother's journey to East Prussia gained for me. She didn't know that it would be her last trip to this faraway place when she set out. It received this designation only subsequently, after everything was long lost, thus distinguishing it from all previous trips, marking not only the end of the country as we knew it, but the end of an era for our family.

This trip, more than anything else, points to my mother's youthful enterprising spirit as well as her courage and joy of life. She had taken heart and tried her luck under the most trying circumstances during those dark days, against all better judgement, and set out on that incredible journey. This wartime story gives insight into the hearts of two young people, who had married during the war, and five years later still hadn't had the chance to live as a couple, and who, just before the collapse of Germany that they didn't yet want to admit was coming, had risked all in order to come together for a few weeks at the most eastern border of the Reich. How conscious they were of any real danger when they planned the trip, I cannot say, but they took a chance, and so this visit speaks of the love of the woman for her man, whom she followed at this most crucial time while leaving her children unprotected in the capital of Saxony.

Some months after the end of the war, when we were at last settled in our own place again, my mother began to talk about the journey among family members. She told us how the trip to Königsberg in the autumn of 1944 had led her past the first refugee treks to the west. People were on foot, with hand carts and baby carriages and heavily loaded covered wagons drawn by horses or oxen. It was then that she began to understand that it would end badly for Germany.

I had seen enough on this last journey to have my own thoughts about things to come, my mother insisted, only no one wanted to listen, and I didn't dare to say much, because I was afraid. You never knew who might pass something on to the wrong people. Even Omi wanted to hear nothing about it. My reports alarmed her. Neither did she want to know that I listened to enemy radio broadcasts after she had gone to bed. She feared betrayal, and even in the last months before the end of the war she didn't want to hear the truth about the

German army and where it had been defeated and pushed back, because she worried about Rolf, her only son.

Getting the special permit required for the train trip from Dresden to Königsberg in November 1944 was an achievement in itself, and bears witness to my mother's strong will and determination. After all, she hadn't simply been able to go to the train station to buy a ticket to this faraway place. How then did she manage to procure the official permit that entitled her to purchase a railroad ticket? What kind of emergency had she come up with, how much power of persuasion did she have to muster in the administrative offices? Had she been driven by love or by daemons when she took it into her head to go on this trip, I wondered, because shortly after her return, Königsberg fell, and soon after that its name disappeared from all maps and the world's memory.

In answer to my question, I found out that my parents had made travel plans immediately after his unit, the signal corps, had received orders in October to be moved to East Prussia. However, the war situation had worsened drastically by the middle of November. The German troops were being pushed back on all fronts, or encircled and cut off from the rest of their units and supplies. Who in the overheated offices of Dresden's town hall, lacking oxygen, had taken pity on her and listened to her pleas on her second visit, and had decided to let her go at such an inopportune time? Could it be that she had simply encountered a good-natured soul who felt for her and understood her longing while ignoring the war and the escalating dangers and had given her a permit to travel east at a time when daily tens of thousands of refugees were already pushing west, and more would join them with every passing day? Just how much did these clerks in their gloomy offices and the citizens of Dresden actually know about what was going on out there? And how much did they believe of what the refugees said? On the one hand, nothing worked anymore, while on the other much was still possible, given the necessary willpower. A strange contradiction.

My mother also had to convince Omi, who didn't particularly care for her son-in-law, of the necessity of that journey, because she would have to take care of us girls. In those months, when all available help was needed and calls went out to the female population to report for work in factories and warehouses, my grandmother didn't want to take time off and stay home for three weeks. Indeed, they hesitated to give her leave, because she was not only hard working and dependable, but also well liked by her colleagues. She was always in good spirits, had endurance, a good sense of humor and a cheerful word for everyone. As I grew up, I got to know her to be that way myself, and as she continued to work in a factory after the war, I heard her colleagues praise her on my frequent visits.

5. One more Romantic Adventure

On the eve of my departure I decided to take the streetcar alone to the main station early the next morning, my mother explained, although Omi wanted to come along to help me with the luggage. There were no more porters available, because all men who were able to work had been called upon to keep things going. However, I convinced Omi to stay home with you and Bettine, and just help me carry the luggage to the streetcar stop. I kissed you before I left, but you didn't really wake up. It was ice cold and pitch dark at five in the morning. The conductor had a stiff left arm from a war injury, but he was nevertheless kind enough to help us lift my two heavy suitcases into the streetcar. In those days, the new streamlined streetcars, called *hechtwagen*, the most modern ones in Germany, were running on the main lines. The drivers sat in their own small cabins, there were seats marked for the handicapped, and every car was equipped with a first aid kit. The seats were covered with dark green leather, the cars were built lower and the platforms raised enough for easy access for baby carriages and bicycles.

Even this early in the morning the streetcars were so crowded that the driver didn't stop at the last stations before the main railroad station. No one wanted to get off anyway. There were schoolchildren aboard, who were actually no longer allowed to take the streetcar, but many had a long way to school because numerous schools had been converted into military hospitals and refugee camps, and the children were taught in shifts in the remaining schools. Sometimes I wondered what those politicians in Berlin would come up with next as we were constantly hit with new regulations amidst increasing deprivation and the never-ending blather of the imminent *endsieg*.

I had no rational explanation for the feeling that was driving me to go on that journey. I simply had to do something, to see something new. The preparations for the trip diverted my heavy thoughts, and there was also the joy over the presents I was taking to Kurt and his comrades.

The two suitcases were heavy, as if filled with bricks. In each suitcase I had a four-pound stollen, Christmas cookies, smoked meat and sausage, and I had saved up my cigarette rations. I also took two bottles of schnapps, which Omi had procured for me after having begged her for weeks, as well as warm underwear, heavy woolen socks, and finally I decided to take along a dark blue pullover I had just finished knitting for Kurt from the wool he had sent from

France in 1940. It was to be a Christmas present, and I wanted to save it for peace time, because Kurt had practically no civilian clothes since he joined the army in 1939 right after finishing the gymnasium to get his military service behind him. Given the circumstances, it was the worst decision he could have made. Most of his classmates had opted to attend university, but Kurt's father Wilhelm – who was actually his stepfather – was a blue-collar worker, and in his narrow-mindedness he couldn't imagine an academic career for his son. Anyway, it was so cold that I didn't have the heart, so I packed the beautiful pullover for him to wear under his uniform. When he came home from prisoner of war camp, the pullover was gone. Kurt couldn't even remember whether he had lost it or it had been stolen.

At the main station I could hardly push through the throng of people across the streetcar tracks to the station with my luggage. The large square in front of the main station was swarming with refugees from the east, who were arriving daily by the thousands in overcrowded passenger and freight trains. After the long, exhausting trip they were overtired and fearful, but they were only allowed to stay in Dresden for twenty-four hours, just enough time to get washed, eat a hot meal, rearrange their luggage and sleep for a night. Then they had to move on.

As I struggled through the crowd, I thought of Kurt and that he was expecting me, so my courage wouldn't leave me. My hands were stiff from the bitter cold. I could hardly curl my fingers around the suitcase handles, and they threatened to slide out of my hands. The cobblestones were iced over, so I didn't dare to walk fast for fear of slipping and falling. With every step I had the feeling that my knees were about to buckle under the weight of the suitcases, when suddenly a man came from behind, took both suitcases out of my hands and left me with just one heavy bag and my handbag.

"Come along," he said, walking ahead of me, "I'll take you to your platform, just follow me. By the way, where are you going?"

"To Königsberg."

He walked fast, taking long secure steps. I could hardly keep up.

"Turn around!" He called out as he hurried ahead with my luggage without looking back, and when I didn't answer, because I was out of breath, he said, "Go back home! Nobody travels to Königsberg anymore, don't you know that?"

And all the time he walked on with my suitcases while I ran after him.

"I must go," I said, but I don't know whether or not he heard me. I never saw his face fully in the crowd. The sight of thousands of refugees and soldiers inside the station frightened me, and I almost lost my composure. Even during those weeks in late autumn it had remained relatively calm in the Fürstenstraße, and I hadn't expected such an onrush of people so early in the morning. We hurried up the stairs as fast as we could, then the man said, "This is your platform. Stay right here, the train will come any minute now." He put down my suitcases and disappeared into the crowd.

Suddenly two young soldiers stood next to me, asking where I was going. I showed them my ticket with the seat reservation. "We'll help you," they said and stayed close to me as we were looking in the direction of the incoming train. The soldiers ran along the train, searching for my compartment, then they helped me on board, pointed to my window seat, stowed away my luggage in the racks above me and took the aisle seats. The train filled up fast with pale, haggard-looking soldiers, worn out from lack of sleep. There were few civilian passengers, and I wondered how far they would travel. The soldiers had large packages with thick slices of whole grain bread and cold cuts and huge pieces of cake and bottles of schnapps. One of them sent around his bottle before the train had left the station. I doubt that any of them ever returned. Whenever I think back on this journey, I ask myself if they knew they were traveling to their death.

The train left punctually. A pale gray morning light lay over the city, and I looked out of the window as we were leaving Dresden, rode through the suburbs and villages and on and on through the endless winter landscape. We hadn't been gone that long when a strange and disquieting picture presented itself as we traveled along the same track that I knew from my trips to Silesia. I hardly dared to let my eyes wander around in the compartment, because I didn't want to look into the young soldiers' faces. In their midst I became aware of the war and felt a kind of shame. Many of them were mere schoolboys, and were already asleep before we had left the city behind us. They had the innocent faces of children, their skin was still soft and unshaven. In spite of the alcohol consumption the atmosphere was depressing. They all seemed to be absorbed in their own thoughts. The carefree mood and the strong spirit of similar trips during earlier, happier times had disappeared. There were none of the obscene jokes that I remembered from older soldiers on my trip to Grandfather the previous summer. They didn't even play cards. I would have liked to ask them where they were going and how they assessed the situation, but I didn't dare to begin a conversation. And they hardly exchanged a few words even with each other. Something strange and inexplicable lay in the air, as if we were approaching a turning point in history. Never before had I experienced anything like it. I hadn't expected such a drastic change, and felt as though I were suffocating. Even the soldiers must have sensed the unnaturalness of this journey that weighed heavily upon us, like the oppressive humidity before the outbreak of a thunderstorm. And all the while I thought of you in Dresden, wondering what you might be doing at that moment, hoping that Omi would take good care of you. I took deep breaths to help me remain calm, and looked out of the window. Now and then I heard the bawl of drunken soldiers from other cars.

The further we traveled from Dresden, the more I became aware of what I saw on the country roads. The sky hung low during our trip east. Suddenly I realized that we were heading directly into the war. We hadn't gone far when I began to see destroyed or burnt-out farmhouses on both sides of the tracks, and it wasn't long before we came upon completely deserted villages. As dusk was falling, it suddenly lightened up in the west as faint light-pink rays of sunlight broke through an opening in the gray sky, and a touch of pink spread over the snow-covered plains. Seconds later it was all over again. In the dim evening light I recognized a destroyed bridge, and fields and meadows laid to waste by the war machinery. Tanks had plowed deeply into the ground, leaving wide dark tracks. We passed shining black tree stumps where vast forests once stood. Fences leaned over half covered with snowdrifts. Hardly an animal was to be seen anywhere.

I had a strange feeling as I saw more and more signs that pointed to the beginning of the end of the war, that revealed themselves in increasingly frightening scenes the further east the train took us. Now and then I thought I should get off at the next station and take the first train back. I looked uneasily at my suitcases in the net above me, but I was weak and couldn't make a decision, so I simply rode on. I hardly ate a bite on the entire journey because of this choking sensation I had in my throat.

Finally we arrived in Königsberg. It was the end of the line, and my suitcases were on the platform before I knew it. Next, I took a narrow-gauge railway to the Baltic Sea Bath Cranz. We traveled along large frozen lakes surrounded by bizarrely bent and snapped reeds, past small birch tree forests, snow-covered dunes with black tufts of grass rising out of them, and on through plains that opened up to distant horizons. It was a landscape that enchanted the eye even in winter, and yet it was very different from the Elbe valley, where soft hills held the gaze of the beholder.

Kurt had come to meet me in Cranz in a carriage with a coachman and a pair of horses. The owner of the estate near Powunden where he was quartered had loaned it to him. I climbed into the carriage, Kurt wrapped a blanket around me, and I leaned back and took deep breaths of the wintry sea air, surrendering only too willingly to a rare feeling of complete bliss. I could smell the snow and felt pleasantly tired. In my daydreams, the ride from Cranz to Powunden mingled with the happy memories of cheerful, serene summer trips of earlier years, transfiguring the somber impressions, because far up there, in that remote corner of the world, the towns and villages, the farms, estates, rivers, lakes and people had remained unchanged.

For several glorious weeks I experienced unreal peaceful days in this far away winter world as it distracted my thoughts one last time before the catastrophe overtook us. How strong our confidence is, how little we can predict the future, how much we want to preserve what we are accustomed to, even if it's already running like sand through our fingers. I was full of hope until Christmas of 1944, even if it was regularly clouded over by dark premonitions that often robbed me of my sleep. How gullible we are, how readily we want to believe that the worst can be prevented after all, and that we shall escape it all once again. How little it takes, even in the midst of great adversity, for us to believe in an intact world.

The East Prussian aristocratic family that had invited me to stay at their estate had had twelve sons, all of them tall strong men with blond hair, blue eyes and high cheekbones. I looked at them often on photographs and family portraits. The two oldest sons had helped with the management of the estate until the outbreak of the war, while the others were far away at German universities, and one of them had already worked as a lawyer in Königsberg. They were all drafted very quickly, one after the other, or volunteered to the great chagrin of their parents. At the time of my visit they had all been killed in action.

Mourning hung over the manor, dark shadows lay on the people's faces due to the senseless deaths of their sons. Few words were spoken. No one wept. The East Prussians are a different breed of people. The man and the woman were alone on the estate with their only daughter, whose husband had also been reported missing in action, the female help and two old male farm hands. They were only able to take care of the most urgent tasks and the animals. They would get through the winter, most of the work was done until spring, the woman said, but added that she didn't dare to imagine how things could continue into the summer.

When Kurt and I were alone at last I tried to discuss the situation with him and what might lie ahead for us. He had to know more than I, and I wanted to hear his opinion. I told him frankly that after what I had seen and heard on my trip, I could no longer believe in a victory. He rebuked me and implored me not to speak a single word about it to anyone ever again.

I was thunderstruck at his response, and asked incredulously, "Can't you see what's going on? Do you have any idea at all what I saw on my way here? Shall I tell you about it? I thought you were better informed."

"Be quiet, Effi," he berated me, "we are at war. I was so looking forward to your visit, I only want to be with you, feel you, kiss you, look at you and talk about beautiful things with you and think of our future. I promise you, it won't be much longer."

"But what will this future be like, Kurt? That's what I want to know! You are living as though you're on an island up here. Can't you hear the distant rumbling of guns at night? How can you sleep? I am afraid."

Even late at night in bed, Kurt didn't want to talk about the recent course of events. He only wanted to lie close to me. His body felt tense while he was sleeping, he moaned, clenched his fists and thrust his arms around, and pushed against me with his legs as he had nightmares. When I woke him up and asked him what was wrong, he said nothing.

"Come on, talk to me, neither one of us can sleep," I encouraged him.

"Walls have ears," he said vehemently, and with that I was to be quiet.

"But I must talk about it. I cannot stand this uncertainty, it depresses me."

He answered, "Not now, later."

"When later?" I wanted to know, "later might be too late."

"You always exaggerate, there is time," he responded. "As you can see, everything is all right so far!"

"How can you say that, Kurt?" I asked upset. "Nothing is all right! I'm worried because of what I've seen."

"Let it be, Effi," he repeated. "You are in no position to judge the situation. We'll drive to the Kurische Nehrung tomorrow. You'll be amazed how beautiful it is out there."

"You know that I am looking forward to it. Don't take things so seriously all the time," I calmed him down. "Be glad I am here, but we have to make plans in case something happens to Dresden after all. We really ought to discuss that tomorrow. I need clarity, you must understand, some sense of security. I cannot count on my mother if the worst should happen. I want to hear the truth from you, how you see things. You and I, we must stick together and trust each other!"

"We'll see about it in the morning," he answered tight-lipped, and turned away from me, making believe he was sleeping.

I was dead tired from the unaccustomed cold and daily work at the manor as I helped the family, and finally I fell asleep as well.

When the woman of the estate and I met in the courtyard the following morning on her way to the stables, she took me aside, touching my right arm lightly as she pulled me behind the barn as inconspicuously as possible. Back there no one could see us. Nevertheless I felt her insecurity. Apparently she had difficulty speaking.

"Is something wrong?" I asked. "Please talk to me, you needn't be afraid," I encouraged her as she remained silent.

While looking around anxiously to make sure that no one had followed us or could see us from afar, she asked me at last in a low voice what I had seen on my trip, what the situation was like in the Reich, and could I advise her? Should they stay or flee? Her hastily spoken questions frightened me even though I was thinking of the war day and night.

To live in constant fear for so many years was horrible. You cannot imagine what it's like unless you've lived through it yourself. Sometimes I wanted to scream because I couldn't speak with anyone. There were moments when I thought I was going mad. As we stood next to each other, I was thinking all the time: she has lost her sons, what else was there? Was that not answer enough? What was she waiting for? But I didn't say that, I simply didn't have the heart. I was convinced that she knew exactly what to expect, and so I only said that things didn't look good, but that I couldn't give her any advice.

The woman must have felt my anxiety, and she slowly turned back to the courtyard. I walked with her so no one would become suspicious and added that she should think about things carefully, proposing that we could try to talk more while working in the kitchen. "There is so much to do every day, and I would like to help with the preparation of the meals and wherever else I might be needed," I offered. "You just have to tell me what to do." She thanked me quietly. We never talked about the circumstances again.

I felt sorry for her. I should have told this good woman more. In spite of my own fears, I had the urgent feeling all of a sudden that I couldn't keep what I had seen to myself and pretended nothing much was wrong. I don't know if I could have survived the death of twelve sons, it simply surpasses my understanding. I cannot forget her fate. To this day I am compelled to think of her. Her husband was a bear of a man, strong and taciturn. He had a broad open face and eyes that looked far and saw much. Why did they not understand the signs of the impending end? I wondered if they talked with each other at night, or if they were silent even then? Or had the death of their sons taken away their will to live?

My mother fell silent abruptly, seemingly lost in thought, and I was relieved. Hoping she had reached the end of her story for now, I was about to walk away, when she said suddenly, "It was betrayal." Her voice sounded strangely shrill. I winced, although she didn't speak loudly.

"What was betrayal?" I asked.

"That I didn't tell her enough. Her questions took me by surprise, she expected me to help her, but I simply couldn't get out any coherent words. When images from the train trip went through my head behind the barn and when I remembered the faces of the young soldiers in my compartment, I was suddenly afraid that someone might see us together or hear us talk and might question the woman later with treacherous intentions about our doings, and that she, in her confusion, might blurt out what she knew from me.

"After that encounter, I no longer felt like going on an excursion that day, and at breakfast I said to Kurt that I would rather go for a walk, far away from the manor, insisting that we must talk at last! He agreed. We dressed warmly and put on two pairs of socks, because the cold penetrated quickly through the soles of our boots and crept up our legs. The walk turned into a hike. Our hostess had given us apples and a package with ham sandwiches when she heard of our intention. But once again, Kurt and I didn't talk about the war. I never felt good again in that woman's presence. I had behaved like a coward."

"You mustn't think that way, Mutti. What more could you have said or done?"

"It was betrayal," she repeated, and nodded with her head as if to underscore her words.

"The betrayal took place on a very different level," I replied. "Besides, you had to survive for us children."

She shrugged her shoulders. "All the same, I failed her."

"Don't think like that. You are not to blame. Maybe the woman wasn't able to flee after the death of her sons? Maybe she wondered why she should go on living so far away from home, and could not find a good reason?"

"Oh, Anne, it was so hard, and we were all so afraid. You had to consider every word before you spoke. You could never be sure who might be listening."

"Exactly. And even if you had told her more, you couldn't have helped her. In the end it was her decision."

"That's true, but it isn't quite that simple. I had seen more than she had, and knew more. All of a sudden I felt responsible for others. Do you understand? She was so good to us. In the midst of the war, she turned those weeks at the manor into a holiday for Kurt and me. I didn't really understand that until later, after we had lost everything in Dresden. I can't even remember whether I thanked her enough for everything she did for us."

"But she knew how horrible the war was," I said.

My mother looked away briefly, but before I could say anything, she continued, "The woman prepared something special for us every night and set it on the small round table with the two wicker chairs in our room. Sometimes we found two slices of moist pound cake and a bottle of Mosel wine, or thick slices of freshly baked bread with homemade cheese. One evening there was a plate with smoked ham and a bottle of Bordeaux. Another time we found a selection of dried fruits, nuts and butter cookies waiting for us, with a pot of hot chocolate standing on a warmer. We always thanked her the next morning, and once she said, 'Why should we save it for the Russians? I am glad you liked it.'

"And what did I give her in return? You cannot imagine the way their house was furnished and how they lived. Everywhere in those huge rooms and in the long halls hung huge paintings and photos of their ancestors in heavy, carved golden frames. His mother was still alive. She was an aristocrat through and through; you could tell by her every move and word. She occupied the seat of honor at the head of the table. For special occasions they set the table in the large formal dining room with exquisite porcelain, sterling silver cutlery, heavy hand-cut crystal glasses, damask tablecloths with matching napkins and tall candles in silver candelabras. Kurt and I were always invited to join them. Never before and never again have I seen such a carefully set table. The food was excellent, prepared with great care. The conversation was discreet, words were chosen carefully; the war was not to be mentioned while we ate, neither the death of their sons. Large soup tureens were brought in, followed by deep bowls filled with steaming potatoes and dumplings, a variety of vegetables, huge platters with beef, or pork and veal roasts, or roasted geese, ducks and venison, as well as an assortment of fish. Once guests were invited, and fish, meat and fowl were served in consecutive courses. The women from the neighborhood had arrived early in the morning to help with the preparations. The food was served by the two old servants, dressed in tails and wearing white gloves, who stood behind us during the meal, passing the platters around for second helpings and pouring the wine. After the main course, they cleared the table and brought the desert plates with matching silverware and brandy. A strong coffee was served to finish off the meal, and the men smoked cigars and drank cognac, which made me feel dizzy in my head. Most likely it was the last great feast they celebrated in the old house."

I never knew what to make of these descriptions because I couldn't imagine such opulence. Once, when my mother seemed very worn out from the memories of her East Prussian adventures, I asked her if she had ever again heard from these people.

"No, never," she answered. "It was as if the earth had swallowed them up. Twice I filed an official search for them, both times unsuccessfully, and for years I looked through the lists of missing persons in the hope that I might come across their names or names of my relatives, but I never found them. I am almost convinced that they stayed on their estate and were driven off by the Russians or killed, because, just like Grandfather, they refused to leave. The estate had been their life; it had been in their family for centuries. It cannot have been long after I left, a few weeks at the most. In January 1945 East Prussia was burning."

After a few moments of reflection, my mother resumed her tale as though driven by an inner restlessness to move ahead.

The distant infantry rumblings sounded especially frightening at night, and the people became more and more agitated. On a sunny winter day, soon after the encounter with the woman, Kurt and I went to Cranz after all. The snow sparkled brightly. He wanted to take me to a Café where they were supposed to serve poppyseed cake. In my heart I still long for the vast open countryside.

On the day after our excursion Kurt had the afternoon off, so we went on a walk at noon, right after we had eaten a bite, because I finally wanted to talk about my trip back. The weather had changed; the sun shone pale. When we were about a quarter mile from the manor we discussed the situation at length for the first time, and admitted to one another at last that things were not looking well. Kurt, however, wanted to wait a few more days and asked me to stay with him for the time being. We still did not dare mention a defeat around Königsberg. The thought was simply inconceivable. On our way back, Kurt told me that they would most likely be moved to Sorquitten in the coming days.

"You are telling me that only just now? That sounds like retreat to me!" I exclaimed. "In that case we should make plans right away for me to go back home!" Kurt calmed me down and suggested that I should follow him in the event of a transfer as soon as he found a place for me to stay.

Suddenly things happened quickly, and within hours he was on his way with his signal corps. I packed my suitcases to be ready when I received a message to join him. When the telegram arrived two days later, I bid our hosts farewell, and the coachman took me back to Cranz. From there I traveled by train via Sensburg to Sorquitten, where I arrived in the evening. The stations along the way were not lit to prevent them from being detected by the enemy. I saw the name on the station placard when we entered Sorquitten, and at the same time heard Kurt calling out loudly, "Sorquitten! Sorquitten!" as he ran alongside the train before it came to a halt. He had come to meet me in his signal car, because trains didn't go to Warpuhnen where he had found lodging for me with a family. His division command post lay in Sensburg, but Kurt stayed with me that first night and later came to see me as often as he could. Frau Werfel was four years older than I, and lived with her mother-in-law and her two little girls in the large house. Her husband and her father were at war. She was surprised when Kurt told her that his wife would be coming to visit him.

I stayed with them for a week. They were warmhearted people, and although their household was small, I helped with the cooking and sewed dresses for the two little girls while thinking of you, Anne. By that time I had been away from home for over two weeks and hadn't heard anything about the latest developments. It was on the fourth evening, after the children were in bed, and we two women were alone in the living room, when Frau Werfel asked me in a hushed way what it was like out there. Immediately I felt hot and cold all over and began to tremble because I was afraid that her mother-in-law or Kurt might return at any moment. It's hard to describe this fear that would overcome me for the slightest reason.

"What would you do in our situation," she wanted to know, "we are directly in the path of the Russians. How long do you think our soldiers can hold them back? What does your husband say?"

Because I didn't answer right away, she told me to my face, "Your husband has radio contact, he must know what's going on!"

Her words agitated me. Perhaps to reassure me she added, "My husband always told me everything, but we haven't seen each other since the summer. Letters from the front are arriving very irregularly nowadays, and they don't tell me much. All I really know when I get a letter is that my husband was still alive at the time he posted it."

"Did you arrange a meeting point in case you must flee?"

"Yes, he has relatives near Hamburg. We agreed to meet there should the worst happen. I wonder if we can still get through? Only yesterday I looked at the atlas, and it's so far away. I have never been there. Do you know Hamburg?"

I shook my head. "The trains are still running."

"We would have to leave everything behind. The house would be looted and taken over by others immediately. Even so, I think of fleeing day and night." The last words she said more to herself, then she added, "I've already laid out everything that we need to take, but no one of my family knows about it yet. All I need now is to find the courage to leave and not look back. But how am I going to tell my husband's mother? And what will I do if she refuses to come along?"

At that moment the old Frau Werfel entered with a tray of glasses and a pot of hot punch. The fragrant scent of the hot wine filled the room, when suddenly I had the feeling that she had been standing behind the door listening to our conversation, and felt the blood rush to my face. Her daughter-in-law seemed startled, too. In order to divert her attention, I was about to ask where she got the cinnamon and cloves, when she said, "It's all right, I am worried, too. The *glühwein* will do us good. Tomorrow we shall see what to do."

She filled our glasses. Kurt returned half-frozen after having tried unsuccessfully to contact the Führer Headquarters in Rastenburg. His fingers were so stiff that he had to let cold water run over them first to warm them slowly. He was ill-tempered. Frau Werfel became anxious, but we didn't dare to ask much.

"Here, hold the glass with both hands and drink, that will warm you up from inside and outside," I said loudly while stepping close to him. His clothes were ice-cold and smelled of fresh snow. "I shall return to Dresden earlier than planned," I whispered.

"We'll discuss it tomorrow, Effi. I want to wait for the signals from headquarters. I'll try again after midnight," he answered nervously.

The Soviet army seemed dangerously close, but the family still couldn't imagine fleeing. Was it because hope continued to get the better of us, or were we paralyzed with fear in the middle of winter, unable to think straight, even though rumors of cruelties committed on civilians by Russian soldiers had been circulating for weeks? What were we supposed to believe? What lay ahead of us? Our soldiers were very tense, even if they continued to joke as they walked past women. Kurt, too, was more restless than ever. At night, we heard far-away rumbles and other ominous noises. The distance was difficult to judge because the vast plains carried the noise over many miles, but there were plenty of other signs that impressed upon us that the war was coming closer by the hour, and that the battles might soon be upon us.

I stayed two more days after that evening. Kurt had to go to Sensburg in-between. It was around the 10th of December. I wanted to be home for the third Sunday in Advent, and because I had to go back to Königsberg to catch the train to Dresden I would need several extra hours for the journey. I packed my suitcase while Kurt drove to Sorquitten to inquire about train connections. That was when he heard that the trains were no longer running according to schedule, but that the train to Königsberg would still leave as scheduled the next day. And so it happened that all of a sudden he hastened my departure and took me to the station the following morning. His commanding officer had also advised him to send me home because things could become ugly any minute. I was tormented by horrible premonitions.

6. The Train through Purgatory

I could only speculate what Kurt was thinking as he stood on the platform in the midst of the pushing and swaying crowd. When the train began to move, slowly pulling out of the station, people suddenly waved with a thousand handkerchiefs. Some women had even brought large white napkins, which they held with both hands, letting them wave like flags. However, the mood wasn't like it usually was at train stations, happy and cheerful, but rather somber and apprehensive. I had found a seat and opened the window. Kurt and I held on to each other's hands as the train left the station, and he ran alongside until he almost stumbled and we had to let go of each other. He continued running alongside the train to the end of the platform, where he stopped and grew small very fast. We waved until we lost sight of each other.

There were so many farewells during those war years, always accompanied by the uncertainty of whether and when we would see each other again. People could hardly tear themselves out of each other's embrace. My head was spinning as I sat down at last and tried to get comfortable. I sat facing forward and looked out of the window until my eyes were dry again.

As we approached Königsberg I became very edgy. Long before we pulled into the station we heard an increasing roar over the noise of our locomotive. Because I had to change trains, I was already standing at the door with my luggage as the train jolted to a halt. To my horror I saw a throng of people on the platform that was much worse than during my departure in Dresden. At the sight of the crowd my spirits sank; this was the catastrophe I had secretly feared. I was more pushed off than stepped off the train, and would have fallen except that the crowd on the platform held me up. I saw sheer terror in people's faces, and was desperately worried about how I would get to my connecting train. For what seemed an eternity I stood pinned between my suitcases, trying to listen to loudspeaker announcements, but they got lost in the confusion and tumult around me. Elbows and fists hit me in the sides and back, suitcases and boxes were shoved against my legs, making me stagger.

There would be a twenty-minute stopover in Königsberg. Kurt had told me that was enough time to catch my connecting train. As he said that at the station in Sorquitten while handing me the ticket to Dresden via Königsberg, making sure that I put it into my handbag, it sounded as if I were going on a trip like every other one. We were both trying to cover up our anxiety, but I could never have imagined what lay ahead of me. When the train to Dresden pulled in, all hell broke loose. The crowd shrieked hysterically, they pushed and shoved, recklessly knocking over and trampling down people while stumbling over luggage as they forced their way onto the long distance train.

I don't know how I managed to get on with my luggage. The onrush was so great that I feared getting shoved aside, but somehow I was able to claim my reserved seat. Before I knew it, the train was full to bursting with refugees and their luggage. No one could keep the people back, neither by command nor by force. They stormed the train with or without tickets. Old people were ruthlessly pushed aside, and children became separated from their parents. A man, whom I remember to this day, was holding a three year old boy high above his head so that he might catch sight of his mother, but he did not find her. Finally another man in our compartment pulled the boy inside through the window. Everyone wanted to get on the train as if it were the last opportunity to leave the town. Many refugees had already encountered horrors on their way to Königsberg, and were starved and half-frozen. Luggage and freight was stacked high on the platforms for transport, but in the end it was left behind because people had stormed even the freight cars. Freight that was already on the train was simply thrown out. Even mailbags were flung onto the platform so more could get on. Others pulled the baggage out of the racks and threw it out of the window to make room for small children.

This is the end, was all I could think. Anxiously I hoped that the train would pull out of the station and prayed that God might bring me home safely this once, and I vowed that I would never go on another trip. Why weren't we leaving, what were we waiting for? The cars were jammed full, I felt like suffocating, and my heart was throbbing hard. I told myself to stay calm and breath deeply while I looked at my wristwatch nervously. From then on my thoughts were only with you and our apartment on the Fürstenstraße.

At last the train began to move and slowly pulled out of the station. The roaring noise of the people that we left behind ebbed off. In a strange dream-like concentration I looked out of the window into the courtyards and windows of the apartment houses, and impressed upon my mind what the people were doing, wondering what fate might be awaiting them. I held my eyes fixed on the towers of Königsberg, and didn't dare to look away even for a second. When they finally disappeared at the horizon, I was sure I would never see that town again, but as it turned out, I was terribly mistaken.

Once the train was on its way, people settled down as best they could. Many fell into a deep sleep from exhaustion. I was dead tired, but couldn't close my eyes because that made me feel dizzy. We headed west for several hours. At times the train slowed to a walking pace; once it even stopped for several minutes in the middle of nowhere. Brakes squealed, the passengers became agitated, but then we continued on.

The battles seemed to accompany us. We heard distant infantry rumblings, now on the right, then to the left of the tracks. That was not a good omen, even though we couldn't see any fighting. I strained to look outside, although passengers repeatedly blocked my view. In the ditches and along the edges of the fields I saw gruesome scenes of the war from past battles and impending death. On both sides of the track lay destroyed and burnt-out military vehicles; I saw dead people and soldiers, frozen horses and farm animals lying in the snow. The roads were crowded with refugees on their way west with heavily loaded coaches and covered wagons. Even without evacuation orders the East Prussians couldn't be held back any longer. The further west we came, the more frequently we saw freshly piled up mounds of earth where people had been buried alongside the highways and the railway embankment. Overturned coaches with broken axle shafts pointing macabre into the sky scornfully reminded me of orthodox crosses. I felt sick when I thought of the future. Now and then I fell into a light sleep during which I was haunted by horrific dreams, from which I awoke frightened to death.

Suddenly the brakes squealed and the train jolted to an abrupt halt. My head flew forward and then slammed back against the compartment wall, giving me a large, swollen bump and a bad headache. The people standing in the aisles staggered, lost their balance and fell on top of each other and on us; luggage and bundles of clothing were flung out of the racks. Frightened, travelers opened the windows and leaned out as far as they could to see what was going on. The fresh air felt good at first, but then it got cold very fast.

Someone said that German soldiers had stopped the train because a Russian division had successfully broken through German lines and captured large areas of Prussian territory while advancing all the way to the railroad tracks just ahead of us. Everyone was in a state of utmost alarm. Men got off and walked to the locomotive to explore the situation and relieved themselves alongside the train. The urine melted the snow making it steam, and soon the snow was stained yellow everywhere. A few crows flew over us appearing like messengers of death. I wanted to go to the toilet, but it was impossible. I couldn't even stand up. There were people sitting on the floor between our feet and in the aisles, and I would have lost my seat immediately. After a while we heard that the train couldn't get through, and that we would be returning to Königsberg momentarily. I closed my eyes and clenched my teeth so hard that my jaws and face muscles ached. I did not dare to imagine what might happen if we weren't able to get out of Prussia. I took an apple out of my handbag and bit into it.

The train jerked to a start, and we headed back. Hours later we pulled into the main station of Königsberg. The conductors had locked all the doors of the wagons from the inside before we entered the station and had forbidden us to open the windows under any circumstances. The train was already overloaded to the breaking point, and they feared that the axles wouldn't be able to carry more. I couldn't see the platforms because of the crowd. The noise was unbearable; it was like a witches' cauldron. The swaying crowd encircled the train, people screamed and pushed, they stepped on top of everything to see better and tried to storm the train even before it came to a halt. In spite of the icy cold men climbed onto the roofs of the wagons, so that we felt them rock, pulling women up behind them. After we had been sitting in the station for about half an hour it had become so stuffy in the compartments that I began to feel sick from the stench and lack of oxygen. The people became agitated, and their faces turned red or ashen. Some vomited and others coughed, and eventually we simply had to open the windows to let in fresh air.

The instant the windows were opened just a crack, they were pulled down all the way from the outside. Immediately women handed us their small children and pieces of luggage, and then tried to climb through the windows themselves. Passengers helped them in, others pushed from the outside. Railroad employees tried to keep them from getting on the train by pulling them back down on their legs until their fingers lost their grip on the window frames and they fell back. Mothers were pushed aside after their children were already on the train, and conductors yelled to close the windows. At some point reinforcements arrived, but they couldn't get through the crowded wagons, and many people succeeded in getting on.

As long as I live I shall never forget the tragedies that took place right before my eyes. A young mother I had noticed in the chaos on the platform directly outside of my window was one of the last refugees to get on the train. Only moments before she had let out a shrill scream that sounded like the howl of a wounded animal, cutting through me to my bone marrow. It pursued me for days, and I still hear it today whenever I think of her. The woman had tied her infant daughter with a square scarf in front of her chest underneath her coat, which she had buttoned up over the child to keep her warm and to have both hands free. On the platform she was pushed so hard by the crowd that her child was squeezed to death by the heavy knapsack that a soldier was carrying on his back. Another soldier, who understood from the woman's screams what had happened, wanted to help. He forced his way to the pile of luggage on the platform, took a carton, emptied it, pushed back through to the woman and wanted to untie her baby to put it into the box, but she wouldn't let him touch the child and screamed even louder, lashing out wildly at him. All of a sudden she was sitting on the floor in a corner of our compartment. Her face was as white as a sheet and she was silently swaying back and forth. She had untied the scarf and was holding the dead infant in her arms. She looked gaunt. Her dry, red eyes stared with a crazed expression at her dead little girl, whom she kissed and hugged without paying the least bit of attention to what was going on around her. Then a man moved in front of her, blocking her from my view, and I felt a great tension unwinding inside of me. When I looked in her direction again later she was gone.

I cannot say how long the train stood in the Königsberg station. I had lost all sense of time, my nerves were tense, and I experienced everything around me as though I was seeing it through a filter, as if I wasn't really sitting right in the middle of it all, but rather as an observer who could get up at any moment and walk away from a bad movie. Hours later we heard that the Prussian areas along the railroad track had been recaptured by German troops, and that we would set out again at any moment. A desperate mother, who was unable to get into our compartment, screamed for her child at the very last moment as the train was beginning to move. A man took the crying girl that had been sitting on the old woman's lap across from me, and whom no one had been able to calm down, and passed her back through the window. Many children left without their parents. I saw some of them later at the station in Dresden, scared and huddled together in small groups, where women from the NSDAP, the National Socialist German Worker's Party, were gathering them up. I've often wondered what became of them. I'm sure most of them never found their parents again. There were so many cruel fates and so much hardship and misery in those days.

When I felt the wheels rolling again underneath me I was relieved, but the subliminal fear, that we might not make it this time either, remained. I wondered whether Kurt knew anything of our odyssey and this madness. Königsberg was a highway and railway junction, but I have no idea what cities we passed through before we finally entered Saxony. We didn't stop at the overcrowded stations, so I couldn't always recognize where we were. When the train went through long, wide curves and I could see the sides of the other wagons, I saw people sitting on the bumpers. They had tied themselves to them so they wouldn't fall off should they fall asleep along the way. Many refugees froze to death. Others lost their strength and fell off the roofs.

You cannot imagine the things I saw; there are no words for it! And whenever I thought things couldn't possibly get any worse, new horrors overtook us. How can one find words for something so incomprehensible or describe the sheer terror of it all? I can only try again and again to speak about it. For the sake of the people who perished I must speak out.

That ride back into the Reich turned into the worst trip of my life. The train was so overcrowded when we left Königsberg for the second time that

I could hardly move my arms and legs, and I had the feeling I was being choked to death when someone pushed a knapsack into my face or pressed hard against me. Again we were forced to stop several times along the way, but then we pressed on, and I was lulled by the rhythmic clacking of the wheels on the tracks as it became night and then morning again. During the entire train ride it was impossible to get to the toilet, which we couldn't have used anyway, because people were standing and sitting there, too. Passengers began to relieve themselves into bottles or other containers and then passed them on to those standing at the windows who opened them and emptied out the contents, but they had to make sure the wind wouldn't blow the stuff back into the compartment. I simply could not do that in front of the other passengers. Many wet their pants. I hardly ate or drank anything. Eventually I no longer felt my bladder.

At the dawn of the new day, I looked into the pale, worn faces of the passengers, and suddenly I got stomach spasms and felt like vomiting. We were surrounded by a terrible stench of sweat, urine and feces. The old woman with deep wrinkles in her face who had been sitting across from me the entire time, quickly held a bottle of Danziger Goldwasser in front of my face saying, "My dear child, take a gulp before you pass out. Can you see the gold sparkle?" And before she let go of the bottle she lifted it for a second toward the dim ceiling light. Her eyes looked wild. We hadn't exchanged even one word up to then. I reached for the bottle and took a sip, and then another. The schnapps, with tiny specs of real gold, burned in my throat. I could feel it go down all the way and took a third gulp. The queasy feeling in my stomach abated, and the alcohol rushed to my head. Another woman, who had been sitting on the floor between our legs for hours so that my legs had become stiff because I couldn't move them, suddenly tore the bottle out of my hand and took several greedy gulps. The old woman gave off a shrill, crazy laugh, seized the bottle, put the cork back in and held it tight, rocking it like a small child. Many people got drunk on the trip.

A depressing hopelessness mingled with fear afflicted me periodically as I sat squeezed into my seat. When we had the worst segment of the trip behind us, and the locomotive was heading toward Saxony after having been refilled with coal and water, rumors had it that this train was the last one to leave Königsberg. I don't know where this news originated. Maybe the engineer had intercepted some wireless message. At any rate, the news raced through the train producing new panic because many families had been separated at the station in Königsberg and were hoping that their relatives would be right behind them on the next train. What was to become of them now? How and where would they ever find each other again? I reproached myself in retrospect for having stayed so long, and looked forward to my arrival in Dresden with feverish anticipation.

From Bromberg on the train stopped again at the stations, letting travelers get off. The woman who had been sitting on the floor at my feet got up with great effort, and at last I was able to move my legs again. When we approached Dresden the train picked up speed since the tracks here were still in good condition. The real impact of the war had not yet reached this part of Germany.

Suddenly, a soldier I hadn't seen before was standing right in front of me. He had his left arm in a sling and wasn't very stable on his legs. In a curve he was pushed against my knees. He had his back toward me and blocked my view out of the window. All I could see was his coat, when I suddenly noticed a louse crawling over his coat collar. I shrieked and literally shook from disgust. What was I going to do if the louse fell on me and I couldn't find it? And who knows how many more lice were crawling about on his uniform? I pulled my legs closer so I wouldn't touch him. My calves were pressing hard against the seat. When I looked up again, the louse had disappeared. At some point, the soldier made his way back toward the center aisle. I searched my clothing, my whole body was itching, but I didn't see any lice.

Finally we entered the main station in Dresden. My legs felt weak. I dragged my luggage out of the train somehow, then left it sitting on the platform, and ran for a public toilet. The suitcases where still there when I returned, and I lugged them to the streetcar station. Back home I simply dropped the luggage in the hall and rushed to the bathroom to urinate again. I sat there for several minutes with my elbows propped up on my thighs and held my head in both hands. It just wouldn't stop. My bladder hurt so badly that I could have screamed. Afterward I ran hot water into the bathtub, got undressed and threw all my clothes into the corner on the tiled floor, because I wanted to search them later for bugs and brush them out over the tub. I climbed into the tub, soaped myself from head to toe, washed my hair and scrubbed away the dirt of the trip with a luffa sponge until my skin was red all over. I ran some more hot water, and then I called for Omi who brought me a cup of coffee. A luxurious feeling went through my body. My muscles relaxed and the warm water made me sleepy. You followed Omi into the bathroom, Anne, and sat down on the stool and just stared at me. I asked Omi for clean underwear and my bathrobe. She hung the bath towel over the heater to warm it up and put the other items on top of the laundry basket while lamenting all the time about what could have happened to me on the trip, and had I ever considered what was supposed to become of her and the children in case I didn't return? "How unreasonable of you," she repeated over and over, "how very unreasonable!" That's when the doorbell rang. Herr Schöne, the custodian, brought in my second suitcase that I had left downstairs behind the front door.

Of course Omi was right, my mother admitted, adding, I often have to think of the people who were left behind in Königsberg, and who had to set out on foot on the long march west. As I relived the last twenty-four hours in the safety of our home, I realized that I had escaped a terrible fate just in the nick of time. Months later I heard that things had gotten much worse very fast because the allied forces detonated the bridges across the Oder river to hold back the increasing stream of refugees. The only way left to safety was to flee across the Baltic Sea, but the Soviets torpedoed the ships crowded with civilians and wounded soldiers, and thousands drowned.

Years later, while we were still in East Germany, people eventually began to talk about the collapse of the German army and the fate of the eastern provinces, and we found out that East Prussia, Pomerania and Silesia should have been evacuated at the latest by the autumn of 1944, long before I visited Kurt in Powunden. However, the leaders of the different districts in Germany had been given strict orders to prevent any evacuation to avoid causing panic amongst the population. The East Prussians were not only forbidden to flee from the advancing Russian troops under penalty of death, they were called upon to oppose them.

After draining the bath water, there was a dark ring around the inside of the tub. I scrubbed it clean and dried it out, then brushed out my clothes over it and hung them on a clothesline I stretched across it to air them out. Thank God I found neither lice nor bedbugs. Those I saw later on the uniforms of Russian soldiers. They seemed to be immune to the vermin.

Before I left the bathroom, I opened the window. When I came out, Omi was busy unpacking my suitcases. I was too tired to help, and just staggered to bed. She had put a hot water bottle at the foot of the bed and brought me a glass of tea with honey. I slept through the night until late the next morning.

As my mother retold the story of her last trip to East Prussia, a longing for a united Europe grew within me in my earliest childhood, long before anyone even talked about the Cold War. In time, Königsberg became a magical word, and I studied its history and the photos and etchings of the town as well as the surrounding countryside. The German romantic poet, Joseph von Eichendorff (1788-1857), who came from Silesia and worked for the Prussian government in Königsberg, wrote about his own journeys by train, describing the kaleidoscope of landscapes flying by and depicted the busy train stations, while he felt caught between the past and modern times. His romantic soul was tired of Europe and its quarrels, and at the same time plagued by a certain fashionable boredom. To escape this universal weariness, Eichendorff, a devout Catholic, set out on his way to visit a hermit, who was supposed to live near a ruin above the woods. However, as he inquired about the hermit's whereabouts, no one on the train, flying through Europe, connecting people, cities and countries at a previously unheard of speed, could give him any useful directions to the hermit's humble abode. And so the poet complained that the people of this new age knew exactly the hour and minute a train would arrive in Paris or Triest or Königsberg, where he did not want to go, but no one could tell him anything about the direction and the distance to the mysterious forest, where he did want to go.

At the time when Eichendorff took that train trip in the middle of the 19th century, Europe was still whole, and thanks to the rapidly expanding network of railroad tracks, its cities had moved very close together. I am convinced that the train my mother took was not unlike the one the poet had taken, and it most certainly rolled for long distances over the same tracks that had been laid during the poet's time. But beyond that there is no comparison, because while Eichendorff, looking from his train window far into the distant countryside, was able to make philosophical observations as he contemplated Europe's future, my mother only witnessed the destruction caused by a war that brought the whole continent to its knees. How much weariness, boredom and misjudgment of the signs of the time had to descend over Europe since the days of Eichendorff, so that World War II could rage across the countries and through its cities and kill millions barely ninety years later, until everything was completely demystified and destroyed by the time of the Advent season in 1944? By then nothing was left anymore that could remind us of the poet's blissfully happy travels.

It was a trip of love and romantic longing, against all reason, her husband said when I asked him about it after her death. And that I have to believe.

7. The Calm before the Storm

Back in Dresden, life became more difficult with every day, my mother continued. We had already experienced a lack of the absolute necessities during the months before my last trip. But what wore me out even more than having to do without those things we had considered indispensable during happier times, was the realization that we had started the war, although after it was all over, it still took me years to understand the full extent of the destruction. My nerves were strained since the summer of 1944 because I was completely left to my own devices and couldn't talk with anyone about the most recent developments. Neither could I ask anyone for advice. The air raids increased, and I no longer doubted that a catastrophe was imminent, wondering when it would be our turn after almost all large German cities had been destroyed by years of repeated bombings.

Hardly anyone talked about it, but I knew that children from the Ruhr area, the largest industrial area in Germany, had been evacuated to Dresden. I should research these events some day. As far as I can recall, there were evacuation plans in place for the schoolchildren of Dresden since the bombing of Leipzig in early December 1943. They called it *kinderlandverschickung,* because they sent the schoolchildren to the country to get them out of harm's way. And just how long were the children supposed to live separated from their parents, I wondered? Would they really suffer less anxiety living with strangers in unfamiliar surroundings, and would they really be safer away from home in case of emergency? And what about the small children who weren't of school age yet, what about their safety? We felt so isolated. In spite of all the circular letters and appeals to the population from the authorities, no one knew anything definite. Things changed from day to day. It could even happen that orders had to be taken back under mounting pressure from the people, and since I had no children of school age, I only heard of the *kinderlandverschickung* from acquaintances. Many of the mothers refused to have their children sent away as they were already suffering enough because of the absence of their husbands, fathers and brothers, and so the children were a comfort to them. Besides, many parents no longer trusted the party leaders and school principals.

I didn't dare to talk about it with friends. I had no time for long discussions anyway, and there were plenty of other worries. I couldn't even talk with Omi because she was too fearful and wanted to have nothing to do with any of it, making believe that the war was of no concern to her. She worked at the factory, and at the end of a long, hard day she was happy just to be home. All she wanted was her cup of coffee after work, some cake and a little music. She had learned to enjoy every free hour and every ray of sunshine.

By the end of 1944, many in my circle of friends began to whisper of the possibility of a complete defeat, and even that sounded like hope. We could no longer fool ourselves; the war was catching up with us in the cities. It came from the front right into our homes, and I must say that I was less afraid of a lost war since my last trip to East Prussia than of a never-ending war. More and more soldiers were killed in action, so schoolboys and old men were drummed together to take their place. I saw the shabby groups gather in the streets, which made me feel uneasy and stirred up anger inside of me. From then on even the letters from the front arrived only sporadically and with great delays.

Such insanity! Just think of it, my mother exclaimed. They still organized marches through the streets with waving flags at a time when there were hardly any men left to take care of even the most urgent repairs, when people began to feel worn out by the grueling circumstances of daily life and no one had the time any longer nor the desire for such parades. Didn't they have better things to do? The only color spots left in our cities were the countless red flags with black swastikas hanging from public and private buildings that even as late as in the winter of 1944/45 tried to give us the illusion of an imminent victory in which I could no longer believe. And yet, even after five years of war, there were still women who stopped on the sidewalks to salute with outstretched arms the diminishing troops and their commanders marching down the middle of the streets. Some continued to walk alongside of them for a block or two with their children, but the joyous mood of the early years was gone. If I was taken by surprise by a parade, I simply looked the other way, pushing the baby carriage a little faster to escape them, and whenever possible I entered a store or disappeared into a side street. But if by some coincidence the parade and I happened to meet head on, and I recognized a neighbor or a relative who sided with the Nazis, I had to stop for the Hitler salute. This gesture always produced a strange feeling in my stomach, but I had no choice. We were simply too afraid of being reported if we did not shout "Heil Hitler!"

My mother imitated the salute at such moments. She stood up suddenly and her right arm shot out as I had seen in so many documentaries and on photographs. The sight embarrassed me, and I wished she would stop with the salute. One day I took courage and begged, "Don't do the salute anymore, Mutti, it looks so out of place, I don't ever want to see it again." I looked away to avoid eye contact with her.

"But that's how it was, the salute was part of it!"

Her words sounded a little defiant and ill at ease. There was something moving and bold in my mother's expression and the way she stood in the middle of the room, her arm stretched out for the Hitler salute. When she became aware of what she was doing, and perhaps realized how strange it must seem to us, she let her arm sink, almost hiding it behind her back, as if to take back the gesture.

This instance remained deeply engrained in my memory, except that today I know I had no idea what was really going on inside of her. I can only guess what she had to overcome and put behind her with that salute. She seemed so alone and vulnerable at that moment. There was something so helpless about her that felt like a dark cloud had descended upon us. Now it was my turn to feel embarrassed. She felt ashamed for something that she had not done often, and then only from fear and under duress. I know she neither followed blindly nor was she an opportunist. She often mentioned how willingly people had used the Hitler salute right from the beginning. Her disgust was real, she had thought about it. Just like everything else that she told us about the war and the postwar years, her words expressed a desperate search for understanding. She was in her mid-thirties when her words and gestures hit me and made me think. I was about fourteen and in the process of forming my own opinions about those years. The way she spoke captivated my imagination. It must have been painful for her to talk about those years, but then again, perhaps talking eased her agony?

After my complaint she omitted the salute. I was relieved, and we never mentioned it again. Today I think that maybe it was good that she demonstrated it to me. It seemed so grotesque, and I had to ask myself what I would have done in her place? What would I have done?

Kurt had promised that he would come home for Christmas, my mother continued at some later opportunity, but I didn't count on it any longer after my return from Königsberg. How was he supposed to make it when the trains were no longer running and the streets were impassable? But then he came after all. His telegram from Berlin reached us on the morning of December twenty-second, and a few hours later he was there. Rolf would arrive the following day.

It was the sixth Christmas during the war. Again I had asked the zoo gardener, who still remembered Papa, for fir branches so I could decorate our apartment in a festive way. I had put fir twigs behind all pictures on the walls and filled several vases with the larger branches, adorning them with tiny colorful glass balls and tinsel. On the morning of the twenty-fourth Kurt brought in the Christmas tree from the balcony to set it up in the living room,

Elfriede Richter, her husband and two daughters, Christmas 1943

and together we decorated it with the beautiful Christmas tree decorations, all of them small works of art that Papa had collected over the years. Finally we attached twenty-four candles holders to the branches and put in the candles as straight as possible. It was a beautiful tree. Even so, I felt miserable at the thought of the upcoming festivities, and as I was bending over the kitchen table rolling out the noodle dough for Rolf, I felt like crying. We had survived so far, I thought, but how would it all end? Rolf always wanted noodles because potatoes caused him severe stomach pains. But for Kurt I had to cook potatoes anyway, because he didn't like noodles. Omi had begun to heat the tile stove in the living room in the early afternoon.

I pushed aside these dreary thoughts, stroked back a lock of my hair that had fallen into my face, and continued with the cooking. Finally I baked a chocolate cake for Kurt, which he preferred even over the best *Dresdner Christstollen* with almonds and raisins. Grandfather's yearly food shipment for the stollen and the festive meals that always took place at our house with the whole family had arrived later than usual. We were already afraid that it might have gotten lost when the two wicker baskets arrived at last with the contents all jumbled up. I had saved enough butter over the previous months just in case because I always wanted to have the stollen ready early so the ingredients would have time to reach their peak of flavor by Christmas.

My mother's mood changed frequently as she told her stories, and even decades later she would suddenly mock Martin Mutschmann's speeches, who was governor of Saxony from 1935 on. His radio addresses were supposed to cheer up the people and make them stick to the party line. On Christmas Eve of 1944 he tried to lift our spirits by claiming that the population could breath easier during the holidays after the successes at the western front. But my mother knew better since her return from Königsberg, and she exclaimed indignantly, "Such idiocy! Mutschmann made fools of all of us! I bet he didn't believe his own words anymore. Today we know that he had a private bunker built on his property in 1943! And I certainly did not observe anything about the population breathing easier either."

In most families the husbands, fathers, sons, uncles and fiancés were not home for Christmas. They had either fallen, were missing in action, had been taken prisoner, or were no longer given home leave. Especially during Christmas people missed them sorely. Besides, the city was overflowing with refugees, and even the Christmas parcels to the front hadn't gotten off as smoothly as in previous years because the railroad lines had been damaged repeatedly by heavy bombing. The trains no longer ran on schedule, nor were there enough helpers to handle more than the most urgent letters and packages. Other more important things had to be transported to the troops. We were among the few lucky families during the Christmas of 1944, if you want to call our situation lucky.

Lieselotte already arrived before noon on the 23rd, my mother continued. She had put her small brown leather suitcase with her things for the night into Rolf's room. When Omi saw that, she ostentatiously carried it back into the hall and set it down next to the front door. I was irritated, and I hoped that she wouldn't start an argument when Rolf came.

Lotte was wearing an elegant dress that she had sewn. She came into the kitchen and asked for an apron so she could help me, but she was so excited that she was of little use. She was no housewife anyway. Besides, she could hardly wait for Rolf to arrive, and looked out of the window whenever she heard a streetcar. So I sent her into the living room to be with Omi, who was sitting in her favorite chair drinking coffee while enjoying popular arias from operettas on the radio. When the program was over Lotte put on Papa's records, singing and dancing along.

Rolf arrived shortly thereafter, young and charming, with a huge bunch of roses for his Lotte. He had presents for all of us, which he passed out right away instead of waiting until Christmas Eve because he was so happy. He wouldn't disclose where he had gotten the roses. We all knew there were no fresh flowers in any of the flower shops. As soon as his hands were free, he embraced Lotte, whirling her through the living room while kissing her happily in front of us. "Come," he said to her, "come to my room, you lovely girl." She whispered something into his ear. He stepped into the hall to get her suitcase, but Omi couldn't keep her mouth shut. This was her apartment and they were not married, she blurted out. "My sweet beloved little mama, either Lotte comes with me to my room or we go to her apartment. What do you think? It's Christmas and so wonderfully warm right here." Rolf flirted with her and took her into his arms. His blue eyes sparkled at her, but Omi wouldn't change her mind. This catholic, Upper Silesian obstinacy! Had she forgotten the days of her own youth? As if she hadn't had any male visitors since Papa's death!

Rolf and Lotte went to her place, and I begged them to come back for supper and handed them a plate of cake. "We'll do it for you, Sister," he promised. After they were gone it was very quiet in the apartment, and you, Anne, cried when your Uncle Rolf left. I had to finish cooking, and now Omi had to take care of you girls instead of being able to sit in her rocking chair and daydream.

The following day the two lovers returned for dinner and the exchanging of gifts. Then they left again. Rolf had to return to the front before New Year's eve. On his way to the station, he came with Lotte to say good-bye, kissing the tears from Omi's face. You were crying, too, Anne, and didn't want to let him go, and we accompanied them to the streetcar stop.

Why did it have to be that way, I ask you, why? Sometimes Omi drove me to despair. And then she cried and mourned over her son's death for the rest of her life. She never got over it. We never found out what happened to him. That was the worst, the increasing pain as hope gradually died, and then the growing certainty that he will never come back. Christmas of 1944 was the last time we all gathered together in the living room. Rolf was with the cavalry somewhere at the eastern front, but we never knew exactly where. The positions changed often, and letters and post cards from the front reached us with great delays during the last months of the war, or perhaps not at all. Rolf loved his horse, which Grandfather had given him, more than anything. In the beginning, he didn't want to give his grandson a horse, although Rolf could only join the cavalry if he had his own horse. He was hoping for healthier, more easily digestible food and better conditions in general. More importantly, however, he felt more secure with a horse. It took a long time until Grandfather gave in to Rolf's request in the spring of 1941, but not before Omi had scolded him and called him heartless. When he gave Rolf the horse, he said expressly, "The horse belongs to you, and not to Mr. Hitler and those scoundrels, don't ever forget that. And when the war is over you bring it back to me!"

There is a photograph of Rolf taken somewhere in the east with his horse, which was also named Rolf just like he. The picture shows a young man in civilian clothes with his head leaning against the head of his horse. It is a thoughtful

Rolf Richter with his horse Rolf, 1944

and open, far from finished face that has been smiling at me for the past sixty years. It would remain the last photo of Rolf. There were no others after that. On the back of it he had written with pencil in very accurate letters: "April 1944. With my faithful horse Rolf – Rolf and Rolf get along very well!"

Rolf was convinced that the horse would save his life, my mother said whenever we looked at the photo, but I dare say that it cost him his life, for Rolf was a strong, well-fed horse, one of the best from Grandfather's stable. Maybe Rolf was killed in action and a Russian soldier took it. But perhaps an even worse fate awaited him after the German army was pushed back. Maybe he starved or froze to death, or died of stomach cramps and bleeding ulcers, or he was captured and taken to Siberia. We received one more post card from him in the beginning of January 1945, after he had rejoined his unit. That was the last time we heard from Rolf. My brother, the poor boy, suffered the worst fate. He never got the chance to be anything but a soldier, and for that he had no talent, as he had often said.

8. Another Wedding

In the winter of 1944/45 even Omi's sisters hardly came by anymore. It was difficult to visit one another during blackout on those short winter days. Besides, we were all occupied with ourselves, with our fears and our fight for survival.

Taking care of everyday life took all of my energy. My thoughts were constantly revolving around the war. At times I felt as though the earth was shaking, as if everything around me was being turned upside down, and I talked myself into believing it was best not to think too much about it all.

During those last months I only visited my best friend Lara Fischer and her family regularly. They lived close by on the Gabelsberger Straße in the direction of the Elbwiesen, the beautiful meadows along the riverbanks. If I had to go out at night during a new moon I could easily lose my orientation, even though I was at home in this city, because there were no streetlights on. The town was engulfed in utter darkness.

Lara's mother, Helene Fischer, was Russian. She only spoke broken German with a strong Russian accent. Her German husband was a merchant in the Russian fur trade and spoke fluent Russian. At the outbreak of the war he was in Leningrad. Long after he should have been back from his business trip, they received news from him that he was well, that they should not worry about him, but that he would be back later than planned. That was the last sign of life from him.

Whenever Russian officers were among the prisoners of war in Dresden, the Gestapo, the secret state police, came to get Helene, and forced her to interpret in court. Back home again at night, she talked about the horrors she witnessed in court, her eyes brimming with tears. The Soviet army had barely entered Dresden when three Russians officers came to get Helene and Lara. They were imprisoned for months and subjected to terrible mistreatment. After their release, they fled to the American zone. Lara's husband, together with their two children, had left the Soviet zone immediately after her detention. Her older brother Alfons had already fled to the Rheinland months earlier. Olga, Lara's younger sister, was not home when the Russians came. A neighbor warned her about what had happened when she entered their street late that afternoon. She never set foot in the apartment again, and after her neighbor had gotten a few things for her from her room, she fled to Heidelberg.

Throughout her life, my mother spoke vividly of the howling sirens that had sounded almost daily air raid warnings since the beginning of 1944. She stressed how people interrupted whatever they were doing immediately to run for shelter, even if the all-clear signal followed shortly after.

The more I researched and read about the history of Dresden during the war, the more it surprised me that my mother never mentioned the bombing of the railroad yard in Dresden Friedrichstadt and other areas of the city a month before on the 16th of January 1945, a few minutes after 12 noon. The scattered bombing had caused several hundred deaths, and a great many people were injured. Hadn't she heard the sirens? Had she missed the rescue operations, the clearing away of rubble and the repairing of houses? Didn't she notice that several streetcar lines had been out of commission for days? Today I believe that the attacks on the 7th of October 1944 and the 16th of January 1945, which had not hit our part of town, simply faded from most people's memory, sinking into obscurity as they were overshadowed by the events of the night of February 13th, and although my mother always mentioned four attacks, and others even speak of a fifth that occurred at noon on the 15th of February, they remained nebulous for me until I read about the bombings years later. Once I overheard an argument between my mother and grandmother, and found out that before her trip to Cottbus to attend the wedding of her husband's comrade, my mother had taken the train to Bischofswerda on the 15th of January to fetch some of his things he had asked for from his parents' apartment. Contrary to her initial plans, she had stayed overnight, and Omi had not gone to the basement with us children, although the air raid on the 16th of January had been in force citywide.

The shrill sound of the sirens was still in my system, even after we had been living in the Federal Republic of Germany for years, my mother told us often. My heart raced whenever factory sirens went off at noon or at the end of the workday, or when the fire brigade came rushing down the streets. It immediately reminded me of the sound of air raid sirens in Dresden, when I automatically looked for shelter, or ran into the nearest park, or sprinted down the street to reach our house. Soon the time came when I no longer dared to go far from our house. During a neighborhood project, our cellar had been officially declared as an air raid shelter for the immediate neighborhood. Its brick barrel vault was stronger than that of other houses, and didn't threaten to collapse so fast in the event of a direct hit.

However, these basements could by no means give adequate protection to all the inhabitants of Dresden. Besides, the city itself was without any kind of defense since the summer of 1944, when the last antiaircraft guns had been moved to where they were needed more urgently, according to war experts, or they lay dismantled and ready for transport, and thus were useless. That the city was without flak is, however, unimportant in retrospect, because nothing, not even the very best defense, could have made a difference against the overwhelming assault by the allies. Besides, there were hardly any men left who could have handled these heavy anti aircraft guns.

As much as she spoke about it, my mother could never understand how a defenseless city could have been attacked with such violence, and even decades later she never disguised her horror over the formidable force of retaliation. Time and again she tried to make some sense of the complete destruction of the old part of town, while the suburbs and industrial areas were spared to a great degree, but found no answer. Even so, she never doubted that we had brought the catastrophe upon ourselves, and blamed the Nazis and their supporters for the war. She denounced those who held the responsibility for the safety of the city for leaving the citizens in ignorance just to keep them quiet, and repeated how her father had prophesied the war as early as 1934. It was as though her father's words lifted the burden a bit of having been an accomplice simply by living in those times. And while she mourned the bombing victims and the complete destruction of the city, I have never heard her utter accusing words against the victors, because the war had been too terrible, the human suffering too great, and all the reasons that are given to this day to explain it, be they political, historic or economic, explained nothing at all in her opinion.

Why did we stay in Dresden, I wondered, why didn't we leave? By the summer of 1944, the inhabitants of Dresden no longer received permission to move away, I was told. But couldn't we have gone to stay with relatives who lived in smaller towns close by? Even if this had meant that the three of us would have had to live in one room while sharing the kitchen and bathroom, wouldn't it have been worth a try? Why didn't my mother attempt it, I asked myself often, until I realized that my question was unfair. After all, what did I know about the hardships of living under such restrictions and how difficult it would have been to stay with two small children in such cramped quarters in a strange apartment, with no end in sight, at a time when everyone's nerves were already worn thin – not to mention the imposition it would have meant for the relatives, even if they had gotten along well with each other? The fact was that in spite of our subtenants, we lived in an elegant and comfortable apartment. The place was warm, we had enough to eat, we went on walks every day in lovely surroundings, and until the 13th of February the hope remained that the city would be spared.

In spite of the alarming warning signs all around us, we hoped for a miracle, my mother repeated frequently. Without the consolation that something would happen just in the nick of time to save the city, we would not have been able to endure. We would've all gone mad, even though I no longer believed in a victory since my return from East Prussia. Besides, there were many reasons why Dresden would surely be spared, she stressed, and proceeded to enumerated them, thus convincing herself anew time and again of their validity: The city had no heavy industry to speak of; it was declared an open city, and therefore undefended. Dresden was world famous as an art and Baroque city, and a special status had been negotiated with the allies to save it. Military hospitals and prisoner of war camps had been distributed throughout town, and it stood to reason that the allied forces would not bomb their own people. Beyond that, mounting fear and increasing uncertainty spawned ever-new rumors about why there would be no attack, which swept through town like wildfire. People even whispered that one of Churchill's nieces was living incognito in the city.

What nonsense, can you imagine that? But people needed something to hold on to, no matter how unbelievable it might prove to be under closer scrutiny. Delusion and self-deception were difficult to separate from truth, and the unrelenting Nazi propaganda confused the people. Even so, we had to count on ever longer and more frequent stays in our cellars from late autumn of 1944 on, not only at night, but also during the day, and soon we received almost daily warnings over the radio about combat aircraft that were on their way to Thuringia and Saxony.

During the Christmas holidays, your father and I had planned to meet in early February 1945 in Cottbus for the wedding of his comrade and best friend, Hermann Dietz. Kurt could no longer get special leave for such festivities, so I wrote him that I was pregnant again. I had known it already on New Year's Eve, but had kept it to myself at the time. When he got the news, he gathered all his courage and asked his commanding officer in Warpuhnen for leave, saying that now that the third child was on the way, he would have to look for an apartment for his family. His commander actually let him go, which in retrospect sounds simply unbelievable. However, before joining us in Cottbus, Kurt had to take a detour via Berlin to deliver urgent messages, which could no longer be radioed.

Life went on, war or no war, and festivities were part of it, my mother explained when she saw my surprise. Cottbus is situated half way between Dresden and Berlin. Trains continued to go several times a day, and I received the special permit for the trip without any problems. When we were sitting together on the evening before the wedding, drinking wine and eating sandwiches, I assumed Kurt would not forbid me to ask questions about the war as long as Hermann was present. And so I changed the topic, mentioning words such as "unconditional surrender," which I had heard on BBC, and I stressed, "I want to know what you think, and don't forget, I am pregnant and very worried under the circumstances."

Kurt bit his lips. "Do you have to bring that up now, Effi?" he asked while gripping my upper arm so hard that it hurt.

"I need to know what may be ahead for us. Don't you understand? You were just in Berlin, so what does it look like?"

"Can't you do something?" he asked instead of an answer.

"It's too late. What are you trying to say anyway? Without my pregnancy you would not have gotten emergency leave. Or did you forget?"

"Things change."

"What are you thinking? I feel fine," I insisted. "Do you have a solution?"

He held onto my arm even more tightly.

"Let go of my arm, Kurt," I hissed, and shook him off. "I haven't told my mother anything yet, she'll have plenty to say once she finds out."

Kurt turned white, fuming, "That's none of Martha's business; I forbid you to talk to her."

"That can hardly be avoided. The day will come soon enough when I won't have to say anything."

"We need our own apartment."

"I asked for an apartment several times last summer," I reminded him, "but I didn't get one. 'You have an apartment,' they told me at the town hall, 'what more do you want? We all have to make sacrifices for the victory.' And they calculated the square footage per person that we were allowed. Besides, I need my mother's help with the children, and we need each other."

"When the war is over, I'll look for a place for us," Kurt said.

"You always say that, but where do you want to find one? There are no apartments anywhere, believe me, only refugees."

I know my words sounded sarcastic, my mother admitted, but I felt a cynicism welling up inside of me like I had not known it until then. At that time Dresden had been declared a closed city, because within a matter of months it had swollen from a little over six hundred thousand inhabitants to well over a million. Our nerves were raw and the war was wearing us down, no matter how much they touted and driveled every day on the radio about the wonder weapon that would be ready any day now and bring us the final victory. For me, any hope of deliverance, nourished far too long by a crazy belief in Hitler's promises, was long gone.

By the time Kurt was to rejoin his unit in Warpuhnen, the Soviet army had broken through and cut off his unit. He was reassigned to another unit in Cottbus, and so my pregnancy brought us luck after all. No one ever returned from his old unit. His comrades either perished or ended up in Russian prison camps.

On the 10th of February 1945 my mother returned from Cottbus.

9. The Storm Begins

Whenever possible, I went on walks with you children, my mother recalled, and the 13th of February was no exception. As we would do often, we went to the Große Garten close to our house, the largest park in the center of Dresden. It was Shrove Tuesday, and one of the coldest days of an already bitterly cold winter. I still remember the streets and paths I took with you, but I did not know that it would be the last time, although in retrospect I seem to have had some kind of premonition. A few hours later, on Ash Wednesday, all of Dresden would be reduced to rubble and ashes.

There was a joyous, almost festive mood in the city. We encountered many young people dressed up with painted faces, who were singing and dancing through town. Their excitement was contagious, and suddenly I wanted to stay in the fresh air as long as possible. Those endless lonely hours in the dark apartment, which I dreaded anew every day, would have to wait. The thought of that unheated space was particularly eerie on that afternoon. I feared the cold, uncomfortable rooms without being able to explain where this heightened anxiety came from, so I delayed our return and decided for once to put on enough wood to get the fire going fast in the kitchen range and not to spare the coal either so it would be warm and cozy quickly.

It was already dark when we reached the Fürstenstraße. The street lanterns had been turned off years ago, the movie theaters lay in darkness, and streetcars, trains, automobiles and bicycles drove without lights. Their headlights had been covered up, and only narrow slits where left open, so they barely lit the tracks or streets. We heard the cars more than we saw them, but we couldn't always trust the sounds either. The sudden shadow of a bike or a car right next to me startled me often enough.

We were very late. Omi had come home hours ago. In order to save a few minutes, I only took the two of you and the baby bag upstairs. For once I left the baby carriage in a corner in the entryway, making sure that it would block neither the front door nor the door to the basement. Normally I took you upstairs and then ran back down to fetch the carriage up to the apartment rather than take it down to the basement, because it was always damp in the cellar and smelled of mold and coal. Besides, the pillows and blankets could easily get soiled down there. On the evening of the thirteenth, however, I took the carriage into the basement, because I had a doctor's appointment the

Elfriede Richter on a walk in the Große Garten in Dresden with her oldest daughter, summer 1942

following morning and would need it for you. The stroller was already stored in our cellar because we didn't need it at the moment. I had put pillows, blankets and extra warm clothing into it just in case, and had covered it with an old sheet. The cellar was getting crowded because when the attacks on German cities increased in the fall of 1944, we were required to empty the storage stalls in the attics to reduce the fire hazard.

Our house had a large, elegant staircase with deep, low steps, a front door with two wings, beveled windowpanes and a colorful art nouveau flower pattern as well as a horizontal window above the door that could be pulled open in the summer for ventilation. It was a fashionable house, and all of the occupants made sure that it was clean at all times. They complained immediately if something was left standing in the entry hall or on the landings, or if someone forgot to wipe up puddles from melted snow or heavy rain. No baby carriages, bicycles, sleds or other objects were to be left in the staircase or block the door to the basement, so that nothing would block our way if we had to rush into the cellar during an air raid. Some tenants became meddlesome, making it their business to spy on others, and reporting to Herr Schöne whatever seemed the least bit suspicious. Thank God he was a good man who listened patiently to their complaints, calmed them down and talked to the other tenants. As far as I know, he never reported anyone.

On the second Tuesday of February 1945, my mother lived through the worst night of her life. Her story always unfolded the same way. She used certain words and set phrases, so I knew at any given moment what would come next. That's how the old women must have told their fairy tales to the Brothers Grimm. Except this was no fairy tale. Her words made me shiver with fear like so many of the old stories, and I often felt like running away. She spoke slowly, chose her words carefully, and stressed every syllable in an almost theatrical way while gazing over the heads of her listeners, perhaps so she would not get stuck. A feverish animation gripped her. It seemed to me that everything came to life again for her, as though she were staring spellbound into that catastrophe. When friends or relatives were among the listeners she sat even more straightly and banned the Saxon dialect from her speech. Only the consonants remained soft as she spoke in an otherwise perfect High German that sounded somewhat rigid at times. Her account of the night of the bombing seemed full of contradictions and confusing details, and although she repeated it often, it always sounded new again. On long winter nights, after the supper table had been cleared, she would retell the events over several evenings, like a serialized novel in the daily newspaper, until it reached mythological proportions for me.

There were times when these memories wore her out more than usual, and she looked at her hands in her lap, seemingly forgetting everything around her. Especially before the hardest part, the bombing attacks, she became very still, as if to gather all her strength and courage. She appeared thoughtful, and there was something dignified in her bearing. Nevertheless I felt awkward as I watched her, and as I grew older I became ashamed of her and all of us. I was ashamed that we had been such fools and had not foreseen that impending disaster, and had thought ourselves too weak in the face of the Nazis to stop those murderers. At times my mother wept quietly in the silence that followed, like a little girl that had lost her way and couldn't find her mother again. She stared into a void and sat there, helpless and alone, looking for consolation, but seldom received any. Occasionally her husband would try to put his arm around her, saying something to cheer her up or divert her, but she didn't let him come close. Instead she just said in a voice full of rejection, her body stiffening, "I see," or, "what do you know?" and moved away from him or pushed him aside.

When things became too unbearable, I hoped that my mother would stop talking about that fateful night, but she seldom allowed herself to become distracted.

I had put you to bed after dinner at seven thirty like most evenings, Anne, she pushed on. Bettine was already asleep. After Christmas I had moved both your beds into my bedroom to have you right with me in case of emergency. Omi was already asleep because she was working the early shift at her factory, and had to get up at three thirty. After the dishes were done and everything was put away, I sat alone in the kitchen, my right ear close to the speaker of the radio, secretly listening to BBC. How I longed to breathe freely again on our walks, when I went shopping, with friends and even at home!

The broadcasts from BBC always began with the same urgent warning: You German people wake up! Then came reports from the front and other war news. My anxiety grew, the words made me shudder, and I felt ice-cold. Before tuning to BBC, I had listened to news from German stations warning the population that English bombers were on their way to central Germany. Their destination was unknown. There was no warning for any specific city. I didn't dare to consider that Dresden might be the target. This announcement was followed by reports from the front, which I doubted because I believed the refugees more, who reported that the Russians were no more than fifty miles from Dresden. There was nothing new from BBC. My hands trembled as I turned the knob back to a local German station, but they offered no new information either.

I was plagued by sinister premonitions. I felt sick to my stomach and very alone. On my trip back from Cottbus three days earlier, I had once again seen the crowds at the main station, which spoke more clearly than anything else of lost battles and retreat. Although I had no illusions, I did not give up hope that the bombers would spare us. There was nothing to be gained by bombing Dresden, I told myself. Besides, it was a long flight all the way from England. I had become weary of our bleak daily life and from worry about people that were dear to me. But the longer the war lasted, the more I lived in fear of retribution, and that we might eventually suffer the same fate as other German cities. The images of my recent travels were stuck in my brain, and the faces of the prisoners of war and the foreign workers that I had seen on the streets of Dresden pursued me. Polish and Russian women were working in Omi's factory. They had already endured much and told horrible stories. Although they were forbidden to speak to each other, especially in their native languages, they did so anyway when no guards were close by. Omi could understand them and secretly whispered Polish words back, slipping them cold potatoes, a piece of bread, some sausage or an occasional bar of soap. She had to be careful not to get caught.

Since there was a long evening ahead, I finally took my knitting, pondering what I had just heard while listening to the rhythmic clicking of the knitting needles. I couldn't get rid of the feeling that something was different, when suddenly the sirens howled into the silence of the night. Startled, I jumped up screaming. Something was very wrong out there. Instinctively I turned up the radio. I still remember this motion, how I turned the button. I was in my warm kitchen, and it was 9:40 p.m. on the kitchen clock. You children were asleep in your beds. I detected an imminent danger in the continuous howling of the sirens, and it paralyzed me for several seconds. I recall no pre-alert, only the full air raid warning.

Unable to focus, I put my knitting on the table. Then I switched off the floor lamp, walked over to the window and pushed the heavy drapes aside. There was a strange light outside, and to my horror I saw target markers, or Christmas trees as we called them, to my left over the old town, whose bizarre shapes were floating down slowly, illuminating the town that lay defenseless below them. British target marking aircraft had lead the bombers unnoticed across Saxony all the way to Dresden, and now they were directly above us. I counted at least five from the kitchen window. I grew ice cold inside and felt a heavy pressure on my chest as I had known it only once during the train ride back from East Prussia. For an instant I feared that my heart would stand still. It was then that I heard the heavy drone of low-flying aircraft.

Suddenly I was wide-awake, and from that point on I did everything automatically. I knew what I had to do; there was no time to lose. Everything happened so fast that any warning for the population came too late. At the first wail of the sirens, loudspeakers mounted on top of cars urged the population to go to the air raid shelters without delay. This time it's our turn. The thought shot through my head with uncanny clarity, and gave me back my inner calm. I ran out of the kitchen, threw open the door to Omi's room and shouted at her to get up immediately, to dress warmly and then help me with you children. "We must get to the cellar at once, all hell is breaking loose out there! Do you hear me?" When I ran to you children, I suddenly heard the hissing sound of the first bombs falling.

Almost simultaneously I heard the fire department trucks and ambulances racing down the Fürstenstraße. The fire engine stopped right below us, and as I looked once more out of the window, because I wanted to see why they were stopping here of all places, I saw flames shooting out of the roof of the house opposite ours. The entire city was awake all at once. As if in a trance I saw the men roll out the water hoses. A jet of water shot up while bombs hailed down around us, and then the jet of water suddenly fell to the ground. Later I heard that the water pressure decreased rapidly throughout the city because of the sudden demand. The fire brigade gave up as explosive bombs, which lifted the roofs off of buildings, hit the entire city all at once, followed by incendiary bombs. Trying to put out the fires was hopeless as houses were burning everywhere within minutes. Ambulances capitulated before the falling bombs. The drivers simply turned off the engines, left the trucks stand wherever they happened to be, and ran for cover into the nearest houses. At that instant I heard the screeching brakes of the streetcar, and the passengers rushed out, running and stumbling in all directions. The burnt-out skeleton of the streetcar was still standing in the same spot when we left the cellar after the second bombing attack. The sight has etched itself into my memory. How often had we taken that line! I saw people run toward our front entrance, which Herr Schöne had unlocked because on the outside wall a plaque had been mounted that identified our cellar as an air raid shelter. Several young people in their carnival costumes, who had populated the streets of the old town all day and were now happily on their way home, fled from the bombs, and I heard their fearful voices inside our house while their steps thundered through the staircase as they scrambled down into the basement.

It struck me strangely as I saw the dark figures run along the street while bombs were crashing into the pavement and houses. The sirens wailed on for some time as their sound intermingled with the penetrating angry noise of the aircraft above us, until they grew silent forever. I felt like I was in the middle of a surrealistic theater production. The tempestuous roar of the bombers drowned out all other noises until there remained only the menacing drone of airplane propellers. The sky above us was filled with bombers. Never again have I experienced such a feeling of terror.

An indescribable mood took hold of me, while I mechanically performed my tasks. For several seconds I had the feeling I was watching myself, having nothing to do with what was happening around me. Strangely enough, seeing events unfold almost as an observer calmed me and helped me make the right decisions. I felt renewed strength well up inside of me. There was no time to lose. While I collected the things we would need in the cellar, the ridiculous rules the Nazis had passed out, and that were hanging on the walls of the ground floors in all houses, went through my head, but what was happening that night brought all these precautions to naught. On leaflets they had even told us that we should put all hangers in the same direction on the coat racks in the wardrobes, opening toward the back, so that we could push them together in case of emergency and lift armloads of clothing out all at once. When the bombs were falling I understood the absurdity of it all. It was to work like this, my mother demonstrated, and she spread her arms wide while lifting imaginary clothes out of an imaginary closet, holding them in front of her for a moment, not knowing where to put them. Then she dropped everything and stepped across the pile of clothes in front of her. Who is going to think of clothes at a time like this, she asked? And how were we supposed to take them along? I am sure those imbeciles had not thought of that. They couldn't have imagined what was happening in Dresden anyway. No one could have imagined it. All bets were off. During that night we all had to fend for ourselves to survive.

I ran back to Omi, who had slept through the noise and tremors. I screamed at her in despair, but she just growled that I should leave her alone and simply turned around to face the wall. I didn't know what to do, so I pulled away her feather bed and tugged at her legs. She scolded me, reached for her cover and wondered what had come over me to treat her so disrespectfully. After all she was tired, and had I forgotten that she had to get up early for work, insisting all the while that she was not going to the cellar and stay up all night for nothing.

"They are right above us, can't you hear the airplanes? This time it's our turn," I shouted. "You must get up, I need you!"

"You go with the children," she murmured, drunk with sleep.

"For heaven's sake," I yelled, "do you want to get killed?"

"Leave me alone, Elfriedchen, please," she begged pitifully, "I am so tired. Nothing is going to happen to me."

I was beside myself. "If you don't come along," I shouted acting upon a sudden impulse, "they'll ask me about you. You know very well that Herr Schöne must make sure that all occupants go to the cellar immediately at the first sound of the sirens, otherwise he'll be in trouble, and so will I. There are spies everywhere, the neighbors will talk. What do you think will become of us if someone turns us in? You'll have us all jailed! The neighbors know you are home and didn't follow the Führer's orders. Besides, you're endangering the girls unnecessarily with your obstinacy."

"The children are better off with me in the apartment than with strangers in the cellar," she answered, "they'll just get lice or we'll all catch pneumonia in the damp cold. And if my Rolf doesn't come home, that will be my death anyway."

"Don't talk such nonsense and get up!" I repeated.

"You go with the children," she mumbled, pulling her feather blanket over her head.

"Why don't you listen to what's going on out there," I shouted all hoarse by then, "the bombs are hitting the houses all around us, this time it's worse than ever before! Pull yourself together, you can't stay here, God damn it, you must help me get the girls downstairs! We need extra blankets, it's colder than usual, and we must take along warm milk for them in the thermos bottle, and you and I need something hot as well." She gave no response. She simply made believe the air raid was no concern of hers. I had to think of a different strategy, so I ran back to my bedroom to get you out of bed, Anne. I put your coat on over your pajamas, put on your shoes and woolen cap, then I put on my coat, lifted Bettine with her warm blanket out of her bed, took the bag, which I always had packed and ready to go, opened the apartment door and pushed you, Anne, out ahead of me and down the stairs into the cellar. You were staggering, still half-asleep.

In the cellar I sat both of you on one of our deck chairs and asked Frau Leberecht, our neighbor, to watch you because I had to run back upstairs. Frau Leberecht had already been waiting anxiously for us and begged me to stay. But Omi was still in bed, and I wanted to get milk for you. The pot with the boiled milk stood on the kitchen table to cool off. I pushed the skin on top aside with a spoon and filled the thermos bottle, leaving the rest on the table for later. Then I quickly brewed coffee for Omi, since there was always hot water on the stove, and poured it through a sieve into a second thermos bottle. After that I ran to her room. She still wouldn't listen. I began to shake her, grabbed her by the legs and pulled hard in my desperation, and suddenly she sat on the floor. She called me disrespectful and said it would be my fault if she didn't get enough rest and then fell asleep later at the machine.

I was scared to death. The noise outside increased, and howling winds were pushing against the windows. I grabbed Omi under her arms, pulled her up and yelled at her to get dressed. Finally I began to hit her until my hands hurt. That helped. When she noticed my despair she began to whine and tremble. Suddenly she wanted to run off in her nightgown. I no longer knew what to do, so I smacked her in the face, screaming, "You must get dressed! If it gets really rough and we have to leave the cellar you can't be in your nightgown!" I had to hand her every single piece of clothing, her underwear, her pullover, cardigan, stockings and woolen trousers, her coat and winter shoes, all while she staggered around and kept sitting down on her bed. It was worse than with a small child.

At that moment there was an explosion and she shrieked, "Holy Mary, Mother of God," while reaching for her rosary on the nightstand. She slipped it into her coat pocket, and before I knew it she was sitting on the edge of her bed again. I pulled her up and dragged her behind me into the kitchen, took the two bottles with milk and coffee from the table, reached for my own coat on the coat rack in the hallway, wrapped a scarf around my neck, put on my good boots, threw a shawl over Omi's shoulders, pressed a hat down on her head and pushed her ahead of me out into the staircase, pulling the apartment door closed behind me. To this day I have the snapping sound of the lock in my ears. We saw an ominous dark red flicker coming through the upper window from the burning house across the street. I don't know who had shoved aside the heavy curtain. When Omi saw the red light and heard the deafening noise coming from the street, she ran downstairs, screaming hysterically.

The cellar was crowded with people not only from our house, but also from neighboring houses, either because they had no real air raid shelter or because they were burning already. Total strangers from far away parts of the city, who were caught by surprise when the sirens went off, had also taken refuge with us. In spite of the crowded condition there was a strange silence. We listened to every noise, trying to explain it or instill courage in one another.

Omi sank down in the deck chair next to yours, Anne. I lifted you onto her lap, spread a blanket over both of you and sat down with Bettine in the other chair.

It was not until that moment, with nothing more to do, that I became very aware of what was going on. It felt as though the world was coming to an end. Even today I still have no words for it.

A man I had never seen before made the lapidary statement that the four corner houses at the intersection of the Fürstenstraße and Gabelsberger Straße were burning. I thought of Lara. He was leaning against the basement wall. His clothes smelled of smoke, and his hat and coat were covered with tiny burn holes.

I would have liked to know more, but I did not dare to ask. Instead I offered him a cup of coffee, which he took eagerly, drinking it down in one long gulp. "It looks bad, it's burning everywhere, and the air is dry and hot," he said when he gave me back the cup. I looked toward the water barrel, which was always filled to four inches below the rim. The water bucket was hanging above it from a hook as always. A lot of water had been used up already, but I couldn't tell how much was left.

While my mother talked, I remembered very clearly that Omi and I were sitting together in the deck chair. I recalled her soft warmth and a trembling that went through her at regular intervals. Then she held me even more tightly, calling me "my darling little Anni, my sweetheart". I buried my face in her body and felt her arms around me and closed my eyes.

We had been sitting in the cellar for some time, my mother continued, when all of a sudden the house quaked. I instinctively threw myself over you while holding Bettine even tighter, but there was only this one jolt, followed by a deathly silence. The tremor had been so strong that I expected the house to collapse over us at any moment. When nothing happened, I dared to look up. People screamed, jumped to their feet and ran up the stairs. Slowly we grasped that a bomb had hit our house. Glass bottles were rolling around in the cellar partitions, jars full of preserved fruit and vegetables had fallen off the shelves and broken to pieces on the stone floor. Behind me it smelled of canned cherries. Pots and pans clattered, and a petroleum lamp hanging from the cellar ceiling swayed back and forth for several minutes, throwing light and shadow over our faces, but the flame didn't go out. When nothing more happened, no explosion, no fire, when no walls came crashing down and the cellar vault stood firm, the stranger said calmly, "That was a dud. We were lucky this time."

His words chased away the fear and loosened our stiff bodies. People who had been about to leave stayed and sat down again. Someone swept the broken glass aside. Others checked their belongings and pulled their children closer. A woman I had never seen before suggested we leave the cellar before the house came crashing down the next time, burying all of us. But the stranger convinced her to wait because it was more dangerous outside at the moment. "Eat and drink something," he advised her, "you'll need it, it's going to be a long night." So she sat down again, pulled both her children onto her lap and sobbed inaudibly.

After what seemed like an eternity to us, the droning of the propellers from the bombers abated and the noise from the street increased. The people became agitated, got up and wanted to leave, then hesitated and listened for sounds from above, trying to explain them.

"I am going upstairs to see what it looks like outside," I heard the voice of the stranger, "I'll be right back."

He was indeed back immediately, reporting that the bombers had left, but that many houses were burning and that the air was full of smoke. People scrambled to their feet. Those who didn't belong to our house wanted to get back to their families and neighborhoods and rushed upstairs frantically. During all the commotion, the all-clear signal sounded.

Nothing had happened to us or our house, my mother remarked, we had survived the bombing, which had lasted about twenty-five minutes. We did not expect a second attack that night. How could we have imagined the unimaginable?

10. Sodom and Gomorra

As people hurried upstairs, I considered what to do next. You were safe in the cellar for the time being, so I decided to go upstairs alone to see what our apartment looked like. I put Bettine in Omi's lap next to you, Anne, and told her to stay put until I returned. She agreed. I wanted to give you some milk, Anne, but you refused to drink anything. Before going, I impressed upon Omi not to leave the cellar under any circumstances and promised to be back as fast as I could.

I took along the little red suitcase thinking it would be safer with me. Frau Becker, who lived below us, left her little girl in the cellar, too. Frau Leberecht also came with us. The Kaufmanns were not in the cellar. I had not seen them for some time. Herr Schöne had hurried ahead of us to see if the attic was burning.

We were faced with a frightening sight when we stepped into the entry hall. Our house seemed unharmed, but a bright red blaze came through the glass panes of the front door. That's why I did not notice right away that the house light would not go on as I turned the switch. I took a few steps toward the main entrance, but then shrank back from opening the door. Instead, I decided to look out of the kitchen window and flew upstairs. We encountered Herr Schöne halfway up the stairs, who announced that for the moment everything looked all right in the attic, and that he hoped that the fire from the roofs of other houses would not spread to ours. He and two other men had poured several buckets of water from the water barrel onto the attic floor. They would replenish the barrel and keep close watch.

When I opened our apartment door, an ice-cold wind hit me, tearing the door handle out of my hand with such force that the door slammed against the inside wall. I stepped into the hall, pushing the door closed with my back. Then I reached for the light switch. Again the lamp would not go on, and I realized that the entire house was without electricity. For the moment, the light from the fire coming in through the window openings was bright enough for me to find my way.

With every step broken glass and porcelain crunched beneath my shoes. I bumped against objects that were lying on the floor and almost fell over an overturned kitchen chair the wind had swept into the hall. As I carried the chair back into the kitchen I stumbled over the radio. I picked it up and set it back on the little table next to the sofa. I wouldn't be able to hear the news anymore, I remember thinking as I was about to close the window, when I noticed that all of the glass panes were broken. The stovepipe was dangling over the stove, giving off a tinny sound when it hit the wall. Soot trickled out of the pipe as smoke filled the room. I stepped onto a chair and put the pipe back into its hole in the chimney. The ceiling lamp swung back and forth in the wind, and I feared that it would be torn off at any moment. I walked from room to room; they all presented the same picture. Due to the enormous pressure of the high-explosive bombs, detonations and the hurricane-force winds of the firestorm, all the panes of the double windows had been broken. Some window frames had been torn off their hinges, others swung back and forth violently, banging against the window openings. One wing lay on the carpet in the middle of the living room. I wiped with my hand over the living room table and felt small pieces of glass, sand and a thick layer of sticky dust. Walking faster and faster, I stumbled over books, broken picture frames and pillows. In the flickering ghostly light I slowly comprehended the full extent of the destruction.

The wind drove flakes of soot, burning pieces of wood and what looked like charred paper through the window openings. Small burning objects got caught in the billowing lace curtains and drapes. The bent venetian blinds rattled and banged against the window casings. The old blankets I had hung on the inside in compliance with the rules for the citywide blackout were blown about or billowed out like sails in the strong draft. Dishes clattered, pictures scraped back and forth on the walls, and the chandelier swung dangerously over the dining table while the crystals jingled whenever the wind blew through them with enough force. One end of a curtain rod in the living room had been torn out of the wall, and the wind slammed it rhythmically against the window frame. The furniture had been pushed around or turned over in the rooms. Even the heavy walnut table with the marble top in the living room had been shoved against the buffet. The two large Meißen porcelain vases, which were a gift from Papa for his wife, and had stood on the left and right side of the buffet, lay broken on the rug. I pushed them out of the way with my foot. Flowerpots had been swept down from the windowsills, and the soil and plants were spilled all over the floor. The window frames in the bedroom were still closed, but all the panes were broken.

I had not expected such destruction, and wondered where to begin with the clean-up. At first, I closed all the doors in the apartment and pushed furniture in front of them so the wind would not be able to push them open again so easily. That cut down the draft considerably. Next I tore down all the curtains and blankets from the windows so they wouldn't catch fire.

Outside people screamed, houses collapsed with a dull thundering sound, and flames hissed and grew taller, surging up from the street on the outside walls of houses. The dud that had shaken the house had come through the roof above our living room and shot through our tile stove all the way to the basement, hurling the upper right corner of the stove into the room, and leaving behind a huge gaping black hole. The custodian found the bomb in one of the cellar stalls and defused it, as he later told us during the second attack.

The wind blew the candles I lit out again immediately. I remembered the petroleum lamp, lit it and walked with it once more through all the rooms. The spooky flickering light of the lamp irritated me, and I told myself over and over: Come on, pull yourself together!

When I was young, I asked myself why my mother embellished her report of the damage to our apartment with so many details. It wasn't until much later that I understood how important it was for her in all the wretchedness that followed to describe once more what a wonderful life we had had, how well we had lived, how fashionably the house had been furnished, and that her father, in his broadminded foresight, had taken such good care of us even beyond his death. To me it spoke of a certain generosity of feeling as well as my mother's deep longing for beauty, the way she described the rooms long after their destruction once more pointing out their original splendor.

The most urgent task was to board up the window openings to protect the rooms from the elements unleashed by men, my mother continued. But what could I use to cover so many windows? There was no time to lose. My hands were ice cold and black with soot. I went to the kitchen to wash them. As I looked down at myself I noticed that I was still wearing my good clothes. I took them off quickly and hung them on the clothes rack in the hall, changed into some old clothes, which were hanging in the broom closet, and put the jewelry next to my golden wristwatch and the red suitcase on the console in the hall under the mirror. Finally, I put on a headscarf to protect my hair from ashes and smoke and cleaned up as fast as I could. As I had walked through the rooms earlier I noticed two window wings whose panes were not broken, a right one and a left one. That was very lucky, because all the windows in the apartment were the same size, and as you looked at the house from the street the windows were all equally spaced for a pleasant look. I carried the two wings into the kitchen, hung them up and closed the window. The silence seemed unreal, the hissing and roaring of the wind was greatly subdued. I swept up the broken glass and breathed a sigh of relief.

After that, I hastened from one room to the next, covering all windows with sheets of tin from Omi's factory, wooden boards or heavy cardboard. Back in the kitchen, I stoked the fire in the kitchen stove, crumbled up some newspaper and put on small pieces of wood. When the fire was really going, I put on briquettes so the kitchen would be warm for you. It seems strange when I think of it today, but I remember very clearly everything I did. I pushed the kitchen table under the window, then I pulled your bed into the kitchen, so that you, Anne, and Bettine could sleep in it. I pulled off the sheets that were covered with soot, put on clean ones and grabbed fresh towels from the closet. Thank God that the doors had not been forced open by the wind. Finally, I poured hot water from the large pot, which always stood on the stove, into a bucket and quickly washed the sticky layer of soot from the furniture and the floor. Even the milk was covered with soot and ashes, so I scooped it off along with the thick layer of cream. Then I poured the milk through a sieve to sift out any pieces of broken glass, covered it and put it back on the stove to heat it up again. Finally I pushed a wicker chair from the hall into the kitchen for Omi and fetched her footstool.

The kitchen was temporarily set up for the remaining hours of the night. I washed myself off quickly and put on clean clothes before heading back down to bring the three of you upstairs, when the sirens went off for a second time. They sounded much quieter, and at first I thought they were coming from far away and were not meant for us, but I soon realized I was wrong, because suddenly I heard the menacing noise of bombers directly above us again. What I had heard was the much quieter wail of hand operated sirens, most likely because the others were no longer functioning. Herr Schöne came jumping upstairs and banged at our doors, drumming us together. I pulled the kitchen door closed behind me so it would stay warm inside, tore my coat off the rack, slammed the apartment door shut behind me and rushed into the cellar. I was scared to death that Omi would lose control and do something stupid when she heard the renewed air raid and I was not there. My only thought was to be with you, so I forgot about the red suitcase. Downstairs I found you the way I had left you, and only then did I realize that I should have changed back into my better clothes and grabbed the jewelry from the console. Strangely enough I found my wristwatch later in my coat pocket. Again the noise of falling bombs drowned out everything else. What had not been deemed possible for all those years, but we had feared since the fall of 1944, had finally come about, and I could not get rid of the feeling that things would end badly.

I looked continuously at my watch, but forgot the time again immediately. Only hours later, when we saw the town lying beneath us from the Weiße Hirsch, the famous restaurant on the hill in Loschwitz on the other side of the river Elbe, did I recall the positions of the black hands of the watch when the attacks had begun and ended. So my brain had registered the time after all.

Things must have been especially dreadful at the main station. Bit by bit I heard the terrible details of what took place there. The two levels, the upper main hall for long distance trains and the lower one for local trains, were overcrowded with refugees at the time of the attacks. There was nowhere to go, so they simply stayed on the platforms and in the halls, sat on their luggage or on the steps, blocking the flight of stairs, while others settled down to sleep in corners or along walls, completely exhausted and discouraged.

Countless people on the streets, who were taken by surprise by the attack, also ran into the station for shelter. Years later, when the authorities tried to figure out why so many people had died in the main station, they realized that it had been built without air shafts leading into the basements and the narrow corridors underground where people had gone for protection. When the lights went out, no emergency lights went on, and people got lost in the darkness of the labyrinth of interconnecting tunnels and walkways and suffocated. Overcrowded passenger trains, ready to leave, were kept in the station on both levels for the safety of the passengers, fearing that the trains might be bombed, or the tracks, switches and signal towers would be hit, causing derailments. At the same time, trains crowded with refugees pulled into the main station while it was being hit severely during the first bombing attack. Many passengers couldn't get off, and days later their charred corpses were recovered from the completely burnt-out railroad cars.

The second attack seemed worse than the first. The noise was deafening as the bombers were now unloading incendiary bombs on us. I feared that our house would collapse any minute and bury us alive, but as long as the bombs were falling, it was not advisable to leave the basement; it would not have been any safer outside. So we stayed, sitting huddled together in our cellar, and ducked automatically when we heard explosions and the rumbling of tumbling walls.

Suddenly we heard loud hacking and pounding against the far wall of the cellar. I imagined hearing voices, at first very faint, then louder, until I realized that people were trying to open up a passage into our cellar from the house next door. Herr Schöne and another man reached for a pickax and a sledgehammer, and began to knock against the wall from our side under what looked like a bricked-up arch. Just a few strong blows, and the opening was large enough. People stepped into our cellar, passing along children and luggage. Behind them, in the black opening, it flickered dark red. Herr Schöne took a small child from a woman as he asked her how many more were behind her while shouting at them to hurry so the opening could be closed up again.

The people came from various houses. One woman told us their house had collapsed over them and how they had escaped through a connection into the next house, where they found they couldn't stay either. Another woman suddenly screamed in despair for her husband, who had been helping others and now seemed to be missing. In the general confusion, they had left luggage behind or had been separated from family members.

"Are you the last one?" Herr Schöne shouted at a man, who had awkwardly stepped through the opening into our cellar. He seemed disoriented and gave no answer as he staggered after the others. The people were very distraught as they sat down on sacks of coal or leaned against the walls, asking for water. Others, who were more courageous, went upstairs to see what it looked like on the ground floor.

"Anyone there?" Herr Schöne shouted into the dark spooky cave. I am sure that his voice did not carry far because of the clamor and roaring all around us. When no answer came, men put the bricks back quickly to close the opening. Our cellar was overcrowded by now.

After a while it began to quiet down outside. The humming of the bombers let off until it finally stopped altogether. I could hardly bear the silence after the hammering of bombs, the rumbling and banging, and was almost more afraid than before. At last the all-clear signal came. The second attack was over. The custodian went up the cellar stairs to scout out the situation. I followed him to see for myself. When we opened the door into the vestibule, we saw to my relief that our house wasn't burning. The cellar seemed secure, having weathered both attacks without any visible damage. Even so, we were afraid that the house might collapse and bury the exit to the street, trapping us inside. I wanted to run upstairs to change into better clothes and get the red suitcase, but Herr Schöne held me back. When I insisted, he dissuaded me urgently from risking it because he could not guarantee that the staircase would hold. I listened to him, but perhaps I should have followed my intuition. Who would have thought that all our planning would come to naught. The contents of the little red suitcase proved to be the greatest loss. After careful consideration, I had to agree with Herr Schöne that we would have to leave the house and wait in a safe area outside for the morning. I don't know when our house caught fire during the next two days. Most likely it burned out from the roof down.

I rushed back into the cellar, put on more warm clothing, and handed a second cardigan to Omi before she put on her heavy winter coat. Then I got you girls ready, put extra blankets, pillows and diapers into the baby carriage, and gave you the last milk to drink, Anne, while Omi finished the coffee from the thermos bottle. I put a jar each with cherries and apricots and two spoons into a bag and set it into the carriage, as well as a knife, some bread and salami – just enough to tide us over, I thought, because in my mind I was sure that we would be back. When all was done, I put the lock back on our cellar door and hid the key under the mattress of the baby carriage. Then I explained to Omi that I would take Bettine in the baby carriage and she would take you, Anne, in the stroller. First I carried a suitcase with extra shoes and a change of clothing for Omi and myself upstairs and deposited it in the hallway, and then I pulled the carriages up step by step. After that I went back to get the three of you. I sat you in the stroller, Anne, and wrapped blankets around you, and laid Bettine into the baby carriage. I lifted the suitcase onto the wooden board I always laid across the front of the baby carriage for you, Anne, to sit on when you couldn't walk the last stretch home anymore as we returned from our daily walks, and tied it down. Finally I took several large cotton towels I had soaked in the barrel of water in the cellar and just lightly wrung out so they would not drip, and draped them for protection against the sparks and hot air over the hood and wax cloth cover of the baby carriage and over the foot muff of the stroller. Herr Schöne had warned us that it was a blazing inferno outside, so Omi and I put wet cloths over our heads and shoulders and tied damp shawls in front of our mouths and noses as protection from the heat and to prevent us from breathing in any flying ashes. We were done faster than I thought. My heart was pounding wildly when I gripped the handlebar of the baby carriage tightly with both hands. All that we possessed had been reduced to these two carriages, the little bit of luggage and the clothes on our backs.

11. Escape from the Inferno

A hellish dark red light flickered through the windows above the front door, and I hesitated to leave the protective hall. I feared that we would suffocate or burn to death instantly. "You must get away from the houses as fast as possible toward the middle of the street, and then make your way down to the Elbe," Herr Schöne had admonished us before running back into the cellar without saying good-bye. Mesmerized, I looked at the flames. My legs failed me and all courage deserted me. I was afraid to step into the burning street. Suddenly Herr Schöne stood beside me again and opened the house door for us. A gust of glowing hot air hit us, and I automatically took a step back into the house. How could I walk out into this blaze with you?

Seeing my hesitation, he pushed me saying, "Go quickly, it will get much worse – for heaven's sake, Frau Bergner, go!" It was as if we had to throw ourselves into the fire. Herr Schöne repeated, "Don't wait any longer, you must go now! You cannot stay here!"

I pulled myself together and said, "Come on Mutti, follow me," as I felt my legs move forward.

The Fürstenstraße was as bright as day. For a moment I thought it was light enough to read the newspaper, and yet it was difficult to see things clearly because of the heavy smoke and thousands of particles flying through the air. The noise and stiff wind almost robbed us of our senses. I could hardly understand my own words. I turned around and saw that Omi was right behind me. We mustn't lose each other, I thought. It was as though we were walking straight to our death.

I shouted to her, "Keep your eyes on me, always stay close to me! Don't listen to others! And for God's sake, never stand still, not even for a second, do you hear me? Scream as loud as you can if something's wrong. Dear God, Mutti, say something, do you understand me?"

To that Omi answered calmly, "Well, Elfriedchen, I am not stupid, of course I understand you. Come on, let's go!"

The town was a sea of flames. Our house was one of the few on our street that still stood unharmed and dark; not even our roof was burning. I saw that when I looked up wistfully one last time as we walked away. And suddenly I knew we would not be back. The fire from the neighboring houses would reach our house any minute at the speed the flames were moving toward each other, merging, leaping up against the walls of houses, shooting high into the sky, consuming with frenzied speed everything that would burn.

According to official orders, we turned in the direction of the Elbe river. The stream of people coming from Johannstadt swept us along. Everyone wanted to get to the Elbwiesen where we hoped we would be able to breathe easier and would be safe from the fire and falling bricks. "Follow me," I screamed at Omi as I was trying to make my way toward the middle of the street, because the sidewalks were covered with heaps of bricks and other debris.

The bombs had torn open the street, blasting deep craters into the pavement that hindered the fleeing people. The street surface was hot and steaming; the soles of our shoes stuck to it with every step. Brick walls collapsed with a roaring thunder, complete outer walls of houses came tumbling down onto the sidewalks in front of and behind us, while some of the bricks rolled all the way to the center of the street. Small and large objects shot through the air and came crashing down unexpectedly, throwing people to the ground. Bodies were lying in the street, some burned beyond recognition. Injured people called for help. I repeated to myself, keep going, we must get away from here, don't think about anything, don't stop, don't look! People shrieked in terror and sank down before our eyes, but how could we have helped? We simply drove around them with our carriages. Once we were even forced to climb over a dead person if we didn't want to get trampled down or separated ourselves. The wet sheets I had hung over the carriages had been dried by the hot winds within minutes, and were flapping in the air. I tied them faster to the hood in order to protect you children at least from smoke and burning particles. Some red-hot object hit me at the hairline, burning my hair, but the wind had already swept it away before I could wipe it off.

Suddenly the people in front of us tried to escape to the left and right when I saw a burning beam rolling towards us down the middle of the street. I had not reacted quickly enough with the baby carriage as the beam rolled directly toward it, singeing the rubber tires of the two front wheels. As best as I could I maneuvered around it on the rear wheels, but then I noticed to my great relief that the tires had not been burned so badly after all, and I could continue to push the carriage on all four wheels.

People merged into the Fürstenstraße from all sides, pushing in the direction of the river. The air got hotter and smokier, and it became more difficult to breathe with every step. I was forced to breathe through my mouth, which was already dry, and my tongue felt like a lump sticking to my palate. My mucous membranes were inflamed, my throat felt so sore that I could hardly speak anymore, and my lungs were beginning to burn from smoke inhalation. The pressure on my chest increased. I panted and coughed, but couldn't find a lozenge in my coat pocket, although I always had some, especially during winter. We couldn't stop to drink something either. I tried to swallow and work up saliva, and then I saw the fire again. The hot gusts of wind seized everything with more force than I could have ever imagined, driving and twirling objects in all directions with ever-increasing speed until they burst into flames in mid-air to be consumed instantly. The storm pulled and tugged at our coats, catapulted heavy objects through the air, lifted entire roofs from houses before our eyes, and carried them several yards through the air before smashing them down at our feet, barricading the street as the beams burned.

Flames shot out of windows and leapt up the outer walls of houses. Roof tiles were flung through the air and hit us on our backs. All the while the raging firestorm swept with unnatural force down into the streets, lifting people off their feet and carrying them along several yards before dropping them again. They screamed, fell to the ground and could not get back up fast enough, and so were trampled to death by the shoving masses. I saw people flare up like torches and burn to death, and no one could save them. It seemed that if you touched them or their clothes, you caught fire as well.

The firestorm tore a child out of a mother's arms right in front of my eyes, throwing it into a burning puddle. She ran after her child and reached for it, only to go up in flames herself, and so they both burned to death. I saw the whirlwind tear the clothes off of people, grab them and suck them along the street, then suddenly change direction, dropping them and leaving them for dead. Others tore their burning clothes from their bodies, running on aimlessly and half-naked. Families held on tightly to each other's hands to keep from losing one another, only to be torn apart by the firestorm, never to find each other again. The smoke grew heavier, and the visibility got worse. I saw hands shoot up to reach for things and hands that dropped things as the wind carried along whatever it could get hold of. Twirling objects were swept away like leaves of parchment until they caught fire in mid-air. Parents yelled for their children, and old people lost their relatives and didn't know where to turn while the roaring all around us drowned out their calls.

We were on the Fürstenstraße, but I had lost all orientation on this street where I knew every house, every wall, every tree, every lantern and streetcar stop. I could not estimate how far we had come, but I suddenly realized that we were headed in the wrong direction. It was an intuition that helped me make the decision to turn around and walk against the stream of people toward the Große Garten. The park was closer than the Elbe, and I knew we would get enough oxygen there to breathe more freely again and would be relatively safe from falling and burning objects. I shouted to Omi, "We are not getting through to the river, we must try to reach the Große Garten!" And we turned around in the middle of the street, against all instructions and previous agreements with friends and neighbors, against all better judgment and the generally accepted opinion that the open meadows along the banks of the Elbe would be the safest place in case of a bombing attack, and headed in the opposite direction. We had to fight hard against the increasing number of people that stumbled toward us from the old town, so we were repeatedly in danger of being trampled.

I didn't think that the allied forces would drop bombs over the Große Garten. When I read reports later I learned differently. Even so, we were lucky we lived on the Fürstenstraße, one of the splendid wide streets of Dresden that had trees on either side and lead through the Große Garten straight down to the river banks. There were wide sidewalks, and in the middle of the street were the streetcar tracks. The wind could sweep down into the street, bringing us oxygen while pulling the poisonous smoke back up into the air.

The further we walked the easier it got, and although the street was covered with rubble, we succeeded in making our way through the debris. The town to our left was ablaze, and many houses were already burning on our right. Surrounded by flames, I had no time to think. The will to escape the fire drove us ahead toward the safety of the park, where the air improved.

It was pure madness. The unnatural brightness of the fire shone into peoples' faces, where I saw sheer terror and agony. The slow realization of what was happening reflected in their paralyzed features and turned their hair gray. That night I witnessed how people lost their sanity, hurling themselves into the flames in some kind of mental derangement. Others were sitting on a rock or squatting on the ground, their faces expressionless, and no one could persuade them to get up and move on. Many were confused and talked nonsense, while lashing out wildly with their arms and tearing their hair out; others called for their children or friends and relatives that were nowhere to be seen. As I observed the madness around me, I felt strangely detached, as though I were watching the events in a film that was unreeling before my eyes, and yet I was right in the middle of it all. Whenever I didn't know how to go on, I looked at the two of you and Omi, which gave me renewed strength and courage to continue.

At last we left the burning city behind us and reached the Große Garten. We were able to walk the last stretch next to each other along the Fürstenallee toward one of the pavilions. There we could sit down and rest and at least have a roof over our heads protecting us from airborne burning objects and the ashes raining down on us. I was completely soaked with sweat from exertion and the heat of the fire.

Sitting on one of the stone benches, I dared to look up into the flames at last. As I saw the full extent of the fire, I doubted we would ever get out of the city alive. We were on a dark island with the city burning all around us.

There were already many people in the pavilion when we got there. I had never seen such people, and felt like a stranger among them. It was as if I did not belong. Even their gestures seemed unreal. They were sitting on the benches or their suitcases, knapsacks, bags and blankets, which they had spread out on the marble floor. Hardly anyone said a word, and when they did speak, their voices sounded hollow as they exchanged news about how they had come here from the various parts of town instead of going down to the Elbe river.

Under the protective roof of the pavilion we survived the third attack the next day in the late morning hours. By then thick black smoke rose from the burning city. The towers of Dresden, whose windows shone red and hollow, stood black in the red and white heat of the fire. Some had become giant torches while others glowed like lanterns. I unwrapped our provisions, fed you two girls and tried to drink something, but my throat hurt with every gulp. Finally I found the cough candies all stuck together in the paper bag. I bit one off, and the lozenge soothed my sore throat. It was then that I knew we had made it. It was like a miracle.

Like a miracle, I wondered? Was our survival really a miracle or was it my mother's presence of mind, her intuition, her courage and her will to survive that rescued us from the flames? Or was it perhaps just plain luck? Wouldn't it have been a greater miracle, or the true miracle, if Dresden hadn't been bombed? And what about the people who perished, suffocated, were burned alive or trampled to death? Where was their miracle? Had they had less will to live, or had they simply been unlucky?

I had never been afraid of the light, my mother said. I always welcomed the morning dawn and the first faint rays of the sunlight, especially in the winter during the war, because they heralded the new day and drove away the menacing dreams. I could take down the blankets from the windows, pull back the heavy drapes and let the daylight in. But during that one night I learned to fear the bright light, the way it illuminated death, forcing me to shut my eyes so I wouldn't see too much. To survive, to escape this living hell, the fire, the smoke and the deadly gases, was all I could think about. The great death had descended upon us and killed every living thing that could not escape the old sections of town. The fire all around us left no doubt that all of Dresden was falling prey to the flames.

We could not really tell when the day began. The daylight was hardly able to break through the thick rain of ashes, and I wondered why they had come a third time. Almost every house was in flames already after the first two attacks. Nothing much of the old town would have remained anyway. The murderous white heat had taken the strength from the iron, had bent and melted it, had burst marble and cracked rocks, and it had made the sandstone porous, hollowing it out, causing buildings to collapse.

As the wild animals from the zoological garden tried to escape, many perished in the flames. I heard the lions roar. I knew the animals and their caretakers well from the time when Papa had worked there, and had continued to visit them after his death.

My mother's storytelling had long ago become a ritual. She officiated over it. We, her family, suffered with her when she spoke about that one night, reliving the horror over and over again. The spirit of the city had remained alive in her and she cast a spell over us by alternately presenting us with the flourishing Baroque city and the dead city of Dresden as she captivated us with her vivid stories of a town that I only knew as an endless field of ruins.

As I grew older I felt both anger and pain when she talked about the bombing, and I did not always listen. Often my thoughts would wander off. On my first trip abroad via Cologne and Brussels to London and Birmingham in the late fifties, I realized for the first time in my life that I had grown up in the midst of ruins. For years I had had nothing but devastation before my eyes. I looked into bombed out houses with huge mounds of bricks and debris piled up in their deserted front gardens, where over the years weeds, flowers, bushes and trees grew through the rubble. I realized that this was not normal, at least not everywhere in Europe. But in Germany every city resembled the other. And yet, as I walked through the bombed out towns, I had to admit that it had been presumptuous to expect mercy for Dresden in the face of all the cruelties Germany had perpetrated during the war.

Our world as we knew it was destroyed when the war came to an end, changing us forever. There was nothing left to build on, and nothing to refer to in the years that followed. We felt like outcasts in a desolate place, naked and rejected. The feeling of being at home never returned; we never belonged anywhere again. Even years later on my many trips it was always shocking for me to see the centers of towns in other European countries without bomb damage. Their elegant beauty confused me. In Vienna, in Prague and time and again in Zürich I saw entire streets with the same kind of apartment houses as on the old photos of the Fürstenstraße. The uniform architecture, in which German cities were rebuilt in the fifties, incensed me. Everywhere the same façades with the same square windows, the same front doors, balconies and roofs, were just cheap imitations of the Bauhaus style.

At fifteen I became impatient with my mother, and one day I said to her, "Can't you leave it alone? Why do you continue to talk about the destruction of Dresden? I can't take it anymore! It has to be over sometime!"

"But it isn't over. It will never be over," was her answer. "You don't understand. You were so little when it all happened."

My mother never gave me the chance to tell her, but I had my own strong visual memories of the many hours we spent in the Große Garten. It was there that my senses awoke. Under the roof of the pavilion I became aware of myself and understood that whatever was going on concerned me, too. I saw the people and paid attention to the things around me, and I recall certain incidents differently that stood out distinctly from my mother's words.

In the pavilion, my mother had lifted my sister Bettine out of the carriage and was cradling her in her arms while staring into the flames. I followed her gaze and became aware of the dark contours of a man wearing a black winter coat and hat, standing just a few steps away from us at the edge of the pavilion looking toward the burning city. Instantly I felt an inner connection to him. An attractive force seemed to radiate out from him, to which I yielded. I got up, walked over and stood next to the man. He did not notice me. My mother called me back, but I made believe that I did not hear her because I wanted to talk about the fire. Fascinated by the spectacle, I tried to get the man's attention. I took heart and pulled at his coat sleeve, but he just continued to look into the flames. I pulled again harder. Suddenly he looked down at me. I had to hear from him what was happening. I wanted to know it for myself. Someone had to talk with me about the fire that surrounded us.

I heard myself say to him, "Everything is burning."

He did not react.

I repeated my words firmer and louder.

Astonished, and as though he were returning from afar to the edge of the pavilion, the man slowly turned to me and repeated, "Yes, everything is burning."

Then he looked once more into the flames.

That was not enough for me. I wanted to know more.

"Why," I asked, "why are so many bombs falling?"

"Oh, little girl, what you are asking, that is a long story," the man answered.

Then we both stood once more silently next to each other, our eyes lifted toward the blazing fire.

"The fire is burning everything?" I asked.

"Yes, there won't be much left when it's over," he said.

"We live over there." I pointed in the direction of the bright blaze. Then I reached for his hand. He said nothing, but he held my hand tight and we stood together for a while. The flames attracted us mightily, they held us captive and did not let us go. We simply couldn't look anywhere else. There was nothing else to see anyway. I could only shut my eyes, but even then everything before me and inside of me glowed red. I opened my eyes again and looked at my shoes, at the stone floor, at the man, then at the city again. Suddenly the fire above the burning houses flared up even brighter for a few seconds. I heard my mother, who was calling me back repeatedly, but I still did not listen to her. When I heard Omi's high-pitched whining, I turned around and saw her sitting next to my mother bent over, her face buried in her hands. She seemed so alone that I pulled my hand out of the man's, ran over to her and forced myself onto her lap. She held me close, and I saw her tears. Her face was completely wet. She cried and lamented over her city while rocking me back and forth. After that I remember nothing for a long time, not until we were on our way through the streets again amongst fleeing people.

In first grade, there was a story in our reader about a summer evening with fireworks for the amusement of a crowd of happy people that were gazing at the colorful sparks that looked to me like large flowers high up in the night sky, or like water spraying up from a fountain. I had never seen a fireworks display, and no one could explain it to my satisfaction. Since I had certain ideas about a fire I thought, no, a firework is like what happened in Dresden. That was the firework! But the children in class laughed at me. So I opened up the book at home and told Omi what a firework display really is, "Just like in Dresden, isn't it?" And I pointed at the picture. She looked at me in horror and scolded me because of my stupid idea.

12. Ash Wednesday

In the meantime it was Ash Wednesday, my mother reminded her listeners. During the third attack, the bombers hit the last houses that were still standing in the center of the city, and finally dropped their surplus over more distant parts of town. When the last all-clear signal sounded, I gathered up our things, stowed them away in both carriages, and then we left the Große Garten to look for better shelter. For one last time I looked in the direction of the Fürstenstraße. The fire would continue to burn for days, reducing everything to ashes like in a huge crematorium.

But which route of escape should we take out of the city? We were surrounded by fire, and the smoke burned in our eyes. First we walked through the Große Garten to the corner of Karcherallee and Stübelallee. Suddenly we were on the Schneebergstraße, and from there we made it through Striesen to the Schlüterstraße. In that part of town only a few isolated houses were burning, and we got ahead faster, continuing through suburban streets in the direction of the Loschwitz Bridge, also called the *Blaue Wunder*, because it was the first steel bridge built in 1891-93, which was hailed as a technical wonder and had been given a light-blue coat of paint. The bridge lay far away from the old town and would probably still be standing and could carry us to safety. My plan was to cross the Elbe to Loschwitz, walk up the steep cobblestone road on the other side to the Weiße Hirsch, and from there continue on the highway to Bischofswerda. We had to get away from the river valley and the wet ashes that fell heavily like rain, blocking our vision. It stuck to our hair and lay on our clothes like a gray-black veil. Breathing was difficult.

On the Loschwitz Bridge I dared to look back for the first time, and saw the blackened spires of the silhouette of Dresden stand like the skeletons of dead giants, surrounded by flames. I had just enough strength left to push the baby carriage without getting its wheels stuck in the streetcar tracks and to make sure that Omi was right next to me. After an arduous walk up the steep hill over icy cobblestones, we reached the Weiße Hirsch in the afternoon where medical orderlies received us. I cannot remember the exact location, but I heard someone call out to us. A man in uniform helped me push the carriage the last few steps to the station they had set up. Under a tent that was open toward the front a large long table had been set up. In front of it stood a huge kettle with hot peppermint tea and a second one with hot porridge. Thank God I had taken along our aluminum dishes and flatware from the cellar. The porridge was our first hot meal since the previous day. We hadn't really noticed our hunger until we smelled the food. The helpers even filled the baby bottle with warm milk and had a cup for you, Anne, but you would not take anything, no porridge, no milk, nothing. You refused all food for days. I could barely make you drink some tea with milk and slip some malt candies into your mouth, which Omi still had in her bag.

As we sat on the bench with our backs toward the city, spooning up our hot oatmeal while constantly spitting out husks, I felt the warmth of the food in my stomach. Finally I turned around and dared to look down over the city and the Elbe valley. From the top of the hill I saw the full extent of the fire. The sky was red as far as I could see. Black smoke clouds lay over the city and rose up from the river valley, drifting heavily over the hills. I stopped eating, got up and took a few steps toward the edge of the road. It was then that I heard Omi's calm voice for the first time in hours, "Come on Elfriedchen, sit down again and eat some more. Don't let the food get cold."

As I stood and looked over the city, I knew that nothing would ever again be the way it was up until the night before. My whole body shook and my hands were ice cold and stiff, but not just from the bitter winter morning air that bit through two pairs of woolen gloves; the cold also came from within. I thought I would never get warm again, and I knew I would never again live in Dresden.

Suddenly I sobbed loudly and thought I was going to have a breakdown. An orderly put his hand on my right shoulder and said quietly, "Don't look back, young lady, the sight will only drain you of your last energies. Come, sit down again, eat up and feed your children." His words brought me back to reality, and I dried my eyes. "You have a long way ahead of you," he added.

He was very young, no more than seventeen. His face was soft and pale, and he was very helpful. He might as well have said, if you look back into the valley, you will become a pillar of salt. Look ahead, up the hill, into a new direction.

Days later I remembered that I had still seen the dome of the Frauenkirche while the young man was talking to me. It collapsed that same day only hours after we left Dresden. In the weeks that followed we could not imagine a future. We could hardly grasp the present. I was filled with just one thought: to get you children to safety, as far away as possible from this place of damnation.

As far away as possible. Rubble and ashes. Sodom and Gomorrah. These words accompanied us from then on, my mother explained. We simply were not prepared for the enormous impact of the bombing attacks. Did the people look back to the Old Testament out of remorse or to find an answer that would allow them to go on living? In the face of the utter destruction and the cost of human lives it seemed no longer possible to think about the war in any way other than biblical terms. Without God there seemed to be no explanation for the complete devastation; with God it was just as difficult to make any sense of it, because how does one measure guilt and punishment? Against whom was the retaliation aimed? What was made right through the destruction of Dresden, and who was being reconciled with whom? Or are these questions, over two-thirds of a century later, still the wrong questions, and therefore continue to be illegitimate?

I looked up dazed from my manuscript and tried to push away the heavy thoughts. Enticed by the early morning sun, I stepped out onto my terrace. Dew covered the flowers and grass in the garden. The water drops shimmered like silvery glass pearls under the bright rays of the sun that had just climbed over the fence to shine onto the lawn, bushes and flowers. Barefoot I stepped onto the cold wet grass. At the tip of each blade of grass hung a full, heavy, crystal-clear drop of water, whose weight bent the blade down in a wide arch. At the slightest touch or puff of wind, the water fell to the ground, and the blade of grass, relieved of its burden, jumped up, pointing straight into the air once again. If a drop was on a young, tall-standing blade, it ran down on the inside like in a drainpipe. As it plunged downward it swelled up as it gathered all the tiny drops that were in its way. On some mornings, when I forgot to roll in the white plastic clothesline that I had stretched over the terrace the previous day, I had two strings of glistening pearls of water. It is incredible how nature can magically turn a practical but otherwise rather ugly plastic clothesline into two long strings of pearls. I walked over to look at the sparkling strings of pearls that were hanging round and full in the sunlight until I could no longer resist temptation and gave the line a quick tug and let it snap back, making the drops fly in a wide arc an inch or two up into the air before they cascaded down and landed next to each other on the deck, forming two perfect rows of water drops.

It was only a game, but once the empty line alarmed me. Irritated, I unhooked it and let it roll back fast, while thinking of my mother who loved pearls very much. She had several strands of various lengths. They suited her well, the light pink hue of the pearls matched her skin wonderfully, and she wore them with pride. Once, as she was getting ready for an evening with friends and went through her jewelry, she took one of the long strands into her hands and, lost in thought, she let the smooth pearls slowly glide through her fingers. Then she said quite unexpectedly, "Pearls symbolize tears. I should not wear pearls anymore. There have been enough tears in my life already."

"Oh, Mutti, that sounds just like Emilia Galotti," I teased her, "how often have you seen this tragedy by Lessing? You aren't superstitious, are you?"

"I'm not so sure," she answered, "because life is a tragedy."

I felt a renewed urgency to continue writing, and returned to the computer and my mother's remarks at the Weiße Hirsch as she was overlooking Dresden.

It was all very well for the young soldier to say that I should not look back, my mother remarked. His words struck me strangely, and for a moment I felt like Mrs. Lot who had giving no heed to God's command and had turned into a pillar of salt because she had looked back, a punishment for disobedience, as is being preached to us women even today. But to look back over the city that is going up in flames and only hours earlier had been our world, is very human. It was important for me to see the entire destruction, because only after seeing it was I able to separate myself from it and look toward a future, which at that moment seemed less certain to me than what was sinking into dust and ashes below us.

A few steps away stood an ambulance around which people had gathered who had come up the hill from the city like us. The orderlies helped as best they could. They cleaned wounds and treated burns by applying some ointment, and then wrapped them with gauze bandages. I watched as they made a sling out of a woman's headscarf for her broken arm. Our eyes were irritated and dry from the smoke and lack of sleep. Our throats were sore. We joined the line and waited our turn because we needed eye drops urgently. The cool soothing moisture felt good. I opened and closed my eyes several times, and then I could see clearly again. Only then did I realize how badly my eyes had been burning. When the medical orderly heard my hoarse voice, he also gave me a spoonful of cough syrup. I opened my mouth not asking how many people had already swallowed syrup from the same spoon and whether they had rinsed it in-between. When helpers saw the two of you, they told us about a farmhouse in the vicinity where we would be able to wash ourselves, get something to eat and spend the night. The NSDAP had already taken provisions there, blankets, diapers, dried milk and other emergency items, he explained.

I was thankful for the information. We left the Weiße Hirsch and set out toward the farm, which we reached about two hours later. The ground of the wide yard between of the farmhouse and the barn was completely frozen, and I remember the cracked ice over once deep puddles. The courtyard resembled a refugee camp. A young woman, who had seen us coming, took us directly to the barn and looked for a good place for us in a corner away from the gate, the cold draft, and the other people. She also brought us two horse blankets to spread over the straw.

"You can rest here," she said, "I will bring you warm milk and cream of wheat for your children. We also have boiled potatoes and fresh buttermilk if you would like some."

The milk was freshly milked. You were not used to the taste, Anne, and didn't want to drink it. I almost despaired. You looked so pale and fragile, but you insisted on milk from the dairy. I mixed some milk into the stiff cream of wheat, and was able to feed you a few spoons. After we had eaten, Omi went to fetch a pail of hot water and linen towels so we could wash and change. I took off my shoes and stockings to soak my sore feet and massage them. Omi got more water to wash our stockings and the diapers and hung everything over a wooden pole on the wall behind us to dry.

Finally I slept for hours, but I woke up again with a terrible headache and stepped outside the barn to breathe some fresh air. My whole body ached. The sky above us was dark red. Black smoke billowed up from the city. The farm woman said that the headache was from smoke poisoning, and gave me chamomile tea in a large enamel bowl. "Breathe in the steam and drink from the tea when it's cooled off," she said, "and soak this facecloth in the tea and put it over your eyes and forehead. That will relax you."

After some breakfast, we continued our journey the next morning along the main street to Bischofswerda, but we could never have imagined the many difficulties and hardships that were in store for us. For a mere twenty-three miles we would need seven days. Kurt and I had covered the route on our bicycles so often in just a few hours as we visited each other! I thought it would be best if we went to his parents', because Kurt would certainly look for us there. Besides, I thought that they would be kind to their son's wife and grandchildren in their need. Omi did not want to come along, she would have preferred to stay close to Dresden, search for a room in the suburbs and look for work, but I needed her and she had to push one of the carriages.

We had not been on the open country road for long, when we heard aircraft engines approaching from behind. The noise frightened me, but on that morning I thought that they were on their way to another target and simply walked on in the middle of the road. There were hardly any cars. The street was full of refugees from Dresden. It took all my concentration to get ahead on the cobblestones, the packed snow and slippery ice. I could feel every cobblestone through the soles of my shoes.

Suddenly I saw how the other people abandoned everything, ran toward the left bank of the street and went down into the ditch. A man yelled at me, "For God's sake, woman, quick, run for shelter," while letting himself roll down the slope. It was grotesque. I stood petrified when I heard bullets whistle past us. They hit the handcart directly in front of us and ricocheted off the pavement. A bullet bored itself into a tree trunk a few yards ahead of us on our right, tearing a deep hole into it. Wood splinters flew through the air, and

I covered my face with my forearm to protect my eyes. People screamed, but before we knew it the spook was over, and the three bombers were only small black specks in the sky. I watched the man who had yelled at us climb clumsily up the steep, snow-covered slope. Then he came towards us with long fast steps. I was shocked when I noticed that his left arm was gone, leaving his coat sleeve dangling empty back and forth with every step.

"Dear woman," he said sternly, "the moment you hear the bombers you must check from which direction they are coming and then get down the opposite embankment or hide behind a tree. The pilots are targeting us. Next time do what everyone else is doing. Grab your children and run for cover."

I looked at the man in disbelief although I had just seen it with my own eyes. Refugees would talk about low-flying aircraft that shot at them as they walked along the highways escaping Dresden for years to come. I didn't know what to think, it was all so confusing, but from then on we also jumped into the ditches as soon as we heard planes. Omi railed against this nonsense when it was especially hard to get back out of a ditch into which we had slipped too deeply. Around noon came so many aircraft that we had to duck and let ourselves fall down the slopes right after having scrambled back up to the edge of the street. It must have been a strange sight from above to watch us scatter, running toward the ditches and getting stuck in the deep snow drifts along the sides of the road, how we were knocked against rocks and milestones or got caught in hedges, lost our scarves, hats and gloves, how we twisted our legs, sprained our ankles and got bruises all over our bodies. Occasionally someone took an unlucky fall into a puddle of ice-cold water where the layer of ice had become thin over the noon hours and broke under their weight. Our shoes and stockings were soaked from melting snow, and our feet felt frozen. The bombers flew low enough that I could see the faces of the pilots in the cockpits, and I thought that they must be able to see us equally clearly.

At certain intersections soldiers had blocked off long stretches of the highway, and we were forced to continue along uneven field paths or unpaved country roads, where it was difficult to push the carriages over clumps of dirt, hard icy snow and negotiate deep, frozen ruts. The wind blew harshly across the plains, biting into our faces. Omi and I were chilled to the marrow of our bones. Although we had wrapped our woolen shawls and headscarves tightly around our heads and necks, our noses were red from the cold and hurt, and our hands were so stiff that we could hardly hold onto the handlebars of the carriages. I tried to keep you girls covered as well as I could to protect your hands and feet from frostbite. Then you decided to climb out of your stroller, Anne, which was not such a good idea. Once you had walked ahead a good distance and remained standing in the middle of the street behind a three-wheeled truck with a flat and watched the men who tried to repair the tire, when we heard more bombers approaching. My heart stood still. I yelled at you to crawl under the truck, but you simply did not listen. That's how you were, if you didn't want to do something, no one could make you.

With time we became more skilled. We heard the aircraft before we could see them, and knew from which direction they were coming. Eventually the sky became silent. I didn't notice it until we had walked for a while undisturbed and one of the men remarked that by now they were on their return flight to England, and wouldn't be back today. I heard his words, but I cannot remember if they triggered any kind of emotion in me. We simply continued to mechanically put one foot in front of the other.

This is what the end of the war looks like, was all that went through my mind. The end, that I had seen coming since my return from Königsberg, and which I had longed for in the hope that we would be spared the worst, came later than expected. I had never dared to visualize what the worst might be. Only as I describe even the smallest details can I hope to understand the events at least a little.

On the second day we stopped early at a farm because I simply could not go on. I had to lie down or at least sit in a warm place. My feet were ice-cold and hurt in the worn shoes. I was afraid of blood poisoning and had to treat my blisters, which burned with every step.

Not all the farmers were as kind and concerned as at our first stop. They had had to put up too many refugees during the last months, and there was no end in sight. I wondered what had become of our house and whether it was still standing, but I couldn't give myself over to such thoughts for long on this arduous journey. At night I had confusing dreams, from which I frequently awoke. Memories of happier days from before the war, when my father was still with us, alternated with visions of the destruction. I screamed in my sleep because the flames were reaching for me in my dreams. Omi tried to calm me.

At one of the farms they had made a big open fire in the yard around which refugees were warming themselves and drying their coats. When I saw the flames, I was overcome by a deadly horror and wept for the first time. In the months that followed I worked through some of the horrors, but other memories I was never able to put behind me. Omi sobbed now and then in her sleep. Maybe she was dreaming about Rolf and her beautiful apartment, of which she had always been so proud.

The following day, we tried to get ahead by train. Once we were lucky and we got to the next station. The second time the train stopped shortly after we had left the station and we all had to get off again. "Maybe the train will continue in a few hours," we were told, but they couldn't promise anything, and so we continued once more on foot. My legs were as heavy as lead. Unexpectedly, a bus came up from behind us. The driver stopped, and without asking where we were going, he told us to get on, he would take us to the next town.

After six days we arrived in Putzkau. We had slept on cots in a school, in drafty barns and empty stables. The people of Putzkau asked us if we were coming from Dresden. When we answered in the affirmative, they wanted to know a hundred details about the bombings, in which part of the city we had lived, what it looked like on the streets, had the inhabitants been able to flee? They asked endless questions, and we were so tired. Someone brought us hot coffee made of barley malt and sandwiches. The people watched us eat and drink, and I became aware of the fact that we were refugees, homeless people who had lost everything and were dependent on other people's kindness. We were so close to our destination, and I suddenly doubted that I could go on. But the food and hot coffee revived me and I felt new energy rise up inside of me.

In the late afternoon, as the sun was about to set, we got to the street that led to the house of my paternal grandparents, Hanna and Wilhelm Bergner. Coming from Putzkau it was one of the first houses of Bischofswerda. When I recognized where we were, I ran away from my mother to the house. The front door was not locked, so I entered and jumped up the two flights of stairs to the second floor and turned the bell at the apartment door. Shortly thereafter I heard familiar voices inside. Aunt Irmgard, my father's sister, opened the door, looked at me, and slammed the door shut again into my face, calling out, "My God, it's Anne!" I was confused and rang again, and this time Grandmother Bergner opened.

"Where are you coming from, where are the others? Let me look at you, you'd better come on in," she exclaimed.

"Mutti is right behind me with Bettine and Omi," I shouted all excited.

Grandmother Bergner couldn't believe that we had survived the bombings. The sky had been red for three nights and days, they said, and the wind had carried ashes all the way to them. "We thought you would never make it out alive. After so many days we no longer expected to see you," they repeated over and over again.

13. A Prison of Death

My mother always ended her account of the bombing of Dresden and our flight from the burning city with these words, "Three bombers crashed during that night into the streets of Dresden. One of them hit the only high-rise building on the Albertplatz, and the wreck lay there for weeks among the ruins for everyone to see." In the midst of all the misery it sounded like a sensation. For years she was horrified by the severity of the attacks and how systematically the city had been bombed. To her it proved how determined the allies had been to beat Hitler in the air war, and she was amazed at their huge weapons arsenal. But not until I was writing down her story over fifty years later did I understand that it was the Americans that had flown the third attack on Dresden at noon on Thursday, the 14th of February, and the fourth one on the 15th.

We had been in Bischofswerda for only a few days when Omi decided to return to Dresden. She wanted to see her city and find out what had happened to our house, and whether the cellar had withstood the bombings. The trains were running again, so she went with me to Dresden early Monday morning, the 26th of February.

The big fires were out, but in several areas of the old town buildings were still smoldering. The smoke curled up through the ruins into a gray sky, airborn particles hindered our visibility, and a strange smell lay in the air, which Omi did not want to explain to me. She was tight-lipped and very different from the way I knew her. The streetcars were not back in service along all the tracks yet. The sidewalks and streets were covered with huge piles of rubble that on some streets had been moved to the sides enough to open a path for people to walk. The center of town had been reopened to the former inhabitants. Those who wanted to access their lots or enter the cellars of their houses had to get the appropriate permits or have some proof that they had lived there if they did not want to risk being arrested for looting.

From the main station, Omi tried to get through the piles of debris and heaps of rubble to our house on the Fürstenstraße, but we were forced to take a detour across the Altmarkt and try to make it from there. At times she ran, pulling me after her so fast that I stumbled, hardly able to keep up, and then again she would stop suddenly and stood rooted to the ground. She was visibly shaken by the vast scope of the destruction. On the Altmarkt, I saw things that I was unable to process, but I understood that dead people were stacked up in huge piles, and many men in uniform were walking about. I pointed at the bodies, asking Omi about them, but she gave no answer, saying only, "shut your eyes, don't look." On the way to our street we climbed over mountains of bricks and debris. It was later calculated that 24 million cubic yards of rubble were hauled away. People had written messages on remaining parts of walls or on scraps of paper tacked to tree trunks with the names of missing family members or addresses where they themselves could be reached. On photos taken by the citizens of Dresden, names, dates and addresses have survived. Graffiti in black and white, born in the hour of need, was written accurately in the old German handwriting or brushed in large awkward letters with white paint, tar, or charred wood and whatever else happened to be available. Omi read the messages out loud, spelled names and places, and tried to decipher any hidden meanings while hoping to find some word about her son.

Finally we stood in front of the ruin of our house. Again, we climbed over piles of bricks and entered the ground floor. The house was completely burned out. We stepped through the gaping opening that once was the front door into the hall. The flames had blackened the walls of the staircase. Fearlessly we climbed down the stairs into the basement. It was pitch dark at the bottom, so Omi lit a candle. We could see that the fire had not penetrated down into the cellar, and we found our partition locked and with everything that we had left behind still in it. Omi stuffed both her large shopping bags and the knapsack with preserved food, kitchen utensils and clothing. To her great joy, she also found the porcelain Melitta coffee filter No 104 for six cups. "We must come back tomorrow to get the rest," she said. Before we left, we sat on a blanket that Omi had spread over a rock outside our house, and in the middle of the devastation all around us, we ate our sandwiches, drank juice from jars of preserves and spooned out the fruit.

Kurt had seen the red sky all the way in Cottbus, and had set out to Dresden to look for us as soon as he received permission to leave his unit, my mother explained. When he saw the Altstadt, he knew that if we had survived he would find us at his parents', where he arrived on the day when Omi and you, Anne, were in Dresden. After hearing Omi's report, he and I went there early the next morning with bags and knapsacks to rescue from our cellar whatever we could. The ruins of the houses were eventually torn down, and the cellars filled in with rubble.

But not all family members escaped the flames, my mother said visibly shaken. Since I had heard nothing from Lieselotte or Rolf, I took the train to Dresden in early March to look for Lotte. She would have known that she'd most likely find us with Kurt's parents, but how could she have contacted us short of coming to Bischofswerda? I also hoped that she might have news from Rolf, after all, he wrote to her regularly. When I entered her street, I saw immediately that her house together with all the others on that side of the street had been bombed. Fear gripped me, and I felt this inner cold again. I hastened down the street, but while I was still running I had this premonition that I would not find her. When I stood in front of the ruin of their house, I could see the rubble inside through the window openings. I was undecided about what to do, so I started to walk around the house to see if I could find any sign of life or messages on the walls that would let me know of their whereabouts. Maybe they had left the cellar before most of the house had come crashing down?

At that moment, a neighbor approached me. He asked me if I were looking for the house owners. When I nodded, he said in his broad Saxon dialect, "Well, then come along with me, I can show you what happened to them."

We walked through the bent wrought-iron gate into the back yard and he led me to a cellar window next to the back entrance.

"Why don't you look inside, my dear woman, but don't you get scared." He wagged his crooked right index finger back and forth in front of my face such that I stepped back in disgust. I bent down to take a closer look through the dusty cellar window. It seemed to me that I saw human heads and bodies, but then again, perhaps my imagination just got the better of me.

"It seems to me that they tried to climb out of the cellar window," the neighbor continued, "most likely after a direct hit during the second bombing attack, which caused the upper floors to collapse and blocked the cellar door."

Right then I understood the cruel truth. Lieselotte, her parents and her sister with her two small children burned to death in their cellar. They had been trapped in the basement, and when the fire came, there was no way to escape. Weeks later they were still clustered together in front of the window, completely charred.

That's when I heard the man again, stressing every word painstakingly in his Saxon dialect, "You see, my dear woman, there are three iron bars in front of each window." He hit them with his walking cane, and they gave off a hollow clank.

I felt sick to my stomach and thought that I saw the charred figures tremble.

"The bars were firmly secured into the wall, so they couldn't bend them apart or tear them out," he commented, supporting himself on his cane. "The bars were supposed to keep the thieves out."

I was prepared for almost anything, but not for that sight through the cellar window. As I stood there, I heard the man shuffle off without saying another word. Later that afternoon I went to the authorities to report their deaths, and asked them to send the death certificates to Bischofswerda. Their names are listed among the bombing victims.

As a child I would walk over to my mother to stroke her softly when she was finished, because I was afraid of her sadness. She took me into her arms and quieted down bit by bit. Later I became ashamed of her tears and the stories she offered to her husband and those family members who had fared better, and then to our new West German acquaintances on the Mosel river, who knew only by hearsay about the bombings of cities, refugee treks and the flight from the Russians.

My mother often suffered from nightmares after she talked about the war. She would grab her down feather comforter, wrap it around herself and run panic-stricken through the apartment screaming, "fire, fire!" I jumped out of bed and saw the fleeing figure run through the rooms into the hall from where she tried to escape into the staircase. When she found the door locked, she felt trapped, screamed even louder and ran back into the living room toward the balcony. Her husband ran after her, but she wouldn't be caught. I closed the balcony door, because I was afraid she might jump over the railing. Her eyes darted about wildly, and her husband took her into his arms and tried to sooth her. Suddenly she let herself sink onto the sofa and began to sob. I made tea, and she drank it sip by sip, gradually calming down.

Only after having spent a week in Dresden several times with her husband after the wall fell in 1989, walking through town for hours revisiting the old familiar places, did she finally get over it and no longer woke up from nightmares about the fire.

As I grew older, I felt increasing shame when we talked about World War II. The reasons were twofold. On the one hand I knew that Germany had started the war, and after five years we were getting back what we had done to others, and that we, as the perpetrators, had neither the right to talk about our pain nor could we expect compassion. On the other hand there was the knowledge that, as far as I knew, no one of my immediate family had said or done anything against Hitler or criticized him in public. No one had belonged to the resistance movement, no one had stood up for Jewish neighbors, or opposed the Nazi regime. To this day I don't know if my mother ever tried to contact people who had been against Hitler and the Nazis, but then again, aren't these late and vain questions from someone who was born after those events took place and who has the dubious good fortune of having only matured enough to ask them decades after the catastrophe?

Kurt Vonnegut was in Dresden as a prisoner of war during the firebombing, and wrote about it years later in a detached, ironic, humorous way in his book *Slaughterhouse-Five or The Children's Crusade*. For lack of more precise words, or because he wanted to point to the banal senselessness of it all, he repeats throughout the book, "so it goes," and "I know, I know, I know." The bombing of Dresden was as insane as the war had been. What particularly amazed me is the fact that even he, the gifted, well-versed writer, for over twenty long years neither knew how to begin his "famous book about Dresden," nor how to write about those fateful days and how to make any sense of it, for what had happened during that night was not easily accessible. To use his words, "There is nothing intelligent to say about a massacre."

"I would hate to tell you," Vonnegut complains about the subject he calls big, "what this lousy little book cost me in money and anxiety and time. When I got home from the Second World War twenty-three years ago, I thought it would be easy for me to write about the destruction of Dresden, since all I would have to do would be to report what I had seen .... But not too many words about Dresden came from my mind then ... and not many words come now ..." What he says about the bombing attacks remains hidden in general observations like, "There was a fire-storm out there. Dresden was one big flame. The one flame ate everything organic, everything that would burn .... The sky was black with smoke. The sun was an angry little pinhead. Dresden was like the moon now, nothing but minerals. Every-body else was dead." And Vonnegut, too, repeats what had been told to the inhabitants of Dresden throughout the war and what they had wanted to believe so very much and used as an excuse to stay, "You needn't worry about the bombs, by the way. Dresden is an open city. It is undefended, and contains no war industries or troop concentrations of any importance."

"*Slaughterhouse-Five* is one of the world's great anti-war books," it says on the back cover, and in the United States it landed on the list of the one hundred most controversial books.

My mother never read Vonnegut's book. By the time I gave her the German version, she had come to terms with it in her own way, and did not want to read anymore what others had to say about it who had neither lived through the war years nor what had followed.

Such a night has never been written about, she repeated to anyone who would listen. Nobody, she insisted, has ever painted such a blazing fire, and who could separate the sounds of madness during the extermination of all living things, who could describe the screams of those who were burned alive and the smells of death or the heat that reached between 1100 and 1800 degrees Fahrenheit in the center of town, thus creating a firestorm of such elemental force that no one could contain it?

A thousand eyewitness reports cannot express the extent of the destruction. Even after everything has been said, the description remains fragmentary at best.

14. The Carpenter's Shop

In the beginning of March 1945 we were given a makeshift apartment in Bischofswerda that consisted of three rooms over a carpenter's shop in the Wallgasse, a narrow, straight alley with small two-story houses and rough cobblestone pavement. The rooms were drafty with the windows facing the alley, and were connected to each other with doors that simply led from one room to the next. To get to the tiny lavatory with a toilet and sink we had to step out onto the landing.

After we had been there for a few days, a coal stove was delivered, which my mother had procured for very little money. Her face radiated when two men in dark baggy pants and shapeless worn jackets brought the range into the kitchen, setting it down in the place my mother pointed out, not all the way against the wall, because the stovepipe had to be attached first. Soot poured out of the pipe stump onto the kitchen floor as the men did not put it down very gently, tilting it toward the back before it landed on its four feet. As it turned out, it was more difficult to find enough stovepipe than the range itself. My mother and Omi walked all over town and to the nearby farms and villages. We needed two elbows and at least ten feet of straight pipe. No one was willing to sell us any. Money was worthless to second hand dealers and farmers, and we had nothing to swap. So Omi took the train to Dresden one morning and returned with full bags and a large, thick rubber mat, which could be used for new soles on shoes. For the rubber Omi was able to barter enough stovepipe from a farmer who had not had any a few days earlier, and she even brought back a sack of flour and slab of bacon.

For a second rubber mat we got several well-cured wooden planks, from which carpenter Petzolt built three pieces of furniture: a large shoe cabinet, a chest of drawers for our gloves, scarves and hats, and another tall cabinet we used as a pantry. All three pieces of furniture were painted in a rich orange and light ocher, the only paint the carpenter had left from before the war, which in those days was synonymous with quality in the eastern zone. Perishable foods were stored in the cellar because we had no icebox. Milk and other dairy products were bought fresh daily.

Soon thereafter, my mother acquired a large zinc tub, which was brought into the kitchen on Saturdays for bathing. Omi would put on extra wood and coal and heat the two huge pots of water and as many small ones as would fit on top of the range. When the tub wasn't being used for bathing or laundry, it was leaning against the wall next to the toilet.

We lived alone in the old building and were complete strangers in that part of town. There was no real front door, just a large factory gate into which an opening the size of a door was cut and secured with hinges. To get to the second floor we had to walk through the large gloomy workshop, where the carpenters would greet me lewdly, calling strange words after me. Whenever my mother talked about our life in that first place, her face was serious, and she never smiled. We had no radio, and there was no music anywhere, just Omi humming Polish folk songs and old hits as she was going about her daily chores. "We had lost all desire for singing," my mother said, when I asked her about it years later. Then she thought for a moment and added, "But I sang you to sleep every night."

There were few children living in the neighborhood, and I hardly knew them because I was only seldom allowed to play in the street. In those uncertain times my mother was afraid that something might happen to me.

Because the war had hardly touched this remote town, life was happier at my paternal grandparents' who were doing well and took things easier. They knew the local people and the nearby farmers, and were informed about what was going on in town, the surrounding villages and on the farms. There was plenty of fruit and lots of vegetables growing in the garden behind their house. Their hens had enough fenced in space to move about freely, and laid eggs daily. When a hen no longer laid, its head was hacked off, and the next day there was a huge pot of chicken soup with homemade noodles, carrots and seasonal vegetables on the stove. There were always five or six well-fed rabbits sitting in the stables in front of their feeding dishes. I talked to them and stroked them and pushed grass, potato peels, dandelion leaves and other delicacies through the chicken wire. As I watched Grandmother Bergner while she cooked and baked, she recited all kinds of children's rhymes, told me fairy tales, sang children's songs or recited short poems. In the months before the Russians came she looked at me mischievously at times and repeated the following rhyme with dark sparkling eyes:

O goodness gracious me,
Said the miller's daughter, you'll see,
When the Russians come, you'd better flee,
Or along with them they'll take thee.

"You better watch out," she kidded me, "when the Russians come, you must run away as fast as you can or they'll take you along, too." I had no idea what to make of her words, but I never forgot the silly verse. Fortunately, no one in our family was taken away.

We lived in an interregnum during those months, my mother would say gravely, as she picked up her narrative where she had left off. The American army, which was in Bavaria as far as we knew and for which we were waiting, didn't come. Instead, endless horror stories chased each other daily about the approaching Red army as it drove millions of refugees ahead of it, whose stories constantly threw us into renewed states of panic. And yet there was a surreal silence all around us. We moved about as if in a vacuous space. People who had been fleeing from the east for months along the autobahn via Breslau, Görlitz and Bautzen arrived exhausted, malnourished, half frozen and demoralized in this remote town. We needed all of our energy for the daily procurement of the simplest groceries like potatoes, beets, cabbage, oats, milk and bread, flour and sugar or sugar beet syrup. Everything was rationed. There was hardly any butter or other fat or meat. I was already overjoyed if the butcher had some bones for me, which made good soup with vegetables and potatoes.

After you girls were in bed at night, I mended our clothes, took apart old dresses, jackets and coats that had been given to me by relatives, turned the material inside out, ironed the seams flat and sewed new clothes for us. Grandmother Schubert, who was a nurse and belonged to the protestant sisterhood before she came to Kurt's grandfather to take care of the household and raise the children after the untimely death of his wife, had given me an ancient iron that I had to fill with hot coals. It was a very tedious process, and I was overjoyed when Omi came home with an electric iron, except that from then on I had to iron late at night or in the early morning hours before the electricity was shut off. We lived with blackouts for years. The electricity was gone without any warning at any time, day or night. In the evenings we lit candles, which were also hard to come by. People saved every scrap of wax and bees' wax to make their own candles. Grandmother Schubert also gave me a large quilted blanket stuffed with unbleached sheep's wool. I took it apart, stuffed the wool into two pillowcases, and took it to a woman who had a spinning wheel. From the spun wool I knitted four pullovers with short sleeves for us; there was not enough wool for long sleeves.

The greatest problem continued to be winter shoes. There were times when one of you had to stay home, because your feet grew so fast and I had no shoes for you, or I took you along in the stroller or wagon wearing house shoes.

We had hardly gotten settled above the carpenter's shop when the next disaster struck. The war seemed to be over, but no one knew anything specific. An atmosphere of paralyzing despondency came over the people. The more time passed, the clearer it became that the Red army would move into Saxony.

I went to see a doctor because I was pregnant. The doctor sent me to Herr Reimann, the owner of the only store for sanitary and medical supplies, who still had a large supply of bandaging materials, baby bottles, cotton blankets, diapers and other items. It was astounding what he brought out of his warehouse after six years of war and was now giving away to the refugees. He also had comforting words and helpful ideas for everyone, and he was one of the few truly practical men that I have ever encountered. During my first visit to his store, he gave me a hot-water bag, a tub for footbaths and a package of spruce needle extract to put into the bath water, hand cream, cough drops, a thermometer, baby powder and gauze bandages. I could hardly believe my eyes when he set all these things on the counter in front of me. "From the public welfare for you, Frau Bergner," he said with a broad smile while putting his index finger over his lips. "The more I distribute now, the less will fall into Russian hands."

While I loaded everything into my two shopping bags, I whispered across the counter, leaning forward, "Do you think they will come all the way to us?" I was afraid of my own words, although we were alone in the store.

"They are advancing," he said. "If the allies don't make up their minds soon, they'll be here in a few weeks, maybe even within days."

That was a devastating thought. Life was completely unpredictable. I was only able to take care of the things nearest at hand. Before I fell asleep after midnight I thought about what I would prepare for breakfast. When I got up I was concerned about what I could cook for the noon meal, but first I had to go shopping. Back home I pondered over supper and how to feed you all and how I would get the rest of the housework done before the end of the day. My nerves were on edge. Omi and I could hardly think of anything beyond our survival. At night, every noise, however faint, startled me out of my sleep. In the end everything turned out much worse than I could ever have imagined in my unbelievable naïveté.

15. The Russians Are Coming

The winter was slowly coming to an end. The days were getting longer again, and the first warm sunshine of spring brought us relief, when the most dreaded event happened, my mother recalled. I cannot remember whether it was a Tuesday or a Wednesday when we received the evacuation order for Bischofswerda for Friday, the 20th of April 1945 – on Hitler's birthday of all days! We had to flee our cities because the Soviet army was moving in, and he was sitting in his bunker in Berlin! That he would commit suicide only a few days later we couldn't have imagined at the time, although I wasn't surprised when I heard about it while we were on our way to an unknown destination, but I felt no satisfaction from the news either. His death had come too late for us.

According to the orders, women with children and old people were supposed to assemble early Friday morning in front of the train station or on the market place, where trains, trucks and buses would be provided for the evacuation. By that time elite troops of the Soviet army were on the autobahn from Breslau via Görlitz into Saxony. "Enemy tanks are advancing," I heard all around me. I was in the fifth month of my pregnancy, and even with Omi's help I would not be able to flee a second time with two small children. And where would we go to anyway? Millions were already on their way west. The country was in turmoil, the streets were congested, and all lodgings were overcrowded. We didn't even own a handcart, only the baby carriage and the stroller, which I had been using for our shopping so I wouldn't have to lug home the heavy potatoes, flour and beets. You have no idea how Omi and I wore ourselves out just carrying the groceries!

I doubted that there would be enough vehicles or space on the trains for the thousands of people who were ordered to evacuate within three days. I was also afraid that we might get separated in the tumult. Therefore, I tried to organize our flight on my own, when I heard quite by accident that a train would be made available solely for the people working for the railroad and their families. This was our salvation, I thought in my despair, and I went immediately to Kurt's parents, whose daughter Irmgard was working at the post office and her husband Georg was with the railroad. They would help us for sure, they couldn't abandon their grandchildren and us.

Omi and you, Anne, were in the kitchen cooking the noon meal when I came back, greatly agitated. Unable to speak I simply let myself drop onto a kitchen chair, propped my elbows up on the table and covered my face with both hands. When you tiptoed over to me, Anne, and put your hand on my arm, I began to weep bitterly, and you wept with me.

"Elfriedchen, you are frightening me, what happened?" Omi exclaimed startled.

"I've been foolish enough to ask Hanna if we could come with them, but she told me straight to my face, 'we can't help you, first we have to make sure that we get away.' With her hands on her hips, her headscarf off to one side, her face red with zeal from all the preparations for the evacuation, and, I am sure, out of anger at me, she added, 'Charity begins at home. We have no room for you'."

"Aren't we part of the family?" I asked astonished.

Her spiteful answer was, "Well, we are already going with Irmgard and Georg, we can't just take along anyone who happens to ask."

Irmgard and Georg were busy sorting and packing, and didn't look up when I greeted them. I was clearly in their way. Wilhelm went to the garden with a tin can full of jewelry and other valuables in order to bury it in the hen house. I was so confused by their hostile rebuff that my words stuck in my throat. As I stood there, forsaken by God and the world, I felt my body stiffen and got stomach cramps. Don't break down now, don't let them see your helplessness, I told myself. That brought me back to my senses, and as I watched their hectic activities, it suddenly looked to me as though they were making extensive plans for a family excursion to the local mountains. There was an excited atmosphere in the air. Rabbits and hens were being slaughtered, because they could not leave the animals behind in their cages, and they cooked and baked and fried. The kitchen was so full of steam my glasses clouded over. While they were stoking the fire they also burned everything that pointed to the Third Reich.

My mother stopped for a moment, as if to recall exactly what had taken place at her parents-in-law's. The memory oppressed her, and she had to reorient herself. During such moments, she was seized by a strong hatred of her husband's family, who had always treated her as an outsider. She was also never able to forgive them for not allowing her to store some of her valuables in their attic before the bombing attacks on Dresden when she asked them in the summer of 1942. She had hoped to take her Meißen Porcelain to a safe place as well as sheets and tablecloths from her dowry. None of it had ever been used and was waiting for better days in large chests. But his family told her to her face that firstly they had no room for her stuff, and secondly they couldn't be responsible for it.

I felt hot and loosened my scarf because I had the feeling I was suffocating amidst this hustle and bustle and their coldness. Glass jars with fruit and vegetables had been brought up from the cellar and stood on the steps of the stairs in the hallway, waiting to be packed. Wooden crates, boxes and suitcases were stuffed with warm clothing, towels and blankets and tied together with rope, ready for transport. More was added constantly. They couldn't decide what to take and what to leave behind.

"Charity begins at home," Hanna repeated as she shuffled past me unmoved and with arms full of stuff. She let me know that I was in her way and should leave. She threw me, her daughter-in-law, out.

I could only stammer once again, "But they are your grandchildren, what is to become of them?" They all pretended they had not heard me and continued to walk around me, giving each other orders how to pack up their things and pushing me aside, all the while stuffing their mouths from the abundance of food, but offering nothing to me. They didn't even give me one jar of fruit or blackberry jam, not one slice of bacon or half a loaf of bread, even though they didn't know what to do with all of their provisions. Their only worry was that something might spoil or that it might fall into the hands of others once they were gone.

I understood that my in-laws saw in us a threat to their own safety. Finally I pulled myself together and left without a word as they carried their valuables past me to hide them in the cellar. We were ordered to leave our houses unlocked so the Soviet army could take possession of them immediately.

On my way home I followed a sudden intuition and I rushed to Herr Reimann. He entered the sales room personally as he always did when he heard the shop door open. He was wearing old clothes and must have been working hard because he was out of breath. I had never seen him that way and just stammered some words. When he smiled at me encouragingly, I took heart and told him about my problem.

"Frau Bergner," he interrupted me, "you can stop worrying. Come to the marketplace with your family before seven tomorrow morning, I have organized a bus for pregnant women and women with small children. Go home, take care of your family and pack just the essentials for the next few weeks. We won't have much space for luggage."

I was so relieved and thankful when I heard this kind offer. There were still good people in this world after all.

The night before our flight I did not sleep well. I dreamed of soldiers in foreign uniforms who kept me prisoner, and of rifle butts striking at me. I could just barely escape the blows. All night long, I heard indefinable noises from the marketplace. I was afraid of what lay ahead for us.

The next morning I got up early, cooked oatmeal and put out the clothes for all of us. While you were eating your hot oats I wrapped up the leftover crumb cake and the cold potato pancakes from supper. You were anxious and fidgety and didn't want to eat. I tried to coax you and filled both your cups again with the rest of the milk. I felt sick to my stomach and had no appetite, but forced down a slice of bread with jam and the milk coffee Omi had put in front of me. I looked at the clock. It was almost six thirty. I hurried you along, making sure that I had not forgotten anything, left the washed dishes in the tub on the kitchen table, shut all the windows, closed the curtains and turned off the lights, and then we left our apartment. We walked the few steps to the end of the Wallgasse and turned left onto the marketplace. I noticed that most people were wearing dark, much too warm clothing in several layers. I began to panic because I couldn't find Herr Reimann right away. Then I heard him call my name and I saw him next to a bus. He stowed away our suitcase, showed us the two reserved seats and pointed to where I could put our hand luggage in the nets above us.

You, Anne, wanted to sit on my lap at the window seat so you could see everything better. Herr Reimann said that we would be leaving within half an hour, and then turned again to the folding table that he had set up next to the bus where he was giving out roasted barley coffee with milk to the people. He had everything well organized. Helpers brought pots of fresh coffee and peppermint tea from his house that was only a few steps away, and carried large pieces of cake in a wicker basket, still hot and smelling of butter. He handed us three large slices on brown wrapping paper. We ate some of it, and the rest I wrapped up for later.

It was a strange feeling as I watched the people outside from my seat on the bus. Many of them had not yet been able to find transportation out of the city, and were frantically running back and forth between the vehicles. Others were sitting on top of their luggage looking detached and forlorn, seemingly waiting for some kind of miracle. The vehicles that had been made available by the city were not nearly enough for the multitude of people who were streaming onto the marketplace from all directions. Herr Reimann spoke to them, offered advice and brought another young mother aboard with a tiny baby and a little girl no more than two years of age. The mother was of a desperate calm. I have seen this kind of expression often on people's faces who were wandering about in the streets, not knowing where to go. The baby boy was screaming his lungs out from hunger. She was not able to nurse him because of an infection on her nipples. Then Herr Reimann came with a baby bottle filled with milk and oatmeal and a tube of ointment for the woman. The child drank the whole bottle and fell asleep. We spoke little. What was there to talk about anyway? No one had any energy left, and we were all occupied with our own thoughts.

From her accent I could tell that the woman was from Silesia. She had been left to fend for herself by the former neighbors from her hometown with whom she had been traveling until two days ago, because she couldn't keep up with them with her two children. She told us that common thieves had taken the baby carriage away from her before they had even left their village. Omi wanted to know where exactly she came from and whether she knew anything about the fate of the people around Ratibor. But the woman just shook her head.

Two older men were walking from group to group, helping wherever they could. On that particular morning, nothing could be heard or seen of the Russians, but there were plenty of rumors. Men kneeled down onto the cobblestones repeatedly, putting their ears to the ground, but couldn't make out any vibrations from approaching tanks. They shook their heads, and couldn't decide whether this was a good or a bad sign. I was torn between fear and hope, although there was no good reason for the latter. Grandfather Valentin was on my mind constantly, and I was beginning to worry because we had heard nothing from him since the delivery of the Christmas shipment. Not even Aunt Lene, Omi's sister, who was not bombed out and was still living on the Bergmannstraße in Dresden, had received any news from him.

Suddenly everything went very fast, and I was torn out of my daydreams. We were ready to leave, the doors were slammed shut and the motor cranked up, but none of us knew where we would end up. Herr Reimann made his way through the crowd on the marketplace at a walking pace down the Neustädter Straße. His delivery van was right behind us. When I looked back and saw the many people on the marketplace that we were leaving behind, I became aware of how lucky we were. For the first time in years there was nothing for me to do. I could simply lean back and let things be. When I closed my eyes I felt dizzy and wondered how we would be able to care for the third child.

The flight was strenuous. We only got ahead slowly, and were often stuck for hours because the streets were overcrowded or blocked off completely. We were stopped, sent back or had to take detours. Bridges that had still been standing the previous day, had been blown up or were so damaged that only one lane was passable at a walking pace, and therefore long lines of vehicles were waiting to take the ferries across the Elbe. Many of the refugees from the east were on foot by then because their horse-drawn wagons had either broken down on the long march west or they were forced to leave them behind because they no longer could feed the horses. People pulled and pushed whatever had wheels, even wheelbarrows were loaded with personal belongings. The inhabitants of Bischofswerda had left their town with overloaded baby carriages, handcarts and wagons piled up so high with stuff that two women had to pull them, while children and old men helped push on the sides and from the back. The smallest children sat enthroned on top of the belongings, tied down with rope. Old women and men, who were too weak to walk, sat on blankets and pillows in the carts, and had clothes in their laps and were holding infants in their arms. Others sat in the very back with their legs dangling down from the open rear ends, while the heels of their shoes bumped along on the pavement as the carts swayed back and forth on the uneven roads. Dented tin cups, water buckets, frying pans, pots and other household items were tied to the carts with leather straps or string, clanging continuously on the rough streets, but the metallic clatter didn't seem to bother anyone. That's how apathetic people had become.

Many refugees were leaving on foot, carrying large knapsacks and lugging cartons and suitcases barely held together with string. They carried sacks over their shoulders and bags with handles that had been repaired with rope, while dragging along small children, who also carried bags and an occasional toy. Men with bulging rucksacks on their backs were riding on bicycles. Often a child or a woman was sitting on the luggage rack or the handle bar. Others were walking their heavily loaded bikes. Bicycles in particular were often snatched from refugees, even by soldiers. Then the people sat with their belongings on the side of the road. At some point, they struggled back to their feet, left behind what they could not carry, and continued on their way, which they didn't know themselves. Others searched through piles of stuff, kept the good things while throwing away inferior stuff from their own luggage. After weeks on the road, the refugees were dirty, flee infested, sick, half-starved and completely exhausted. They were chased away and driven from one place to the next. No one wanted to take them in. They neither found peace nor could they rest anywhere. Occasionally a rickety old truck putted past us. Wagons drawn by an ox or two cows trudged along. The animals were reduced to skeletons so you could count their ribs. The farmers had gotten down from the coach boxes to lighten the load and were walking alongside with expressionless faces, their backs bent. Sometimes a goat, tied to a wagon with a long rope, was trotting behind trying to find some grass at the wayside. The people were mute; I seldom heard them mutter a word. No one laughed. Repairs on vehicles took days, if they were possible at all. There were no tools and no workmen and no spare parts, and the wagons had been weakened during the long march west. Again and again wooden spokes broke, and if the people did not notice it in time, the wagons broke down completely.

Once I became witness to such a breakdown and won't ever forget the noise of the slowly collapsing ox-drawn vehicle. Fascinated, I had watched as the wooden spokes of a wheel slowly broke under the load, how the steel band sprang apart and rolled clanging along the street, and how the ox tried to walk on, but the wagon leaned over slowly toward the center of the street while the load began to shift and slide down. I saw how the people came running to prop up the wagon by putting a block of wood underneath the axle to prevent a second wheel, or worse yet, the axle from breaking. A scraggly dog was running amongst the people, sniffing at everything. People chased the dog away with sticks and stones, and it howled pitifully when it was hit.

The devastation on the streets surpassed everything I had seen only a few months earlier on the streets of East Prussia, my mother continued. Broken vehicles had been abandoned alongside the road, having sunk deep into the rain-soaked shoulders, or slid halfway down the embankment into the ditch, or tumbled onto lower-lying meadows. The contents of suitcases, cartons and crates were strewn over the ground. Decrepit old people had been left behind. Their lifeless eyes persecuted me for years.

No filmmaker has ever successfully reproduced this chaos. In all the movies that I saw about the end of the war, it always seemed to me that I had seen it before, only better and more true to life.

Again we heard the humming of aircraft above us. The noise of the airplane propellers made us tremble, and just as on our escape from Dresden, we spent the nights in barns. The farmers had had to put up so many refugees over the months, spread out straw and hay for the night, bring porridge and boiled potatoes and warm milk for the children, that often enough they, too, were at the end of their wits. Their provisions were beginning to run low, and with it their charity.

I made it as comfortable as possible on the bus for you girls, and put a blanket on the floor between our feet for Bettine where she could sleep. I played with you and tried to amuse you and keep you quiet. We were all in a depressed mood. Herr Reimann tried to get news of the whereabouts of the Soviet army. We asked refugees how far the Russians had advanced, but the information was often contradictory because the situation changed hourly.

Eventually I lost track of how many days we had been on the road. One day had run into the next, and I had to think hard to calculate the date. Finally we reached Sebnitz where Herr Reimann procured lodging for us at an estate that the NSDAP (National Socialist German Worker's Party) had turned into a shelter for women with children. We were lucky to find beds with clean sheets for all of us, and we could clean up and wash our clothes. Herr Reimann parked the bus and the medical truck in the barn so no one would see the vehicles.

The following morning we heard that a group of Hitler youth had shot dead and robbed two Russian soldiers and an officer not too far from us. The news frightened us terribly, and we feared retribution. Those louts were still steeped in illusions of the Hitler youth movement, unable to understand what was really going on in the east.

We had already been there for a few days when one morning, as we were sitting in the large dining room for breakfast, Russian soldiers arrived in the courtyard. When they banged against the large entrance portal we were expecting them to kick it in and feared the worst. Herr Reimann signaled us to be silent and motioned us to go upstairs swiftly. Then he stepped outside pulling the portal shut behind him. I looked down from behind a lace curtain because I wanted to see what was going on. As far as I could tell, the Russians had come to take over the building and wanted to force their way in. Herr Reimann held them back with words and gestures. They used no force, but they made an awful racket. One of the soldiers pointed his rifle at him. Herr Reimann remained steadfast and asked them to come back with their commander. When they were going to push him aside, he lifted both arms, like the pastor in church during the benediction. The soldier lowered his rifle slowly and said something to his comrade. Herr Reimann seemed in control of the situation. He must have filled them with respect, because they calmed down and marched off.

When he came back inside, Herr Reimann told us to finish breakfast quickly and then pack our things just in case so we would be ready to leave, but he hoped to be able to speak to the commanding officer and that he would let us stay.

The commander arrived shortly thereafter with two other officers in their military vehicle. I went to the window again when I heard it stop outside. Herr Reimann greeted them in front of the house, walking towards them. The driver remained behind the wheel as two of the officers got out and spoke to him. I could not understand anything, but things seemed to take a peaceful turn. Suddenly the Russians turned around, climbed back into their vehicle and drove off the property in a wide curve. Some soldiers came that afternoon with a flatbed truck to get hey from the barn, as well as beets and potatoes. Herr Reimann knew they would be back and did not go outside again. We stayed for another week, but the Russians never returned.

One morning, we walked to town very early, because we had heard that the NSDAP was in the process of emptying out one of their warehouses, distributing everything to refugees and victims of the recent bombings. When we arrived many people had already assembled. I could hardly believe my eyes when I saw the full warehouse. We were given children's clothes and new shoes. When they noticed that I was pregnant, I also received two dozen diapers, baby blankets, rompers, bath towels, shirts, bottles, nipples and even a rattle. Everything was brand new. I was so happy about the unexpected gifts that I forgot our dismal situation for a moment. I could never have imagined that there were still such well-stocked warehouses with such a large selection of items. At that time I chose the name Viktoria for the unborn child. I knew that it would be a girl again because I felt exactly as I did during my previous pregnancies.

Omi went back the following day. She was lucky and came back with full bags a second time. Now at least I had the most necessary things for the unborn child, and even the two of you were taken care of for a long time to come.

I remember that I got new shoes, which I wore while Omi put my old ones in the bag. Little white labels with the red letters NSDAP and NSV (National Socialist Public Welfare) were sewn into all the articles of clothing. When I learned to read, I asked what these letters meant. I did not understand my mother's explanation, but I knew the sequence of letters from her stories. She pronounced them so quickly, and everybody seemed to know their meaning. It took a long time before I realized that they stood for organizations of the Third Reich.

A few days later, Herr Reimann decided to return to Bischofswerda, my mother went on. It was not really safe anywhere anyway, and it made no sense to try to go further west. As far as he knew, the streets were open. Most people agreed to return. The young woman from Silesia had recovered and had joined a trek from her area on their way west. We longed for our own beds and private space, no matter how humble, after so many nights in one room with twenty beds and the large kitchen where we cooked the meals that we ate together in the dining room.

Herr Reimann looked after the bus in the garage daily. The gas tank was filled again and he had scrounged several canisters with extra gasoline. We left Sebnitz one morning at the break of day undisturbed by the Russians, and drove back to Bischofswerda along narrow country roads via remote villages, and arrived back home in the afternoon. We stopped on the marketplace at the same spot from where we had left. The town was deserted. We got off quickly and collected our luggage. As it turned out, our flight from the Russians was all for nothing. Omi and I couldn't carry all the new clothes, so Herr Reimann offered that we could leave the rest with him and pick it up later. Before our escape, he had nailed wooden boards in front of the two large shop windows for protection. He was sure that his store had been looted, but he found everything the way he had left it.

Over the following days we learned bit by bit what had happened during our absence, and that many inhabitants had not returned yet because there was no reliable information. News traveled slowly. Later I heard that people had entered the unlocked apartments in many neighborhoods after the evacuation and before the Soviet army came, and had taken whatever looked good to them. They looted whole streets, leaving the houses and apartments in disarray as they searched for valuables. They smeared the walls with shoe polish and spread toothpaste over chairs and tables, broke dishes and glasses and emptied the contents of fruit jars on the floors. Russian soldiers, who patrolled the town day and night by twos in the months to come, were quartered in apartment houses where they were supposed to have caused havoc. House owners talked for years about the devastation and looting. "Nix kultura" was a common remark about the toilets, which they tried to use for washing their hair or feet, and were angered because there was not enough flowing water. We laughed about it and repeated the "nix kultura" mockingly.

We also found out that many inhabitants of Bischofswerda had simply fled to the nearby woods or hidden in the more out of the way villages to observe the developments from there. At night they sent spies to the autobahn where part of the Soviet army would most likely approach. Others tried to get information from the railroaders, because they figured that the greater number of Soviet troops would arrive on the trains that they had confiscated from the Germans, since the Russian tracks were wider than ours, so their trains couldn't come onto German territory. Many inhabitants returned secretly under the cover of darkness and hid in their garden houses and tool sheds, or even just stayed in their houses. They came to replenish their provisions and get clean underwear, blankets and towels.

The people who had been hiding in the vicinity were the first to return to their houses after it became clear that only a few hundred Russians would remain in town. Shortly after that, the population was allowed to return except for those whose houses had been confiscated for Russian officers, who were hunting down Nazis and other war criminals, and were to establish a provisionary order. The displaced house owners were given temporary lodging in other empty apartments. Even months later, horrible scenes took place when the rightful owners came back and found their apartments occupied by other people. Many didn't return, however, but fled to the western zones, to Bavaria or the Rheinland. The villas the Russians occupied had belonged to wealthy families, industrialists, merchants, academics, or high-ranking party members, who were smart enough to realize that the Soviets would be looking for them.

Nothing happened to our small family, my mother always finished with a sigh of relief. Our simple apartment had remained untouched, and we were able to live in it again, and one day Kurt's parents, Irmgard and Georg were back, too.

Bit by bit I heard the whole story of their flight. On the afternoon of April 20th they had taken their luggage in two handcarts to the evacuation train, and were told to take back a heavy wooden crate with household items. The things they took along were of little use to them, however, because the train did not get very far. Their flight turned into an odyssey. In Radeberg, the locomotive was taken away from them. Hours later they got it back, but they could not continue on to Dresden, from where they were supposed to go to Glashütte. Several times they were stopped in the middle of nowhere, because the next town was either closed off, or a railroad bridge had become impassable, or enemy tanks were on the advance. At other times they received no permission to enter a railroad station, but they were rerouted and sent on a sidetrack, which ended in a forest. Finally they arrived in Cobitz. That was the end of their train trip. They had to carry their luggage through heavy rain to the banks of the Elbe and were forced to leave more behind. Thousands were already waiting to get across the river ahead of them. In Pirna they made it across at last, then wandered around aimlessly for weeks until they ultimately arrived back in Bischofswerda.

In retrospect what happened during those days resembled a caricature of the Third Reich. But come to think of it, the Third Reich had already been a caricature of life.

Whenever my mother spoke about the flight of her in-laws, she stressed what a blessing it had been that they had not taken us along. We could not have survived those hardships. In spite of that insight, she could never forgive them, nor could she forget the humiliation she had suffered. It overshadowed the rest of her life.

16. A Child is Born

After our return we tried to live as inconspicuously as possible, my mother continued. When we went shopping, we encountered Russian soldiers patrolling the streets by twos and threes. Sometimes they stood together in larger groups discussing something. I always walked past them as fast as I could. They paid little attention to me. Curfew was at 8 p.m.

Omi worked several times a week on the nearby farms. The farmers paid her by the hour and gave her two meals for the day, and she always got an extra portion to take home in the evening. The soups were very nourishing, and we ate everything with a voracious appetite. Soon the days came and went with an eerie normalcy.

Even though my mother was not particular happy about it, I frequently walked alone from one end of town to the other, to be with my paternal grandparents while taking care of all kinds of errands along the way. The adults had instilled in me never to speak to strangers or Russian soldiers, and never to accept anything from anyone I did not know, nor go along with anyone. I am not sure how much I understood at four years of age, because I remember a situation when I disregarded this admonishment. I still recall the corner where the Bahnhofstraße and the Stolpener Straße meet at a right angle, next to the little park with the fountain in the middle, called Käthe Kollwitz Park. There a group of children had gathered in front of a Russian soldier. A second one was standing a step behind him. When I approached them with curiosity, I saw the first soldier handing out candies to the children. When he noticed me, he motioned me to step up, and I couldn't resist the candies. I knew that I was doing something forbidden when I stretched out my hand and felt the soldier's fingers, but the temptation was too strong and the soldiers were so friendly.

Early one morning, Omi took me along to the railroad station in Bischofswerda, where countless refugees camped out every day on the large square while waiting to move on to some unknown destination. It was a warm sunny day. Omi was wearing a light colorfully printed summer dress and open shoes without stockings. She had boiled a large pot of potatoes in their skins the evening before, and the next morning she poured them into an old shopping bag and took them along to distribute to the refugees in exchange for information from Silesia. She walked amongst the people, asked them where they were from, paused here and there to speak with those who claimed to be from Upper Silesia and talked about her son and her family. For what seemed useful news she would hand out potatoes.

Soon she felt especially drawn to a raw-boned woman in rags, who was sitting on the pavement surrounded by her meager belongings and several uncombed filthy children. Her haggard face, the red circles around her sunken and yet piercing eyes and her disheveled long hair attracted my attention. Her appearance was repulsive, yet at the same time the woman made a deep impression on me. That's what I thought the witch in Hänsel and Gretel must have looked like. I tried to pull Omi away, but she pushed me aside impatiently, which was unusual, and I had to make sure that I would not lose her in the crowd. The witch eagerly entered into a conversation with Omi and must have given her some desired answers, because all of a sudden she filled the woman's skirt, which hung like an open net between her spread out knees, with the rest of the potatoes. "For you and your children," Omi said, and wanted to know more.

But from that moment on, the witch paid no more attention to Omi. She stared at the cold potatoes, took a long knife out of a pocket of her skirt and reached for a potato, held it up for a second, cut it in half, speared it with the tip of the knife and devoured the entire piece unpeeled. It looked to me as though the witch was gulping the potato halves down without chewing them and with a greed that I had never seen before. I watched aghast as the potatoes, one after the other, vanished into her mouth, like into a gaping hole, and was dismayed to see that she wasn't giving any to her children, who were squatting around her, hoping with every potato the woman took that it might finally be their turn. They tried to reach for them, but she pushed the children away as she continued to eat them until even the last one was gone, murmuring all the while, "So many potatoes, so many potatoes!"

The grotesque scene affected me deeply. I felt sorry for Omi and would have liked to comfort her, but didn't know how. That's when I heard her scream, "You unthankful bitch, you, you brood of Satan!"

The witch gave off a shrill laugh while waving about wildly with her knife in our direction before she let it disappear again into her skirt pocket and sank back into a stupor.

Other refugees approached us saying they had news from Ratibor in exchange for potatoes, but we had none left.

When we came back home, my mother scolded Omi, calling her irresponsible for giving away so many potatoes. Omi sat down on a chair and wept for her son. I leaned against her. She pulled me up on her lap and rocked me in her arms.

Curfew was still in effect in the summer of 1945, and we had to plan our days in such a way that we were home before nightfall. Grandmother Bergner had to make sure to send me home early enough, but often we'd forget the time when we were in the garden. On other days we stayed too long at a farm or the hours slipped away from us while we looked for mushrooms in the woods. Night set in before we knew it, and it was too late for me to start on the long way home across town. I had to spend the night, and we could only hope that my mother would not be too worried, because there was no way to let her know that I was all right.

The Soviet army immediately took over the entire town. My mother's voice sounded weary as she talked about what life was like under such circumstances. Whenever they felt like it, soldiers walked through the town hall, the post office and the schools where they looked into the classrooms, asking all kinds of questions. They demanded entry into hospitals, walked through the various wards, wanted to see everything and be part of every decision. They gave commands, and ordered the doctors and nurses around.

We were still living in the Wallgasse, and after you children were in bed I settled down for an evening of sewing. Grandmother Schubert had given me her beautiful sewing machine saying, "You need it more now than I." For me it was the greatest gift of all, and I was overjoyed by her generosity.

The second of August was a quiet night. The monotone rattle from the sewing machine filled the room. My thoughts were with the unborn child, and I wondered how I would be able to manage three small children. The clock from the town hall struck ten, I counted the strokes. From afar I could hear the boots of the Soviet night watch beat on the pavement in regular intervals as they made their rounds through town. They seldom entered our street, but the echo carried the impact of their boots over to us. After it had been quiet longer than usual, or at least so it seemed to me, I became restless. My heart began to beat faster as I waited for the renewed pounding of the boots.

Suddenly I felt the razor-sharp pain of beginning labor in my pelvis and lower back. Seconds later the pain was gone, and I hoped contrary to all experience that I had been wrong. But within minutes the pain was back, returning in ever shorter intervals and growing stronger. There was no doubt, the labor pains had set in with full strength, and I had to expect the birth of the child within hours. It felt like my lower body was being torn apart and my back was burning hot.

I said to Omi, who was just about to go to bed, that we would have to prepare for the birth immediately. Under the circumstances, I was adamant that we stay home, but Omi would hear nothing of it. When she saw my determination, she began to lament and finally threw up her arms in despair.

"Stay calm," I shouted, "get extra sheets and towels and light a wood fire in the stove for hot water. There is enough newspaper next to the wood, and the matches are on the board above the range."

When she finally understood, she panicked, running around aimlessly, imploring me to go to the hospital, as she repeated, "Please help us, Holy Mary, Mother of God."

"Stop your catholic whining," I shouted, "it's caused enough discord in our family already. God will be with us if we don't lose our heads." I was really incensed at how she let herself go.

She fell to her knees in the middle of the kitchen crying, "For heaven's sake, Elfriedchen, the child can't come here, I cannot help you, we've got to go to the hospital."

"I'm going to do it all, you are only supposed to help me, why can't you understand that? Children are being born every day all over the world," I said, and grabbed her by the shoulders to bring her back to her senses. A few days earlier, I had already packed my bag with everything that I would need for myself and the newborn in the hospital. Of course I had hoped that I would be able to walk to the hospital by myself during the day so that Omi could stay with you girls. Now Viktoria had surprised me and thwarted my plans.

Suddenly, Omi put on her jacket, slipped on her street shoes that were standing next to the kitchen door, picked up the bag, took my hand and was about to pull me out of the kitchen. I was afraid to go out at this late hour, because I had heard many fearsome stories and rumors about what happened to people who were picked up by the Russians. Two women on the street in the middle of the night during curfew, that couldn't go well. And because the labor pains were so sharp and followed so fast one after the other, I feared that I would not make it all the way to the hospital anyway. My first two births had gone fast and without complications, and I was sure that it would be no different this time. I was healthy and strong and I knew I could do it.

Again, I explained to Omi that I knew what to do, and assured her that everything would go well and fast, judging by the way the labor pains were coming and from the pulling in my legs, but that I would need her. She flatly refused to help me, and remained determined to walk with me to the hospital. She even threatened that she would leave the apartment, should I not come along. I didn't even bother to ask where she was thinking of going.

When she moved toward the door, I lost control and screamed, "For heaven's sake, pull yourself together. In the morning you can get the doctor or the midwife."

I thought that I had convinced her, when she screamed, cursing Kurt. Then she sat down on a kitchen chair and began to wail, like at a funeral. There was nothing I could do, all persuasion was in vain. I went to you, Anne, and explained that your little sister was going to come most likely during the night, and that Omi and I would have to go to the hospital to get her. I promised you that Omi would be back soon, but that I would not come home until later with your little sister. I left the light in the kitchen on for you and kept the bedroom door open. Then I put on my summer coat, took the bag and waked out of the house with Omi.

I was more afraid of the Russians than of the birth. We tried to walk as fast as possible and stepped as lightly as we could on the cobblestone pavement. Even so our steps echoed loudly between the houses in the narrow alley. We had barely walked a few feet, when two soldiers yelled at us from afar in Russian and German, "Stoi! Halt!"

At first I couldn't see them because they were standing in the shadow of a house entrance. I stopped and held my belly with both hands. Omi wanted to walk on and pull me along, but when she took another step, the soldiers stepped into the center of the alley about thirty feet away from us, threatening us with their drawn rifles, yelling once more, "Stoi! Halt!" The light of the moon shone on their faces, and I saw the rifle barrels aimed at us.

"For heaven's sake stop, Mutti!" I whispered, and I held Omi's hand tight. We were both shaking. She called out some Polish words while pointing at my stomach.

The soldiers yelled anew, "Stoi!" as they were marching in step toward us, their rifles pointed at us the entire time. When they were about ten feet away and I could see their faces, they came to a halt. One of them lowered his rifle, took two more steps towards me and touched my stomach with his right index finger. Omi said in Polish that we had to get to the hospital because the child was coming. The soldiers talked to each other briefly, and then signaled us to follow them. I didn't move, so they took us between them. One of the soldiers touched my left arm lightly, and they accompanied us to the clinic. I almost thought that they enjoyed walking with us along the dark streets. I hardly dared to look around, but I saw for the first time, just how many soldiers were out and about at night. We had to stop several times so they could explain to their comrades where they were taking us. They always pointed to my stomach and laughed. The labor pains stopped on the way to the clinic.

The hospital lay quiet and dark before us. A dull glimmer of light shone from only a few windows on the ground floor. When one of the soldiers wanted to open the large entry portal and noticed that it was locked against orders, he cursed loudly. I felt terribly sick by then and was hardly able to stand up anymore. My legs were giving out from under me. The other soldier knocked so hard against the door with his rifle butt that it reverberated from inside. After that, everything seemed even quieter. The people inside are holding their breath, I thought. The soldier yelled commands in Russian and German, and then there was the sound of doors opening and closing inside the hospital. I heard steps and subdued voices behind the portal. The outside light went on, the key turned in the lock and the door opened hesitatingly just a crack. The pale face of a nurse appeared who kept her body hidden behind the door. The soldier kicked the door wide open with his boot so hard that the nurse was barely able to let go of it and jump aside in time. Then the soldiers shoved us in. When the nurse saw me, she knew what was going on.

A great commotion spread through the hospital as lamps went on and doors opened and closed again. In the meantime the physician in charge had arrived, whom I knew only by sight. I am sure he was relieved when he saw the reason for the untimely disturbance. He thanked the soldiers in Russian and asked them politely to leave. I had the presence of mind to turn to the doctor and said, "Please, the soldiers must accompany my mother back, my two little girls are alone at home." They actually did that, and so everything turned out all right.

The maternity ward was on the ground floor to the left of the main entrance. The nurse who had opened the door led me to an empty bed in a nearby room, where she helped me get undressed and handed me a nightgown out of my bag. Then she laid me down on the bed like a child and listened intently to the heartbeat of the unborn. She frowned because it took her a moment to find the heartbeat. She was satisfied, but my abdomen was very hard, like a huge pumpkin, and hurt terribly. My hands and feet were ice-cold, although it was warm in the room.

"You must relax, Frau Bergner, so the child can come," the nurse said to me while stroking my forehead. "Take deep breaths and think of nothing but your child. I'll get you a cup of chamomile tea."

The hot tea calmed me. Another nurse brought a hot-water bottle for my feet and a second blanket, which she spread over me. After a few minutes I felt the warmth in my legs, and the labor pains started again slowly, but nothing happened. The birth process had been interrupted. My body was in shock and only the piercing pains continued. My state remained unchanged throughout the night.

The nurse kept coming back to listen to the child's heartbeat, which remained strong, but beyond that there was little she could do for me. The nurse suggested exercises for stimulation. In the morning, they brought me a tray with my breakfast, which I did not touch. Just the smell of the food made me feel sick, so I asked for some tea.

Once the day had begun, they had little time for me. New patients were brought into the ward, and other women gave birth, but nothing happened with me. During the late morning, the two Russian soldiers entered my room, followed by a nurse. I recognized them right away, and was surprised how young they were. From then on they came every day in spite of the protests of the hospital staff. Even the operating room was not safe from them.

The baby didn't come on the second day either. My condition remained unchanged. There was no medication for the pain and no injection to induce the birth. The nurse in charge of the ward came by regularly. She made me do knee bends and other exercises to bring some movement into my lower body. In the afternoon they put me into a bathtub with hot water and massaged my body under water. My breasts were hard and swollen and hurt terribly, and the nipples were bright red and inflamed. The milk had already come in, and a nurse showed me how to squirt it out. She set a bowl with chamomile tea on my nightstand, soaked a towel in it and put warm compresses on my breasts.

In the afternoon Omi knocked at the window from the outside. She had come with the two of you to bring me more nightgowns, towels and facecloths as well as my hand cream. You girls were not allowed to come in, so Omi stayed outside with you, passing the things to me through the window. I couldn't eat anything and asked the nurse to wrap my cold-cut sandwiches for you to take home. I heard you shout with delight, Anne, when you held the package in your hands, and from then on your first inquiry was always for the sandwiches. I couldn't stand up long and went back to bed. We shouted a few more words to each other through the open window, and I asked Omi to bring more cream from Herr Reimann.

With the cream I massaged my abdomen in a rotating motion, and noticed that the baby moved slightly, but my belly stayed hard like a medicine ball. The skin was bluish and itched terribly. It was a hot day, and I was bathed in sweat from the physical exertion and the stifling heat.

During the third night my strength failed me. I couldn't go on, and was beginning to think that I might die in childbirth. I had been struggling for over fifty hours already. The night nurse was sitting at my bedside almost the entire time. I had not been able to sleep since my arrival, neither had I eaten anything except for a few spoons of porridge or yogurt and some slices of melba toast dunked in peppermint tea. I was admonished repeatedly to do certain gymnastics, to squat and to walk around. During that third night the kind nurse who had admitted me was back. She was horrified that I had not given birth yet and examined me. Then she scolded the other nurses for their negligence and pointed out the danger to the unborn child.

"Frau Bergner," she whispered while bending over me, "you cannot go on like this. I am worried about you and the unborn child. I am going to get a shot for you, but you mustn't say anything to anyone about it, not even to your family! You must promise me that! Not one word! If someone finds out about it, I will be punished severely, I may even be sent to prison. And I don't have to tell you what happens to women in prison. We get women every night in the early morning hours who have been raped. They have bruises all over their bodies. Especially when they try to defend themselves they are mistreated even worse. Their lower bodies and legs are covered with blood, often there are several layers, all dried up because the men ravaged them several times. Some arrive with internal injuries, and we don't have enough penicillin or other medication against infections. The syringes are counted and locked up, but I know where the key is, and I'll take one for you at an opportune moment. It'll work then, I promise."

She stood up, put her finger on her lips and repeated, "You swear, not a word!"

Within minutes she returned with the syringe, which she had hidden in the pocket of her white apron. She pulled the door shut behind her.

"All right, Frau Bergner," she said, "I am going to stand in front of you so that no one can see what I am doing should anyone enter the room unexpectedly. In that case, we'll both make believe I am massaging you." Then she gave me the shot. After she had pulled out the needle she rubbed the area explaining, this way the puncture is not so visible. "It's a little high on the hip, but I couldn't risk it any lower, in case someone would become suspicious during the birth. We are going to run a tub of hot water for you to relax your muscles, but first I must hide the syringe. I'll get it before I go home, we can use it again."

As I was lying in the tub I could feel the cramps slowly subside. The hardness went away and the contractions started again. The injection was beginning to have its desired effect. I stayed in the water for thirty minutes, and then the nurse helped me out. Even so, the baby was not born until the next morning. The especially sturdy midwife, of whom I'd been afraid the whole time, yelled at me that I should think of the baby and push harder instead of being such a sissy. Tears welled up in my eyes because I was so exhausted. Finally Viktoria was here. I heard her scream immediately. "It's a girl," the nurse told me as she held her up so I could see her. I knew it would be a girl, and was glad it wasn't a boy.

Viktoria was tiny but healthy, and incredibly sweet. She had five fingers on each hand and five toes on each foot. The delayed birth had not hurt her. I was so happy when I held her in my arms at last, and forgot about all those terrible hours, but I am sure that we would have both died without the help of that merciful nurse.

On the day after Viktoria's birth the two Russian soldiers came again, wanting to know whether it was a boy or a girl. When I answered happily, "A girl," they said, "Nix gut, Junge besser," laughed and marched off. I often wondered what became of them.

When Omi came with you and Bettine in the late morning of the fifth of August and called for me from outside of the window, another woman who had since been assigned to my bed gave you the good news. I had heard you, too, but I was two rooms further down to the right. Omi lifted you up, Anne, so you could look through the window. On the second day after the birth I felt strong enough to get up and walk over to the window. It was a beautiful summer day, and we were all healthy. Your first question was again, "Mutti, do you have more sandwiches?" I smiled, walked over to the nightstand and fetched the package for you.

On the eighth day after the birth, Viktoria and I were finally allowed to go home. You brought the baby carriage we had rescued from Dresden. I had cleaned it and outfitted it completely new. It had not been easy to get two new rubber tires for the front wheels. I had asked everywhere in Bischofswerda, when one day Herr Reimann called me into his store, producing four new wheels from underneath the counter. "If the clamps are too tight, just bring the baby carriage over and I will mount them for you," he said smiling. I had lined the hood with pink silk from Grandmother Schubert. All the way around the hood I had fastened wide ruffles, just right for a girl, and there was even enough silk for a pillowcase.

As I came down the six steps in front of the hospital with the baby in my arms you shouted for joy when you saw your little sister, Anne. Although you were hardly able to look over the handle bar, you reached for it, and neither Omi nor I were allowed to touch the baby carriage. If I had to straighten the carriage out a little because you were about to hit something, you pushed my hand away immediately.

17. A POW Returns

When I think of those sunny August days during our first summer after the war, I remember feeling the warm wind blowing through my hair as I made my way home to the Wallgasse along country lanes and rutty paths, through meadows and past fields. I carried a bunch of summer flowers from Grandmother Bergner's garden. I could never get enough, so the bunch had become very large and I could hardly grip it with one hand. Grandmother looked for twine to make it easier for me to hold the flowers, but as would often happen during those years of want she couldn't find any, and I tied the flowers together with long blades of grass.

How I loved these solitary walks! I wanted to pick a bunch of wild flowers too, and finally I was unable to resist the white daisies with the large yellow dots in the center and the long stems of trembling grass. To pick them I had to put down the garden flowers. Soon I had two bunches of flowers, and still had half the way home ahead of me. After a while my hands hurt, because I held the flowers so tight. I followed the deep narrow tracks in the path that were cut into the dirt by large wooden cartwheels, still filled with rainwater here and there, or I stepped into the deep imprints of horseshoes in the soft ground. My hands relaxed, and the bunches of flowers seemed lighter.

Finally I was home. The light was dim in the old workshop, because the large iron-framed factory windows were so dirty that they filtered out most of the daylight. Coming in from the bright sunlight, my eyes adapted slowly to the semi-darkness, and I walked as fast as I could through the deserted hall and up the stairs.

I held the flowers straight up in front of me so that my mother would see them right away as I entered the kitchen, because I had decided that both bunches should be for her. I had not quite climbed to the top of the stairs and was about to call her so she would open the door for me, when I heard an unfamiliar voice coming from the kitchen, and then the strangely changed voice of my mother, drowned out by Omi's loud scolding. I was frightened, and suddenly I knew: the unfamiliar voice – that was he! I stood still on the last step and leaned against the stone wall, feeling its coolness run up and down my back. I let my hands with the flowers sink, not knowing what to do.

I'm not going in there, I must run away, back to the grandparents, I thought. I could visit them whenever I wanted and stay as long as I wanted. Should I just put the flowers on the floor in front of the door? But by then it was already too late. The kitchen door opened and Omi came out, hurrying toward the stairs. When she saw me, she dried her eyes quickly with her apron, took the flowers and pulled me into the kitchen without saying a word.

There I saw the dark contours of a figure, whose face I couldn't recognize right away against the sunlight that was streaming into the room through the two windows behind him. It smelled like a man, and I detected the smell of food, which was laid out on the table. My mother stood to the left, holding my new sister in her arms. Her face was wet with tears. Then she touched the forehead of the child in her arms with her lips. She held the child securely in her arms, but she looked as if something terrible had happened. My eyes went from the man to my mother and then to Omi, who was busying herself at the stove grumbling: What a terrible man, what a bastard!

I walked over to Omi and asked her for two vases for the flowers. Details of the hours that followed I remember only vaguely. But I will never forget my mother's distress, which touched me deeply. The garden flowers stood on the table at supper, and the daisies were in a glass jar on the windowsill. The evening sun shone through them into the kitchen.

After the fire-bombing of Dresden our life had changed very dramatically. Even geographically we were so far removed from everything that had once been our life, that with the loss of my first home, my father had disappeared too. I only remember hearing now and then, "When Kurt returns...", and hoped that would never be. And suddenly he was back. I cannot recall whether or not he embraced me or had brought me anything.

Omi had promised to cook noodle soup for supper because she had gotten a can of beef, but then there was no soup.

When I was fifteen, I asked my mother while on a walk how it had happened that her husband had come home from the American prisoner of war camp already by the end of August 1945, and what it had been like for her. She had alluded to his return every so often. Nevertheless, my question surprised her, but then she gave me a detailed account of how she had experienced the day she had looked forward to with anticipation and mixed feelings. As would often happen, I became her confidant, and she added candidly all those parts she usually left out in front of company. She talked about the very private things that took place between her and her husband: how he took away her freedom by taking over control of everything immediately after his return, how he undermined her every decision, how he ridiculed and mistreated her, how she was unable to defend herself against him, how she submitted to him, and how her love eventually died. She spoke of his restlessness, his hectic movements, his outbursts of rage, his cutting voice, the arbitrary orders he shouted out abruptly, tolerating no contradiction, and which scared and disgusted me too, so that I ran away from home as often as possible, either to relatives or simply into the fields and nearby woods. He did not know how to awaken confidence in us women and build a loving relationship. But to others we looked like a normal family, and no one would ever have imagined the extent of our troubles.

While my mother talked about his homecoming, memories about how unhappy I felt after his unexpected appearance surfaced again. I had often asked myself why his return did not produce raptures of joy in our home as I had witnessed repeatedly in other families and the way I had seen in the fifties on the weekly 20th Century newsreels in our local cinema, and the way authors wrote about it in their novels set in that time? Millions never returned, and other women waited in vain for years for their husbands and mourned for them. Most never found another husband, and they had to work in factories or as saleswomen and take care of the children and the household in the evenings and on weekends.

Kurt made sure that no real joy surfaced when he returned home, my mother said, as if to answer my unspoken question. It had been a quiet afternoon because the workers had left the building around noon. I was bathing Viktoria to prepare her for the night. She was a good child, and although she was only three weeks old, she already slept through the night if I took enough time to nurse her and didn't put her into her crib until around seven. That's when I heard someone open the house door and let it fall shut with a bang. At first I thought it was you, Anne, but then I recognized his heavy steps and his panting breath as he was climbing up the stairs. Although I knew it was Kurt, he scared me when he tore open the kitchen door without knocking. Involuntarily I took a step back.

"Good God, how you frightened me," I cried out. "How can you storm in like that? Why didn't you knock first or at least call my name?"

But he just laughed, saying that he wanted to surprise me. He let his heavy knapsack fall on a chair, set down his old suitcase next to it and hung his worn dark brown jacket over the back of the chair. Then he gave me a kiss saying, "You have no idea how I've missed you, every day I thought only of you." As he talked he looked around the kitchen.

Just before he entered I had lifted Viktoria out of the tub and wrapped her in a towel. I held her close, trembling all over. In those days we were easily alarmed when we heard the heavy steps of men or unfamiliar noises outside our doors. The fear was still in my bones from the days of the Nazis, and only went away slowly over the years.

In Dresden men from the Gestapo had come repeatedly, two at a time, and had stepped in cadence through our large staircase. I never found out why they came, and didn't dare to talk about it with the neighbors. Once I was in the hall, right behind the apartment door, when I heard them come. I counted their steps and looked mesmerized through the colored glass of the apartment door into the staircase as I saw two male figures coming up the stairs. My heart skipped a beat, fearing they would stop in front of our door and ring the doorbell like mad. I held my breath and clenched my hands so hard that my fingernails dug deeply into my palms. I could see their faces coming toward me across the wide landing, but through the glass they just looked like light ovals. They made an awful racket. To my relief they walked past me up to the next floor. At times they climbed all the way to the attic, and after a while they came rumbling down again as loudly as they had come, leaving the house without knocking at anyone's door.

Once they must have been drunk because they jostled up the stairs, knocking against the railing and the walls, laughing strangely. I felt nauseated. As far as I can remember, they only knocked once very hard at the Kaufmann's door on their way down from the attic. When the door was opened, I heard the men yelling an order. It remained quiet for a moment. Shortly thereafter, they left the house with a third person. I looked out of the living room window and recognized Herr Kaufmann walking between them down the street. I didn't see him for months after that. One day he was back. He looked at me nervously when we met on the stairs, as if he were ashamed of something. I felt sorry for him and came to my own conclusions, but I never dared to speak to him, and the Kaufmann's never said anything either. The house we lived in belonged to Jews. Herr Schöne, the custodian, secretly told me that they had left Germany for New York shortly after Hitler took over power. I don't know whether the Kaufmanns knew them or were in touch with them.

Every time the Gestapo came, I prayed that the danger might pass us by. In the house in the Wallgasse we were the only tenants, the war was over, and the Nazis could no longer harm us. Instead we were afraid of the occupation troops. Terrible things happened every day. They called it purging. It was not until we had lived in West Germany for years that this reaction of ice-cold fear whenever I heard male steps on the street behind me or in the staircase slowly subsided. I was still frightened even though friends and acquaintances or the postman didn't ring the doorbell so long or knock so recklessly, and didn't wear boots either, nor did they make such an abominable noise.

Immediately after a brief greeting, Kurt began to unpack his old rucksack and the battered brown suitcase, which he had tied together with string. First he took out foodstuff, which he spread out on the kitchen table. There was a bag of sugar, a slab of bacon, a salami out of which some bites had been taken, some coffee beans in a small paper bag, perhaps enough for three pots, a loaf of dark bread, real honey in a special honey jar from a bee keeper in the Harz mountains, a bottle of linseed oil and about three pounds of lentils. Some of the groceries he had received from a farmwoman, for whom he had worked several days. He also had a large bag of powdered milk, a sack of dried beans and a small white linen sack with flour. I was so overjoyed that I put Viktoria down into her crib, looked at everything and was about to put it the pantry so we could set the table for supper.

That's when he said, "Just a minute, I want to divide up everything first. Half of it is for my parents and Irmgard should get something too." I thought I had not heard right as he began allocating food portions, asking me for paper bags or bowls. He reached for the scales on top of the cupboard, which Grandmother Schubert had given me for Viktoria, and set it down on the table.

"I have no spare bags. What exactly are you doing? How can you give away any of these groceries? We have so little ourselves as it is, and now you are here too."

"Half of it is for my parents," he stuttered excitedly. "They've earned it," he added dryly when I looked at him in disbelief.

"What do you mean, they've earned it?"

He gave no answer.

"They have everything they need, they suffer no shortage, they don't even know what hunger is with all the provisions they've hoarded in the kitchen and the cellar. They have a dozen hens in the garden and rabbits, they have connections and time to go to the farms, they don't need this. We are your family now, you are my husband, you have three small children, how can you give away anything? I beg of you, think of us."

"I can give my parents whatever I want," he responded.

"Let me tell you something, in case it has escaped you: your parents never helped us in the least! As far as they were concerned, we could have all perished," I shouted.

"Why must you always exaggerate, Effi," he retorted, "I'm barely home and we are fighting already. I can do with the food as I see fit. It was given to me, I worked for it. When is supper ready anyway? I am starved. And after supper we'll go to straight to my parents, and we'll take them their part."

"Have you lost your mind completely, Kurt? You want to give half of this food to people who never gave me so much as one egg? They've never had anything for us, and I am supposed to go along and leave the children alone?"

He didn't react. I spread both hands over the food on the table to make him understand that he should stop dividing it up, but he just pushed me aside.

"Please don't give the food away," I begged him, "the children need it, can't you understand that?"

"My father is sick," he hissed angrily.

"He is old, the children are small, they need it so much more."

He looked at me saying, "Get out of my way, I make the decisions here, not you."

So I yelled, "All right, go ahead, go to your dear parents and your precious sister, you prefer them over us anyway, just go, get lost, see if they want you, but they don't, they couldn't care less about you, they just take from you. You take from your own small children and throw it at them. Then you are the good son and the good brother and you'll beam with pride all over your face while we go hungry. But I'll never forget nor forgive you for what you are doing."

You have to understand, Anne, he was so pleased that he could take something to his parents, but he received nothing in return, not a single jar of preserved fruit or vegetables, of which they had hoarded row upon row in their cellar. The shelves were bending under the weight, every jar neatly labeled showing the year and contents. And every year more was added. Later they had to dump whole shelves full of the stuff. Can you imagine! How could he do that, how could he take food away from his own small children? But I know why he did it! He wanted to show them that he was a man, that he knew how to procure things, he wanted to ingratiate himself with them even though they had endangered us terribly. Let me tell you a little story that shows you into just how much trouble they had nearly put us.

I was at home alone one morning when I suddenly heard a man's steps on the stairs and then a knock at the kitchen door. I was just changing the baby and asked frightened, "Who is it?" A male voice answered that he had come to ask me some questions. I began to tremble and shouted to the man through the door that he would have to wait a moment. Then I wrapped Viktoria into a cotton blanket and opened the door, holding her in my arms. The man was in police uniform. The blood rushed out of my head and I felt dizzy.

"Don't worry, young lady," the policeman said. "I only came to tell you that you must report to the police station at eight tomorrow morning, room 6." He held an official paper in front of my face, "Here, you must sign right here, and I'll take the paper back with me."

"But that's impossible," I said, "as you can see, I have three small children. I cannot leave them alone and I can't take them along either." The three of you were very quiet. I said nothing about Omi living with us. Thank God she was out at the moment.

"Yes, I can see that," the young policeman said, "but I have a summons for you."

He held the paper out to me again, but I did not take it. "What is it about," I asked. I was surprised how calm my voice sounded.

"Here, read for yourself," the policeman said.

"I can't read that so fast. Can't you see I have work to do? Besides, I would have to get my glasses first," I responded, "I am not sure where I left them."

"They have a few questions for you."

"Who has questions, what kind of questions?"

"Where you are from, what you are doing here, where your husband is."

"Who wants to know? Who sent you?"

"The city. You are not the only one."

I knew that I must not go there under any circumstances. I thought, once I am there they might not let me go again. I had to gain time, and I already saw us fleeing town.

"Who wants to know what about me? I don't know anybody here," I said.

"Something was brought up against you, that's all I know." The young man was very kind. The situation obviously made him feel uneasy.

"Don't you see, I cannot leave. My husband is a prisoner of war. Please tell me, who denounced me, and what did they say against me?

"Well," he said hesitatingly, "you don't need to search far. Your husband comes from here, doesn't he?"

He looked at me again, hesitated, and then made a decision. He put the paper he had been holding in his hand all the while on the table. "You are not at home, I am simply going to leave it here. I'll tell them I shoved it under the door." He wished me a good day, turned around, left the kitchen and pulled the door closed behind him. I heard him walk downstairs while counting every step. Then the door down below opened and fell shut again. After that there was a deadly silence.

I felt my legs go limp. My whole body trembled. I had to hold on to the edge of the table, and almost dropped the baby. My eyes went to the paper on the table. I've signed nothing, I thought, and put Viktoria into her crib. Then I took the sheet of paper, and without taking a closer look I burned it in the kitchen stove. I watched as it began to burn, how it came to life, how the flame shot up high for a few seconds, how the paper curled up, burned with a blue flame, and slowly turned to black ashes. When nothing but a thin, wavy, black-blue shape was left, which trembled and fell apart, a deep calm came over me, and I knew that the danger had passed. Never again was I harassed by the authorities in that or any other matter, but I heard the locals whisper about a purge.

I know who had denounced me, who harbored evil intentions toward me: those people on the Gartenweg! They would have wanted to see me gone. They didn't care what would become of you children. Most likely they had a skeleton in their closet, and wanted to divert attention by denouncing me.

On the first evening of his homecoming, without any thought for our life as a family, I was supposed to go with Kurt to his parents. He also demanded of me, "From now on I want you to put the children to bed right after supper. I need you, I want to be alone with you, and your mother must leave at once."

"My mother is living with us. Where is she supposed to go?" I asked. "Besides, there's still a lot to do in the evenings after the children are in bed."

"What are you doing all day long," he wanted to know, "how come you are not done with your work after supper?"

I gave no answer. If he had to ask such a question, I couldn't explain it to him, I thought. This homecoming was different from all those years before when he came on leave. This time he would stay. For the first time since our wedding we would live together, day after day, as a married couple and a family. I had longed for it so much and had pictured our future in the rosiest colors. Life with Omi was not exactly easy either. She was a complicated woman.

Even if things had turned out very different from the way I had hoped, living in my own apartment had given me new energy. After all those terrible months I had a chance at last to plan our life the way I thought best under the circumstances, and Omi had helped without saying much. But then he came and took over everything. I had not expected that, I was stunned. He didn't allow us even one hour of happiness, no peace and quiet, no time to get used to each other.

Anxious misgivings befell me the very first evening, but because every day was so full of work, I had no time to really think about it. Even so I could not always suppress memories from earlier times. I remembered how opinionated he was, how he wanted everything to go his way, and how he found fault with whatever I did. He knew everything better, and nothing pleased him. Soon all joy was gone out of our lives. We no longer laughed in his presence, no longer teased each other, and sang no songs. This initial anxiety after his return turned into desperate disappointment. I couldn't find a way out, and soon I didn't even have the energy anymore to be happy with you children when he wasn't home. He had hardly entered the apartment coming home from work, and taken off his shoes and jacket, when he started in on me. He even wanted to tell me how to shop, how to plan the meals, when and for how long to go for a walk with you and how often I should clean the apartment.

In Dresden I used to think his nerves were giving out from the physical exertion. I was sure all of that would change once the war was over, and he would calm down when we were living together. I thought that we would love each other, be there for each other and that many problems would go away on their own. During the day I tried to push my doubts aside, and when I was finally in bed at night I fell asleep right away from exhaustion.

What my mother was telling me was not new to me. I had witnessed how she lost her vitality, her cheerful disposition and her power of judgment bit by bit. He ridiculed her so often, made her out to be inexperienced, and did not take her seriously. Who can put up with such criticism for years without suffering psychological damage? She became insecure and depressed while working far too much in order to do everything the way he demanded it of her. In the hope of pleasing him, she tried for decades to prove to him what she was capable of.

Things got much worse that first evening, my mother continued. After he was done dividing up the food, he asked, "When do we eat?"

"At seven," I said, "after Viktoria has been nursed and put to bed for the night."

"From now on I want supper at six, otherwise we don't have much of an evening, besides I'm hungry by then."

I thought that I had misunderstood him, and explained patiently, "I can't get things done by six, that's too early, especially in the summer, and if I put Viktoria to bed before seven, she won't sleep through the night."

To that he answered unmoved, "Then organize your day better."

The one has nothing to do with the other, I thought, but let it go for the moment, because I didn't want to argue about that too on our first evening. I already didn't know anymore whether I was coming or going. Viktoria was screaming, so I picked her up again. You had hidden in the bedroom, Omi was standing quietly at the stove, frying potatoes with onions and preparing linden blossom tea. When Viktoria was in her crib, fed and diapered, she fell asleep immediately. I set the table, put out butter in celebration of the day, which I spread thinly on the bread for you girls, and sliced tomatoes and cucumbers. Omi brought the fried potatoes and we sat down. I had no appetite, only a gnawing hunger. I didn't touch any of the things he had brought, and he did not put any of them on the table. We hardly talked as we ate. You and Bettine were scared and didn't say a word. Omi didn't join us at the table. Instead she ate her plate of potatoes on a chair next to the stove.

While we were eating I understood that the fear of the Nazis, caused by their insidious terror, had simply shifted in our family after the end of the war. From the day of his return, the oppression continued from my own husband. The transition had taken place seamlessly.

At his insistence, my mother accompanied him to his family after supper after all. When they were in bed my parents argued late into the night. I tiptoed to Omi and snuggled up next to her under her blanket. In the quiet of the night, the bitter exchange of words sounded even shriller. Omi pulled me close, kissed me and stroked my face and hair. I relished her warm body and was happy.

When I woke up in the morning, I was back in my bed. I had forgotten about the argument between my parents, when I suddenly heard his relentlessly scolding voice coming from the kitchen.

The next morning Kurt demanded all the money from me, my mother continued. I had to hand over everything to the last pfennig, as well as our joint savings book. He did it in front of my mother, and was not the least bit ashamed to treat me like a stupid child. And to top it all off, he was distrustful of me, questioning several times if I had really handed over everything. He looked at the savings book, counted the bills and asked, "Don't you have more, shouldn't there be more?" I can hear those questions to this day.

"More, how can there be more? After all, we had to live. Are you forgetting that we lost everything? Why don't you look around? We needed money for that!"

I was so proud of what Omi and I had achieved. Six months after we had been bombed out we each had our own bed again with a mattress, a pillow for everyone, a feather bed and sheets. We had a wardrobe, a large kitchen table and six chairs, the stove and an old green kitchen cupboard. It had been so difficult to get these few things together. After all, we needed everything: cups, plates, pots and pans and flatware. Almost daily something was added. Once I found an enamel bowl and a set of four ceramic bowls in different sizes at a secondhand dealer. I was always so happy whenever I managed to get hold of something.

"I know about your generous way of housekeeping only too well," he cut me off sharply while standing in front of me with distorted features. His thin, bluish-white lips disgusted me. When I saw how tense he was, all I could do was ask, "Just what do you mean by 'generous housekeeping'? Do explain that to me! We hardly have the bare necessities."

"Well, at your parent's house there was always such a bustle. Your mother didn't know how to keep house and spent money left and right while your father watched helplessly, and then he had to figure out how to pay for it and make ends meet," he said. His voice broke as he shouted these malicious words at me. He must have forgotten that Omi was standing at the stove, overhearing every word.

"Do you have any idea what you are saying?" I asked indignantly. He had always enjoyed being at our house, and he ate more than any of us at the meals. During this exchange of words, he continued to search for money in pots and cups, opening tin cans and other containers, just in case I had put some away after all. When he found nothing, he counted the bills once again and then proceeded awkwardly to put them away into his worn wallet.

"What are you doing?" I asked horrified.

"I'm putting away the money," he said deliberately calm, "can't you see that? I am here now, and from now on I am going to budget the money. Besides, I need some, too."

"And with what am I supposed to go shopping today?"

He looked at me uncomprehendingly.

"I must go grocery shopping right after breakfast," I explained.

"I thought you went shopping yesterday?"

"My mother and I have to go shopping every day, everything is rationed. Besides, I never know what might have come in," I explained. My words irritated him. He wrinkled his forehead as he thought about what I had said.

"How much do you need?" he finally asked.

"I don't know. I buy what I can get for the food stamps. I must buy milk for the children daily, per child I get half a liter, and as long as I am nursing I get milk, too. Sometimes something comes in unexpectedly, like cheese or cucumbers, and I must buy it right away before it's all gone. I always take along extra money, just in case."

"Don't you have a shopping list?"

"That's of little use these days. Besides, I know what we need."

"How can you manage the household that way? I don't call that planning!"

"What are you saying?" I asked exasperated. "There's no other way. How can I plan? I have to take what I can get. You've never been shopping in all your life, especially not now, after the war. It was already difficult enough during the war. If I don't jump at every opportunity, we'll all be missing out. And no one knows when there will be a new shipment of soap, onions or whatever it may be. If they have carrots or green beans I buy as much as they will give me for a family of five, six with you now, or kohlrabi or cabbage. Only then can I plan our meals and have a little variety. People are standing in line daily in front of the stores. They join every line and then ask the people in front of them what's being sold. Even the groceries for food ration stamps I must buy immediately because everything is gone in no time."

Kurt simply had no idea what shopping was like in those days and how much physical energy and nerves it took. He remained unmoved. Other women had more understanding husbands who helped whenever they could, and who were glad when something extra was available.

"Come on, now, Kurt," I begged him, "take whatever you need and give me back the rest of the money."

That's when he said, "I'll go shopping with you from now on. You spend the money too easily; I cannot trust you in money matters."

I was speechless. Imagine, he actually said that to me! He had only just come home the night before, and behaved as though I knew nothing about running a household. But it was he who had no idea.

I looked at my mother, her hands were trembling, and she was rubbing them so that I wouldn't notice. On that afternoon I understood better what his homecoming had meant to her. Finally I asked, "What money did he take away from you?"

Well, she said, there were his wages from the revenue office where he was employed since his high school graduation, which I got after our wedding because he was in the war. At the time he was glad, even proud, that we got his money, as he always said. We had both our names on the bank account. But I also had my own money in a separate savings account that Papa had opened for me when I was just a little girl. I deposited most of the money Papa had given me for my birthdays and Christmas into that account. Rolf and I had also inherited some money from him, and I put the money into that account that was left at the end of every month while I was working at the post office before you were born, Anne. I saved everything I could because I knew that Kurt and I would get married some day, and he had nothing at all. He came from a poor working class family. When we got engaged, I had no idea what I was getting into. I had always thought that an easier life would please him because he had poured out his heart to me so often, telling me how he was suffering in the cold and loveless atmosphere of his parents' home. It was such a miserable and primitive life, and I thought that he appreciated better things.

You know, Anne, I didn't understand that I hadn't just married beneath my position as far as money was concerned until after he returned from the prisoner of war camp. Papa had warned me about him from the very beginning. He was against a marriage. "That can't go well," he used to say, "the differences in your backgrounds are too great, even if he graduated from the gymnasium at the top of his class. If I didn't know better, I would never have guessed it. He has no manners, he always sits by himself in a corner, he is so unfriendly and never opens his mouth. He lives in a world of his own. There's something wrong with him. I advise you, leave him alone. He'll never change. He doesn't know how to be with people. Believe me, he's not good for you."

Papa was right, but I didn't want to believe him back then. I really thought that I knew better, and that I could help Kurt. I was sure that he would change and that everything would go well if I just loved him enough and stood by him. I imagined it all in such vivid colors. He would often tell me that I was the only person whom he trusted and who cared for him.

He loved the meals that Omi cooked, but he ate in silence without looking up from his plate until it was empty. She always offered him a second helping, and never needed to prod him. We always had wine or beer with dinner, and Papa wanted white bread with every meal. Even on weekdays we set the table carefully with a tablecloth, nice porcelain and silverware. At Kurt's home everything was thrown onto the old kitchen table. The bent flatware lay crisscross on the table next to chipped plates and tin cups for the malt coffee or peppermint tea. Only his father got his weak brew, which Irmgard or Kurt had to fetch for him in a pitcher every evening from the pub. Kurt's comrades from school, who sometimes invited him to visit, came without exception from well-situated families, and ever since then he longed for a better life. I took him along to the opera and to concerts in Dresden. It was all new to him. Afterwards we would go to the Italienische Dörfchen for a glass of wine. He was not accustomed to that either, but he enjoyed it and began to open up when we were alone together.

After Papa's death I altered his suits, jackets, pants and shirts for Kurt, who owned nothing but his worn school clothes. It had always been important to Papa that his suits were of a perfect cut and made of English woolen fabric of the best quality. With the suits he wore the finest maco shirts. He also had several pairs of gold and silver cufflinks with real pearls and diamonds. Kurt looked good in Papa's clothes, and was thankful for them. Rolf only wanted Papa's golden pocket watch, which burned with everything else.

Because Papa had never been out of work, and consequently we did not suffer hunger during the inflation of the 1930s, and since I always wore beautiful clothes, Kurt thought that I was spoiled and was spending money unnecessarily. But I was already sewing my own clothes by the time I was sixteen. I also took apart the dresses and suits that no longer fit Omi or that were no longer in fashion, and altered them or made something new out of the material for myself.

I simply cannot understand how things ended up the way they did. It all began very harmlessly. I was fourteen, when Kurt and I met for the first time at my confirmation on Palm Sunday. He was a distant cousin and almost exactly two years older than I. Out of politeness, my mother asked him to stop by the next time he was in Dresden. He was back the following weekend riding his bicycle from Bischofswerda. From then on he came every weekend, and we never let go of each other again. We did so many things together, went on bicycle tours and long hikes in the Elbsandsteingebirge and the Oberlausitz. In the evenings he joined us for supper, and soon he stayed overnight in the room where Herr Pollack had lived.

That all seems so long ago now. Anyway, only a few years later, he demanded that I hand the savings book over to him. The next morning he took it to the bank to have it changed over into his name. Because they couldn't do it without me being present, he came back and said I had to go with him. I delayed it for a few days, because I didn't want to do it and because Omi was gone for several days, and I couldn't leave the three of you alone. But eventually I had to go. A woman was sitting behind the counter. She looked at me with a strange expression. When he was busy at another counter, she asked me, "Why are you doing this?"

I couldn't answer her. My mouth was so dry that I was not able to get out a single word. I felt so embarrassed and humiliated. Today I think this woman knew what was going on in families and with men returning from the war. From then on I was completely dependent on him. He didn't spend the money on himself, she added in a low voice, as if to excuse what he had done. It wasn't avarice either that drove him to take everything away from me. But he believed in all seriousness that he knew better simply because he was a man, and he never gave in.

My mother was mentally worn out from his miserable scolding and petty interference in everything she did. Daily life was already difficult enough in those years. Even when her husband was doing nothing but yelling at her, complaining about at all the things that dissatisfied him, she was sitting on the couch knitting or mending our clothes or darning socks. Now and then she wiped away a tear, cleaned her eye-glasses, which had steamed up, and said weakly, "Why don't you stop at last, can't you see I have no more strength left?" After that he was quiet for a few minutes before he started again. Even in the middle of the night I was awakened by the man's scolding and her heart-rending sobbing. And there was Omi's irritated voice asking for quiet, telling him that he should let her daughter sleep. After all, her day had been long and hard enough. Everything sounded louder and more threatening in the silence of the night. I lay in bed, my eyes wide open, thinking about the words that were coming through the door quite clearly. My mother had picked up my little sister, who was crying. I heard her speak to her softly. The man ordered his wife to put the brat back into her crib and push it into the kitchen or out into the hall and come back to bed; he needed his sleep. She did not listen to him, but nursed the baby and changed her diapers.

At the full hour I heard the town hall clock strike. It drowned out the agitated voices from the room next door. I got confused as I counted the chimes. Was it three or already four? Later I heard the bells of the nearby Catholic church. I counted six chimes.

At breakfast he continued, "You are spoiling the children. I need a quiet night and a well-rested wife. I don't want you to get up at night." As he spoke, he sat stiffly in front of his plate full of hot oatmeal.

"You should have thought of that before you got me pregnant for the third time," she once shouted. "Besides, if I let Viktoria scream we can't sleep either."

"She'll stop once she learns that you are not coming," he countered.

"Right, and then she gets a rash, and I have no baby cream. Before you came she slept until five or six in the morning, that's when I got up anyway, and after I took care of her she was satisfied until ten. She's still so little. If I put her to bed as early as you want it, she must be fed and changed during the night."

"What kind of new methods are those anyway? Other women let their children cry. That's the only way they are going to learn to sleep through the night."

"You just be quiet," my mother shot back. "I know how things were at your house. There was very little love. Grandmother Schubert always talked about how you were sitting in a corner all by yourself weeping. I learned much from her also concerning infant care. I won't let my children cry at night and become sore and suffer hunger."

"You are a hysterical woman who thinks she knows everything better, but you know nothing at all," he yelled.

She looked straight at him saying, "I see, but of course you know it all, and you seem to think that you can terrorize me! I am taking care of Viktoria the way I took care of Anne and Bettine. It doesn't take that long, and if you wouldn't carry on like that, we would all sleep much better."

"You'll see soon enough how your children turn out with your upbringing. They won't thank you for it later, mark my word. And you call this a marriage? Why don't you show some consideration for me? I came back from the war completely burnt out. You can't even begin to imagine what I've been through."

"How dare you speak to me like that after everything we suffered through! Do you really believe that our life was a bed of roses?"

When he lifted his hand toward her, Omi stepped between her daughter and him unexpectedly, threatening him, "Don't you dare touch her or I'll inform the authorities about you!"

"That I would like to see," he mocked her, taking two quick hard steps in her direction. But he did not dare to touch his mother-in-law. Instead he said in a threatening tone, "What do you want here anyway, you are not part of our family, you washerwoman, you."

Omi would not be intimidated in spite of the insult, and said calmly but full of contempt, "I am sure you know what I can bring up against you. Washerwoman is right, or would you like to slave in the washhouse? Besides, once I am gone, who will protect Elfriedchen from you?"

That hit home.

"Throw your mother out," he raged, "I won't tolerate this woman in my house any longer. I won't survive it if I have to spend one more day under the same roof with her."

"Don't be ridiculous, how am I supposed to manage without my mother? Besides, it's *our* home! She's staying! You know very well that I need her."

"She's in my way," he screamed, "I am here now, I'll help you."

"What do you know about helping? I'm still recovering from Viktoria's birth. For the time being my mother has to stay."

Years later my mother said, "I felt so miserable and weak. I wondered what was to become of me. I was not recovering fast enough from giving birth, and I was concerned that my milk would dry up from all the hard work and the daily worries. What would I give the baby then? There was hardly any formula for infants, and it was given only to women who couldn't nurse. Viktoria was still too small for cow's milk. From that day on he repeatedly demanded that Omi had to go. He said he felt watched all the time, and that he wanted to live freely with me. But he was not home during the day and knew nothing about the groceries and the many other things Omi procured from the local farms and merchants and how she slaved tirelessly for us. She was in her early fifties and full of energy, and she loved us, her children, more than her life."

My mother remained steadfast. She refused to let Omi go. He implored her to listen to reason, as he called it, and out of respect for him. And when this didn't get him what he wanted, he kneeled before her and declared that she was his queen, that he worshiped her and swore by everything that was sacred that he could only live with her alone in the apartment, that he had to have her for himself, that her mother was too argumentative, and that she spoiled the children on top of it all.

Unfortunately, Omi left us soon after his return after all, and went back to Dresden, where she found a spacious room with kitchen privileges on the second floor of one of those large old villas with a pretty front yard and a high iron fence around it, not far from the Loschwitz bridge. The room had a large stone balcony facing the street, a high ceiling with a rich stucco pattern and a chandelier on which several of the light bulbs were burned out, as well as a huge deep blue tile stove. She had also found work in a factory. I visited Omi often all by myself on the weekends. Later my mother told me that he had thrown her out.

18. Sickness and Disease

After Omi's departure my mother seemed weaker with every day, and complained of difficulties swallowing, even when drinking. Her husband barked at her to pull herself together, but her condition worsened by the hour, and it became hard for her to do the most urgent housework. Soon she could hardly take care of the baby anymore, and rested on the sofa in the kitchen frequently, sighing loudly with her eyes closed. When she got up she dragged herself through the apartment, holding onto the furniture and looking strangely white. Cooking had become a major chore. She vomited frequently and was running a temperature. I helped wherever I could and ran errands for her. She sent me to buy milk from the local farmer because it was better than the milk from the dairy, and it was closer. After cooking the milk, a thick layer of cream formed on top, which we loved to eat. I went to the pharmacy for her and bought yogurt at the dairy where I heard that they were selling *Harzer* cheese, a cheese made of skimmed milk, at eighty pfennigs per pound. I told my mother about it, and she gave me enough change to buy two pounds.

When I returned my mother made two sandwiches for us. After the first bite she said, "This cheese tastes bitter, what awful stuff is this?"

"No, it tastes good," I said, chewing happily.

Puzzled, she examined her tongue and throat in the mirror, and saw a strange coating she couldn't explain. She finished her bread with the cheese and sat down again. The following morning she felt so sick that she only got up to care for my new sister. When my father came home from the post office, where he had found employment a few days earlier, there was no noon meal, and no table set. He was about to get angry when she called him from the bedroom with a weak voice and asked him to get Dr. Kowalski right away. My father's description of his wife's condition must have sounded urgent because the doctor came along immediately in her old Mercedes. She had hardly entered the bedroom when she said, "You have diphtheria, Frau Bergner, I don't have to examine you, I can smell it. You must get to the hospital immediately! I am taking you with me."

Then she looked at us children one by one and determined, "The infant must come, too, she has nasal diphtheria. Why haven't you come to me with her? That's irresponsible not to seek treatment for such a small child, she could have suffocated! Are you aware of the fact that the new-born is critically ill?"

"Dear God," my mother wailed, "I've been terribly worried for days. The little one was breathing with such a rattling sound, her nose was completely stuffed up, and I pulled long slimy stuff out of her nose with tweezers, almost like tubes, which went deep down into her throat."

My mother described such situations lively and colorfully, without being excessive. Her husband, who did not have this talent, and whose world was a reasonable, logical, emotionless and boring place, always felt uneasy when his wife talked in such a descriptive manner, and would cut her off, as he did then, saying, "Stop that already, we are not interested in your exaggerations!"

"But that's how it was," she defended herself. "You saw yourself how much I took out of Viktoria's nose!"

"I am sure Dr. Kowalski doesn't want to know about that now," he sneered.

"On the contrary," the doctor said, "I do want to hear about it, Herr Bergner. As a matter of fact, I must know about it, because it supports my diagnosis. And now help your wife get ready."

My father was quiet after that, not daring to question the doctor's authority and her resolute orders, and did as he was told. He got a clean nightgown and a towel, and put it into a shopping bag with my mother's bathrobe.

"Don't forget my cream, comb and my toothbrush," my mother reminded him.

Dr. Kowalski took my little sister and wrapped a blanket around her.

"How long will my wife have to stay in the hospital?" he stammered helplessly when he realized the seriousness of the situation.

"You'll have to count on two weeks at least, until the danger of infection is past and she's gained back her strength."

"And what am I to do with the two older children? I have to go to work."

"You'll have to think of something," Dr. Kowalski said unmoved. Then she put the baby into my mother's arms, took her bag, and led her down the stairs.

"You better ask my mother to come until I'm back home again," my mother suggested.

I ran to the kitchen window to watch her get into the car with my baby sister. Right after the car had disappeared, my father buttered several slices of bread for all of us and washed some apples. Then he left my sister Bettine at his parents' for the afternoon, and took the train to Dresden with me. When we arrived at Omi's, she had just gotten home from the factory where she was working the early shift again. Omi didn't want to come at first, because she treasured her newly found peace and freedom in her beautiful large room in the city she loved. But we needed her and I begged her to please come, and eventually she let herself be talked into it. "Out of compassion for the children," she insisted, "and only as long as it is absolutely necessary." I wanted to take her with us right away, but she said that she could not come before the late afternoon the following day, because she had to go to the factory first to let them know, and to take care of some other things.

The next day I waited for her all afternoon in front of the house, and when I finally saw her with her suitcase, I happily skipped toward her. She put the suitcase down and hugged me. Even before we reached the apartment she pulled a paper bag filled with deep red raspberry candies out of her jacket pocket. She also had our favorite butter cookies for us as well as a bottle of glue, colored pencils and a roll of large sheets of heavy light pink paper from the factory to draw and paint on. We loved her dearly because she always brought us such treasures.

I followed my mother to the hospital only three days later. It was the same hospital where Viktoria was born. Omi took me there. They put a child's bed next to my mother's so she could take care of me and I wouldn't feel so alone.

Every evening after the lights were turned off, the nurses came, opened wide all the doors to the rooms and sang good night songs in the hallway. I knew the songs from my mother, but in that strange environment I paid better attention, and understood for the first time the meaning of the words of the lullaby "Guten Abend, gute Nacht" with the melody by Johannes Brahms that end with the words: "Tomorrow morning, if it pleases God, he will wake you again." The nurses always sung it last. I took the words literally and became agitated. "What does it mean, if it pleases God?" I asked my mother, "I want to wake up, I don't want to die. I am going to wake up all by myself tomorrow morning, right?"

"You mustn't be afraid, Anne, it's only a beautiful old song." My mother took me in her arms, "Don't you remember I sing it for you every night, too?"

"But now I don't like it anymore, I don't ever want to hear it again. I am going to wake up whether God wants it or not."

"Oh, you silly little girl," my mother said. "God wants both of us to wake up again tomorrow morning, and your little sister, too, and all the people in the whole wide world as well."

Viktoria was in the infants' ward, and my mother and I walked over to her several times a day to feed and change the baby. The nurses were glad about the help. They were quite sympathetic and broadminded at the hospital in those days, and whatever was lacking as far as medication was concerned, they tried to make up with much understanding and consideration. Even years later my mother would talk about the physician with the greatest respect, because he made sure that there was enough food, fruit and fresh juices as well as medication, and he came by daily to inquire about her well-being.

After two weeks my mother was discharged with the urgent recommendation to take good care of her health, not to work too hard right away, and to rest whenever possible, reminding her that her state was still very precarious. After she left I was moved to the children's ward for another week.

During the early years after the war, we children caught all of the contagious diseases, from diphtheria and whooping cough to chicken pox and measles, which often took a life-threatening turn due to lack of medication. And often enough we had to stay inside the house because of a high fever or an ugly sore throat. For the fever we were given ten or twelve tiny white sweet-tasting quinine pearls, which my mother counted out and offered us on the palm of her left hand. She was generous and always gave us two or three more. I counted them every time, and was happy about the sweet pearls, and we always got well again.

When I was allowed to go home at last and my mother felt better, Omi went to Dresden to visit the cemetery and to withdraw money from her bank account. It was then that she found out that one of her accounts had been 'plundered', as she called it. "It was empty, completely empty!" She couldn't grasp it. "My good money, simply gone, and no one could tell me what had happened to it! Those scoundrels, they stole it from me! There was still money from Grandfather in that account, which went back all the way to the days of the Kaiser. Not even the Nazis had dared to touch my money!" The disappearance of her money was never resolved. She was not the only victim.

Omi also told us horror stories about the demolition of the ruins of beloved buildings in Dresden. Countless ruins that could have been rebuilt easily enough were systematically detonated or torn down, often because their former function did not fit the ideology of the "New Germany" and for lack of money. Streets and squares were renamed. One day, Omi took the streetcar along the Fürstenstraße to the zoological garden, as she would do frequently, except the Fürstenstraße was no longer there. It was suddenly called Fetscherstraße. To her it seemed like robbery, because the changing of the names gave her the feeling that everything was lost now with a finality that was hard to accept, and she never got over it.

I walked often with my mother and grandmother through the streets of Dresden. In the Old Town only grass and ruderal flora grew for years amongst the ruins and on the cleared areas. Right in the middle of the weed-covered grounds and between monuments and ruins, a small herd of sheep was grazing one day. I never forgot that sight. Later they reminded me of the Baroque poems from the time of the Thirty Years' War from 1618-1648, sinister premonitions that seemed to foreshadow things to come for Dresden. Will there always be this senseless destruction, because we cannot prevent people from conjuring up ever-new reasons to fight yet another war, I wondered? Will we always have to live with the "vanitas, vanitatum, et omnia vanitas!"

There was new hope, my mother said, as if she had guessed my thoughts. Much seemed possible in the early months after the end of the war. Although life seemed to be in a continuous provisionary state, survival was the motto of the hour. We were facing new problems daily that demanded all of our energy and imagination to solve. We couldn't compare our situation to any events from the past, so we could not fall back on anything we knew. People just took a deep breath, knuckled down and cleaned up. Everywhere, women and old men worked tirelessly. They had listened to the appeals to clean and stack up bricks in the bombed out cities, to clear the streets and cart away rubble, and no one complained that the work was too hard. They even began to sort the stones of the destroyed Frauenkirche in Dresden to prepare it for rebuilding. For their labor people received a hot meal out of huge kettles, which smelled temptingly good as we happened to walk past. Resolute women in old dresses and aprons and old men in worn jackets were passing out soup or porridge, scooping it with large ladles into battered tin containers. The bronze statue of Martin Luther was put back on its pedestal in front of the Frauenkirche, and the reformer once more held out his Bible patiently to all who passed by. In September of 1945 there had not yet been time to come down hard on us, to capture the people's thinking and indoctrinate us with these 'new' ideas. We were looking for a better future at a time when the yearning for freedom and a new beginning had not yet been suppressed by communist party propaganda and misconceived Marxist ideas. However, just two years later everything had changed completely, and we encountered names like Walter Ulbricht, Otto Grotewohl, Wilhelm Pieck, August Bebel, Rosa Luxemburg and Karl Liebknecht wherever we went. We learned that Ulbricht and his comrades had been trained in Moscow during the war in order to lead us all into a bright new future. Soon after there were signs everywhere that things were not going as expected. The SED leadership (Social Unity Party of Germany) even stopped the rebuilding of the Frauenkirche. The pile of rubble that once was the Frauenkirche with the Luther monument in front of it became an anti-war memorial, and became one of the most photographed sights of Dresden after the war.

My Omi had also cleaned and stacked thousands of bricks shoulder high and several layers deep on the wide sidewalks for the rebuilding of the city.

On my desk stands the photo by Robert Capa, showing sixteen women of all ages from the back, their hair pinned up or held together with headscarves, surrounding a large, open wagon loaded with bricks. They are pulling and pushing the heavy load toward the Victory Column in Berlin in the spring of 1945. Trees without leaves, many of them torn apart by bombs, are standing on either side of the wide empty boulevard. The women are wearing shabby dresses with skirts reaching down to the middle of their calves and aprons tied around their waists, old cardigans, worn jackets and downtrodden shoes, heavy socks or thick long stockings. Amongst the women are two or three old men. It is a dismal sight. The goddess of victory is flying high above them with outstretched wings, but she is so far away that nothing connects her with this group of hard-working, ragged people.

19. A New Apartment, a New Hope

My mother often proudly told us how she began to look tirelessly for a real apartment with a kitchen and bath right after she had recovered from diphtheria. She had implored Omi to stay at least until she had found a better place. Omi gave in and stayed. Every day my mother walked to the town hall, went from room to room, knocked on closed doors, entered without waiting for a response, and would neither be put off nor turned away. If the answers were evasive or negative she would say, "Thank you for your help anyway, I'll be back tomorrow. Perhaps an apartment will turn up for us by then." She explained to the clerks how sick we had all been and pointed out that the rooms in the Wallgasse could not be heated adequately in winter, nor was there enough coal and fire wood to heat such a drafty place with ice-cold floors located over a carpenter's shop.

The men in the offices looked surprised at this young resolute woman. It never occurred to them to deny her entrance. I think that with time they even enjoyed seeing her. She carried a fresh wind into the stale atmosphere. They got up behind their desks when she entered, took a slight bow and began to believe in miracles themselves, just because she knew that there was an apartment for her family somewhere in town. Exactly where this apartment might be was up to them to find out, she told them.

And so it happened that by the end of September she was offered a spacious apartment on the Goldbacher Weg, which was beautiful beyond all expectations. It had a large square kitchen, two very large rooms, a big hall and a real bathroom with a toilet, a sink and tub and gas heater. The kitchen had only a simple deep sink mounted on the wall with flowing cold water only, and we had to wash the dishes in a large enamel basin on the kitchen table, but that didn't seem so bad to us at the time.

After the move, Omi returned to Dresden for good and from then on came to visit us every Saturday morning. She talked to us children about Rolf, helped her daughter where she could, and returned to Dresden after the noon meal on Sunday. She always arrived with heavy bags, bringing us whatever she had managed to get hold of during the week and knew we could use well.

At that time she began to look for Rolf, her boy, as she called him, and to whom she clung tenaciously with all of a mother's love and pride, with renewed energy. She went to the authorities in Dresden and to the Red Cross to add his name to the list of soldiers who had not returned, and gave them her own as well as our new address. Daily she listened to the announcements of missing and killed soldiers on the radio, whose names were read for hours on end. My mother helped her, but they never found even the slightest trace of Rolf, until finally, years later, all hope of finding out anything about his fate had died. Omi's pain and despair over the loss of her son never went away; it just became more subdued over the years and surfaced less frequently, and instead of shedding a river of tears she just sobbed quietly while her eyes shimmered wet.

What is it like, I wonder, when a human being who is so close to us disappears without a trace, and we never hear from him again, because no one in the entire world can tell us anything of his whereabouts or give us any information about his death, since no one we know or shall ever meet was there? We shall never know where Rolf met his fate, nor how it came to him and what he was thinking in the last moments of his young life, and how deep the loneliness must have been. Or was he lucky and died within seconds, without knowing what was happening?

The sorrow over the traceless disappearance of a loved one may subside given time and seem to become bearable as the years pass, but a void remains, because with Rolf we also lost a wife he may have married and any children they may have had. When Omi finally stopped her search after many years and had him listed as missing in action, the pain broke out anew and seemed as strong as during the first months after the end of the war. She had his name and the dates of his short life chiseled and painted in gold at the bottom of her husband's gravestone, leaving enough space between the two for herself. I went with her often to the Johannisfriedhof to visit the grave where she always talked to both of them, her husband and her son, while pulling out a weed here and a blade of grass there before we watered the plants, laid down a wreath or put a fresh bunch of flowers into a glass jar on the grave.

Rolf was my only uncle, and because I often heard others talk about him I missed him very much and wove my own stories around his life. We elevated the young man with the blond hair and the blue eyes in our memory, and when I was young I constantly searched for him in the faces of other men on the streets. It is an East Prussian face with even features that seems like the face of a stranger to me in spite of the four photographs that my mother got from her mother, and now belong to me. At times we became confused and began to doubt him who left us without saying good-bye, and whose fate remains a mystery. I wonder who will have the photos after me and look into his face then, and whether they will know anything about this man who only lived to age twenty-three?

Shouldn't war make such a loss, one repeated tens of thousands of times, more bearable? People were mourning the deaths of their sons, husbands and fathers everywhere. That's what war is all about, I thought. We started it, so what could we expect? It had hit everyone, even us and him. Nevertheless we needed comfort, and for a long time we wanted to believe that Rolf had been seized as a prisoner of war, that he had been lucky enough to survive with the help of others, but that he had simply lacked the opportunity to send us a sign of life. We wanted to believe he had found a woman far away from home, that he had begun a new life with her and was speaking a new language, that he was thinking of us, but that one day it was no longer important to him to let us, his old family, know that he was all right.

We had heard of men who were living a new life in a foreign country under an assumed name. At some point in time, a message would reach the first family, because someone had met a German in a far-away land, and after his or her return they would search for the family and bring them the good news. The relatives were relieved, and if they were lucky the two families would finally meet, and everyone would cry for joy. The members of each family would learn some words in the other family's language. All were happy, they took photos, and promised to visit one another again soon. And they thanked God that everything had turned out well after all.

In the apartment house on Goldbacher Weg lived three families on the ground floor and another three on the second floor, where we occupied the apartment in the middle. There was another smaller place under the roof with slanted walls and three mansard windows facing the street. Toward the back was the drying loft and a storage space for each apartment, separated by wooden slats. The woman who lived up there with her two children painted tin soldiers for a meager living. I visited her often and played with the figures that stood in straight lines on wooden boards and trays all around her and wherever there was an available surface in the room, waiting their turn to be painted with the next color or to dry.

For the first time since their wedding my parents had their own real apartment. The furniture came together astonishingly fast. Relatives and acquaintances who had not been bombed out brought us furniture out of their basements and from their attics, and one aunt even gave us a small table with a marble top and a floor lamp from her living room, which my parents took along wherever they moved. My mother cleaned and polished the furniture with a polish that she made of oil and vinegar until everything was gleaming to her satisfaction.

On the white-washed walls in all the rooms a flower and garland design had been applied with a rubber roll to resemble wall paper. In the bedroom, the design had been applied in a deep cornflower blue. In the living room the garlands were light green and in the kitchen they were bright yellow. When I had nothing to do and was expected to be quiet, because my father demanded unrelenting silence when he was home, I contemplated the designs on the walls. I followed the simple garlands as they ran up and down the walls in eight inch wide stripes and noticed how they moved apart by as much as half an inch, leaving a white stripe, just to come back together again and even overlap, so that the blue, green or yellow was more intense there. And because I had a vivid imagination, I seldom fell prey to boredom.

One day, a complete living room set arrived from my grandparents'. Because of the lack of apartments, they had to turn over two rooms of their three-room apartment to their recently married daughter Irmgard and her husband Georg after their first child was born, so there was no more room for the furniture. However, we children did not benefit from the furniture. From that day on, we were no longer allowed to go into the living room without permission, because the furniture had to be treated with the utmost care. We only used the room on holidays like Christmas, Easter and birthdays and when relatives or friends came for coffee and cake. At times, my mother would disappear into it with a neighbor woman, pulling the door shut behind her after admonishing us to be good. Throughout the year, we children were restricted to the spacious kitchen and the large bedroom, which contained all of our beds, one large table, two dark wardrobes and a huge chest of drawers.

To complete the household my mother continued to be very enterprising. She tried her luck stopping in craftsmen's shops and small factories until she had found all the things we really needed. Once she came back with six ivory-colored supper plates that had tiny blue flowers with two leaves and a stem printed on them. Another time it was an earthen vessel, or second choice clay vases and bowls from the local ceramics factory. She found wooden cooking spoons, old silver plated coffee spoons, children's clothes, shoes, sewing utensils, black twine, nails and thumbtacks. And she was always on the lookout for an extra ration of vegetables, cheese, soap or honey. She managed to get hold of yogurt when others said there was none, and often came home with full shopping bags and nets, smiling happily. Her hands were marked with dark red and white welts from the bags' handles that had cut deeply into her palms. She rubbed her hands and massaged her shoulders and feet, and forgot the pain because we had enough to eat again. Often I came along to help her carry the bags. Occasionally we had to stop along the way and set them down to catch our breath.

There was little fat or oil and hardly any meat available. We were always hungry and ate unbelievable amounts of potato pancakes made of raw grated potatoes, which my mother fried on the large hot stovetop in order to save the oil for home fried potatoes. When she had flour she would make a batter for pancakes with one egg and milk in a huge bowl which she also baked on the stovetop during particularly hard times. We sprinkled sugar on the Plinsen, rolled them up and stuffed them into our mouths. I preferred them that way to being fried in a pan with margarine, which stank so badly when heated that I stayed out of the kitchen. We were elated when a mill owner filled a bottle with linseed or rapeseed oil for us. For supper we would pour the oil over a bowl full of hot boiled potatoes and sprinkle them with salt, or dunk large chunks of rye bread into a bowl of oil which my mother had placed onto the kitchen table.

"I never could stand dunking," my mother interrupted me as I talked about those days, "but Kurt was used to that from his family. They lived like day laborers when they were amongst themselves. A pot was placed in the center of the table and everyone dunked."

I had to smile because we dunked a lot during the early years after the war. We even dunked little pieces of old, very dry bread into hot sugar milk or milk coffee or into a glass of runny sugar beet syrup. During those first years after the war, everything revolved around food, warm clothing and solid shoes.

20. A Visit from the Past

It was early spring of 1946. The day was cool and dark, so the kitchen lamp was still on, and I was helping my mother with the dishes after the noon meal, when there was an unexpected knock at the apartment door. We stiffened from fear and did not move, and then there was a second louder knock. Bettine and Viktoria were taking their nap. My mother's hands trembled. She put her finger on her lips to signal me that I should be quiet. Who could it be? When we heard no sound from the staircase and the knock was not repeated, my mother said, "Stay here and be quiet." Then she tiptoed out of the kitchen leaving it open just a crack. One of the beams of the floor in the hall creaked when she stepped on it.

"Is anybody there?" she called. I heard a woman's voice that I recognized.

"Dear God, Frau Leberecht, you are still alive!" My mother exclaimed, "I never thought I would see you again. What a surprise! Please do come in, take off your coat, here is a coat hanger. May I take your hat and umbrella?"

"My dear Frau Bergner, I am so glad to see you alive and well," Frau Leberecht shouted excitedly on her part. "I've been thinking of you and the children and your mother ever since we lost each other on that terrible night after we left the cellar. How did you ever make it out of the burning city with the two children? I was so worried about you!"

The two women entered the kitchen moments later. My mother asked me whether I remembered Frau Leberecht. How could I ever forget the woman in whose apartment I had spent hours almost every day? I shook her hand and curtsied.

"Please sit down with us in the kitchen for a moment," my mother said, "I'll make coffee and finish the dishes quickly. Then we'll go to the living room and talk. You do have some time?"

Frau Leberecht looked at her wristwatch. "Yes, my train for Bautzen leaves around six. I am on the way to my daughter's, and decided to stop by."

"How did you know that you would find us here on the Goldbacher Weg?" my mother asked.

"My dear Frau Bergner, I knew that your husband's family lives in Bischofswerda, so I inquired at the town hall, and they gave me this address. I tried my luck and here I am. I hope you won't hold it against me, but I couldn't have announced my coming."

"How can you even think that, Frau Leberecht? I am so happy and relieved to see you," my mother responded. She was glad that Kurt had gone back to work early that day. He would not have liked the visit of our former neighbor. He disliked all dealings with his wife's friends, no matter who it was, and wanted no one to visit us in our home. It was like a mania with him, some sick jealousy. There was something obsessive in the way he put pressure on the whole family while thinking that his behavior was normal, that all men were like him.

When the coffee was ready we went into the living room. My mother set the small table with the marble top in front of the couch, poured the coffee and offered milk and sugar.

"I am so glad I found you, Frau Bergner, it is so good to be able to talk with you about our life in Dresden." Her cheeks glowed bright red.

"I feel the same," my mother agreed, and her face radiated even years later when she spoke about the visit.

Frau Leberecht was the only neighbor whom we met again after the bombing. I listened spellbound, and did not take my eyes off the two women. On that afternoon my mother laughed often. She was so joyful about our old neighbor's visit that she completely forgot about me.

"You are so quiet, Anne," Frau Leberecht said turning to me. "Are you sure you remember me?"

I just nodded. Frau Leberecht had not only been a good neighbor, she had also been my friend, and I loved her almost as much as Omi. I was quiet because I wanted to hear every word. The visit of the elderly lady brought back long lost memories that built a bridge for me to the days before the bombing and recaptured almost forgotten events for me. I would have liked to ask her about Inge, the girl who was my age, and who had lived with her mother on the floor below us during that last winter in Dresden. Inge and I sat together for hours on the sofa in their living room with our dolls and my teddybear. We invented all kinds of stories to cheer each other up. Often we would sit in complete darkness; we didn't even have a candle. Only a faint glow came from the radio that we had turned on low, and which cast a pattern of light through the round holes of the back panel onto the wall behind it. These round dots of light took on oval shapes and stretched out into elongated ellipses the further away they were cast. A second glow of light emerged from behind the kitchen door that stood just barely ajar as her mother worked in the kitchen, and ran through the hallway into the living room. After a while, our eyes got used to the darkness, and we were able to see the outlines of the dark brown furniture.

Frau Leberecht and you, Anne, were good friends, my mother said, evidently thinking she had to remind me. Can you imagine that we didn't even know until this very moment whether we had made it through that inferno, and we told each other how we had left the burning city, and what decisions had guided us. During that afternoon, we both realized once again what a disruption the bombing of Dresden had caused in our lives. Frau Leberecht was always happy to take care of you when I had to run an errand, and you loved to go to her.

In February of 1943 you had this terrible accident in her kitchen. You were just eighteen months old. I had taken you to Frau Leberecht because I wanted to run quickly to the bank and get milk on the way back. Frau Leberecht was cooking chicken noodle soup, your favorite. I dropped you off at the door and rushed down the stairs.

As Frau Leberecht explained later, the two of you went to the kitchen to taste the soup. She let you have a sip, holding her left hand under your chin so no bouillon would drip onto your dress while you were slurping the soup. Careful, it's hot, she said to you, while blowing lightly so it would not splatter. Then she asked you if the soup needed more salt. It was like a game, you always wanted more salt. Frau Leberecht would laugh and turn toward the kitchen cupboard to get the saltshaker. But on that day you couldn't wait, you had to try the soup again immediately. So you must have stretched out both arms and pulled the pot forward, and suddenly it fell off, spilling the boiling soup all over you.

When I entered the house, I heard you scream at the top of your lungs. Frightened out of my wits, I put the milk can down and jumped upstairs, taking two steps at a time. Frau Leberecht was already waiting for me with you in her arms, stammering incoherently. One look at you and I knew that your life was in danger. You had a laceration across your forehead where the pot had hit you, as I found out later, and your entire face was scalded. I grabbed you, ran into our apartment, fetched a cotton blanket and wrapped you in it while I jumped down the stairs, through the front door and ran across the street to the streetcar stop, where a streetcar was about to leave in the direction of Dresden Neustadt. There were no taxis available during the war. When the streetcar conductor grasped the situation, he reacted immediately, telling the passengers that he would try to drive straight to the military hospital without stopping along the way. Whoever didn't want to go that far should get off and wait for the next streetcar.

At the military hospital the doctors had specialized in the treatment of burn injuries, and were leaders in the field. The hospital was full of soldiers who had suffered all kinds of burns at the front. When the staff saw you they rushed you immediately to the operating room. You had been screaming uninterruptedly during the entire trip. A nurse wanted to pull your woolen pullover over your head, but the skin on your face was bright red and full of blisters. In some areas your skin was hanging down in shreds. I yelled at her to work faster and told her to cut off your clothes so as not to damage your skin even more.

The doctors looked at the wounds and said they would like to try out a new method that would make new skin grow back and heal smoothly without the build-up of scar tissue. They gave you a general anesthesia and began to work on you right away. The procedure lasted over two hours, and then one of the doctors came out and assured me that everything had gone well, but that he couldn't promise me just yet whether you would survive. "Even if your daughter doesn't die of the burns and the skin heals without any infections, it's too early to predict whether she will survive the shock," he explained.

I must have looked alarmed, and he put his arm around me. "We'll wheel your daughter into the room next door in a few minutes. You can stay with her until she wakes up."

When they brought you in and I saw your face, arms and hands completely covered with white, damp gauze wrappings, I almost fainted. Lying on that gurney you looked as if you were dead. The doctors had pulled all of the scalded skin from your face and covered it with damp mull cloths that they would keep wet. Their hope was that this way smooth new skin would be able to grow. Only under your nose did they leave an opening for you to breathe. During the coming weeks, the mull was exchanged every few hours. I sat down on a chair next to your bed. I can't recall how long I remained there. Now and then someone entered the room to look after you. One of the medical orderlies brought me a cup of coffee saying, "Here, please drink this before you fall off the chair."

After what seemed like an eternity, you moved ever so slightly. I ran out of the room calling for a doctor. He looked at you for a long time, felt your pulse, listened to your breathing and said, "For the time being her heartbeat is strong and regular. We'll know more in a few hours. Her chances for survival will increase with every day. I think it would be best if you went home now and got some sleep."

Leaving you was out of the question. I wanted to stay during the first night, so I asked for a more comfortable chair. They set up a plank bed for me next to yours with a blanket and a pillow. Someone brought me a bowl of soup. There was no way to let Omi know how things were going, but I was sure that Frau Leberecht would tell her the essentials.

The doctors did their very best. We were so lucky because your face could have been disfigured forever. Everything healed very well. The scars on your upper right arm and your neck were caused because the wool of your sweater retained the heat of the bouillon longer and damaged the skin deeper. When I was finally allowed to take you home again, I had sewn all new clothes for you as well as matching clothes for your doll. I showed you the doll and tried to cheer you up, but no matter what I said, you turned your head away. Not even the faintest smile appeared on your face. When I wanted to stand you up to get you dressed, your legs simply slipped apart, and I had to catch you to keep you from falling. You had to learn to walk all over again. After your stay in the hospital you remained very shy for a very long time.

I remember how I spent what seemed to me to be an eternity alone at the hospital in permanent darkness. I only heard unfamiliar voices and strange noises, or felt the vibrations of approaching and receding steps. I pricked up my ears when someone knocked against my bed and waited for someone to speak to me. Now and then I wanted to say something, but as far as I can recall I remained silent. I knew when my mother was there, but I seldom reacted to her voice and touch because I was upset with her for leaving me alone for hours. I also seem to remember how she once asked someone if the child still knew her. I sorted things out for myself as I tried to assert myself against these strangers who grabbed me and tied my hands to the slats of the crib to prevent me from scratching the itching new skin on my face. During those long three months, I learned that I belonged to myself, and that there was something inside of me that neither the doctors nor the orderlies could touch as they stood around my bed talking about me, bending down over me and discussing what to do next, as if I were not there.

It must have been a large room, and somewhere to my right must have been windows, because it seemed lighter on that side, or perhaps it was a large lamp whose light shone through the bandages over my eyes. The day came when they removed the bandages and put mittens on my hands, which they tied around my wrists. At least I could move again and comfort myself through my own touch. Although I could finally see again, I have no happy memories of those weeks. I experienced a gray, oppressive environment, faces that remained shadowy, and windows through which the light fell dully into the large room. I don't recall any sunshine. These lonely hours were a shock to my soul that no one had considered. They only talked about the shock of the scalding and my mother's angst.

My sisters had woken up and came into the living room. Frau Leberecht had not said much while my mother was retelling the story about the accident. I've often wondered why, of all the stories she could have told during Frau Leberecht's visit, it had to be that one.

At around five o'clock, my mother became agitated. Her husband would be home soon, and she had to think about supper. Frau Leberecht noticed her restlessness, and looked at the pocket watch she kept in her handbag, exclaiming, "My goodness, I must run if I don't want to miss my train to Bautzen."

The two women quickly said good-bye, and my mother showed her friend to the door. Then she hurriedly cleared off the table and washed the dishes so no traces of those few happy hours were left. She swiftly prepared supper as she murmured, "Quick, quick, quick, where is the sharp knife, Anne, go get the bread and cheese from the pantry, hurry up, put the plates, forks and knives on the table and a tea glass for everyone. I still have to boil hot water for the tea, and you girls go wash your hands!" Moments later my father entered the apartment.

He was always suspicious, and noticed right away that something was different. With sparse words my mother talked about Frau Leberecht's visit. He had a ravenous hunger just as always, and was in a bad mood. We were sitting at the table looking in silence at our plates, and I had a guilty conscience without knowing why.

I never saw Frau Leberecht again. Once, when my mother came back from Dresden after a doctor's appointment, she said that she had visited Frau Leberecht, and again she looked happy.

21. Secrets and Illusions

Not long after Frau Leberecht's visit, daily life had regained some kind of normalcy when unexpected new problems within the family surfaced, my mother told me as she let her story unfold to reveal new secrets. One day Kurt forbade me to speak with the neighbors in the house, even if we should meet by accident in the staircase. A "good morning" or "good evening" was enough, he stressed; every additional word was already too much. I was not to allow myself to be drawn into any conversation with anyone while sweeping the stairs, as I was fetching something from the cellar or while hanging up the laundry behind the house. He even forbade me to stop and gossip, as he called it disparagingly, while I was shopping.

Kurt justified his orders on the assumption that I would give in to the temptation to spilling family secrets, or pass on facts from his work as personnel manager at the post office that he discussed with me at night. That was nobody's business, not to mention that I could endanger him. Things got even worse when he was called into his supervisor's office and was told that he would have to take notes on anything suspicious that would come to his attention about his colleagues and enter it into their personal files. He was also supposed to put certain questions to them and record their answers. Every three months he would have to deliver detailed reports to Berlin. Kurt resisted, saying that he was not suited to the task of being an informant, but was told that he had no choice in his position. "Try to contain the damage as much as possible," his supervisor suggested, "just write down a lot, even if it's completely apolitical. Whatever they make of it in Berlin is up to them."

From then on, Kurt would spy on me continuously. He listened behind closed doors, peeped through keyholes, and sneaked after me wherever I went. "Have you lost your mind?" I asked him, when he followed me down the staircase on a Saturday morning, and then rebuked me in the apartment for having talked to Frau Steinbacher who lived below us. "Why do you think you can forbid me to speak with the people in the house?"

"Because I cannot trust you," was his answer. "Besides, you are wasting your time. You keep saying yourself that you never get done with housework."

His words angered me. "How do you think we survived the war? Do you really think that I don't know what I can talk about and what I have to keep to myself? I dare say I got plenty of practice in keeping silent. You were away at the front. What do you know about life at home? And as far as housework is concerned, it never ends, I can work as much as I want, and there's always more to do. Frau Steinbacher just shared with me that they have onions at the *Konsum* (the state run grocery store), and two pounds of rice for every family without food stamps as long as the supply lasts. I'm going right now to get our share!"

"You're staying here," he said harshly, "you've already been shopping today."

I untied my apron, put on my street shoes and a cardigan and said firmly, "Give me money right now, otherwise I'll scream so loud that the whole house will hear me." The rice was a welcome change in our daily diet. Rice cooked in milk with sugar, cinnamon and melted butter was one of his favorite meals.

My mother was always very nervous around noon when the time approached that he would enter the apartment. She stood in front of the stove, bent over the pots and trembled because the soup would not come to a boil or the meat was not yet tender. Sometimes he was a few minutes late and she made it just in time, but the pressure that he put on her day in and day out was tyranny. It was inhuman. She dropped things simply because she didn't know what to do first.

The noon meal didn't only have to be on the table punctually, but the food had to be just right, not too hot so he could start eating immediately without burning himself, and not too cold either. "I need my nap before I have to throw myself back into my work!" he yelled whenever the food took a few more minutes, and blamed her because her lack of punctuality was costing him precious minutes. He looked at his wristwatch in a theatrical manner, saying that she had no idea about the stacks of files and paperwork that landed on his desk daily, and that he couldn't even begin to explain to her the pressure he was under at work.

When he was thundering around again one day, because the noon meal was not quite ready when he entered our apartment, and began to stalk through the kitchen in his house shoes, which looked really funny, all the while driving his wife to vexation as she stood in front of the hot stove leaning over a pot, stirring the contents with a wooden spoon while her glasses were all steamed up, she suddenly screamed, "You beast, you! Can't you see that I'm at the end of my rope? Why can't you leave me alone? The coals are damp, and the fire is not hot enough, so I can't cook any faster!" The wooden spoon barely missed him, hitting the wall behind him.

That drove him into an even deeper rage, and he lost control. I can still hear his hand slapping her upper arm, for she had learned to duck so he would miss her face to protect her glasses. If she was not fast enough the glasses flew through the kitchen from the sudden hard blow, and I would run to get them and hand them back to her. She sobbed while looking at the frame, and then bent it back into shape ever so carefully. Then she cleaned the glasses with her apron before putting them back on slowly.

What surprised me is that after his outburst she stayed in the kitchen and continued to cook while saying to us children, "Come on, be good, sit down." She never did anything to put an end to his ruthless behavior. Strangely enough, she didn't protect us children from him either. On the contrary, if we didn't do what she wanted from us during the day, she would threaten us saying, "You just wait until your father comes home tonight, I'll tell him how bad you were again, and he'll spank you!"

After years of such rebuke, I began to stutter in the presence of friends, acquaintances and even strangers, my mother confided in me as she did often. I became inhibited in public, and was no longer able to look at people directly. Soon I hardly dared to greet the neighbors anymore, and began to evade anyone I knew. As soon as I recognized someone from afar, I disappeared into a side street, even if it meant taking a detour, and if I could not escape or hide from them, I kept my eyes to the ground, pretending I didn't see them. If a neighbor greeted me anyway, or asked me if they could walk a distance with me, as people would do back then, I told them that I had to hurry because the children were alone at home, and then I ran so fast that no one could keep up with me. I would break into a cold sweat, and pearls of sweat collected on my forehead. Friends who saw me in this state thought I was sick. They gave me good advice and reminded me not to overexert myself, but they had no idea of my real problems.

I could no longer keep up with even the simplest conversation and was always searching for words. I wracked my brain, but couldn't form complete sentences. My voice just gave out. People looked at me in a friendly and invitingly way, waiting patiently for an answer, but I just stood there paralyzed. I trembled at the most well-meaning questions, and if the wind blew cool in the shade, I felt chilly and caught colds easily. People must have thought that I had gone mad. No one could have known that I had a crazy husband, because he was always friendly to everyone and bowed deeply as he raised his hat politely. He was respected in town. He had passed the baccalaureate with honors at the top of his class. This Kurt Bergner is a bright fellow, the people would say, he'll go places, while behind closed doors he beat into me every day that I should not talk to anyone at all. When he came home at noon he questioned me in minute detail about my shopping and whom I had seen in town. At night he wanted to know everything all over again, and would scold me if I admitted that I had spoken with neighbors and acquaintances. But how was I supposed to find out what was going on in town?

I decided I would not tell him everything any longer, but he harassed me until my resistance broke, and didn't stop until I had given him another complete description of the day. These interrogations depressed me and caused me to suffer from nightmares. If I left the apartment while he was home, he wanted to know where I was going and why now and whether it was really necessary, and then he spied on me. Seconds after I stepped out into the staircase, he opened the door quietly just a crack to see if I had indeed gone to the basement or into the garden. He followed me noiselessly. If I talked with a neighbor, he called me back, saying that he had to speak with me right away, that it was urgent, and then waited for me directly behind the door. When I opened the door, he pulled me inside brusquely and furiously hurled insane questions at me. If I didn't return immediately but continued to talk to a neighbor because I knew what he was up to, he came and stood right next to me, his arms folded across his chest, leaning slightly forward while bobbing up and down like a child. He interrupted the conversation and dominated it with his opinions until the others took their leave, irritated. If I was on my way to the cellar to fetch potatoes, he pulled the bucket from me. "I'll get the potatoes," he would say, "but first we must talk." He could hardly contain himself until our apartment door was closed before yelling, "God damn it, you know that you are not to speak with anyone! I can't stand it when you talk to others while I am waiting up here for you. How often must I tell you that?"

"Other men let their wives talk," I defended myself. "None of them would think of running after them or calling them back. Why can't you let me be?"

"I don't care what other men do. When I am home you belong here with me. I don't want you to talk to the other women about us!"

"Don't be ridiculous. Your mother and Irmgard talk to their neighbors all the time, and your father says nothing."

"You are different," he dared to say to me, "you lack judgement, you could misspeak and betray me. I want to know what you are saying, otherwise I don't feel safe. How can I be sure you don't pass on important information when I tell you about my work? Those are state secrets. I really shouldn't be talking to you about them, because we are bound to secrecy."

"Then don't tell me about them, for God's sake! Keep your stupid state secrets to yourself. Besides, I know what's dangerous. I kept quiet under Hitler, too, and I knew a lot from listening to BBC and from Frau Fischer and my visits to you."

"That's just what I mean! It was irresponsible of you to continue to visit the Fischer's. You exposed us all to great danger. You could have been questioned by the authorities."

"They needed me, they needed someone to whom they could pour their hearts out. I learned a lot from what happened to Frau Fischer and Lara. Not everyone remained silent and looked the other way."

"How dare you speak to me like that? I did my duty. I was under oath. I was not allowed to say anything."

"What kind of an oath is that in such a criminal country and for such a war! You kept your eyes and ears closed so you would get through unharmed. You didn't care what happened to others."

"That's not true. I thought of you and the children, so you would be safe!"

"I made sure we were all right. If I had followed your advice and if I had done what Hitler and his cohorts ordered, we would have perished under that hail of bombs."

"Why don't you stop your ignorant blather," he cut me off. "You were in no position to judge the situation. What did you know anyway?"

"Enough!" I screamed finally, "As you can see, we are alive."

Often we fought so loudly that the neighbors could hear us, and Herr Steinbacher from below would knock at their kitchen ceiling with a broomstick, my mother recalled. The other occupants complained to Herr Polenz, the friendly elderly owner of the building, who lived in the apartment to our left. No one dared to approach Kurt directly, they always complained to me only. Even Herr Polenz kept out of Kurt's way. He would ring our doorbell the following morning, after Kurt had left the house and say, "Frau Bergner, you are such a beautiful woman, you are so diligent and you take such good care of your household. Your children are always dressed in lovely clean clothes and are so well behaved. Don't let your husband get the better of you, and don't argue so loudly late at night. Please think of the other occupants. You are disturbing the domestic peace."

I stood hiding behind my mother while Herr Polenz was talking to her, and saw that he was holding a bright red potted cyclamen that he had grown and gave it her when he was finished. My mother was touched and apologized, mumbling a few indistinct words. Another time he brought her a bunch of flowers from his garden or onions, which were hard to come by in those days. Onions in particular were very coveted because they added such a wonderful flavor to the otherwise monotonous meals. We loved my mother's mashed potatoes with fried onions and a bowl of green salad.

After an especially dreadful evening, when my parents had quarreled late into the night, Frau Steinbacher came up to us the next morning after the man had left the house. I was sick and had stayed home from school. My mother, who was already peeling a large bowl of potatoes for the noon meal, dried her hands on her apron when the doorbell rang and walked to the door. From Frau Steinbacher's words I had guessed that she had not come to borrow a cup of sugar or an egg, so I crouched down in the corner next to the cupboard.

The two women entered the kitchen. My mother offered Frau Steinbacher a chair. She sat down at the narrow end of the kitchen table and spoke persuasively to my mother, explaining in a friendly but blunt way that her husband could not take these nightly fights any longer that often dragged on long after midnight. He was suffering from heavy war injuries and phobias, which were made worse by this loud screaming and the heavy steps. Unable to sleep, he was restless all night, keeping her awake as well. "My husband and I would never dishonor each other in such a way," she said, "I would never allow myself be beaten, and should that ever happen, I would divorce him. But my husband would never do that. We love each other far too much. And our children."

My mother didn't say a word. She sat slightly bent forward at the kitchen table, her hands folded in her lap. I can still see her sitting like that. When Frau Steinbacher stopped talking, my mother took off her glasses very slowly, almost awkwardly, and put them carefully down on the table next to the bowl of peeled potatoes. Then she reached for the bottom of her apron and wiped her face with it. Frau Steinbacher put her hand on my mother's left arm. I looked spellbound at the two women. Suddenly, my mother began to rock back and forth slowly and trembled violently, and seconds later she began to weep uncontrollably loudly. I had seen her dissolved into tears before, even when she was all alone, but never in front of a neighbor, and never before did she appear so forsaken. Frau Steinbacher was startled. She had not expected such a reaction, and began to comfort my mother, putting both her arms around her.

"Frau Steinbacher," my mother said at last as she straightened up while drying her eyes with a handkerchief she had taken out of her apron pocket, "if you only knew what you are saying." Her sobbing ebbed down. "I cannot defend myself against my husband. I don't know what to do. I have three small children."

"Why don't you just let him talk and don't say anything in return? That will stop him, it'll take the wind out of his sails," the neighbor suggested.

"Believe me, I would like to keep quiet, but he demands an answer from me. If I say nothing, he runs after me from room to room, and keeps on talking until I cannot stay quiet any longer. And then he starts all over again. He simply won't let go. I've tried to lock myself into the bathroom, but he'll keep banging on the door and won't leave while he alternately threatens me and begs to open the door until I finally unlock it. Then he comes bursting in like a wild animal and starts beating me. If I remain steadfast and don't open the door, he'll sit down on the sofa eventually, waiting coolly until I come out, and then he'll start all over again. Usually it's over the housekeeping money. Before he goes to work he puts it on the kitchen table for me for the day instead of giving me the money at least for a week, because he thinks that I would spend it all the first day. Often he forgets about the money."

Frau Steinbacher stroked over my mother's hair.

"I feel so embarrassed," my mother said, "I'm always afraid that he will hit me because I've done something against his will. He says that I anger him to the point of rage."

"You must get help, Frau Bergner. Talk to Dr Wedemann. Go to him late in the afternoon, when his office hours are over. He'll make time for you, he'll be able to advice you. He's a good man."

"It won't work in the evenings, my husband will want to know where I'm going."

"Tell him you have an appointment because you are not feeling well."

"And what am I to tell the doctor? How am I supposed to begin?"

"Just talk, he'll understand without your having to explain too much, and he'll ask questions. The conversation will flow by itself. Believe me, you are not the only woman. Doctors hear such stories frequently these days. It would be wrong not to go because you are ashamed. The doctor will treat everything confidentially. Besides, the whole house knows what's going on anyway."

I couldn't stand seeing my mother so sad any longer, so I got up, walked over to her and put my hand on her arm.

"Good God, Anne," Frau Steinbacher exclaimed. "I didn't see you! If I had known that you were in the kitchen, I would not have said anything. Well, I have to go now. Tell me what the doctor said, promise me that you'll see him soon. I am worried about you, Frau Bergner."

My mother tried to get up.

"Please stay where you are, I can let myself out."

A few moments later the doorbell rang again, and the neighbor handed my mother a pot of real coffee.

The evening was peacefully for once, my mother continued, so I didn't mention the housekeeping money to Kurt. I wanted to wait for a more favorable time, but the following morning he left the house once more without giving me the daily allotment. I forgot about it with the baby crying while I was preparing breakfast, and again I had to walk the long detour to the post office to get the few marks before I could go shopping. He sat tall behind his desk as I entered the office. He puffed himself up and grinned, making believe he had no idea why I had come.

Once my mother was especially angry with him about his method of handing out the household money daily. While she was shopping she saw that they unloaded a truck full of the best early potatoes right onto the sidewalk in front of the *Konsum,* and people queued up immediately. They had carried out the large scales, but that took too long for the sales woman. She knew how many pounds were on a full fork, and filled them right into shopping bags and sacks as the people held them out to her. My mother stood shaking in front of the pile of potatoes. Such beautiful new potatoes and she couldn't buy any because she had no more money left!

"Why didn't you come to the post office," he asked, "I would have given you enough for the potatoes."

"Walk all the way to you with the heavy shopping bags? What are you thinking?" she screamed with dismay. "I can't leave the baby alone that long either. Besides, my breasts were swollen and hurt, it was high time to nurse her. If only something like that were to happen to you just once! I want the money for a whole week from now on!"

"It'll be gone within two days," he answered unmoved.

"What are you taking me for, you are making me so mad! Did you ever go hungry? Have I ever frittered away money? I want to take care of us in the best way I can, but you attack me from the rear, making things even harder with your mistrust and ignorance."

"Who can tell what you'll spend the money on if you have it all at once? You don't know how to budget."

"Oh God, you devil, you Satan!" she screamed, and tried to shove him away.

He gripped her arm and turned it behind her back so hard that she winced from pain. "I'll teach you how to behave. You and your mother, you frustrate me."

When he noticed me watching he let go of her. She crouched on a chair in front of the table, sobbing silently while rubbing her arm. Then she pulled me close. I was perhaps five and a half, and was wishing him away. Although I couldn't understand everything, I suffered with her, and knew that we could have used the potatoes.

22. The Housekeeping Money

These gloomy days were followed by happier ones with a certain regularity, and are documented in the photos he took on sunny days when we went on long walks. On one of these black and white photos my mother is leaning against the trunk of a birch, smiling into the camera. She is wearing a light white summer dress with a tiny floral print, shoulder pads and a wide skirt with four tiered flounces. Her medium brown hair falls in lovely soft waves to her shoulders. She is in her late twenties, and very attractive and sensual. It is a romantic picture, and I wonder how life really was back then, and how it could have been under different circumstances. As a child I was proud to have her as my mother.

Not long after their fierce arguments about money, my parents planned an all day hike with two other couples. The men also worked at the post office. Since the women would prepare the food to take along, my mother had to ask her husband for extra money. This time he put it promptly on the table. After all, everyone was also invited to supper at our house. Omi had come from Dresden for the weekend to take care of my two younger sisters while I went along on the hike.

One of the men always drew pictures for me, such as children at a fair riding on a carousel or holding balls attached to a string, which I couldn't understand because I had never seen balloons. But I had once seen children on a farm play with a pig's bladder, and so I asked if a balloon was something like that, to which he nodded. He drew fast. The pencil flew over the paper. I liked to watch him, and envied him for his talent.

During the hike, my mother and the other two women would either walk ahead or keep their distance behind the men. The women were engaged in vivid conversations, laughing frequently. He did not like that, he wanted to know what they were talking about, and would have preferred to walk with them. At times he tried to catch up with them, but the men kept him back while teasing him, saying, "Let them be, Kurt, the women want to be amongst themselves, too, now and then." He could not understand that, and was tense, but he had to acquiesce.

I ran to my mother, and she allowed me to walk next to her. Intermittently the conversation came to a halt. My mother lowered her head, muffled her voice and checked to see if the men were at a safe distance before she continued.

At times she turned to the side, blew her nose and blotted her eyes. It was as though black clouds had darkened the blue sky, and I stayed closer to her side, pushing my right hand into her left while trying to understand her words better, whose true meaning did not become fully clear to me until years later.

For the noon meal we rested on a sunny meadow with a brook winding through it. We sat on tree trunks at the edge of the forest amongst the heather and bright yellow-blooming broom and tall grass. While my father was getting water for us to drink from the brook, we unwrapped our sandwiches, hard-boiled eggs, apples, tomatoes and large slices of crumb cake, and laid everything out on two dishtowels that were spread before us on the grass. My father always took many photos, and I still have those black and white prints with jagged edges that poke into my thumb and fingertips. On one of the photos we are bathing in a lake within an area marked off for swimming. On another photo we are hiking along a narrow path.

I also remember walking alongside long stretches of completely desolate autobahn. The straight light gray band attracted me irresistibly, while at the same time I wondered why there were no cars. When I felt no one was looking, I would step out into the middle. The branches of the trees on the center median and along both shoulders reached far over the lanes. Once while I was walking along the right lane, an old black delivery truck came up from behind. I had heard the noise of the motor behind me for a while already without paying attention. Suddenly a loud honking startled me, and I jumped aside. The truck straddled both lanes as it passed me. I followed it with my eyes until it disappeared from sight.

Long after we had left Saxony I looked at a map, and understood that I had been walking on an original stretch of autobahn built by Hitler, which, coming from Dresden, passed by Bischofswerda and continued via Bautzen to Görlitz, and from there across today's border between Germany and Poland on to Breslau.

After our picnic, we continued our hike. The men joined up with the women, and my mother seized the opportunity to talk about the household money.

"Tell me, Hildegund, how does Hermann give you your household money? Once a week, once a month or every day, the way Kurt does it with me?"

"That's nobody's business," my father said sharply, "one doesn't talk about money."

"But I want to talk about it," my mother retorted. "So, Hildegund, tell me, how do you get the money?"

Hildegund looked a little embarrassed, then she said, "Hermann gives me no household money. I withdraw whatever I need from the bank, or he brings it home if it's convenient."

My mother looked at her in amazement.

"Did you hear that, Kurt?" she asked, and continued without waiting for an answer, "Do you want to know what Kurt does with me? He puts the money for the day on the kitchen table for me every morning – if he doesn't forget it – and on Saturdays he gives me something extra for Sunday. How am I supposed to plan for anything if I only have the money for a single day at a time? I can never buy anything in quantity, and I am left in the cold when something is for sale like those wonderful potatoes the other day."

There was an awkward silence. Her husband tried to signal his wife to be quiet, but she did not let herself be intimidated this time. "If you are really our friends, then tell me if what Kurt does is correct?"

"Effi, maybe we should talk about it tonight?" Hermann asked.

"No, Hermann," my mother said firmly. "I want an answer from you right here and now!" And she added while looking toward her husband, "The other day they had full-length slips for sale. I wanted so very much to buy one, but I had no money. So I ran to Kurt as fast as I could to beg for some, but by the time I was back they were all sold out. I've had to mend all my underwear already, and if my mother wouldn't bring me some new pieces now and then, I wouldn't have anything to wear anymore. Those slips were so beautiful," she lamented, and turning to her husband again she said, "You seem to forget that all of our things burned in Dresden!"

After that outburst, my mother stopped as abruptly as she had begun.

"It isn't the way you tell it," he said.

"Oh, how is it then? Are you accusing me of lying? Believe me, Hildegund, it is the way I said it." My mother's voice sounded sharp.

Hildegund said quietly, "Kurt, if it's the way Effi says, you can't do that. You cannot give her the money for only one day at a time. How is she supposed to go shopping for a big family? That's impossible. I would never stand for that. Hermann, you talk to Kurt! From man to man."

Hermann spoke slowly; he seemed to consider every word. "It goes without saying that we both have access to the money in our bank accounts. Hildegund takes care of everything, and so she spends the most money. I am glad that she does the shopping on top of her professional work. Shopping is hard work under the present conditions, and there are only two of us. I can't imagine how much more difficult it must be with three small children as well. Hildegund and I trust each other completely in money matters. The way she plans things, we always have enough at home. Every day doesn't work, Kurt, I have to take Effi's side. Effi is such a great housewife, and works very hard. You won't find such an efficient and competent woman again anywhere, so don't make it harder for her than it already is."

My father said nothing that afternoon when he realized that he was outvoted. I ran away, walking along the edge of the forest, and observed them from afar. In those days the forests were swept clean. Not even the smallest branch was lying on the ground because people carried everything home. They had even broken off the dead branches from the trees as high they could reach since they made excellent kindling wood.

For supper my mother had prepared a large bowl of potato salad and two bowls of herring salad, one with herring tidbits and lots of onions and one with herring in tomato sauce. We ate it with bread and butter, and so the evening ended happily. My mother felt exuberant and entertained us splendidly. They all praised her for having laid out such a rich table, agreeing that she had outdone herself once again. He sunned himself in the praise given to his wife, helped himself generously, and allowed the evening to end harmoniously after everyone had left. Even when they were in bed at last, I heard her clear happy voice and his darker one. From then on he did give her the household money for an entire week. Not very long after that day, Hildegund and Hermann fled to the west.

23. Abortion

My mother never conformed completely to her husband's will in other areas either. As Frau Steinbacher had suggested, she did gather all her courage one day and went to see the doctor, who had already helped her so much since we came to live in that small town.

Dr. Wedemann was an elderly gentleman. His house was a refuge for women who were alone in their need, and who came for advice and some good words, but older people also trusted him. He not only treated their illnesses but also listened to their worries, and counseled and encouraged them. For special female patients he opened his back door after dark. He never sent anyone away.

After the war, Dr. Wedemann found himself facing a completely new set of problems. Curfew was the least of the chicaneries. Medicine, injections, even cotton, antiseptic gauze and bandaging material were hard to come by during the Soviet occupation, or no longer available at all, and because he wanted to keep his private practice, he was discriminated against with the supply of the most necessary items. "If one of these days things don't work anymore, I'll close my practice," I overheard him say to my mother.

She took me along often, although I didn't understand why she went to him until she told me about it years later. One particular visit I remember very well. I was about seven or eight when the doctor invited my mother and me into his elegant library next to his office. The ceiling had a beautiful stucco design, especially around the gleaming brass candelabra. When my mother noticed how intently I was looking at the stucco, she said, "The ceilings in our apartment in Dresden had the same rich stucco decorations." I had learned a new word, and faintly remembered something from long ago. A tall window with cream-colored lace curtains and dark green velvet drapes faced the garden. The heavy dark brown furniture and deep leather chairs impressed me. "Walnut, everything real leather and walnut," my mother said in admiration when the doctor stepped into his office to get something for her, which she quickly dropped into her handbag. On the armrests and the headrest the surface of the leather had cracked into hundreds of tiny squares and rectangles. I let my hand glide over it and felt the broken leather with my fingertips. In front of the window stood a heavy desk behind which the doctor would sit to write something down. Now and then he would get up, take three measured steps to the huge bookcase, whose doors were of amber-colored glass, unlock a door and reach for one of the heavy books bound in leather or linen with gold lettering. He would hold it in his left hand while leaving unhurriedly through the pages until he had found what he was looking for. Sometimes he would reach for a second book. It seemed to me that he did all of this without paying any attention to us, and when he was finished he showed my mother a picture in the book and explained something to her, to which she barely nodded.

After having helped me twice already, I was again close to despair, and felt embarrassed to go back to Dr. Wedemann so soon, my mother said to me as we were sitting together talking about those years in East Germany. Dr. Wedemann looked at me with piercing eyes that made me feel very strange indeed, and while stressing every syllable, he explained that I had to make absolutely clear to my husband that with my weakened physical condition and the unbalanced nutrition and lack of vitamins in our diet in those days, every additional pregnancy would be critical, if not fatal, my mother continued, becoming visibly agitated. I told Dr. Wedemann that I didn't know how to talk to my husband about it, to which he repeated, "You cannot risk another pregnancy, Frau Bergner. Besides, three children are enough in today's times. Think about the future, when the children are bigger. Your husband must wait with intercourse until you have regained your strength. At the very least he must make sure that the seminal emission does not go inside of you. Perhaps you should bring him along next time, I'll talk to him."

I explained to Dr. Wedemann that he would not come with me if I disclosed to him why he wanted to see him, and if he knew the reasons for my visits, he would forbid me to come again. He insisted on his rights several times a week. Whenever the desire came over him I had to go to the bedroom with him. He was of the opinion that he was getting for himself only what every wife owed her husband. Even in the middle of the night he wouldn't leave me alone, no matter how exhausted I was or how deeply I was sleeping. I couldn't scream or fight him off because you children and the neighbors would hear me. There was no point in pleading with him, because at such moments he was not himself. He would have put his hand over my mouth and hurt me if I had tried to push him aside or tried to dissuade him. I had to let him do his business whenever he felt like it. Sometimes I didn't even really wake up, and he was done by the time I came to. When he was finished, I got up and staggered to the bathroom praying that it was not too late. I felt disgusted with my own body, and I prayed that God would show some mercy and help me, and not let me get pregnant again. When I returned to bed, I heard him breath calmly. He was fast asleep again, as if nothing had happened, while I was worried sick.

The doctor had listened to my explanations dispassionately, my mother recalled, and finally interrupted me saying, "Frau Bergner, God has nothing to do with it. You must be realistic and think of your health!" Then he stepped behind his desk, opened one of the drawers and pulled out a package. He often reached into his drawers to get little bottles, tiny paper bags and small jars. He helped wherever he could with medications and tonics. He filled out prescriptions for juices, because we had no garden, and for ointments to heal my raw hands caused by doing the laundry with the harsh soaps, and he prescribed pain pills and quinine for fever as well as laxatives, and told me which herbal teas I should ask for in the drugstore to soothe my nerves and be able to sleep better.

I glanced at the package he was holding out to me, and was shocked when I saw what it was. I wanted to give it back to him and almost stuttered as I said, "Dr. Wedemann, I cannot take that, my husband refuses to use condoms. He claims that it robs him of his feelings." To this day I don't know how I managed to utter these sentences. I had never spoken such words in the presence of a man, my mother said blushing. But Dr. Wedemann was not impressed. Instead he repeated sternly, "Tell your husband that this is pure nonsense. It's all in his head. He can do it if he wants to." I was unable to explain to the doctor how powerless I felt.

After Dr. Wedemann had finished his speech, he dismissed us in a friendly manner, took us to the front door, unlocked it, and my mother and I whisked out. I heard him lock the door behind us. We hurried silently through the streets in the evening dusk. The lamps in the houses lit up the interior of the rooms. Here and there, the drapes had not been pulled closed yet, and I could see the people inside going about their work. A woman stepped up to the window as we were passing by and pulled the curtains closed impatiently. Our eyes met for a second, and I seemed to detect a hostile expression in her eyes, as if it was my fault that I could look into her living room. I wondered how the people lived, what they were doing, and whether they could perhaps surmise where we had just been. My mother's eyes were fixed on the cobblestone pavement, and she was not paying any attention to what was going on around her. As we hurried along the streets it could happen that she forgot to greet an acquaintance and was startled by the "good evening," which she felt was extended in an overly friendly yet reproachful tone.

You must understand, Anne, that I had already tried to explain to Kurt during the war that two children were enough in such insecure times. His response was that we have to be careful, but that he needed me especially right now more than ever, that he had been thinking of me day and night out in the field, that the war had only been bearable because he had me, and without that he would not have been able to endure it. He was in a frenzy as he spoke, and appeared to be mad while I choked with fear, unable to get a single word out.

On the weekends it could happen that I had to send you children out to play, no matter how cold it was outside or if it was raining. You had no weatherproof shoes and no good protection against the rain, but at such moments he didn't care, because he wanted me. He was shaking all over if I didn't get you out fast enough. When I was finally able to call you back inside, you were frozen stiff and your noses were running. Once in a while you rang a neighbor's doorbell. Frau Rosen, a very kind elderly woman, always took you in if she was home. I think she guessed what was going on, and I felt ashamed when I couldn't find you and had to ring the neighbors' doorbells. They let me know in no uncertain terms that it was irresponsible to send you outside in such bad weather.

If I didn't return with you right away, Kurt went crazy. I couldn't tell him that you went to the neighbors or he would have beaten you, so I had to come up with excuses, but at least you were warm and dry. At other times you walked away when it took too long, and I caught up with you on the way to his parents' house.

I recall vividly how the three of us stood in front of our house, and how I suggested to my sisters that we should ring Frau Rosen's doorbell. She always invited us in, helped us take off our coats, caps and gloves while asking all kinds of questions. I had a bad conscience while sitting in her kitchen because my mother didn't know where we were. Frau Rosen gave us cookies and peppermint tea, and when we were done she brought out her huge box of toys.

I was already trembling before you girls had left the apartment, my mother went on agitated. At times I thought of running away, but how could I leave? I had you girls to think of. There was no place for us to go, not anywhere. He dragged me into the bedroom, pushed me down on the bed, and pulled off my panties himself because it didn't go fast enough. He didn't care if my silk stockings got torn, so I took them off quickly myself. Just imagine, I took off my stockings so he wouldn't ruin them, while I didn't even want to be with him! If I didn't come willingly, he used force and grabbed me so hard that my arms were covered with bruises. Even when I didn't feel well he pointed out that it was my duty, after all we were married, and besides, how much longer was he supposed to wait? He insisted that he loved me and needed me, otherwise he couldn't concentrate and work right.

"And what does your behavior have to do with love?" I asked him. Instead of answering me, he smacked me in the face so hard I could still see the marks of his fingers on my left cheek hours later. He didn't even leave me alone during my period, and if I didn't quickly put a large towel over the sheet or when he disheveled everything in his crazy haste, everything was smeared with blood that would run down my legs and drip onto the floor when I got up. I took the sheet off quickly so that the blood would not seep through the blanket that was covering the mattress, and I washed out everything under cold running water. Getting bloodstains out was difficult in those days because of the poor quality of the washing powder, if there was any. Often we had to use hard soap, which did not lather, stank, and was rough on the hands. The women even hung up their cotton sanitary napkins on the clothesline so the sun would bleach them. They didn't care if the men saw them, but I always felt embarrassed for them. Everyone in the house knew when they had their period.

"For heaven's sake, Mutti, you really made it hard for yourself. What do you want to do in such hard times? Besides, we learned in school that the sun doesn't only bleach things, it also disinfects. I bet that except for you no one thought much about the pads."

"I'm not so sure about that. The men often made suggestive remarks."

"So what, men are stupid anyway. I remember seeing the sanitary napkins on the clothesline. Once, when we were both looking out of the kitchen window, I asked you what they were. The whole line was full of them, each of them secured with a huge wooden clothespin. That left an impression on me, the way dozens of them hung on the line. You said they were diapers. Surprised, I asked, diapers for a baby? But you gave no answer. That wasn't right either."

"You were still so small."

"I was old enough to ask about them. You could have simply said that women need these things."

"And if you had asked further questions?"

"You would have thought of something. Besides, I didn't believe your answer about the diapers, and I'd heard people talk about worse things. You were always so agitated how the women could hang them up like that, visible to the whole world. 'The women have no shame,' you said indignantly, and this got me really curious. Anyway, it had nothing to do with impropriety or a lack of shame."

"Leave it be, Anne," my mother begged, but then she continued to tell me more.

It had been a very dull day when I knew I had to go to Dr. Wedemann again. I entered through the back door as always, and when he saw me in the waiting room, he most likely guessed the reason for my visit, and took me to the library, whispering that I should come after hours in future. I listened to his steps as he walked away and opened the door of the practice, then closed it behind him.

And there I was, sitting in the dark, alone with my thoughts, shaking from fear. I didn't dare to turn on a lamp.

It seemed like an eternity until I heard his footsteps, and a moment later the door to the library opened. We hurried into his practice without switching on the light. He made sure that the drapes were closed completely. No one was to know that there was still someone with him. Then he took care of me quickly in the dimly lit room. He seemed uneasy and rushed more than usual. When I looked at him questioningly, he said tersely that he suspected that someone had denounced him and he was being watched, and that he was not going to do it for a while. It was my third abortion.

Right after the procedure I felt that something had not quite gone the way it should have. The pain was much greater. Dr. Wedemann warned me that I would bleed more heavily, and that I should lie down right away at home so that the blood could coagulate faster. He gave me two packages of cotton, which I put into the shopping bag I had taken along. I was afraid that the blood might run down my legs on my walk home, and put an extra layer of cotton into my panties.

"Remember, Frau Bergner, this was a miscarriage! And take care of yourself, go to bed right away, put a pillow under the hollow of your knees and drink a lot of juice and tea." The doctor opened the back door, and there I was, all by myself. I had stomach cramps and felt like vomiting.

I had barely gone a few steps, when I saw a figure appear from behind a bush. I was scared to death, then I recognized Kurt. I had left the house before he had come home from work, and was not expecting him. Especially since I had not told you, Anne, where I was going, only that you had to take care of your two sisters and that I would be back soon. Kurt grabbed my right arm, and hurried me along while driveling about how worried he had been about me. I complained that I could not run that fast, besides I had the awkward feeling that the sanitary napkin and cotton were slipping with every step. I dared not moan, but would have liked to lean on his arm. He continued to hold my upper arm so tightly that it hurt. I tried to shake it off, and when I didn't succeed, I hissed, "Take your hand off of me, you are hurting me!" He continued down the road like a maniac until I stopped and said, "Either you let go of me and we walk normally, or I'll sit down on this wall right here. Haven't you noticed that I have no strength left?"

That worked. His let go of my arm, and I could put mine on his for support.

At home I fell onto my bed completely exhausted after I had washed myself off. When I sat on the toilet, the blood came running out of me dark red. I asked Kurt to bring me a cup of tea and a wet facecloth that I wanted to put on my forehead, because I felt dizzy. It took forever until he came with the tea, placing the cup and saucer in my hand, then he disappeared again. I couldn't drink much of it because I could hardly keep myself up, so I put the cup on the nightstand and let myself fall back into the pillows. I closed my eyes as a deep tiredness enveloped me. Suddenly he stormed back into the bedroom and said, "Get up and get dressed; we are going to the movies."

I felt strangely light-headed, like in a delirium, when I heard him say again, "We are going to the movies right now."

I lay very still and whispered, "Please leave, I am not feeling well." But he continued to besiege me. I could hear his words, but did not understand their meaning, and said, "I am so cold. Come, lay down next to me, please, so I'll get warm, or bring me a hot-water bag."

Instead, he began to shake me, repeating all the while, "We must go to the cinema so no one will become suspicious!"

"Suspicious of what?" I asked bewildered.

"Of what you just did."

I didn't understand what he wanted, and said, "I cannot get up, you go without me," blinking at him drowsily. He was white as a sheet. Suddenly he took both my arms and pulled me out of bed with such a jerk that I almost fell on the floor. I barely came to sit on the edge of the bed. Then he threw my clothes at me, my coat, gloves, scarf and hat. As I looked up I noticed that he was fully dressed to go out. He left the bedroom and returned with my shoes, and said, "Come on, hurry up, or do you want to endanger all of us?"

"Why do you want to go to the cinema?" I asked finally.

"So that people will see that everything is all right," he barked.

"If I go with you, everyone will see that I am sick. I can hardly stand up," I answered, but he forced me to come along.

On the street I could barely keep myself up, I felt weak in my legs and staggered. I could have doubled over from pain. Kurt had to carry me more than I walked. When we were sitting in the cinema, I felt the warm blood running out of me and how it got cold. I felt faint; it came over me in waves. I closed my eyes and almost slid off the seat. He pushed me and whispered. "Sit up straight, what are the people supposed to think if you are lying half over me?

Someone behind us hissed, "Quiet!"

To this day I don't know what film we saw. On the way home the cold crept up my legs, and I was completely soaked. At home, I sank down on the bed and didn't get up again. He had to undress me, bring me clean things and wash my bloody underwear. I was too weak to care anymore.

Two days after the abortion I got an infection and fever of which I almost died. When the fever climbed higher and higher, he got scared. He went everywhere looking for help, except he didn't say why I was so sick. When my health worsened, he finally went to Dr. Wedemann, who came after office hours. He had been expecting complications, but he was very surprised that it was so bad and how weakened I was from the large loss of blood, and reproached me for not having sent my husband sooner. After the doctor urged me to tell him exactly what happened, I finally divulged the truth. He held my hand mumbling something about irresponsible behavior, and that there were no good drugs available. Then he told Kurt to give me fruit juices and grated carrots so that I would have enough vitamins, as well as herbal teas from the pharmacy to sooth me, adding, "Herr Bergner, your wife must stay in bed if she is to get well again." As he wrote a prescription for quinine to lower the fever, I was wondering who would prepare the tea for me, because Kurt was so inept at everything concerning the household. He either made the tea too weak or it was bitter and half cold, because he had let it steep too long.

Finally Dr. Wedemann turned to me and repeated in Kurt's presence that another pregnancy could cost me my life. He wrote a second prescription, which he handed to Kurt saying, "Try to get this from the west. You do have relatives or friends over there?"

Hermann Dietz sent us the medicine along with lemons, coffee and chocolate, but by the time the package finally arrived, I was already feeling better again.

When my father had gone to the pharmacy the next morning, I watched my mother drag herself moaning from her bed through the hall to the bathroom. She crawled more than she walked, and tried to hold onto things whenever possible, sighing and lamenting. I suffered as I watched her, and did not know what to do. When she was back in bed, I said, "Mutti, we must tell Omi to come."

"Oh, Anne, Omi can't help me either," my mother whispered.

"Yes she can, and she can cook for us and be good to us," I insisted.

Two days later Omi did come. He had telephoned her factory. I knew then that everything would be well again.

Omi couldn't stay long that time, my mother interrupted me, but she did come every Saturday afternoon to help out with the housework. Saturday evening she soaked the laundry in the kettle in the washhouse, and washed it Sunday morning. Sunday afternoon she took the train back to Dresden, and he had to hang up the laundry. I watched him from the window, and had to explain to him time and again that he had to hang the sheets and tablecloths straight on the line, so that they would not be pulled out of shape. He was much taller than I, and yet he went about it so clumsily that he barely got the laundry on the line without dragging it on the ground. Even so he made believe housework was child's play, something that he, a man, could do on the side, when in reality he knew nothing about it. He did little during those weeks except sweep the kitchen floor and polish the shoes regularly. He was not even capable of making mashed potatoes.

When Dr. Wedemann came by again, he wanted to know how I could have gone to the cinema the same night. Even in retrospect he was worried that I could have become so sick that they would have to take me to the hospital, and then would have found out the real reason for my illness. I didn't want to answer, but finally admitted that my husband had forced me. How can your husband force you to do anything, Dr. Wedemann wanted to know, shaking his head.

After the doctor had left, I was once again alone with my worries about the three of you. What was to become of you if something should happen to me? I was so weak that I was soaked in sweat several times a day. I suffered from anxiety attacks and felt dizzy when I tried to sit up in bed.

Frau Steinbacher was the only one who helped me. She put a cooked meal on the kitchen table every day, came into the bedroom, opened the window and said to you, Anne, "We must let some fresh air in. Close the window again after a while." She also brought me tea, helped me change my nightgown and supported me on my way to the toilet. She was my guardian angel. If it had not been for her, things might have ended in a bad way.

Years later I finally understood that my mother had not been 'sick', although she had been close to death. She was very susceptible to all kinds of illnesses during those years in East Germany, and continued to be critically ill often. She would lie in bed for days, and if we talked to her she barely opened her eyes and could hardly lift her head. I became scared because I feared that she might die. I sneaked to the bedroom and stopped on the threshold for several minutes before I dared to walk to the foot of the bed and looked at her intently until she noticed me. Her eyes closed, her hands limp on the blanket, she whispered to me what I was supposed to do. Her brown hair lay in soft waves around her white face.

Two months went by until I had regained enough strength to take care of you and the household again, my mother explained. I got up in the mornings against the doctor's advice to cook the noon meal and look after the most urgent things. All Kurt had to do was get breakfast and prepare supper for you. He sat in his office all his life and never knew how hard housework was. Just to get three meals for five people on the table each day was an achievement. I did my best to make them nourishing and tasty. He wanted variety when nothing was available, as if there had ever been variety at his parents' house! We had many blackouts during the day in the early years after the war because the factories were supplied first. Even the gas was turned off frequently. If they announced it ahead of time, I cooked before daybreak and wrapped the hot soup or a casserole into blankets, set it into my bed and covered it with the feather bed so the food would still be warm at noon.

Whenever we had these conversations, I asked my mother why she put up with so much from her husband.

"You have no idea," she would say. "How could I have defended myself against him? What should I have done when he wanted something from me in bed even when I was exhausted and afraid of yet another pregnancy? If I shoved him away, things only got worse. He pushed my upper body down with his left forearm across my chest so hard I could have screamed from pain. He pressed his sharp elbow so deep into me that it stabbed me like a dagger between my ribs. With his left arm he held both my hands and forced my arms down behind my head, then he pushed apart my thighs with his legs and knees. And all the time he panted and squeaked, "I love you, your body is holy to me, I cannot live without you, I need you, you are the only one, you are my goddess." When he was done, he let himself fall on top of me so I almost suffocated, and I had to scream at him to get off of me. Although I could hardly stand up straight from cramps because he had penetrated me so hard and deeply, I got up, ran to the bathroom and washed myself out. I was desperate. He just wouldn't leave me alone. For years he took me and forced me."

Sometimes she startled herself because she was telling me things that a mother does not normally tell her daughter. Slowly I began to understand how miserable life had been at home. Even so, my mother continued to take care of the household in an exemplary way. The meals were ready and the table set when he returned from work. During the summer there was always a vase with flowers in the middle of the table, and during the winter it was decorated with a small pot of bright red cyclamen or pine branches and a candle. And so there were times when life was like that of any average family, and we learned how to present things in a pleasing way, and understood that even the simplest meal tasted better at a well-set table. My mother usually had a surprise for desert, like a vanilla pudding with fruit, or blueberries we had gathered in the forest, or cream of wheat with cherries, a large bowl of plum or apple compote, depending on the season, and of course cake or a plate of cookies. But even during such moments he might grumble about her extravagance, and that she was spoiling us children with the sweets.

"He always managed to ruin those happy moments," my mother said, "before he finished his plate in a hurry and took a second helping. He loved deserts."

24. The Minister and the Priest

By the summer of 1946, we had settled down as well as possible in this small town. New surroundings and events supplanted old memories. Instead of the Große Garten and the meadows along the Elbe river, we had the vast open countryside around the town. My mother was very athletic and swam a thousand meters every morning in the nearby public pool as soon as it was opened for the season. On most days she went early in the morning while we were still asleep, and was back before it was time to wake us up and get us ready for school. During summer vacation, we children were at the public pool every day from early morning until supper. Year after year we spent the most beautiful summer days there, or so it seemed to us because there we could forget about the difficulties of everyday life and the troublesome political developments.

In the afternoons, when her husband was back at the office, my mother joined us. I was happy when I saw her coming in her upright springy step, and I ran with her to the large pool with the five-meter diving tower, sat down at the edge and let my feet dangle into the water while I watched her. I was not the only one. She attracted the eyes of many young men. She looked wonderful in her well-fitting bathing suit, and showed off her figure in her two-piece sun suit after she had swum several laps. She was a great swimmer and basked in the general admiration. The men applauded spontaneously, spurred her on and called out, "Come on girl, show us what you can do, let's race each other, the winner gets a kiss!" They didn't want to believe that I was her daughter. She swam to me and wanted to lure me in. She laughed and was in high spirits, and the two vertical lines on her forehead above her nose had disappeared.

Those bright summers remained vivid in my memory, and as I look back, my mother appeared transfigured. I wonder if I am the only one who knows how things were back then during these endless, hot, sun-filled summer afternoons at the public swimming pool, and how happy she was.

On Sundays, our family went hiking for the day. The mood was subdued from the very beginning, because he always found fault with something. The sandwiches were not ready on time, the apples not washed and dried, he couldn't find the rucksack, and where was the blanket, where were the tin dishes and the pocketknife? "You are incapable," he scolded his wife, as he ran seemingly aimlessly from room to room, looking for things that he couldn't find. "You can't even plan a Sunday excursion. I was looking forward to it all week as I was sitting at my desk with work piled high, and was picturing how beautiful the early morning hours would be, and then we can't get away. We've already missed the first train. Why is nothing ever in its place?"

"The first train is too early, you said that yourself, and the day is still long enough," my mother replied.

"But it gets hot at noon, I want to have arrived by then. Why didn't you prepare things last night?" he shot back.

"I worked uninterruptedly all day yesterday. I went shopping, cooked dinner and baked a cake for today, and I helped the children with their homework. After supper I had to iron six shirts for you for next week. Two of them I had to mend first. When should I have prepared for today? Can you explain that to me?"

"You are never organized," was his stereotypical answer.

"I see! I guess it doesn't count that I got up at five this morning to cook soup for tonight so that we can eat right away when we get home tired and hungry."

My mother was braiding my hair as she talked. I sat on a kitchen chair, and the more he complained, the more she pulled and tugged at my hair. I whined and held my hair. She became impatient and complained, "Your hair is so straight, it always slips away and doesn't frame your face in nice curls like Christine's." He looked at me and scolded me for not wearing the right shoes.

When we left the apartment at last, he took such long steps that we had to run to keep up with him. We stumbled on the cobblestones, fell and scraped our hands and knees. He scolded us, pushing us ahead of him, yelling at us to keep our eyes open and pay attention as we walked, and to lift our feet so our shoes wouldn't get scuffed. We marched through town feeling depressed. We were not allowed to laugh or speak or pick up a bright piece of broken glass or a temptingly colorful pebble. We did not dare to reach for a blossom or the berries on the bushes we passed, nor look left or right. Instead we kept our eyes to the ground, hardly aware of where we were going. I was ashamed in front of the people we encountered, and would have preferred to go to my grandparents'. At the station we were hurried along again, and ordered to go to the gate and wait there for him; he would follow with the tickets. Finally we were sitting on the train, confused and downcast, as we rode into the open countryside. I didn't want to meet his eyes, and so looked out of the window. As I saw the landscape fly by I began to enjoy the train ride, but all too soon we arrived at our destination and had to get off.

As the years passed, I began to feel desperate, and although Dr. Wedemann was always there for me, giving me mostly practical advice, I began to doubt him. Eventually I took a step that I had pondered in my heart for some time, and went to the pastor. Perhaps he would be able to help.

After Kurt had left for work and you were on your way to school, I took Bettine and Viktoria to a neighbor one morning and stole myself to the parish house of our Lutheran pastor.

Like a sinner, I thought to myself, as my mother was talking.

When I rang the doorbell, the pastor's wife opened, and I was suddenly so flustered that I could only stammer, "May I come in, please?" Without giving her a chance to step aside, I squeezed past her into the dark corridor. The woman looked at me surprised, and shut the door behind me. I was glad to be inside because I did not want to be seen by anyone. There is so much slander in small towns. People talk ill of others without giving it much thought and pass on half-truths. Today I know that a parish house is like a reservoir for all kinds of gossip. I thought I was safe there but I was so naïve and inexperienced in such matters.

The pastor's wife led me into her husband's study where she pointed to the chair at the table near the door. Then she walked away with fast, short steps and called her husband. I shivered in the coolness of the room, which didn't just come from the cold walls, and wrapped my cardigan more tightly around me. I would have liked to get up and leave, but it was already too late. It was an unpleasant situation. I heard a door squeak that hadn't closed completely, and had the feeling that she was planning to eavesdrop. The pastor entered the room, motioned me to stay seated and shook my hand with hasty politeness saying, "Good morning, Frau Bergner, I am glad that you found your way to us. What brings you here?"

His stilted manner of speech sounded strangely pious. I tried to find the right words, and said something about being forced in bed, that he was imposing his will on me, and that I didn't know how to go on. I was about to explain things in more detail because he was looking at me with such a strange expression, but suddenly he waved his hand impatiently, stopped me in the middle of a sentence and began to talk. I heard his voice, but didn't understand what he was saying. His face became blurred before my eyes.

"I cannot understand you, Herr Pfarrer," I said.

That's when he said firmly, "My dear Frau Bergner, why don't we put it all into the Lord's hands right here and now. Let us not tempt the Lord by talking too much about our problems. Remember that the heavenly father knows everything already, and does not need to hear it again. You must trust the Lord our God completely in your marriage as well. He will always be with you and give you the strength to carry the load that he has given you to bear. Your family is so blessed that your husband returned from the war."

That was the end of our conversation. His words sounded like utter mockery. I wanted to get up and run out of the room, but instead I stayed put like a sheep. I had hoped that he would help me in some way and show me that he took me seriously, so I would no longer feel so forsaken.

I was still sitting on the chair, paralyzed, when I heard the pastor say, "Frau Bergner, let us pray now and ask for strength and protection, and for his benevolence." He folded his hands theatrically. The subservient tone of his voice sounded disingenuous. I could tell that the situation did not suit him. And I had actually thought that such a man of God could help me! I didn't feel like praying, so I kept quiet. He didn't notice that I was not participating. Finally he quoted the verse, "I can do all things through Christ, who strengtheneth me," and explained to me that God leaves no one alone, we simply must want to believe and trust him. I said goodbye quickly, because I felt as though I was suffocating, and ran off.

"Your problems surpassed his imagination. The doctor was the better counselor and a true friend," I pointed out.

"And what about practicing charity?" she asked pointedly.

"A noble idea, nothing more," I said.

After the debacle with the pastor, my mother visited a fortuneteller. This woman did not prophesy her the usual things like a long life and happiness in marriage, or a new love and riches, but that she would die young. From then on, my mother foretold us her early death often, especially when she was unhappy, when her husband asked things of her that went beyond her capabilities, or when we children would not obey her. Her words upset me greatly. She spoke quietly and with an almost clairvoyant presentiment, as if our disobedience were to blame for her early death. I believed her, and at the same time I didn't. Perhaps she used the prophecy to compel us to obedience, but I wonder if she was aware of the effect her words had on me when I was a small child. The words, "I shall die young," produced strange associations within me. They reminded me of stories in old children's books from the 19th century, where the mother had died much too young of an indefinable fever, leaving her helpless little children behind in poverty. For my mother, however, this prophecy was like a promise, in which she believed for decades, clinging to it steadfastly during especially bleak times. The knowledge of an early death seemed to ease the burden of daily life for her. She used the prediction of an early demise to create an island for herself where she could retreat. Evidently it was a comfort to her that this man would not be able to touch her anymore in a not too distant future. Whenever he mocked her or when she felt misunderstood she said, "I won't grow old, I know that I shall die young." She even told her doctors about it because it seemed to explain her frequent illnesses. They contradicted her vehemently and called it superstition and irresponsible nonsense, at which she felt offended. The homeopath, however, took her more seriously and agreed with her, repeating that she would indeed not live a long life, especially not if she stayed with her husband.

Today I am almost inclined to believe the fortuneteller was no dilettante after all. On the contrary, she was wise enough to understand that my mother would not find what she was looking for because she was not going to go get it on her own. And perhaps the fortuneteller was clever enough to detect in my mother's demeanor and speech an unfulfilled romantic desire and a certain weakness, and so, with her prediction of an early death, she made things easier for the otherwise strong woman. She showed her a way out, which would either come about through malnutrition, infectious diseases, or overwork, or my mother would live long enough and forget it all some day. However, it is also possible that it was just a simple coincidence she had encountered this woman who had dished up a blatant lie for her.

My mother had stayed away from the Catholic church to honor her father's wishes, but when the meager words from the protestant pastor proved to be less than helpful, she looked to the church of her childhood for consolation. The priest greeted her in a friendly manner, and was pleased to help this lovely young woman regain her equilibrium. The mass with all its rituals, the Ave Maria and the rosary were not quite as familiar to her as the sermon, the Lord's supper and the hymns of the Lutheran church, but they fulfilled her longing for mystical love.

During the Advent season she once took me along to the Catholic church. They had set up a beautiful manger that was altogether different from the carved wooden figures and candleholders from the Erzgebirge, the local Iron Ore Mountains, that stood in our Lutheran church. We entered the Catholic church stealthily as my mother held my hand tightly. I had never been in that church, but I knew that Omi went there very early on Sunday mornings while we were still asleep. Sometimes she would quickly disappear into the church when we were walking through town. She left me standing outside and asked me to wait for her and not run away because she just wanted to say hello to Mary.

And now my mother went there with me. It was dim inside. The smell of incense filled the church. She led me down along the left side to the manger and began to explain to me the life-size figures from the Christmas story. Her voice sounded different, solemn and full of expectation. I found the restrained explanations peculiar, because I knew the story and whom the various figures represented. After a while my eyes got used to the light, and I saw people kneeling devoutly in the pews, when a young priest came toward us from the other side of the church. His gown impressed me. It was so fancy, not at all like the simple black one that the pastor wore at our church. The priest greeted my mother in a most friendly manner while looking at me lovingly.

I noticed a trembling go through my mother as she gazed at him. Then she said to me, "Wait here for me, I'll be back shortly," and walked away with the priest. I looked around some more, admired the stained glass windows, and then left the church. I had to wait for her a long time, and my feet got cold in the falling powdery snow that covered everything, and reminded me of the fluffy powdered sugar on top of the *Dresdener Christstollen* that we ate every afternoon.

I never asked my mother what she was looking for in the Catholic church or why she took me along on that day. However, I do remember clearly the deep disagreement between my parents afterward, from which I seemed to understand that she went there to look for help from a man of her own age.

Her husband raged. The word "treason" fell, and he screamed, "I know how you are! I forbid you once and for all to go there again. How dare you talk about our marriage and other intimate matters? That's nobody's business!" I expected him to loose his composure and beat all of us, one after the other. He stood in front of his wife, demanding obedience and a confession. She was supposed to repent, ask for his forgiveness and swear to be faithful, but she would not speak. He hit her in the face. She took it in silence. He went on deep into the night, with an interruption at the supper table as we sat at our places, stared at our plates and swallowed down our food, not daring to even look at each other. Furtively I grimaced toward my sister, who gurgled with laughter. He leaned toward her across the table yelling, "Quiet!" I took a sidelong glance at him. He looked grim, and I lost respect for him a little more with every passing day.

My mother appeared so very unhappy, and swallowed her food in silence, while mine almost got stuck in my throat. She was afraid of him. When I finally understood that, something broke inside of me that never healed again. I knew instinctively that she was at his mercy, just like we girls, and that she trembled like we did. She didn't seem like my mother at that moment, but more like an older sister who had to submit to him, and who had to obey him and do what he demanded of her. When I saw her sitting across the table in all her unhappiness, her face became blurred, but I suppressed the tears, because if he had seen them he would have forced me to say why I was crying, and I would not have known what to say. I suddenly realized I had no words yet for that, and she would not have had the strength to stand by me and protect me. Today I would call it a witch trial.

That summer and winter I seized every opportunity to get out of the house, especially when he was home, even if it meant that I would have to do some work. I was barely six years old when I helped lift the heavy wicker baskets full of wet laundry into the handcart and pull it to the meadow behind the house, where I would help my mother spread out the sheets and tablecloths on the lawn for bleaching. If the laundry dried too fast, I would water it with a watering can. Bright white laundry, hanging from clotheslines for the world to see, was synonymous with being a good housewife. Women who had gray sheets and underwear were looked upon as lazy. Other women whispered behind their backs and pitied their husbands. It could happen that my mother would take a less than white old sheet to the attic for drying because she feared the judgement of the neighbors.

To me it always seemed like a miracle to see spots lighten up and disappear from the laundry under the rays of the sun. In winter, the laundry froze on the clotheslines. The towels and sheets hung stiff as boards on the lines. We were not to touch it, or worse yet bend it, because then the fabric broke and got worn faster at the creases. And even if the sun did not shine, the laundry dried slowly during the noon hours. When we brought the ice-cold laundry into the apartment, it always smelled so wonderfully fresh, and the scent lingered for hours.

As long as we lived in Bischofswerda, Omi came once a month to help with the 'big' laundry. She was so small, even fragile, and yet she was very stalwart and strong-willed. My mother was also slender-boned and not exactly tall, and I wondered where both women got their physical strength and tenacity.

In front of the wash tub on the floor was a large wooden grate, so that they didn't have to stand in the water on the cold stone floor. The tub stood on sawhorses in front of the two small windows that looked out into the back yard, but were steamed up most of the time. The whole washhouse was filled with white-gray steam. I could hardly make out anything when I entered, and called out to my mother and grandmother. I can still see them bent over the washboard. Their hands were raw and red, and they were completely soaked from sweat and steam, which at times almost burned their forearms. When they heaved the boiling laundry out of the large kettle with that giant wooden spoon and carried it about ten feet to the wash tub, the hot water ran in streams down over their feet and onto the floor. I helped by moving the laundry around in the kettle with a huge tamper-like gadget on a long wooden handle to loosen the dirt.

Bleaching and hanging the laundry up to dry was equally heavy work, and finally it had to be ironed, which took another day. My mother and I stretched and pulled the sheets and tablecloths to give them back their shape. It was a tall stack, and she stood tirelessly all day long and far into the night to iron one piece after the other. She used the weight of her body and pressed down on the iron with both hands. Before he came home she had to prepare the evening meal and removed the blankets that she used for padding from the kitchen table. After supper she continued until the last piece was done. It was easier to iron the laundry right after it came off the line when it was smooth and still slightly damp.

25. Without a Trace

Although it did not take long to settle into our apartment, we soon realized that we were at a great disadvantage living under Soviet occupation, and that the people in the west were much better off. We listened mostly to RIAS Berlin (Radio in the American Sector), and experienced life under the Soviets as a twofold misfortune after the disaster of the war and the postwar misery. My parents discussed the political developments and commented on the posters and banners in honor of the Soviet Union, as well as the massive anti-capitalistic propaganda. The larger than life heads of Lenin, Stalin, Marx and Engels, assembled in unity in front of the waving Soviet flag with its hammer, sickle and star, as well as the posters and banners with Karl Liebknecht, August Bebel and Rosa Luxemburg, dominated the streets of our town. In unison they looked straight ahead into a promising future, symbolizing the "New Germany" that was to appear on the horizon, and was proclaimed and hailed anew every day in glowing words at school, in the work place and at assemblies. Soon political jokes against the Federal Republic surfaced in the daily newspapers. Shaking his head, Grandfather Wilhelm showed me caricatures of Konrad Adenauer, Robert Schuman and Dwight D. Eisenhower. I was never sure whether he was shaking his head over our side or those in the west. In spite of a severe lack of paper, cloth and other materials, as my mother would point out indignantly, red flags and banners with socialist slogans hung from public buildings by the dozens, and posters with party programs were glued to fences, walls, house fronts, ruins and wherever else there happened to be space. There was a giant mural painted over the entire windowless side wall of a three-story house on my way to my grandparents' that particularly impressed me. A returning German soldier in a shabby uniform and knapsack, whose right leg had been amputated above the knee, was coming towards me on crutches, walking erect, with bright open eyes. Next to him stood in huge letters, with each word on a separate line, "Nie wieder Krieg" (Never again War). Since I could read the words, I must have been in second grade. I was convinced that there would never again be a war.

For years to come we encountered men on crutches who were missing a foot or a leg. Others had lost a hand or an arm, and their jacket sleeves flapped back and forth with every step if they hadn't put it into a pocket. Men who had lost both legs sat in wagons pulled by a woman or two children, and it always seemed to me that they were especially big, strong men, because their upper bodies appeared so tall with their short leg stumps, at which I couldn't help but stare. Sometimes they had both legs amputated at the hips, so they could hardly keep upright. Pillows had been stuffed all around them, and a wooden board lay across the top of the wagon to keep them from falling over. Many veterans wore black eye patches, others had an arm in a sling, while still others hobbled along the streets with canes.

Judging by the wonderful things we received from my father's comrades in West Germany, we all knew that we had really been unlucky that the Russians had come to Saxony, although we had all hoped for the Americans. Soon we had memorized the advertising slogans we heard on RIAS Berlin for western food brands, cleaning products and luxury items such as coffee, cocoa, chocolate and cigarettes, and we learned and sang the latest western hits. That life was better in West Germany I also knew from other children in my class who received packages from over there, boasting of their contents during the breaks. My aunt and uncle in Birmingham, England, sent us Cadbury chocolate, black tea, coffee beans, raisins and butter. The butter was salted, which my mother could not understand at all.

These packages from England were always a huge event. My parents received a notice from the postman, and had to go to the customs office to pick them up. On rare occasions they were given the package intact, but most of the time the customs officials spread everything out on a table. The contents of bags were poured into bowls, cans were opened, and chocolate broken into pieces. Nothing seemed safe from the inspectors. They even cut into the butter. In the end it was all put back into the package and wrapped up with paper twine as well as possible before my parents put it into a shopping bag to carry it home. Chicanery, my mother called it. Even so it was better than Christmas when the contents were laid out on the kitchen table, and we smelled the foreign flavors and ate the first piece of chocolate, which we were not allowed to chew, but were admonished to let melt slowly on our tongues. My father watched us children as we ate the chocolate to make sure that we let it melt slowly. If he saw us chew, he scolded us, and then took a piece of chocolate, put it into his mouth and showed us how to do it right. Later, when we were in the west, we seldom had chocolate because there was no money for such luxuries.

As time past, my father and Omi alluded to colleagues who had fled to the west overnight or on the weekend while no one at work had suspected anything. They didn't find out about it until one morning when another one of their colleagues didn't come to work, and were surprised that they hadn't noticed anything questionable.

One day, my beloved homeroom teacher did not show up for class. We were sitting at our desks waiting for him, and were beginning to get restless.

Several boys and girls left their seats and opened the classroom door to look for him, when a very young woman entered. She introduced herself, and said without further explanation that she was our new teacher, and was looking forward to it. The news alarmed me, and I was seized by a romantic sadness that stayed with me for days, because I knew instinctively that I would never see my teacher again.

When I came home from school, my mother already knew of his disappearance. It was the talk of the town. She also told me that the authorities had gone to his mother's immediately, but she hadn't known anything about her son's plans to defect. Soon classmates went missing, some of whom I had known well, and I tried to imagine where they might be. I decided that I wanted to leave also, and go where I could buy chocolate, oranges and bananas, and where people were free. I cannot say what I imagined when I heard the word "free", but I was sure of one thing, there would not be any "Junge Pioniere" (Young Pioneers) in the other part of the country.

The Young Pioneers met in the afternoons in the classrooms of our school, but I never joined them. I can't really explain why I didn't participate, but I didn't want to put on the blue scarf, nor would I ever wear one of those tiny metal pioneer pins. I simply had a strong aversion to such things. The other children soon came to school wearing their blue scarves, and many of them wore them all the time, no matter where they went.

One day Grandmother Bergner asked me, "Where do you have your blue handkerchief?"

"I don't have one," I answered.

"Well, if I were you, I would get one real fast."

"But I don't want one," I insisted. It was the first time I had said out loud that I didn't want one. "I'm not in the Young Pioneers anyway, so I don't need one," I added when she looked at me in amazement.

"I thought you wanted to go to university some day? In that case you'll have to join the Young Pioneers."

I considered her words, and then answered with conviction, "I'll go to university, you'll see."

Grandmother Bergner looked at me amused, "Well, if that's so, you have no choice, you must join the pioneers, whether you want to or not."

I never joined, my parents never talked to me about it, and I got my degrees in California.

Our new teacher invited me frequently to join them in the afternoons, but I was never impressed enough to go. Finally I went, because a girl friend had begged me to, adding that they always had a lot of fun. When I entered the classroom, all of my classmates were already there, sitting in their usual assigned seats. I walked to my place, the only one that was still empty, and sat down. When our teacher entered moments later, she saw me right away, and after the Pioneer greeting, "Be ready – Always ready", she welcomed me personally. She said she had been waiting for me, and was glad I had come at last. We sang several songs, whose lyrics I didn't know well, or not at all, but all the other children sang them with gusto. The teacher talked a lot and asked many questions, but I cannot remember much except that we were supposed to paint the Young Pioneer symbol, "JP" with the red and yellow flames on top.

"Do you know what it looks like?" she asked me. Of course I did, but perhaps I didn't respond right away. In any case, she sent me into the large hall, and said that I should take a good look at the symbol, which was hanging above the landing of the stairs to the second floor, and then come back and describe it to the class. I recognized it immediately, you couldn't miss it, but suddenly I became unsure, perhaps because the whole thing seemed too simple. So instead of returning to the classroom, I ran up and down the stairs and through all the halls of the huge building, convinced that I had to look for something I had never seen before. I was gone for a long time, and when I reentered the room the teacher pretended she hadn't noticed. I sat down quietly and began to draw my emblem. I never went back, and no one ever asked me again.

It must have been in the summer of 1948 when I noticed that my parents were secretly talking about something until late at night in the kitchen by the dim light of a table lamp and closed windows. It often took me a long time to fall asleep, and because their voices were so low I sneaked into the hall and listened behind the kitchen door. I heard words like "flight" and "Berlin" and "West Germany", as well as the names of friends who were living there. From then on I asked my mother often when we would be going to the West. By 1949 my parents had given up hope for a new Germany on the territory of the German Democratic Republic.

As I recall, my questions did not surprise my mother, and she explained to me that they would have to think carefully about it, and that I should not mention it to anybody, not even to the grandparents. I guarded the secret, and years passed during which my parents tried to decide whether we should take the risk and flee or stay. They watched the political developments closely, wondering how bad things might become under Soviet occupation. I remember that they began planning our flight in earnest in 1949. They sought advice from a few chosen friends and colleagues. My parents never spoke to me directly about these plans, but I heard much and asked my mother about it when we were alone. This gave me the feeling that I was contributing to the decision to flee, but I also knew that I would miss my homeland, so I kept my eyes wide open as I walked through town to impress upon my memory every house, wall

Elfriede Richter with her three daughters in Bischofswerda, 1950

and fence, every bush and tree in every garden, and even the different patterns of sidewalk paving stones.

My last birthday in East Germany was a very special day. My mother baked several sheet cakes and a cake with real chocolate glaze, and invited family and neighbors in the afternoon for coffee and cake. There was not enough room at the dining table for all the guests, so some sat on the sofa in front of the small marble table and on additional chairs in front of the large window. The guests praised her cakes, the conversation was lively, and my mother was in high spirits as she walked repeatedly with a large pot of coffee from one person to the next, refilling their cups.

Two weeks later, on a Sunday, my father took me on an extended walk through town after the noon meal. Before we left the apartment he awkwardly put a roll of film into the camera and hung it around his neck. We had just stepped out of the house, when he took the camera off again to take photos of the front and the back of the house. After that we walked to the cemeteries, where he took photos of Grandfather Wilhelm's gravestone, who had died two years earlier, and those of other relatives. When I asked him why he was taking photos of graves, which to me seemed an odd thing to do, and he answered evasively that Martha had brought him enough film from Dresden. It sounded strange that he called my Omi Martha. He also photographed the town's sights and his high school.

Finally we reached his mother's place in time for coffee and cake, but first, everybody had to step out onto the balcony so he could take more photos while there was still enough daylight. Suddenly his mother asked, "Kurt, are you thinking of leaving?"

Her straightforward question took him by surprise, and he shot back too fast, "No, what gives you that idea? Don't you think I would tell you about it?" His words did not sound very convincing, but perhaps it just seemed so to me because I thought I knew better.

"Well, I just wondered because you're taking so many photos. Where did you get the film anyway? I thought there was none for sale," his mother said.

"I got it from Martha. She managed to get several rolls in Dresden, and so I decided to take some photos right away."

He took two more photos, and then we sat down around the kitchen table, ate enormous amounts of cake, and took our leave sooner than usual. On our way home, we stopped by the railroad station, where my father bought two tickets for the Monday morning train to Berlin. He had to show his identification as proof that he was eligible to buy tickets to Berlin. Carefully he put the small beige cardboard tickets into his wallet. After supper he disappeared into the bathroom for hours to develop the films.

That Sunday was different from all other Sundays. Two suitcases suddenly stood in the bedroom, and into one my mother put my clothes and underwear. In the middle of a hot summer she packed long stockings, pullovers, wool socks, my scarf, gloves and winter boots. She had let the seam out of my winter coat and hoped I would not grow too fast so it would fit me until the end of winter. I watched her and finally asked why she was packing my clothes, to which she answered, "You and your father are leaving with the first train for Berlin tomorrow morning." Her voice trembled slightly, and she did not look at me.

"I knew it, I knew it!" I exclaimed excitedly. "Tomorrow is a school day, and I am going to Berlin!" But at the same time I had a strange sad feeling, which dampened my joy, although I couldn't have said why.

My mother put her right index finger on her lips, "Not so loud, and don't ask any questions. Your sisters mustn't find out about it until you are gone, so no one will betray us at the last moment."

I cannot recall how the day ended. Perhaps I walked for the last time along the fields and over the meadows as I had done so frequently. Maybe I went to the quarry to stand once more at its unsecured edge, shuddering while looking down into the huge deep hole while trying to imagine that I could fall to my death should I take just one more step. I always took some small stones and threw them down into the crater while counting the seconds until they hit bottom. On the way home I may have picked one last bunch of wild flowers, which my mother would have put into a glass vase and placed on the table. But it's also possible that I walked to Grandmother Bergner, taking the long way around the town, passing through the fields and meadows, and then sat in her kitchen or accompanied her to her garden, and simply walked home in the evening.

The following morning my mother woke me while it was still completely dark, whispering into my ear, "Come on, Anne, wake up, we must hurry!" She helped me get dressed, watched me eat my oatmeal in the kitchen, and then accompanied us to the station while holding my hand. The fresh, cool morning air drove away my sleepiness. Inside the large station my mother hugged and kissed me, and then she turned around fast and ran off before my father and I stepped out onto the platform, where we waited in complete darkness for the train.

As we said good-bye, my mother whispered into my ear that Omi would be on the platform at the main station in Dresden, and that she would bring us cold-cut sandwiches, apples, cookies, and most certainly a bag of candies for the train ride to Berlin. I knew the route well, and stood at the open window as the train was entering the station. From afar I saw Omi wave, and I waved back enthusiastically. We got off the train, and while I pressed myself against her, she gave my father something flat wrapped in paper, which he put into the inside pocket of his jacket. They stood close to each other and exchanged a few words in low voices. They seemed to arrange something, and unlike other times were in agreement. Moments later Omi kissed me and hugged even more tightly than my mother had done an hour earlier, wiping away her tears with a handkerchief. Then it was time to get on the train to Berlin, which was standing on the other side of the platform. We had hardly boarded when it pulled out of the station. Omi and I waved good-bye to each other. When I could no longer see her, I sat down and opened the package to see what she had brought for me. I ate one of the large sugar cookies from her baker, and as I was chewing I began to grasp that I would not see her again for a long time, but my imagination was not sufficient to understand how much I would miss her and how alone I would feel from that day on, because I wasn't only going away from her, but from my homeland and all the people I had ever known. My Omi had always been there for me. She had not only shared my joys, but I could go to her with all my hurts and worries, or when I was sad. She always knew how to help, and calmed me down and made it all better. From that day on I've lived with a feeling of homesickness. It abated as the years passed, but never went away completely. I could not imagine the inhuman border that would soon separate us. Perhaps that was why I went forward and wouldn't have turned around for anything in the world, because I was so convinced that I wanted to go to the other part of Germany, of which I knew very little, but into which I was putting all my hope and trust. Besides, my mother would soon follow with my two younger sisters, and this eased the pain of parting.

At the time it was still possible to exchange East German for West German money at a rate of 3 to 1, and I learned later that Omi had paid for all five airplane tickets out of Berlin. The money had been in the flat package she had given her son-in-law at the railroad station in Dresden.

In East Berlin, my father and I took the S-Bahn, the public transportation system that continued to serve both East and West Berlin until the wall was built on the 13th of August 1961, to the Hellwig's. Herbert Hellwig was one of his former colleagues from the post office who had been transferred to Berlin. He and his wife, Ilse, lived far out in a suburb, and we had to walk several blocks from the end of the line to their house. I knew the couple from hikes we had taken together before they moved away. They were living in a nice duplex that belonged to her parents. The house was surrounded by a large garden full of fruit trees and a swing, and on the right side there was a fence and a gate that led into a small private forest. My father left me with these people with the usual admonitions to be good, saying he would pick me up again as soon as possible. He was about to leave when Ilse said, "Come, Kurt, sit down and eat something first," and he gulped down a large plate of steaming home fried potatoes and a fried egg, followed by a large cup of peppermint tea. But after that nothing could keep him any longer. From later reports I know he took the S-Bahn back to West Berlin, where he stayed for three weeks in a refugee camp. On Friday, 12 October 1951, he came very early in the morning to get me, and brought me a bar of chocolate.

"The chocolate is only thirty pfennigs," he said excitedly as he held it above his head so that everyone could see it.

"Well, yes," said Ilse, "but that's West German money. For us it's three times as much."

"That's true," my father conceded, "but it's real chocolate. And soon I'll be earning West German marks."

Ilse looked at him strangely, but said nothing more.

My suitcase was packed, and moments later we walked very fast along the deserted street toward the S-Bahn station.

"Not a word," my father warned me, "you are not going to say a word at the station or on the train until we are on the other side."

I nodded and wondered what exactly he meant by "the other side", and had butterflies in my stomach during our ride all the way to the American sector. That this was our destination I didn't understand either until much later.

From the S-Bahn station we ran straight to the travel agency at the Kurfürstendamm in West Berlin. It was the first time that I entered a building in the west. Everything looked different. There were colorful posters of cities, islands and mountains on the walls with names I had never heard before. My father greeted a man who was sitting at a desk behind the counter. He got up when he saw us, but stayed behind the barrier as he held out his hand toward my father. The two men seemed to know each other. I was looking around the room as they were speaking when I heard something that aroused my interest. The travel agent said to my father before he handed him the flight tickets, "Herr Bergner, I must point out to you once more and ask you to consider very carefully what you are about to do. If you fly to Frankfurt am Main today with your own tickets paid with your own money, you will not be entitled to any kind of help or assistance from the West German government in finding an apartment and employment. The state will help you only if you and your family go through the refugee camp here in West Berlin and wait your turn. In that case all five of you will be flown to Frankfurt at the expense of the Federal Republic."

"I cannot expect my family to spend weeks in a refugee camp," my father replied, "we've been through enough already. First the fire-bombing of Dresden, then the evacuation when the Russian army moved in, and a difficult new beginning. That's enough."

"Just remember that it will not be easy to find an apartment and work."

At that my father laughed and said, "It cannot possibly be more difficult than starting over in the eastern zone. Don't worry, we'll make it." The man gave my father the tickets, which he immediately put into the inside pocket of his jacket where the money from Omi had been before.

"All right then," he said before we left, "in a few weeks my wife will be here with the two younger girls to pick up the three remaining flight tickets."

"You can count on us, Herr Bergner. I wish you a good flight."

"Thank you very much again, and good-bye," my father said, touching the brim of his hat with his right hand.

On the wide sidewalk outside the travel agency stood a fruit stand on wheels with a colorful umbrella, where a man was selling bananas and other tropical fruit that I had never seen before. My father walked over to the stand and said to the vendor, "We just came from the east, could you please give me an especially nice banana for my daughter?"

"They all say that," answered the fruit vendor, "but here I have an extra large one," and he handed it to me. I did not know what to do with the bent yellow thing. My father took it from me after paying for it, and peeled it halfway. Then he gave it back to me, looking at me with great expectation. "Go ahead, eat it," he encouraged me. But this first banana did not taste good to me, so I gave it back to him. He took it and finished it with a few big bites.

Not long thereafter we were sitting in an aircraft from Air France, and at 3:45 p.m. we took off for Frankfurt am Main. I still have my flight ticket. It cost DM 48.00.

It was not until years later that I understood that fleeing the Soviet occupied zone on the second Monday morning of September on the first train to Dresden, and then on to Berlin, would be one of the most important events of my life.

A few hours after your departure, around 9 a.m., there was an impatient, prolonged ringing of our doorbell, my mother continued her story. The police stood in front of our apartment door. I had not expected them so soon.

"Where is your husband," the two policemen wanted to know, after they had made sure that I was Frau Bergner, although I knew one of them. He didn't let on, though, so I answered just as Kurt and I had previously discussed it. "My husband is on his way to the Main Post Office in Berlin, just like every three months. I am sure you know that."

"We don't believe you," said the policeman I didn't know. "Maybe you can tell us in detail what you were doing during the last forty-eight hours?"

"What do you mean?" I asked.

"Why don't you tell us about the conversations between you and your husband and the preparations before he left."

"Nothing out of the ordinary comes to mind," I said.

"Would you like us to help you along? You were seen together at the station early this morning," the other policeman interjected.

"I accompanied my husband to the station as I often do," I answered boldly. "If you don't know where he is now, then I don't know either."

They remained polite, but said straight out, "We have to assume that your husband is about to flee the German Democratic Republic."

"Then you know more than I," I heard myself say, and was surprised how calm I was.

"What will you do in the event that your husband doesn't come back, and instead you receive a message from him from West Germany?" they demanded to know.

"In that case I shall have to follow him with the children, I'd have no other choice. My children need a father, and I love my husband. We are a family."

"If I were you, I would think it over carefully and not repeat what you just said," warned the policeman whom I knew.

Strangely enough, they asked no further questions. As a matter of fact, they suddenly seemed to be completely disinterested. I didn't become afraid until after they had left and I heard the front door close behind them. My hands trembled and my legs felt weak when I returned to the sewing machine to finish the dress that I was making for you, Anne. I had taken apart one of my old ones. Several days later I was summoned to the police station for more questioning. Again they wanted to know what my plans were, now that they knew for a fact that my husband had fled the republic.

"I know nothing about it," I said, "I haven't heard from him."

"We can help you out there," said the older of the two policemen in the office, and handed me a sheet of paper across the table.

When I did not reach for it right away, he said, "Go ahead, take it, the letter is for you."

I recognized Kurt's handwriting and read the letter. It did not say much, just that the two of you had arrived safely and that I should go ahead and do everything as planned, which sounded very incriminating. I had not expected a letter from him, and felt the blood rush to my face. I knew that Kurt would not be able to write anything specific. We had agreed upon an address in Berlin where I should go once we were there. I knew the people; they were friends of the Hellwig's.

To this day I do not know what to make of my visit to the police station, but I was free to leave again after the interrogation was over. I received two more letters from Kurt that he had addressed to Omi in Dresden, who brought them to me. I could not tell whether or not the authorities had opened them. Once I knew that you had arrived safely in the small town on the Mosel, I began to dissolve our household.

During the three months that remained, my mother shipped everything that could be taken apart, folded together and wrapped from the local post office to the address of my father's wartime comrade, Jürgen Gehring, in Cochem on the Mosel. A few weeks after our arrival, we received packages daily with clothing, curtains, pillows, sheets, dishes, pots and pans, flatware and kitchen utensils, feather beds, blankets, towels and books, as well as disassembled pieces of furniture like small cabinets, chests of drawers, tables, lamps, two nightstands, book shelves and six dining room chairs. She sent clothes pins, wicker laundry baskets, the iron and ironing board, our toys, a doll carriage, the dollhouse with its furniture, the sleds and a wooden wagon. Even so, in the end it was so very little that we were able to rescue from one German State to the other. My doll bed, which Aunt Irmgard had given me after we had been bombed out, along with my dolls, was one of the first shipments to arrive in the other Germany. I was overjoyed, and my father glued it back together for me in a carpenter's shop. The larger pieces of furniture, our beds, the stove and stove pipes, and the rug in the living room, all items which she had procured with such great effort and a lot of luck, my mother sold with a heavy heart so she would have money to buy food, because she no longer received any money at all, and no more food stamps either after her husband had fled. Once again Omi had to help out. Every evening, my mother sewed until late into the night. She undid several of her dresses and made new ones for me. Once a large package full of clothes arrived, and her husband lifted one of her dresses, made of a turquoise colored cotton with a tiny white design, out of the box, and was about to breath in her scent, when he suddenly let it drop forlornly, because she had made it into a dress for me, and the second and third one, too.

"How could you do that?" he complained to her later, "I loved to see you in those dresses. The turquoise one was one of my favorites. You cannot possibly imagine my disappointment."

"It no longer fit right," she answered. "Besides, the cut was old-fashioned. I had so much time during those long evenings, and did not want to give myself over to doubts and heavy thoughts, so I knitted and sewed as much as I could. Besides, my mother brought material for several new dresses for me."

My mother also sent beautiful ceramic dishes with artistic flower and leaf designs like I have never seen again anywhere else. Even in Bischofswerda they stopped using these skillful patterns long ago because they are so labor intensive, and therefore too expensive. She also bought hand-carved and painted wooden figures from the Erzgebirge, which my parents used as gifts for the help they received from people in the west, who knew little of the real value of the wooden smokers, nativity figures, angels, Christmas pyramids and the beautiful pottery.

She had numbered all the packages. There were over one hundred of them, and they all arrived in good condition. Nothing got lost or broke during the long journey from east to west.

The upper part of the sewing machine she could not entrust to the post office, because it not only had an inestimable value to her, but it was one of those items that were forbidden to export. She would tell us often how she smuggled the heavy sewing machine in a suitcase to West Berlin, and how she carried the suitcase as if it were as light as a feather, so neither the Volkspolizei (East German people's police) nor spies in civilian clothes would become suspicious, and stop her and ask her to open the suitcase. If they had seen the sewing machine they would have guessed that she was about to flee to the west. Her heart beat so loudly that she thought everyone could hear it, she often said, but the sewing machine had to come along. She was sure that she would find another sewing machine table for it. She also found a mechanic in Cochem who would file those large needles for the old machine. They were at least two inches long and no longer for sale.

Herr Hausmann, whom I could trust and who had helped me with the disassembly, wrapping and mailing of the larger pieces, pulled the heavy suitcases to the railroad station in his handcart and lifted them into the compartment, my mother continued her description of events. For his help I gave him the furniture I had been unable to sell as well as several hundred pounds of coal and potatoes that were in our cellar. Omi had spent the last days in Bischofswerda, and accompanied us to Dresden, where she helped us onto the train to Berlin. Everything had gone very well up to that point, but on the train from Dresden to East Berlin I suddenly feared that one of the conductors or officials in uniform who constantly walked back and forth through the train would become suspicious. As it turned out, however, we were very lucky, because a large group of young people from the FDJ (Free German Youth) was going to Berlin with us. Without asking any questions, they had simply helped us with the luggage in Dresden, and had lifted our suitcases along with theirs onto the luggage racks above the seats wherever there happened to be space, and it looked like our things were part of their luggage, which the inspectors did not check. Because they all helped, they did not notice that we were traveling with seven suitcases. When asked, I always pointed only to the one suitcase in the rack above me. The tickets for the three of us were in order, and they never asked for any other papers, which one needed in those days to take the train into East Berlin.

Many passengers had to open their suitcases for the inspectors. The closer we got to Berlin, the more passengers were taken off the train at the stations and lead away. Among them was an elegantly dressed woman in her mid-forties, wearing a fur coat and leather boots. Two men in uniform led her past us, one in front of her, the other behind her. Her face was ashen.

One of the controllers asked me if these were my children as he pointed to Bettine and Viktoria. I answered in the affirmative. He wanted to know why we were going to Berlin. I told him that we were planning to stay with friends for a few weeks who had a house with a large garden, which would be good for the children, and that I had to recover from protracted pleurisy and general weakness. He believed me. Besides, it was true. Travelling with two small children, the top of the sewing machine in one suitcase and six others filled with dishes, shoes, summer and winter clothes and two shopping bags full of provisions and things that I had stuffed in at the last minute, could have easily gone wrong.

When we arrived in East Berlin, the young people from the "Free German Youth" took all the suitcases down from the luggage racks as a matter of course and set them on the busy platform, because we had reached the end of the line. The platform was busy, and no one paid any attention to us or asked any tricky questions. While I was still thinking about what to do next, I saw the sign for the luggage depository. At the same moment, Ilse was coming toward us.

"I am so glad to see you," I said relieved. "Please wait here with the luggage and the children while I take four suitcases to the luggage office, two at a time. I'll transport them to West Berlin tomorrow morning. The rest we'll take with us to your place."

"You cannot go there twice, Effi, they will notice that," Ilse said. "You take the first two, and I'll deposit the other two."

The following morning I took the S-Bahn to the railroad station and picked up the first two suitcases to take them to the Tempelhof airport in West Berlin, where I dropped them off again at the luggage office. I was gone for three hours, and when I was back there were different people working behind the luggage counter, so I could get the other two suitcases without anyone becoming suspicious. The spies that traveled along on the S-Bahn always walked through the trains by twos while looking searchingly at the passengers. They asked questions, wanted to see identification cards and other papers, and demanded to see the luggage. I looked out of the windows and pretended their doings did not interest me in the least, as if travelling by S-Bahn with two suitcases was the most normal thing in the world. At the stations they were always the first ones to jump off the trains. They walked along the platforms, suddenly ran after people, returned, stopped passengers, and when the train left again they jumped on at the last instant. They led away men and women with suitcases and briefcases, but there were also people with no luggage at all that disappeared with them behind closed doors.

On the 10th of December 1951, we left for the airport early in the morning. It was still dark, and again we made believe we were only going to West Berlin for a few hours, which was still possible in those days. We still had two suitcases with our clothes and hand luggage. The other five I had already taken to the airport. Ilse came along. I was relieved when we finally arrived in the west. I felt strange, and in spite of all the excitement and anticipation, I was filled with a deep sadness. The day was cold and wet, and everything in West Berlin was unfamiliar. I was nervous and shivered, but even so I had to display optimism and express confidence, if only for the sake of Bettine and Viktoria. We said farewell to Ilse at the Kurfürstendamm. Both of us knew that it would be forever, but we made believe we would see each other again really soon.

We took a taxi to the airport. It was my first taxi ride since the beginning of the war. The taxi driver was very friendly, and helped me with the heavy suitcases. I didn't dare to talk to him during the ride, but he guessed what was going on. After unloading our luggage, he wished us a good flight and lots of luck, and mentioned that he himself had just recently arrived in Berlin from Magdeburg. He patted me on the shoulder saying: "Cheer up, young lady, it'll all work out. The worst is behind you." His words helped me. I had some money left from Omi, so I was able to give him a good tip. There wasn't much time left, and we had to hurry to catch our plane.

Without the help of Ilse and Herbert Hellwig we would never have made it. I was worried the whole time that someone might report them. I was also afraid that someone in Bischofswerda might betray us after all, and that they would come any moment and take me away. Especially at night every noise frightened me. The Hellwigs had been very courageous to let us stay with them. You never know what the neighbors might see and how they'll react. Ilse's husband soon embarked on a big career in East Berlin, and one day a letter arrived in which he asked us not to write them anymore. I wonder how they fared. Ilse was very sensitive; you could tell just by looking at her. I always felt sorry for her because she couldn't have children. She suffered terribly because of it.

That we left East Germany so early is proof of the fact that my parents did not simply go along with the communist regime, but were critical of the new men in power. The new beginning, which turned into a huge economical and political disaster for the eastern part of Germany, had disappointed them almost from the beginning. But more importantly, it drove many people into a moral dilemma. There was no doubt about where the better future would be for us.

On the 10th of December, my father took the train to Frankfurt am Main very early in the morning to pick up my mother and sisters at the airport. He had several things to take care of before their arrival. I would have liked to come along, but we had no money for a train ticket for me. I could hardly wait to see my mother again, and did all kinds of things to pass the hours after school. Finally it was time to go to the railroad station with the Gehrings. Jürgen had not expected so much luggage. He had to make the trip twice with his motorcycle and trailer.

"Of all the suitcases, the one with the dishes, which I had guarded like the apple of my eye the entire trip, slipped out of his hand as he was lifting it into the trailer," my mother wailed often. "I heard right away that something had broken, and felt sick inside as tears sprang to my eyes. I could not believe such carelessness."

26. Care Packages from the East

When we arrived late that night at the Gehring's, hungry, dead tired and dirty from the long trip, and I saw the small uncomfortable room that smelled of mildew, where all five of us would have to live for the time being, my world collapsed, my mother recalled. The endless walk from the station into the narrow valley had already seemed dubious to me. If I had known what was awaiting me, I would never have left the bright, spacious apartment in Bischofswerda. Never would I have given up what we had there to begin all over again for the third time within just a few years. Kurt had described everything so beautifully: a small side valley of the Mosel river, vineyards on the one side, trees on the other, a stream and a mill right behind the house, the Mosel wine and the abundance of food in the stores. And then we arrived at a ramshackle place, and didn't even have money for the most essential things.

The room was barely two-hundred square feet, a single room for all of us to eat, sleep and live in. In one corner stood a small iron stove to heat the room. In the mornings I would boil water on it for coffee and tea, and in the evenings I would put on a large pot for hot water so we could wash ourselves. We had a couch, a double bed, a two-door wardrobe about four feet wide, a chest of drawers, a table pushed against the couch, three chairs and a footstool, and our suitcases for storage. That was it. Two of you children had to sit on cushions on the couch for our meals. The two small windows opened toward the back, where the sun hardly reached them. The room was gloomy even during the noon hours. There was no running water in our room, and the only toilet in the entire house for thirteen people was on the landing of the second floor, and always occupied. I would often stand waiting behind the apartment door, which I had opened a crack so I could hear the toilet door open and rush upstairs.

Our life took place in those tight quarters for the next ten months until we were given our own apartment by the city. Even so, we were unbelievably poor during the first years in this godforsaken place on the Mosel. For years I didn't want to acquire much of anything because I couldn't bare the thought of losing everything for a third time. The people who visited us could not understand my thinking. They had always been living in the same place, and through all the wars their houses had been safe with all of their valuables. Their cellars and attics were stuffed full of things they no longer needed. We, on the other hand, had not only lost most of our material possessions, but also beloved relatives and friends.

Kurt could not find regular work for years. The post office would not employ him because he had been employed at the revenue office in Dresden right after graduating from high school, and the revenue office in Cochem refused to take him back because he had worked at the post office in Bischofswerda. Beyond that he would have had to prove to the West German authorities that he had to flee East Germany for political reasons. But there was no one in the west who could attest to that. The travel agent in Berlin had been right after all.

For five years Kurt worked as a day laborer for the winegrowers in the villages along the Mosel. He helped fell trees, split wood, shovel coal. He lugged bricks to repair and build supporting dry walls in the vineyards, and during the wine harvest he carried the heavy baskets filled with grapes down the steep hills over the sharp-edged slate gravel into the winepresses in the cellars, ruining his back and his shoes. During the summer he helped out at the tourist office and tried his luck as an insurance salesman, but in those years, farmers and small business people were still suspicious of any kind of insurance.

When there was no work at all for several days, and he could bring no money home, he had to go to the unemployment office. He always tried to avoid it for as long as possible because he felt ashamed of standing in line with the other people who were out of work, visible to everyone.

During those years when we were as unbelievably poor as never before, Kurt began to give me the household money on a daily basis again. It hit me hard, because I was so careful and thought twice about every mark before buying anything, and would have never wasted even one pfennig. Whenever he could, he insisted on shopping with me after work. That had the advantage that I didn't have to carry the heavy bags all by myself, but he rushed me. Since the shops closed early in those years, I had little time to look at the merchandise more closely, to check things out at other stores, and compare prices so I could decide where I would get the better bargain. Without hesitation or consideration of quality, he always reached for the cheapest item.

As always, the greatest help came once again from Omi in Dresden. My mother had barely arrived with my two younger sisters when the first packages started coming. From the time of our escape to the west until her grave illness, of which she died in 1964, she sent us three or four packages a week to the great surprise of the mailmen who wondered what good things could possibly come from East Germany. The packages contained everything she could find: material for dresses and drapes, underwear, nightgowns, socks, stockings, sheets, pillowcases, blankets, tablecloths with matching napkins, dish towels, hand towels, candy by the pound, noodles, sugar, flour and cookies. She sent house shoes, plastic sandals that never lasted very long, and books from second hand stores, amongst them such treasures as the collected works of Goethe, Schiller, Lessing and Fontane, as well as the novels of the great Russian poets, which are all still standing on my book shelves today. She sent writing paper, envelopes, pencils, scissors, kitchen brooms, wooden cutting boards, clothes brushes, dinner plates, soup plates and bowls of all sizes. During the colder months we received smoked sausages and smoked meat. She used all her free time after work to go to the stores in Dresden, and stood in line until she had what she was looking for. She bought whatever was available and thought we could use. It proved as difficult to procure the sturdy cardboard boxes, wrapping material and heavy string that would survive the long trip to West Germany as it had been to find many of the items, because everything was always in short supply in East Germany. She also sent us toys, board games, doll carriages, a scooter with air tires, as well as dozens of the carved wooden figures, pyramids and smokers for Christmas from the Erzgebirge, where the women would make them in their homes while the men worked in the mines. She found beautiful vases, pitchers and bowls in pottery factories, wooden candle holders, carved boxes with lids, silver bracelets, necklaces, rings with semi precious stones, amber jewelry and the first wrist watch for me. Many of these items I still have today, and whenever I see them I think of her. These were regular care packages making their way to us in the other direction. It was like a cornucopia, which emptied itself week after week for over a decade onto our kitchen table. How would we have ever made it in the west without her help?

Citizens of the GDR were only allowed to mail one package per month to West Germany, but we got several every week. When she came to visit us for three weeks in the summer, she would tell us how she took the streetcar to far away post offices after work, no matter what the weather was like, so no one would notice how many packages she actually posted. She rode to Dresden Neustadt, and all the way to Radebeul, Radeberg, Weinböhla or Klotsche, and had to hurry with the heavy packages so she would be there before the post office closed. She was so frugal and modest, and needed so very little for herself. Everything she gave to us, her beloved children.

When I came home from school I saw the contents of a package spread out on the kitchen table. "That's incredible, it's like a miracle!" I exclaimed as my mother brought me my noon meal. I did not know then that these days with her were numbered, and that I would never again experience her like I did at those times when I loved her so very much. Within a very short time this intimacy between us was lost forever.

"You are right, it is a miracle," she would agree. She sat down next to me, her left elbow propped up on the table, resting her face in her left hand and had her legs crossed. Often she was quiet and very restless. I didn't know what to say either, and thought of other things. Seldom would she ask me about school, and if I told her something, she would not really listen, but looked out of the window or studied her well-manicured fingernails, which she filed daily. I saw her, sensed her closeness and breathed in her eau de cologne. Sometimes she mentioned that we still had to buy a pound of coffee and mail it to Omi. For all the packages, Omi wanted nothing in return except one pound of coffee beans every two weeks. Now and then she asked for half a pound of cocoa and a bar of chocolate or a pound of raisins, but usually she wanted just coffee. It was difficult enough for us to send her the coffee, because we had hardly any money.

In the late afternoons I would run to the post office before closing time to mail a parcel for Omi. One of the clerks was Reinhold, who was working behind one of the counters since he'd had a bad motorcycle accident, and could no longer deliver the mail. He was always glad to see me, and I arranged it in such a way that I could go to his window, even if I had to wait longer.

I loved the smell of real coffee, the only luxury Omi afforded herself every afternoon, and often watched her make it, a ceremonial act she took very seriously, and did not want to be disturbed. First she got the bag with the coffee beans and the old wooden coffee mill. Then she carefully took the porcelain Melitta coffee filter, an invention from Dresden, and the coffeepot from the cupboard. The porcelain filter had survived the bombing unharmed in the cellar, and Omi guarded it like a treasure all of her life. Finally she counted the coffee beans into the hollow of her left hand – thirteen per cup and some extra beans for the pot – and poured them into the old-fashioned coffee mill. She sat down on a kitchen chair and put the coffee mill between her thighs to hold it steady so it would be easier to grind the beans. When she was done she would knock at the mill from all sides so all the coffee powder would fall into the small drawer. After warming up the coffeepot with boiling water, she took off the lid, put it on the table and set the bright white porcelain filter carefully on top of it, where it sat on the pot like a crown and put in the filter paper. Then it was time to take the little drawer with the ground coffee, that smelled so wonderfully aromatic, and empty it into the filter. After that she brushed all the remaining coffee powder from the mill into the filter so nothing would get lost or stay in the mill, which could otherwise spoil the flavor of the next batch of coffee. At last she poured boiling water very slowly over the ground coffee so it could steep and unfold its full aroma. Between pours she covered the filter with a saucer so no heat or aroma could escape. She even covered the spout of the coffeepot with a cloth napkin to keep all the steam inside.

I shall always remember the way she sat in her upholstered chair at the round living room table after this procedure. Laid out before her she had her Meißen porcelain coffee set for one person with the hand-painted flowers she had found quite by accident in a store in a suburb of Dresden after the bombing, and had bought right away. The set consisted of a coffee cup and saucer, a cake plate, a sugar bowl with the Meißen rose on the lid, and a creamer. Behind the coffee set stood the ivory-colored Bavaria porcelain coffeepot with gold trim, covered by a blue cozy to keep the coffee hot. The woman sat at the table absorbed in thought, dreaming of far away places, or perhaps she was just enjoying the coffee and the bliss of the moment. She rarely put down the cup between her small sips of the strong hot brew.

Her slow dreamy movements fascinated me. For years I watched, hypnotized. When the first cup was empty, she put it down on the saucer, stood up to lift the cozy carefully from the coffeepot, poured the second cup, added half a spoon of sugar and a few drops of heavy cream, and stirred it devoutly. Before she picked up the cup again, she ate a forkful of cake and praised it, saying, "Elfriedchen, your cakes are heavenly, no baker can bake like you!" Omi would not allow anyone to distract her while drinking her coffee. She appreciated no conversation and paid no attention to questions from her grandchildren. This time belonged to her; it was sacred to her. She could easily sit in her chair for an hour and retreat into her world.

The housekeeping money was very tight during those first years after our flight, and my mother once more needed a lot of imagination to cook good meals for the five of us. In a butcher shop she was once deeply humiliated when the butcher's wife said to her in front of a store full of women customers that she couldn't always just buy bones for vegetable soup and a ring of *bockwurst*. She was ashamed of her poverty, and would have liked to buy a roast or *schnitzels* now and then. Those customers who bought huge amounts of sausage and meat every week were given a bag full of bones or a whole ring of sausage courtesy of the butcher, and she was not supposed to buy them?! My mother never went back there, and soon found another very friendly butcher in an out-of-the-way street, who always served her politely.

After asking around, my parents found a carpenter in Cochem who also had a small furniture store, and was willing to sell furniture to us on an installment plan. In her great joy my mother must have told some neighbors about it. The Goedeke family, who lived below us, was scandalized by the mere thought of it. Self-respecting people didn't buy things on installments, and they spread the news around town so that we heard about it from third parties. But the war had not come to the Mosel valley. What did they know about our problems?

Once Frau Goedeke happened to see as a large box with a brand new radio was being delivered to us from a mail order store, and she asked my mother, who never had a ready answer and never knew how to defend herself: "How are you going to pay for it?" These words spoiled her initial excitement about the beautiful radio that would finally allow us to take part in the things that were happening around the world. It soon became the center of our family life. We listened to music, the news and all the new entertainment programs. However, I had to secretly listen to AFN, the American Forces Network. My father would not tolerate American voices in his living room. I turned it on every afternoon as soon as I got home from school, and understood every word within a very short time.

One day, my father heard that the Americans at Hahn airport needed office help, and were looking for Germans with some knowledge of the English language. Discarding all prejudice, he tried his luck and offered his services. He filled out several forms and was hired the same day by the "work order section." From then on, he took the train daily from Cochem to Bullay on the Mosel, from where he rode to the base with some German colleagues in their car. At night he would tell us about some aspect of the life of the American families living in the housing area. We could neither imagine their carefree life nor the abundance of everything they seemed to enjoy. The taste and look of the food from this far-away world remained forever foreign to us. From the outside we marveled at their large apartments in which the lights seemed to be burning permanently. They were supposed to have flowing hot and cold water, large bathrooms, built-in kitchens stocked with Rosenthal porcelain, pots and pans and flat ware. The central heating was left turned on day and night, and when it got too hot they simply opened the windows. My father described American bread as white and soft as cotton, already sliced and in the shape of a large pound cake, but not quite as sweet. He promised to bring home a slice if he ever got hold of one. He told us about flat, round patties of ground beef the Americans called "hamburger", fried unseasoned and served on soft round rolls with a soft crust. The women went shopping with their hair in huge curlers, and he imitated their excited voices over the telephone when the gas or electricity failed while they had a cake in the oven. The taste and consistency of those cakes he could describe even less accurately than the bread, but he knew that the dough was mixed from a powder in a package to which water was added. My mother looked at him skeptically, and said, "But every cake needs butter and eggs."

Her husband was glad to have a secure position at last. He gained the confidence of his employers and learned American English. Economically, things were finally better for us. After years of the most severe want we were able to buy a few things we had desired for a long time, and we all got new shoes. My mother took care of the family and the household with renewed diligence, and continued to sew tirelessly. The sewing machine remained her most important tool, and everything should have gone well from then on.

When my father came home from work and entered the kitchen, his first move was always to lift the lid from the pot, and although it smelled wonderful, he asked gruffly, "Why are you cooking noodle soup today instead of potatoes? You know I don't care for noodles, they don't satisfy my hunger."

"But I made the noodles from scratch. I thought some nice, thick soup would do us good during this cool weather, and there will be enough for tomorrow. This saves me time."

"How much time can it take to cook?" He asked disparagingly. "I thought you loved me. Why didn't you make a roast with potatoes and vegetables?"

"That's not a roast, it's meat for boiling. I was glad when the butcher brought it from the back room and offered it to me at such a good price."

In the end he enjoyed the soup and took a second helping.

During the afternoons my mother always sat in front of the sewing machine. She knew how to create something new for us from the most unlikely scraps of material. Sewing was not only her greatest talent, but also her passion. I would often watch her when she sat at the old machine, bent over her work while her body moved rhythmically as she tread on the pedal while guiding the material toward the needle. She worked tirelessly, was always in good spirits, and could hardly wait to see another piece done. After trying it on, she might change a seam or adjust a dart, and then finish the remaining work by hand, the seam of the skirt, buttonholes and the buttons. Finally she steamed the new garment and tried it on again. She turned to the left and right in front of the mirror to appraise her work. Pleased, she took it off and put it on a hanger, her face beaming with joy because it had turned out far better than she had dared to expect. She was just as happy when a cake turned out better than ever. We praised her and ate one slice after the other.

She altered our dresses, found a piece of material that matched the old dress well, and with much imagination and skill created a new one. She wracked her brain over the most complicated patterns, and spread them out on the material from an old article of clothing she had taken apart. She moved the pattern around and puzzled over it until it fit. She never gave up, but got nervous because time passed so quickly over the tricky work. I was looking forward to the dress that took shape beneath her nimble fingers, and that I had to try on every now and then. Usually she basted the pieces together, but now and then she would just pin them together to save time, and I had to stand very still so the pins would not prick me, and hold my arms straight up into the air while she pulled the unfinished dress down over my head. She got impatient easily because I slowed her down with my wiggling. If she had material left, she would make a bow for decoration or a matching band for my hair. There were few women who could sew such beautiful dresses for their daughters from scraps of material. Her husband called it "magic".

"Let's see what magic you worked today," he would say in a patronizing manner.

"Magic, oh my God! What do you know about how much work it is and the nerves it costs!" she exclaimed indignantly. And then she would show us her hands, which were red and swollen because she had been sitting at the sewing machine all day long. Her wrists and shoulders ached, and when he happened to overhear her, he would put her down instead of praising her work by saying, "Why do you sew for so many hours? You know no limits! Why do the girls need so many dresses anyway?"

Often my mother was under time pressure to finish a dress, especially right before some family festivities. For each of our confirmations she not only sewed the confirmation dress, but also something new for all of us. She worked through the nights, and on Palm Sunday she got up at five in the morning to prepare the festive meal. She peeled potatoes, cleaned the vegetables, put the roast in the oven, so it would braise while we were in church, and whose wonderful aroma enveloped us as we opened the front door. Cakes and deserts were ready for the afternoon coffee. She invited Lara and her husband as well as Hermann Dietz and his wife Editha to such family gatherings, who lived in different towns several hours away. After the noon meal we all went for the obligatory walk. Upon our return the table was set for coffee and cake, and in the evening an abundant supper was prepared, while my mother reminded us of her father's legendary hospitality.

And then there was this one Saturday in the mid-fifties that brightened her life. My parents returned from town walking arm in arm. My mother's eyes sparkled and she could hardly contain her excitement as she shared the good news that they had just bought an electric Pfaff sewing machine with zigzag stitch, which would be delivered that very afternoon. It was a wonderful machine that allowed her to sew the most difficult things. She had been able to try out a similar model in the shop that worked like a dream, was quiet and very easy to handle. Herr Goeppel had even taken the old machine as a trade-in, and had assured her that the new Pfaff machine was just as good, and would sew much easier and faster than her old Singer machine in Dresden. They had chosen the best cabinet in light oak for the new machine. The top opened up to give her a large surface area to work on. "At last the days of treading the pedal and the loud rattling are over," she sighed happily. "I can really step on it now, and don't have to worry anymore about the needle breaking!"

Once I asked my mother how she had learned to sew so well. "Well, it was important to Papa that I knew everything that I would need some day for my family and the household," she explained. For my eighth birthday he bought me a Singer sewing machine, and taught me how to sew according to the instructions from a book. Can you imagine that, Anne? He, a man, sat next to me and made sure that I did everything right! I had to execute the various stitches very accurately on scraps of material. Then I learned to baste, sew seams and buttonholes, always under his supervision. Omi could not sew, and was not interested in it either. She did no needlework at all, and would only sew a button back on if it was absolutely necessary. Twice a year a seamstress came to us for a week to sew new dresses for her and me, to alter old ones and mend whatever was torn.

One day, Papa came home with a little suitcase. It was the same one into which I had put the most important papers and my jewelry in the summer of 1944. The suitcase contained everything that I would need for sewing. There was a removable insert with partitions Papa had lovingly filled with all kinds of useful items. There were buttons covered with white linen for pillowcases, expensive buttons of all sizes and colors for blouses, dresses, jackets and skirts, silk and cotton ribbons in various widths and colors, an assortment of sewing needles, a box of pins with colorful glass heads, rectangular pieces of cardboard with silver and black snap fasteners, as well as hooks and eyes, a yellow measuring band, sewing silk in the colors of the rainbow, plenty of spools, sewing scissors, a pair of buttonhole scissors, a ripper, basting yarn, a piece of tailor's chalk, a silver-colored metal thimble, and as a big surprise, a Meißen porcelain thimble with a tiny pink rose and gold rim.

First we sewed doll clothes, then pillowcases so I would learn to sew long, straight seams. We hemmed linen towels and men's handkerchiefs, and finally we sewed an apron. After that Papa went shopping and brought back material for skirts and dresses for me. He was always so happy when he could give us something that we enjoyed. He bought patterns, which we pricked out on paper, enlarged or reduced as necessary, and then cut out. Any changes we drew on the material with tailor's chalk.

When Omi saw how good I had become, I had to sew everything for her as well. From then on the seamstress did not have to come anymore. Omi was overjoyed and glad to save the money. "You are so much better," she would always say, and when we had visitors she would show off her newest dress with the comment, "Just look how well my Elfriedchen can sew!" But she was also very impatient. Whenever I had begun a dress for her, she wanted it finished right away. She came to check on my progress, and I was hardly allowed to get up. She set a plate with a slice of cake and a cup of coffee on a small table next to me so I would not have to interrupt my work. When the dress was finished, she put it on right away and strolled up and down the Prager Straße with her women friends.

The women in that small town on the Mosel river recognized my mother's many talents, and when asked she would gladly explain an especially difficult detail. Her suits were always a perfect fit. No tailor could have done it better, everyone assured her. On Sunday mornings she would sit straight as a queen in church. The people on the street looked at her admiringly, because she was a beautiful woman who radiated self-confidence, and her body moved very subtly with every step. She cut her own hair fashionably short. Her eyes looked about freely, and she believed in life. No one was dressed as elegantly as she, and the neighbors admired her three daughters, who frequently wore new dresses. But there were also women who envied my mother, while others shook their heads in disbelief saying, "How diligent you are, Frau Bergner! How do you do it?" Others would give her somewhat suspicious glances, because as a newcomer and a protestant they thought that she walked too upright, and her steps seemed too secure. She held her head ever so slightly to the left, giving her a gentle womanly appearance. At such moments I sensed her satisfaction and pride. Even her husband basked in the admiration that was extended to her when they walked down the street arm in arm, while he lifted his hat reverently in all directions, greeting the passers-by.

All too often, however, just after they arrived back at home, his mood could change abruptly. His face darkened, and he asked distrustfully, "Why did Herr Hofe greet you so overly friendly?"

"Who is Herr Hofe?" she asked surprised.

"Herr Hofe from the revenue office, who else?"

"I don't know any Herr Hofe. And how is he supposed to have greeted me?"

"Friendlier than necessary. I cannot stand it when other men stare at you lustfully!"

She looked at him with indignation. "Are you out of your mind? Do you have any idea what nonsense you are talking?" Her words aggravated him even more. It upset him when other men looked at her admiringly in passing, and yet he enjoyed it secretly, because this much he knew, even if her never conceded it to her: his wife was more beautiful than the other women, and more competent.

My mother had high hopes for life, and was ready to work tirelessly and give everything in her power to reach her goals. She knew how to furnish the apartment comfortably and brightly with the few things we had. But as the years went by, she tolerated his jealousy, often erupting unpredictably, and his narrow-mindedness less and less. He hurt her feelings with the harsh words he spewed out so thoughtlessly. It didn't make things any better when he calmed down again after his tirades and begged her to sit down on the sofa next to him, and solemnly assured her that he needed her and would perish without her. The one was as extreme as the other, the scolding every bit as much as the ensuing protestations of love and devotion. Both disconcerted her and weakened her psyche, because the peace never lasted very long, often barely a few hours, at most a day.

After the sewing machine, other electrical appliances for the household followed: a vacuum cleaner for the new living room carpet, and a refrigerator, the first one with a modern flat door. At last the food would keep for several days! Leftovers had always been a problem, especially in the summer when even the cellar warmed up. Soups got a tinge, the milk turned sour, and the sausage began to smell bad already the next day, but my mother just couldn't throw away food. She would fry the sausage with onions to cover up the taste, but no one wanted to eat the sour smelling soup. When he reproached her saying, "Why do you cook so much?" she would answer, "I thought you would eat more, you always eat more!" Then she stood leaning against the cold stove and ate the soup right out of the pot. I felt sick just watching her. Usually nothing happened, but sometimes she looked strangely pale and had to vomit, and felt sick for hours.

27. Tyranny by Radio

Toward the end of the fifties, my father received a letter containing good news. His former superior at the post office in Bischofswerda had fled to the west, and was willing to testify that, as a personnel manager, my father had to collect information about his colleagues and report it to Berlin, a circumstance that was incompatible with his principles, and left him with no other choice but to flee the Soviet zone.

For the last time my father filled out a myriad of forms and went to various government agencies in Koblenz and Bonn. This time things moved swiftly. It didn't take long before he was employed by the revenue office in Cochem, and subsequently sent to Bonn three times for training, three months each a time, over a period of two years. These months were the happiest and most carefree ones for my mother, my sisters and me. We enjoyed a freedom we had never known before. Life was wonderful without him, and my mother admitted that she, too, found it liberating. She became softer and looked younger, felt more at ease, and had more time for us. Strangely enough, however, she seemed to miss him after a while. She had no women friends with whom she could talk about the things that were important to her. He did come home every Friday evening, and since he only wanted to spend time with her, my sisters and I were free to do whatever we wanted. On Saturday mornings my parents went shopping together, and often didn't return until after we were back from school. On Sundays they went on long hikes without us whenever the weather permitted it.

For the first time since our flight from East Germany, my father received a decent salary with benefits and health insurance for the entire family. He could expect promotions and pay raises at regular intervals, and would receive a good pension one day. Life seemed calculable. He faithfully and meticulously did his daily workload at the revenue office. His wife called him the born civil servant. Finally my parents could breath more freely. They had arrived.

The easygoing mood didn't last, however. After he returned from his final session of schooling, he very quickly fell back into his old behavioral patterns, belittled her "fantastic plans", as he called them, and forbade her once again to buy anything without his express approval. After all, he earned the money, and therefore he could judge best how it was to be spent. Every night after supper she was to be there for him exclusively.

Life was monotonous. There were hardly any diversions in that little town, and plagued by homesickness, my mother would talk more and more frequently about her many visits to the theater and opera in Dresden. The only place my parents went regularly was the cinema. Once my mother returned very excitedly, after they had seen the film *Salaire du peur,* which had impressed her deeply. Another time they took me along to see *La strada.* I sat next to her and could feel how she got carried away. She spoke with great intensity about the fates of the people in this film, stressing that she couldn't imagine such a life, but didn't understand how small her own world was within the confines of our tight apartment. Without becoming conscious of it, she preferred to adapt to her life by reading many books, and then dreaming about them while he claimed responsibility for everything except the housework. Whenever she complained about it, he said that he only meant well, that he was taking care of everything so she would not have to worry about it.

"But I do want to know about it," she insisted, "I have a right to know!"

"I don't want you to wrack your pretty little brain over these things. Other men don't do nearly as much for their wives. Why aren't you glad that I'm so considerate?"

Once again he settled financial matters without discussing them with her. He only showed her various forms, insurance policies and other contracts if he needed her signature. At such times, he would stand next to her to watch her sign, and didn't find it necessary that she read the small print. When she insisted that he allow her to read the form, he answered that it would take too long, and she wouldn't be able to understand the complicated language anyway, and besides, didn't she know that she could trust him completely? He assured her that he was telling her all the important things, stressing that he was acting in her best interest.

"But I am part of the family; we are married! I want to know what's going on. I have ideas, too, and I don't always want to stand there completely ignorant. I want to be able to withdraw money from our account instead of you always bringing it to me or standing next to me when I am at the bank. This makes me feel insecure, so I get all flustered and do everything wrong!" She sounded very unhappy.

During such moments he made a show of being generous to appease her, and actually explained something to her, but usually he just did what he thought was best on his own, and eventually she gave up.

One day he joined a book club. From then on he chose the books for our birthdays and Christmas from the meager offering of those early days. Books we never liked from authors we had never heard of that stood unread on our bookshelves gathering dust. My mother said she wanted to select books herself in bookstores, so she could take them into her hands, leaf through them, and read a page here and there before buying them. "What good are cheap books if they don't interest me, to say nothing of all the other things you order without my knowledge. You treat me like a child, but I am your wife."

He burst out laughing. Her words amused him. "Of course you are my wife, and I always discuss everything with you."

"No, you don't! Frequently I don't find out about an order until it arrives in the mail, or you bring things home for the household. Often enough you hide the items in your closet because you know very well that I don't want them. A good sharp knife from Solingen steel is better than those ridiculous gadgets that never work anyway and are a lot of trouble to clean. That stuff just looks practical and seems to be child's play during demonstrations, but I can work better and faster with a good knife."

"All right then, in the future we'll decide together," he said, reaching for the book catalog.

"That I would like to see. From now on I want to buy my own books," she insisted.

"They are asking exorbitant prices in bookstores. When will you come to your senses?" he tried again.

"The book club does not have what I am looking for," she countered.

"Yes it does," he protested. "Here, have you gone through the latest catalog yet?" He picked it up from the living room table and held it out to her. "You just have to look through carefully. I've already marked some interesting titles."

She pushed the catalog aside saying, "Those books you can read yourself. I am looking for very different topics."

From that day on she went to the largest bookstore on the market place in Cochem to secretly order books, and paid for them with her household money. She was well read, but she was alone with the subject matter, because her husband read no books. He was satisfied with the local newspaper and the travel brochures that he studied for hours.

The owner of the bookstore knew my mother, and was horrified when she heard what she wished to order. She pulled her away from the other customers and tried to change her mind, but my mother insisted on her choice. Among them were books with scandalous contents for that time, like Henry Miller's *Tropic of Capricorn* and *Daphne and Chloe* by Longos. Both were listed on the Catholic church's index of banned books, which people in the fifties still adhered to in this small catholic town. One afternoon my mother told me incredulously that the owner of the bookstore had said she could order the books for her only because she was protestant. "Lutheran," she had replied, "we belong to the Lutheran church." And to me she exclaimed, "Can you imagine that they would say something like that to me in a bookstore? Isn't that very strange indeed? Just think of it, if I had remained catholic, if Papa had gone along with the nonsense of his wife's catholic relatives, then I wouldn't have been able to buy these books in Cochem!"

The order took a while. When the small book by Longos finally arrived, the owner fetched it wrapped up from the back room so no one could see it, and it was handed to my mother discreetly over the counter. The storeowner was appalled when my mother unwrapped the book in the store to take a look at the book before paying for it. My mother was amused by her behavior.

She had bought that love story when she herself was still young and of classical beauty. The book has been standing on my own bookshelf for years now in such a way that I can see the drawing of the lovers on the front cover. One day my mother gave me the pretty little book, saying, "Here, you take it, I don't need it anymore." I was usually happy about such gifts, but when she gave me *Daphne and Chloe*, it seemed to me as though she had finished with life. My poor dear mama, how much she had desired a true love of her own!

Another time, out of the clear blue sky, she asked me as she entered the room, "Anne, can you imagine having breakfast in the nude with your friends?" And since I didn't answer immediately, she explained, "Henry Miller does that with his women." She was very beautiful as she stood in the middle of the living room wearing a light dress, laughing freely at her own question. No, I couldn't imagine that, at least not in the prudish atmosphere of our home. I was surprised that it impressed her how free others were. She, too, was born to be much freer. What held her back? Why did the small and narrow in her life continue to win out? Why was it stronger than her desire to pursue greater things?

Her husband would frequently talk admiringly about the wives of his colleagues, about sales women and the women in the neighborhood. He praised them, added how good-looking they were and how well they dressed, boasting that he could imagine a life with any one of them – without paying any attention to how this might affect his wife's feelings.

"Sure, you think that you could live with them, but would they take you?" She sneered back at him after she'd had to listen to such idle talk more than once.

"You must admit that Fräulein Bachmann always looks very good," he bragged as if playing his trump card. Her first name was Felicitas, he told us, and she was the department secretary.

"You call this looking good? She's all shriveled up! And what about me, don't I always look good?" she challenged him, deeply hurt.

"Fräulein Bachmann and I never fight."

"Are you living with her? Do you call her by her first name? No woman would be able to live with you, I can tell you that much, especially no woman who is financially independent! You make all the decisions, you always think you know better. Other women would not put up with that. But you seem to think you can treat me any way you like, and then, to top it off, you set others up as an example for me!"

"And no man could stand living with you," he countered, genuinely surprised by her reaction. "You can be glad that you have me!"

"Sure. You are free to go whenever you like. Felicitas Bachmann, this frigid woman, who has never been with a man, she might even take you in."

"How dare you say that? How would you know?" he protested.

"I can tell by looking at her. She longs feverishly for a man. She would gladly take any man at all."

"What's come over you? That's reprehensible. That's slander!"

"You started it. And, by the way, how come you know so much about her?"

He tapped his forehead to indicate to her how stupid she was.

"I know you find other women more interesting. You would get along famously with every one of them. They all would esteem you more highly than I. But were you ever by any chance together with one of them? Or why would you praise them so? Or would you like to try it? Why don't you admit it!" My mother sounded hurt.

"Why don't you stop already? Don't exaggerate all the time!" He tried to brush things off. "Whatever you might think, Fräulein Bachmann is very competent, extremely pleasant and quiet."

"Of course! And how am I? You are so mean, so unbelievably mean! You've always been mean to me. You have no idea what you are talking about!" After that outburst she cowered down on the couch and began to cry.

"Do you always have to sulk? Every little thing gets you upset," he said, annoyed. She continued to weep.

After a while he said, "Come on, stop your weeping, I didn't mean it that way."

"And how did you mean it? That's no small thing. Just go ahead and make light of it. You look at other women. Don't you think they notice that? You take away my honor!" Then she lifted her head, wiped away her tears with the back of her hand, and said, "None of them can do what I can! And you, you don't know what you owe me, your wife, and how to behave properly."

I hated the way he called Frau Bachmann Fräulein just because she was not married.

I often wondered why my mother couldn't let go of the things that poisoned her life. Why did she have to talk about them over and over again? Once, when we were alone on a walk through the vineyards, I asked her why she clung to her past so tenaciously.

"Anne, you don't know what it's like. You don't know what it means to be married to such a man. No matter what I did, he yelped, 'I'll cure you of that yet!' He wanted to 'cure' me of everything."

"Why don't you leave him then? You don't have to stay with him!"

"And how should I do that? What would we live off of? What are you thinking?" she asked, looking completely defenseless.

"We're grown up now, we'll help you," I insisted. "I know how unhappy you are. You just have to have a little courage for a new beginning. Staying with him takes courage, too."

"But you are all still in school."

"Yes, but we are on your side. Just try it, I know it'll work."

She gave no answer. She always became silent when my sisters and I tried to suggest to her that she leave him.

"Everything would have to be divided up," I said. I wanted to lift her spirits, and show her she had a choice, that things didn't have to stay the way they were.

"How are we to divide up everything? We would have to move into smaller apartments and buy more furniture." She shrugged her shoulders in a way that told me that for her the discussion was over.

"That can all be solved," I said, "you just need to have some faith in yourself. We won't need much to start with."

"I can't," was always her answer, and then she suggested, "come, let's walk some more in the sun before we return to the valley."

We continued our walk in silence, staying close enough to each other along the narrow path that I could smell her Mouson Lavendel, the eau de cologne I liked best. I still miss the scent. All her things, the dainty lace and maco handkerchiefs she took out of her skirt or coat pockets for me because I never had one along, her blouses, scarves and pullovers, everything smelled of it. I loved to walk with her arm in arm when we went window-shopping or along the Mosel promenade. It was wonderful to feel her warm body so close.

The radio we had been so happy to get soon became an instrument of tyranny. The longer we had it, the more dictatorially he treated his family. He marked all the programs he wanted to hear in the weekly radio guide using different colors depending on the kind of program it was and its importance to him. Shortly before the evening program began, usually classical music, he told us to use the bathroom and get what we might need for the next two hours. Then we had to sit down and remain quiet. He looked at the clock, and punctually at eight he pushed down the ivory-colored button, and would no longer tolerate any noise. My mother was not allowed to continue working, especially not at the sewing machine, because the clatter disturbed him. She was to sit next to him quietly on the couch. The slightest noise, every little movement, even the clicking of knitting needles irritated him. We only had the one room in which all family activities took place. During the cold months we had to do our homework there, too.

He sat completely motionless during the entire concert, leaning against his wife with his eyes closed. His face looked like a mask. His legs were stretched out into the room with his right food crossed over the left. His world was in order. He had what he wanted exactly the way he wanted it.

When my mother was under pressure to finish a garment she pleaded with him to let her continue to sew. If she needed it for an invitation or a festive occasion, he might allow her to go on, but otherwise he forbade it. So she got up again around midnight when he was fast asleep and worked until she was done.

Because she acquiesced, the outer appearance of a good marriage remained intact. The neighbors in our house said nothing, and no one in town became suspicious that anything might be amiss because she had become an artist at hiding her real circumstances, and maybe he thought all families were like ours.

Almost daily my parents walked arm in arm through the pretty town that had by then become a favorite tourist attraction. She picked him up at his office in any kind of weather, and they quickly went shopping together. Only when it was pouring rain or during a heavy storm did she stay at home. Then he was disappointed and asked, "Why didn't you come today? I've been waiting for you all afternoon. Don't you know how I look forward to seeing you? The mere thought that you are meeting me makes my work bearable."

The women in their aprons, who were standing in groups in front of their houses or leaning on their kitchen and living room window sills talking about the latest gossip, looked at her in wonder as she approached, and whispered after she had walked past with light quick steps at exactly a quarter to five, dressed elegantly and greeting them in a friendly manner. None of those women would have ever thought of picking up their husbands from work.

I blamed him for our bleak and joyless life and supported my mother, but I could not understand why she left me to fend for myself so often, and didn't even help me when it would have been easy for her. She never talked to me about menstruation. She told me nothing about the changes I should expect in my body, and gave me no books to read the way other mothers did with their daughters. The girls in my class brought along such books, and they whispered about them during a break or after class in small groups, exchanged experiences and looked at the pictures and drawings. I didn't join in because I was inhibited and because I felt ignorant. I didn't even dare ask any questions for fear they might laugh at me.

All my mother did was look at me searchingly from time to time, asking me if everything was all right. I had no answer for her. I only had a vague idea from the girls at school. They all had their period, that much I knew. I saw their blood-stained underpants when we were sitting on the terrace floor at school or on top of the tables in an empty classroom if their skirts had crept up and thought what luck that no boys were present. When I was little, my mother had taught me to always pull my skirts over my knees and keep my legs together tightly so no one could see my panties, but why didn't she tell me more when I was older? We had no books at home, no encyclopedias and no magazines where I could have read up on it.

When I was thirteen, I went to the Black Forest for three weeks with my girl friend Gisela and her parents, and my mother put a large package into my suitcase.

When she noticed my questioning glance, she said, "Just in case."

"What's in the package," I wanted to know, and reached for it.

"Just leave it," she said, "you'll only mess up everything."

"But what's in it?"

"You'll know when you need it."

"When I need what?"

"Sanitary pads."

"But I don't need any."

"The time will come, you'll see."

"What do you mean? What will come?" She gave me no explanation and simply walked away.

I looked at the package's contents and tried to figure it out. I thought, I don't want that anyway, and hoped that I would never need those things.

Gisela had discovered the package in my suitcase right away, and asked, "When is your period?"

I didn't know what to say.

Since she was very practical, she said in her high spirited manner, "When did you have it last? We can figure it out."

I gave some date.

"In that case we'll have it together," Gisela shouted happily. "We'll enjoy some wonderful days on the lawn chairs in the sun and have them serve us drinks and food!"

I had no idea when that would be, and decided to watch her.

When our vacation was over, I brought the package back home. My mother helped me unpack the suitcase, reached for it without comment and returned it to her wardrobe.

On a particularly hot summer day in September, I felt strangely unwell as I was walking home from school. At first I thought it was the unbearable heat, but then I noticed a painful pulling down my inner thighs, and it was hard to stand up. I thought I was sick and went to the toilet. There it came out of me like never before, and when I looked, the water in the bowl was red. Blood was dripping onto the toilet seat, the floor and ran down my legs. I knew that the sanitary napkins were in her bedroom and that I would need them now, but when my mother was at home, I couldn't just enter it.

I cannot recall what I said to her. Maybe I showed her the blood in the toilet bowl, maybe she understood me without words. At any rate, she whisked into her bedroom to get what I needed. Then I was alone again. She simply left me. I went back into the bathroom. Instead of being relieved that I now was like all the other girls, I thought the whole time, my father must not find out about it! I begged my mother not to tell him. "If you mention anything to him, I won't be able to stand it. I don't want him to know!" Suddenly I no longer trusted her.

She was about to walk away, but turned around once more and looked at me ambiguously, her head tilted slightly. In that instant I saw treason in her eyes. "Please," I begged, "please don't tell him, I'll do anything, just don't tell him!"

Instead she said, "You have no idea about the things that men want to know. You'll find out soon enough." With these cryptic words she walked away.

I ran after her. "Men," I said breathless with fear, "but not he! And what do men want to know anyway?"

Why didn't she take me into her arms, sit down on the sofa next to me and explain to me that this was the most normal thing in the world? Instead, she always thought that I was too thin and too susceptible to any kind of illness. But I was very athletic. I had a lot of energy and stamina. I had goals, and was ready to fight for them. Unfortunately she had no vision for my life. She did not see me as a woman in a new age with a new role. On the contrary, she passed the old limiting values on to me. I was to marry and have children to fulfill my destiny. I was angry with her.

"That's the way it is for women," she would say.

"No, it does not have to be that way!" I yelled. I was stunned, and decided that I would never again share a secret with her.

I had been living in California for years when my mother and I once sat together with a glass of wine. She was discontented with the way her husband was planning their days. I wanted to change the subject, but nothing came to mind, when suddenly I remembered the incident with the sanitary napkins, and asked her, "Why didn't you ever talk to me about having periods? You left me completely in the dark."

She looked at her glass of wine.

"You didn't even give me anything to read," I added.

"But I had no books, what should I have given you?"

"Things weren't quite that limited anymore in those days," I protested. "There were pamphlets at the pharmacy. I noticed them when I knew what they were about, and there were little folders in the packages of napkins. Why didn't you help me and give one to me? Can you imagine how ashamed I felt?"

I was surprised how deeply this still bothered me. I had said more than I intended, but because she was just sitting on her chair in silence, it burst out of me.

She avoided my glance. At last she said, "I simply could not talk about it. I just couldn't."

"But it's the most natural thing in the whole world. It has to be that way. It was your silence that turned it into something stupid, something that only happens to women, like a curse. The idea of sin and uncleanness resonated in your lack of words, something that men and the church try to make us women believe, while this change in our bodies signals life! If it's a secret, then it's the greatest secret of all, because it contains all that is human and holds all hope for the future. It's a sign that everything starts all over again and again without end. It's a wonderful secret don't you agree? I've thought about it often. How is it possible that a mother doesn't tell her daughter about it?"

"I don't know, Anne, I can't remember. You are right, but that's how things used to be back then." She looked very distraught.

"But you told him about me!"

"I couldn't have kept it from him," she defended herself. "If he had noticed it on his own, he would have created a scene."

"You could at least have waited for a few weeks. The two of us could have made a pact and become aware of our power as women. It would have united us!"

"Your father broke me. He suffocated everything inside of me."

"What do you mean by 'my father'? He was your husband! You told him everything the very same evening. You pulled him into the bedroom saying, 'Come along, I must tell you something.' And all the while you looked in my direction, and I knew what you were up to."

My mother was surprised.

"I listened from behind the door and hated you for it. That was not normal! You explained nothing whatsoever to me, but you talked to him about it as though it was the latest gossip. You could have given me some time to get used to it and regain my self-confidence, but instead I felt so ashamed without knowing why. He was never a father to me. Never! You always talk about your Papa. You had a father, I didn't."

"But I had to tell him, he always said that he wants to know everything."

"What you are saying sounds so incredible. It wasn't a great secret, but it was a female matter. You knew that I couldn't stand him. You yourself were afraid of him, and then, in spite of everything, you always sided with him against us girls."

"You talk as though you understand everything. I would need more money from him from then on to buy more napkins."

28. Addiction

By the end of the fifties, now that we finally had enough money to buy some new household appliances, the housework had become easier, and my mother had some free time in the mornings or afternoons. Most likely she didn't really know what to do with these extra hours, although she read even more. I hardly ever saw her without a book unless she was sewing something. Because her husband always interfered in her friendships, she didn't let any women become close to her anymore, and thus began many years of loneliness for her.

Her motivation to continue working so tirelessly diminished. She took some money from the household budget for a bottle of wine, which she got from the winegrower next door – a table wine without a label. The following morning she would return the empty bottle and bring back a full one, or she would send us. I noticed her drinking during summer vacation. At noon she was often just barely able to bring the meal to the table. Afterward she took the usual nap with her husband without resisting any longer as she used to in earlier years, and didn't wake up again for hours. He got up after thirty minutes as usual, and because she didn't stir, he let her be and went back to the office while she slept off her inebriation. Later she would also send us for beer in the pubs. Before he came home she hid the empty wine and beer bottles in the kitchen cupboard behind pots and pans or underneath the sink. She hid them in buckets, in the broom closet or in the deepest corner of her wardrobe. Soon she hid the bottles so carelessly that we found them as we opened the closets. Sometimes she would forget her hiding places and searched for them feverishly. When I happened to witness her putting the empty bottles into a shopping bag to return them for the deposit, she looked at me intensely for several seconds to make sure that I wouldn't talk. We reached an unspoken agreement, but neither one of us was fully aware of what was going on. We simply didn't understand the imminent danger. She was weakened and insecure, and I thought she was drinking to drive away the feelings of loneliness and to numb the pain of a life that was slipping away from her, and that she had envisioned very differently. Because she often didn't feel well she would go to bed for hours with a clear conscience. Soon she slept the afternoons away.

When she woke up at last, it was time to think of supper. In the beginning she felt embarrassed that she'd slept for so long. She feigned an indisposition, mumbling something about stomach cramps or a migraine headache. But soon she got used to her extended afternoon naps, which shortened her days, and stopped making apologies. Instead she complained constantly about various pains and talked about ever-new illnesses that befell her more and more frequently, and helped her get all the wonderful pills and tablets the doctors prescribed to her only too willingly, without warning her enough of their side effects. She increased the dosage as she needed it, swallowing uppers and downers to make her feel good. Later, Valium became her drug of choice, and for years she couldn't go to sleep without laxatives and sleeping pills, falling into near unconsciousness as she combined alcohol with drugs, thus increasing the effect, and thereby drowned her sorrows. The drugs gave her a feeling of lightness, which must have been tempting after years of struggle and hard work. With the pills she could flee from her dark thoughts for a while and continue to believe that she was still in control of her life.

She found new doctors, asked for more and more medication, and soon she had a shoe carton overflowing with pills, tablets, dragées and drops. When her husband noticed the countless packages, he took away the carton, and from then on administered the pills to her as prescribed. At first she resisted, but soon enough she accepted it, and from then on she was dependent on his judgment and goodwill. In the evenings she begged for hours for more until she had the number of pills she wanted.

"Come on, give me one more," she would ask.

"You already had two," he said.

"Two are not enough today, I need one more. Or give me one from the others."

"Two are more than it says on the instructions for use. Here, why don't you read it yourself."

"You and your instructions. Dr. Arenz assured me that I could take more now and then should I need it."

"But you take more every day. Your body is already used to the higher dose."

"Not every day, but today I need more; I am in great pain."

When he didn't give her the extra pills, she was restless and couldn't sleep, so that he would give her more late at night after all. At times he even urged her to take more so he could sleep.

Her addiction to pills soon became serious, but what felt even more repugnant was having to listen to her beg for the pills, and watching how he apportioned them to her, how he debased her, and how he became infuriated when he found out that once again she had gone to other doctors in spite of his forbiddance, and had asked them to write prescriptions for her. My mother could describe her pains very believably, and the doctors soon realized that she would leave their offices as soon as they prescribed the drugs for her.

When he found a new package, he would hold it up triumphantly. If she wanted to grab it from him, he lifted up his arm so she couldn't reach it. She jumped for the package, and sometimes managed to snatch it from him. He demanded it back, and threatened to go to the doctors to forbid them to write prescriptions for her behind his back, or to the pharmacists who would give her larger packages as she pleaded with them, or give her pills in advance if she promised to bring the prescription by later. She threatened back that he hadn't seen anything yet should he dare to do that.

Both of them played this game, although he had the more insidious part, and both forgot that they were gambling with her health, because even under his supervision she took too many pills.

For my last three years of high school I had to take the train to Koblenz, because the local school didn't offer the higher grades. I got home very late every afternoon, and would find my mother sleeping on the couch. I was distressed because she hardly breathed and didn't move when I touched her or talked to her. She didn't even wake up when a fly walked across her face. I watched for a while as she tried to drive it away with her eyes closed. Then I went to the kitchen to eat the food she had put on a plate for me, and slowly I began to suspect what was going on. I plucked at her blanket, she moved a little and pulled it back. I talked louder until she opened her eyes at last.

"Wake up, Mutti, make coffee," I said.

She looked confused, surprised that it was already so late, got up quickly and went to the kitchen to make coffee. I was famished after a long day at school and set the table in the living room for the afternoon coffee and cake. After we had finished, she changed to pick up her husband.

During meals she drank the glass of wine or beer her husband poured for her, and never asked for more. This made it that much easier for him not to pay attention to her drinking problem. "She has a good life," he would say, "I wish I had it as good." But didn't he wonder how fast a case of beer or wine was emptied? And didn't her change in manner trouble him? Often she continued to drink in the kitchen after the meals until she staggered while doing the dishes. Then she crawled along the walls to the bathroom, and from there she barely made it to her bed and let herself fall into it. He said little, and only got irritated when she ruined his plans because she felt sick, when she dropped things, smashing them on the floor, or when she lost her balance and suddenly found herself sitting on the carpet with a childish grin on her face. She struggled to her feet awkwardly, saying she had stumbled. At such moments he would talk to her in a hurried and didactic way, holding her by her upper arm. She brushed his hand off indignantly, denied with an offended tone that she was drinking, and said, "You are hurting me, get out of my way. I don't ever want to see you again!"

One day I realized that she would never be able to shake her alcoholism by herself, because drinking made life more bearable for her as she lived in this permanent twilight, which dulled her senses. I carried this knowledge around with me for a long time until I said to him, "She drinks too much and takes too many pills, can't you see that?" He made believe he hadn't heard me, but the medicine cabinet and the new little red suitcase she had wanted for Christmas were full to overflowing. And where did he think she got the money for the alcohol? Why didn't he want to know that? Hadn't money always been the cause of so many fights? It even happened that he admitted that he was glad when she disappeared into bed for hours on Sunday afternoons because then he had some peace.

Soon enough, however, the time came when no one could overlook her drinking any longer, and when he found empty bottles he held them out to her with a triumphant smile, shouting agitatedly, "I was right after all, you are drinking secretly! Here I have the proof!"

She put him off and said wearily, "Leave me alone. What do you know anyway?" And she drank even more than before.

29. Betrayal

It happened one sunny Sunday right after the noon meal. My parents were in the living room about to go for a walk. He was wearing shorts and very short beige socks, which she didn't like because they made him look like a schoolboy, brown sandals and a short-sleeved shirt. She wore a light summer dress with a wide skirt that enhanced her figure. Whenever I think back, I remember among all the dark impressions this image of a very beautiful woman full of life. In spite of all her problems, there was something about my mother I didn't see in other women that made her stand out. It wasn't just her physical beauty, rather there was something in her being, and in the way she moved. I wonder if she knew that about herself? When I look at photos of her from those years I am reminded again of this certain something.

That particular Sunday had been uneventful up to that moment, when suddenly a quarrel flared up between them that escalated within seconds. I was sixteen and sitting at the desk doing my homework. Since I was used to such eruptions, I didn't let it disturb me, but I wondered why they weren't talking a little more quietly. Everyone in the whole house must hear the shouting. I asked them to tone it down, but they paid no attention to me.

Then it was quiet for a moment, like the calm before the storm. My mother said something that must have provoked him even more, because I suddenly heard him yell like crazy, "Answer me! You are supposed to answer me, you damned woman, you!" He lost control and jumped toward her, blocking her way to the hall, and was about to strike her.

I got up and looked at him. I knew this animal-like posture – like a tiger before it leaped upon its prey – this wrath that burst out unpredictably and with such elemental force that it terrified us all over again every time it was unleashed.

Something held him back from hitting her. Defamatory words flew through the room, dark threats and bitter accusations, which he did not take back. They seemed to have forgotten everything around them. Suddenly, with a hysterically shrieking voice, he ordered his wife, "Go into the bedroom, you whore! Off with you!"

It sounded like a curse, and I shuddered at this vile command. My mother grew silent, but did not move.

"Do what I tell you!" he hissed threateningly. His face was white and contorted. His eyes looked dark. "Into the bedroom with you! What are you waiting for?"

He's lost control of himself, I thought, and caught my mother's eyes. Her face was pale and twisted with fear. I looked from her to him and back to her again.

"Into the bedroom, I said!" His voice grew louder, cruder, his body towered over her.

She began to whimper.

Again he thundered, "Off with you!" He raged and tried to drive his wife toward the bedroom like an animal, but even then she did not move. She simply stood there, afraid, waiting, letting herself be pushed by him. His voice broke and his eyes were wild with fury.

I neither knew what to say nor do, but I had an idea of what was about to happen. I knew his wretched outbursts only too well. That's how he had acted all his life toward his wife and three daughters. I was standing behind the desk now, but they were unaware of me. The man's upper body was leaning toward her, his right arm already lifted up against her. The woman looked around helplessly, unprotected, paralyzed. When her frightened gaze recognized me, she pulled herself together and walked toward the bedroom without uttering another word. He followed her. I stared after them and took a few steps toward the door. For the first time I felt myself in the role of the observer. I experienced everything completely aware of the situation.

He kicked the bedroom door wide open and pushed her hard inside. Before the door closed behind them, she began to give off pitifully whining sounds. I could hardly bare it. I stood right behind the bedroom door, gathered all my courage and opened it a crack. They did not hear me. It was then that I saw the bent-over back of my mother between the chest of drawers and the foot of their marital bed. She had bowed her head down low and was protecting her face with her arms.

He saw me, stopped as he was about to hit her, and seemed to understand what I saw.

"Get out! Close the door!" He screamed in my direction. My mother turned around. Our eyes met.

"Leave her alone," she shrieked and stood up straight, now that he desisted from her momentarily.

I wanted to press forward toward him without knowing what I would do. He pushed me back so hard and fast that it hurt, and threatened, "Get out of our bedroom!"

"What are you doing?" I called out angrily, and took a step backwards.

"That's none of your business! Get away from here! Leave!"

I did not move.

"Away!" He screamed to my face. I thought he would hit me, and was ready to defend myself. He took another step in my direction while pushing his wife aside. I escaped his grasp and returned to the living room.

The door was hardly closed behind me when I heard his yelping unmanly voice, "Take off your glasses! Stand up straight and take your arms away from your face. Look at me, you are supposed to look at me! Take off your glasses!" There was silence for several seconds.

Then he yelled again, "For the last time, take off your glasses, you damned woman, you. I'll show you, I'll teach you obedience!"

She must have taken off her glasses, and almost simultaneously I heard him slap her, hard and loud, time and again, into her face. After each slap I heard a terrible cry from my mother. He beat her and beat her and cursed her and cursed her. I heard how her body fell against the furniture, then she slumped to the floor with a loud thud. She screamed under his beatings.

Suddenly it was over. I only heard her sobbing, which ebbed slowly until it subsided altogether.

I was still standing right behind the door. There was a deadly silence. What had happened to her? I heard the wooden planks under his steps. He tried to step softly. The dry silence seemed eerie after the beating. I held my ear to the door and heard him again. I was shocked by his soft low voice. He was talking to her in a soothing, comforting way. It seemed that she didn't let him come close. Then I heard him approach me on the other side of the door. Suddenly he stepped out of the bedroom alone. I had taken a step backwards, but was still close to the door. He pretended he didn't see me, pulled the door shut after him, crossed through the living room and stepped into the hall. Then he opened the kitchen door, went in and closed it behind him.

Quietly I entered the bedroom and saw her kneeling at her side of the marital bed. Her body was shaking from her heavy sobs. I looked up. In the center above their bed, high up on the wall where the eyes don't look right away, hung the catholic cross, made of blond beech wood with a silver Jesus and the INRI in silver letters.

I touched my mother lightly. She did not react.

"Mutti, talk to me?" I pleaded.

"Go away," she said, "leave me alone."

"Why?" I asked, "why do you put up with that?"

"He is so mean, so unbelievably mean," she said.

She pulled herself together and stood up clumsily. She was unsteady on her legs and blind with tears. Then she reached for her glasses on the chest of drawers. Her hands were shaking as she put them on. He had had the presence of mind to think of her glasses! That meant he had hit her with clear intent, I thought. We went into the living room. He had returned from the kitchen.

"You miserable man, you bastard! You worthless, demoralized barbarian, you dog!" She spewed out the words while rubbing her upper arms and body.

He said nothing. Instead he sat down in an upholstered chair, turned on the radio, searched for a station with classical music, took the newspaper, spread it out in front of his face, and acted as though nothing had happened.

I observed how calmly his hands held the newspaper, and felt disgusted. From that day on, whenever I see his hands I have to look away, otherwise those memories from so long ago will come up again, and I feel anger rise within me. I never wanted to see him again. But it was difficult to ignore someone who is in the same room. He remained there as a shadow.

Her face was bright red from his slaps and embarrassment. Her left eye was suffused with blood and swollen. She let herself fall onto the couch. I fetched a towel, held it under cold water, folded it together and gave it to her.

"Put the towel on your face," I said, "it'll help."

She took the cold, wet towel with one hand, and with the other removed her glasses and put them on the table in front of her. She put the towel over her eye and put her head down on the backrest of the couch. I was very agitated. It was horrible to see her sitting on the couch, beaten and forsaken, and hear her moan almost inaudibly.

"Would you like me to make some chamomile tea?" I asked her, feeling so out of place.

"No, don't bother," she whispered, "it's all right."

"Nothing is all right," I responded loud enough for him to hear. I bent down over her and asked again, "Why do you put up with that? Why do you let him beat you?" She just shrugged her shoulders.

I sat down on the couch next to her in such a way to shield her from his view. He sat motionless behind his newspaper as if he had nothing to do with her emotional and physical state. But perhaps it was even worse, perhaps he thought he was right? She stroked my hand as if to comfort me. I went to the kitchen, put the kettle on the gas range, and got the chamomile tea from the cupboard.

Why did he drive her like an animal into the bedroom of all places? Why not into the kitchen? How can they ever sleep next to each other again in a room where such horrible things took place? How could they ever close their eyes in peace again in that room?

As I was thinking about what I had seen, I suddenly realized that he had always been like that. I remembered the nights when I was small and woke up, and could hear the sounds much more clearly through doors and walls. I used to suffer terrible anxieties in the dark, and Omi, too. When it became too much, she would get up, walk next door and demand silence through her mere presence. The following morning she called him a "barbarian" and a "scoundrel", followed by a torrent of Polish swearwords.

I soaked the towel in chamomile tea, and put it on her forehead and eye. Then I fetched two glasses of white grape juice for us. She took the glass, drank it, got up and went to the bathroom, where she stayed for a very long time. After a while he got up and knocked at the door, and said, "Come on, open the door!"

"Go away," she screamed. He waited for a few seconds and knocked again.

"I don't want to see you. Leave me alone!" She called through the locked door.

"Come on, open it," he repeated, "be good again!"

Those words upset me. "You are the one who beat her, and now she's supposed to be good again?"

"Shut up," he yelled in my direction. "Who asked you anyway?"

He turned toward the door again and said for the third time, "Unlock the door, Effi. I didn't mean it that way."

"Then how did you mean it?" I asked.

He gave no answer, but stayed in front of the door.

Finally she came out. He wanted to reach for her, but she escaped his touch.

"Leave me alone," she repeated, "I never want to see you again, you miserable inhuman brute, you!"

"Come on, I want to go for a walk." He ran after her.

She entered the kitchen and started doing the dishes.

"You can do that later, I want to go for a walk now!"

She continued to work in silence.

Impatiently he said, "Please come now, Effi! It's already much later again than planned. We never get away on time!"

After five minutes he was back and demanded, "Leave the dishes and come with me. I want to go!"

"And how am I supposed to go out looking like this?" She asked pointing to her swollen eye. "What are the people supposed to think?"

"If someone should ask you, you can say you ran into something," he remarked offhandedly.

"But she didn't," I said.

"Get lost!" he yelled at me.

About ten minutes later they left the apartment together. She had combed her hair over her eye. I couldn't believe it. He was satisfied that they got away at last, and that she went with him. I watched them as they walked down the stairs, she two steps ahead of him. They exchanged small talk. Nothing indicated what had taken place. Then I looked out of the living room window and saw them cross the street, enter the forest, walk up the winding path and finally disappear amongst the bushes and trees. Why had I not come to her aid? Why didn't I attack him from behind? Why had the two of us not hit him after I diverted his attention? Why hadn't I thought of that? I never forgave myself, and to this day I cannot understand what kept me from stopping him. Together we could have defended ourselves against him!

After I had witnessed my father's brutality toward his wife that afternoon, I understood that he had degraded her so deeply in her humanity that she was no longer able to protect herself from him. Time and again she took it without defending herself. She even seemed to expect it, and yet she was always afraid of the next time. She always shrank back in sheer terror, even when no beating was coming, and was never prepared when his fists did come down on her. She never seemed to have a plan to escape his blows.

As my mother and I were sitting together many years later, I summoned all of my courage and asked her about that particular Sunday. She had not expected my question. Then she asked, "What was I supposed to do? How could I have defended myself against him? If I had hit back things would have become even worse. He had much more strength than I, he was as strong as a bear!"

Her words about the superior muscle strength of men startled me. "But why did you stay with him, and why did you take off your glasses? Why didn't you simply run out of the apartment instead of letting yourself be pushed into the bedroom?"

"He would have run after me."

"Into the street? For everyone to see?"

"Perhaps not. He would have turned around at the front door, and his anger would have grown immeasurably."

"How do you know that?"

Instead of an answer she asked, "And how long should I have stayed in the street?"

"It would've been better to run away than let yourself be beaten. I would have run after you, and we'd have returned arm in arm. He wouldn't have dared to touch you."

She remained silent.

"Why did you take off your glasses?" I asked again.

"I needed my glasses. I can't see anything without them. When he was that crazy with anger, he didn't care if they broke or whether he would injure me even more if I kept them on. You know how expensive frames and lenses were in those days!"

"Good God, Mutti, what intolerable conditions we lived under. I cannot understand why you stayed with him. That hurt me, too."

"You are right," she said, "of course I thought of you. But back then things were different. I didn't know what to do. I was all alone with the three of you. It didn't get better until you were older and didn't need me so much anymore. He was always jealous of you girls."

"How can that be? That's sick, that's criminal behavior!"

"Oh, Anne, you simply don't understand."

"That's right, I really don't understand."

"You have no idea what goes on in some families."

"But not hitting you! He even said that you deserved it."

"Those were hard times back then. We had so little money, and I had such grand ideas at times."

"What are you saying, Mutti? Do you also believe that you deserved it?"

"Afterward he always said he was sorry, and promised that he would not do it again."

"And you believed him?"

"Anne, just let it be. It won't make things any better today. Why don't you give me a glass of wine? I need one now."

I thought, if I give her a glass of wine, she'd want more and get drunk. And if I don't give it to her, she'll get it herself and get drunk anyway.

Elfriede Richter with her three daughters in Cochem, 1954

30. Suicide

Not long after this terrible Sunday, my father was waiting for me when I came home from school. He opened the apartment door when he heard me coming. That was strange because his noon break was long over. I was not happy to see him, and tried to sneak by him. Suddenly I stopped short. The silence in the apartment was suspicious. Something was wrong.

"What's going on?" I asked. "Where is Mutti?"

Instead of giving me an answer, he wanted to embrace me, but he lacked practice. I stepped aside, and our bodies just barely touched. I was aware of my reaction, and suddenly I felt compassion for him. He was strangely pale, and his eyelids twitched.

"Why don't you come inside first," he said, "and close the door behind you."

"What happened? Tell me already, what's going on?" I spoke louder.

He directed me into the kitchen. "Why don't you sit down."

"But I don't want to sit down, I want to know what's the matter with Mutti. Don't keep me in such suspense!"

"Well, she's in the hospital. You can go visit her later."

"In the hospital? Why is she in the hospital?" I asked suddenly scared. "What happened? How come she's in the hospital?"

I was about to ask, what did you do to her, when he said, "The doctors don't know that yet. She fainted this morning. Frau Goedeke heard something, a dull thud, then everything was quiet. So she came upstairs to see what was wrong. Luckily the apartment door was not locked."

"And Mutti had fallen onto the floor?"

"Yes."

"When did Frau Goedeke hear that?"

"Around ten. Mutti lay face down on the kitchen floor and was unconscious. Frau Goedeke called for an ambulance, and then she called me at the office. I went straight to the hospital."

"Why does it smell of gas here?" I walked over to the stove. "Is there a gas leak?"

"No, everything is all right."

"I'm going to the hospital right now. What is her room number?"

"She is in the emergency room. You must stop at the front desk and ask for Frau Bergner."

"Emergency room, why is she there?"

"It may have been an accident. They didn't know all the facts yet."

"What kind of an accident? Here, in the kitchen?"

"We'll find out later."

"Come on, talk to me, you must know a bit more than that! Did she stumble or fall off a chair?" She always stepped on a chair when she wanted to get something from the top shelf. I was dumbfounded. "When can I go to her?"

"At 4 p.m. are visiting hours. Make yourself a sandwich," he said.

I had a sick feeling in my stomach. He stood in the middle of the kitchen, restless and undecided. Then he lifted his arm abruptly, looked at his wristwatch and said, "I must go back to the office. After work I'll go straight to the hospital. You don't need to wait for me with supper. I might be home late."

"We'll be with her," I answered.

He walked toward the door saying, "All right then, until tonight." I heard the front door close behind him. His steps echoed from the sidewalk through the open kitchen window. Then everything was quiet.

When I entered her room at exactly 4 p.m., I saw only her. Her bed was next to the window, and she was sitting up straight and smiled at me shamefaced. Sunshine flooded the room. The curtains of the two windows had been pulled aside all the way exposing the view toward the mountains behind the hospital that were covered with bushes and fruit trees. I felt insecure, and remained standing at the foot of her bed. I looked at her but couldn't find anything in her face. It was so beautiful and open, and she looked at me almost happily, which confused me.

"Mutti, what's going on?" I asked.

"Oh, Anne, nothing, everything is all right again."

"And why are you here then?"

"Don't ask now, I'll tell you later. Come, sit down on the bed and give me your hand."

We talked haltingly about everyday things. The really important things we avoided. When he entered the room an hour later, she greeted him with a smile. I saw her smile first, then I turned around and saw him.

I got up from the bed and said, "I'm going home now. Do you need anything, would you like me to bring you something tomorrow?"

"Yes, Anne, bring me some fruit, grapes would be good. Wash them thoroughly and let them drain well!" As I was leaving, I heard her say to him, "Give her some money tonight for the grapes."

When I stepped into the room the following day, Reinhold was with her. He looked handsome, young and tall, like the hero in a movie, with his black hair and dark brown eyes. He was from one of the villages on the Mosel. The people here looked different than in Saxony. Many had French names.

I was surprised to see Reinhold. I had noticed that they talked together when he was delivering the mail, and that my mother liked to see him. After his motorcycle accident he worked at the counter in the post office. I had expected her to be alone, and wanted to ask her why she was in the hospital, only now we couldn't talk. She had patted lightly with her hand on the spot I was supposed to sit, and I did so obediently, but I felt strange somehow, because this way Reinhold was sitting on a chair behind me, and I could not see him when they were talking with each other. Her face was radiant as she looked at him. I got up and stood at the foot of her bed. Now Reinhold was next to me. He looked at my mother the whole time. He, too, seemed happy.

Reinhold stayed. I thought I ought to go. "I'm going now," I said loudly, "I have lots of homework today. Maybe I'll come back later, after supper." As I was about to leave I remembered the shopping net with the grapes that I had put on a table. "Oh, yes, here are the grapes," I said and put them on her nightstand.

"Thank you, Anne," she said pushing some items aside to make room for them. Then she moved a large bunch of flowers so that she could see them better.

"They are from Reinhold," she said in answer to my inquiring glance.

"Do you need anything for tomorrow?" I asked, already at the door.

"Stay a little longer," she begged suddenly, "I am so glad that you are here."

But I felt awkward in Reinhold's presence, although I liked him. It felt strange to hear them talk so intimately. Then again I thought it was also exciting. I kissed her, and said, "Until tomorrow, get well soon, it's no fun at home without you."

"Come back later, Anne," she pleaded.

"I'll try."

"Please come!"

"All right then."

In the staircase I encountered Frau Goedeke. She asked me how my mother was doing, and looked at me strangely. I would have liked to hear from her what she knew and what she had heard, but I was too shy to ask. I never spoke with our neighbors except when they asked me a question. We had already been living in the same building for five years, but we knew little about each other's lives. Everyone in Cochem was catholic, only we were protestant. That divided us more from the local people than if we had come from a foreign but catholic country.

At suppertime my two younger sisters and I sat alone with my father at the kitchen table. We missed our mother terribly; after all, she was always with us. It felt uncomfortable to be just with him. No one spoke, although I was sure that he wouldn't have forbidden us to talk that evening. We hardly looked at each other and ate fast so we could get up again. Because I wanted to know what was wrong with my mother, and had yet to receive a satisfactory answer, I asked so suddenly that I surprised at myself, "Why is Mutti in the hospital? She doesn't look the least bit sick. What really happened that morning? Why was she lying on the floor?"

He stared at me. It was obvious that he didn't know what to say.

"Come on," I demanded, "say something!"

"Well, the doctor said that she suffers from gas poisoning," he said with great difficulty.

"Gas poisoning? Here in the kitchen? And that was the accident?" I was shocked.

"She had opened the oven door and turned on the gas, and it escaped," he explained, but I hardly listened to him.

"Was she about to bake something? Was the oven broken?" I pressed on. I did not yet want to think of another possibility.

"I don't know exactly."

"What did she tell you?"

"We have not talked about it yet. She must get well first."

"She turned on the oven, but did not light it?" I asked.

"I don't know. I must talk with the doctor first."

"You should above all talk to your wife."

We got no further. So it was gas. And I slowly began to realize what had happened. Then I heard myself say, "Did she do that?" Suddenly I could imagine why she was lying so strangely on the floor, with the oven door open. She had turned on the gas and put her head into the oven. The fate of a battered housewife.

I ran back to the hospital right after supper. This time, my mother and I were alone. She was happy to see me.

"Anne," she said smiling.

"When are you coming home, Mutti?"

"Soon, at the latest the day after tomorrow."

"Not tomorrow?" I was disappointed.

"I need another day. I must rest a little more. I still feel dizzy when I get up."

Although we were alone in the room, I leaned toward her and whispered, "Why did you do that?"

She didn't answer and looked out of the window. Then she looked at me.

"Why?" I repeated.

"I simply couldn't take it any longer," she said. Her face was suddenly gray and gaunt. She seemed tired and sad.

"My God, Mutti," I gasped, "you must leave him!"

"And what is supposed to become of you?"

"What's supposed to become of us if you stay?" I retorted, and wondered how I could have been so fresh. "We'll make it, you'll see." Then I added, "He would have to pay."

"It's not as easy as you think," she responded.

"No, not easy, but easier than it is now! You can go to work and we'll help with the housework. We'll go shopping and clean the apartment. What do you think?" I looked at her expectantly.

"We shall see," she said almost inaudible. It sounded cryptic and not exactly hopeful.

"Don't ever do that again!" I begged her, and since she gave no answer I added, "You have no idea how terrible it is without you. Please do come home tomorrow."

She smiled self-consciously. "The doctor will come by later to discuss my discharge with me."

"Tell him that you must go home!"

"I'll tell him."

"You cannot leave us alone with him, we need you! It's not nice without you."

"Yes, Anne, but it's so hard!" She answered chagrined. Her smile was gone, she frowned while staring straight ahead, then at her hands, at the blanket, out of the window.

"You have us. We are on your side!"

"Yes, I know." Her voice sounded unhappy. Then she said, "Tell me what you did today."

I thought of the apartment, how empty it was without her. We always ate the same food for supper: rye bread, cold cuts, cheese, a cucumber, tomatoes and radishes.

She was lucky that time, said the doctor, her husband and everyone who heard about the accident. Two days later she was back home. I was glad. Her attempt to take her own life would have been forgotten soon enough if it had not happened again.

When she was in another deep crisis years later, and the two of us were still at the kitchen table after breakfast on a Saturday, she talked about her suicide attempt in Cochem. The physician had sat at her bed and had tried patiently to get her to speak. He wanted to know her reasons. He listened to her, helped her order her thoughts and gave her careful advice about what she could do so she would not try it again.

"Did you want to attract his attentión?" I wanted to know, "or were you looking for clarity by trying to commit suicide?"

"I don't know, Anne, I cannot answer your questions, really, I can't. I only know that everything seemed so senseless to me, and I saw no way out. I didn't want to go on living. Everything was so hopeless, and the future looked so bleak."

"And what did you tell the doctor?"

"I couldn't admit to a suicide attempt. I had heard that the police would have to be notified in such cases. So I let everyone think that it was an accident with the old gas range."

"And the doctor believed you?"

"Oh, Anne, I have no idea, but he left after a while."

Nothing changed in my parents' marital life after that incident. The days came and went, and soon everything continued the way it had been before. That must have been harder for my mother than the decision to put an end to her life. After all, what remained for her after this act of desperation? Soon she drank even more and slept even more deeply on the couch in the afternoons. We got used to it and let her be. When I mentioned the suicide attempt to him after her death, he could not remember it.

"It was her first attempt to take her own life," I said.

"I know nothing about that," was his answer. "No one told me anything."

"But we all knew it, besides, how else would she have gotten the gas poisoning?" He shrugged his shoulders and looked away.

"The next time she took too many pills," I said, "and they had to pump out her stomach."

On certain days my mother was driven by an anxiety that remained a riddle to me for a long time. An occasional smile flitted across her face, then she looked at me with a questioning yet elusive glance. That told me she was concealing something she didn't want to talk about, and yet she had trouble handling it by herself. When I entered the kitchen her hand would quickly slide into her apron pocket. Once she rushed past me with a letter as I entered the apartment and disappeared into the bathroom. After a long while I heard how she tore it into small pieces and flushed it down the toilet.

"From Alfons," she said to me when she came out of the bathroom.

Alfons, Lara's older brother and a friend from her life in Dresden, was living in Düsseldorf, and they had been in contact again for some time. He was the love of her life, and I am sure her husband knew that. I am almost certain that their love never found physical fulfillment. Knowing glances, conversations about times long ago, a quick embrace as they greeted each other or said good-bye, or a nervous touching of hands as they walked passed one another had to suffice.

How sad that she couldn't keep the letters from Alfons. She needed them so much! I would have liked to help her by hiding them amongst my things, but for some reason I never offered it to her.

Now and then Alfons came for a visit. He traveled much on business, but Cochem lay in a remote place, and he had to add several hours to his trips if they wanted to see each other. Once they met for a few hours in Koblenz. They had to plan the meeting well in advance, and had to postpone it several times because she couldn't find a good enough reason to take the train to Koblenz. Alfons wanted to take her to a restaurant, however she refused because she was afraid that someone might recognize her. But who was supposed to see her, who knew her in Koblenz? And so what if they did? Or did she want to be completely alone with him, walk close to him, talk softly, or just be silent and feel each other's presence? They walked along the Rhein and up the Mosel, sat down on a bench to watch the ships or had a cup of coffee and a slice of cake in a Café, which she didn't finish because she couldn't get anything down, as she later told me. In the evening he accompanied her to the railroad station, and she went back to her old life. He waved good-bye on the platform, then boarded the next train to Düsseldorf, back to his wife whom he no longer loved, and left soon afterward. My mother stayed married. A divorce still tarnished a woman's reputation in the fifties. She was unable to live with the pressure from society as a divorced woman.

I liked Alfons' endearing way. He was always elegantly dressed and very charming. The way he spoke reminded me of my home country, although he didn't speak with the Saxon dialect. He sent me books regularly that I still have today.

Later when we were living in Worms, it was easier for him to interrupt his travels for a few hours, since the city was on the main railroad line. One afternoon they met for a glass of wine in Heidelberg, walked along the Neckar river, and later had dinner with Lara. My mother returned by train shortly before midnight. When she was back, her husband was relieved. That evening we had left him alone in the living room. We didn't want to be with him without her. He reproached her for staying out so late.

Eventually there came a time when my mother resigned herself to the way things were, and asked Alfons not to come anymore, and not to write her anymore either. They never saw each other again.

He died suddenly much too young of a heart attack. When we received the news of his death, he had already been buried, and I didn't know what to say to my mother. His name never came up again in our conversations.

31. Prayers in the Cathedral

Omi visited us again in the summer of 1959, as she had done every year. We always looked forward to her coming. The day of her arrival was like a celebration. She had written us early enough to tell us which train she would be taking from Dresden, and when she would arrive in Wartha, the last railroad stop in East Germany before the "Iron Curtain" border, assuming everything went well. From Wartha on nothing was predictable anymore, because no one knew how long the train would be stopped at the border between the two Germanys. As in previous years, she had relied on us to look up the connection from Bebra, the first railroad station in West Germany, to Frankfurt am Main, and then on to Cochem. But the arrival times for trains from Dresden in West Germany were vague at best. East German summer and winter train schedules were frequently not passed on to West Germany. That summer my mother had received incorrect connection information at the station in Cochem, where the employees had tried to figure out train schedules, scratching their heads and shrugging their shoulders. They made phone calls to Frankfurt, but no one could say for sure when the express train from Dresden via Wartha/Bebra would arrive in Frankfurt am Main, so they had given her a later connection from Frankfurt to Cochem via Koblenz.

We had just left the house to walk to the station, when we saw my grandmother coming toward us completely exhausted after the very long walk from the station. I was shocked when I saw her on this hot summer afternoon lugging her two heavy suitcases. When she noticed us, she stopped and put the suitcases down. Before she could say a word, I realized we would never be able to make good that we had failed to be at the station on time.

Seldom have I seen Omi angry, but in this moment she was very upset, and scolded us for having been so careless and extremely unkind.

"You let me walk with my heavy suitcases all this way in this summer heat. All year I've been looking forward to see you again, and as the train was pulling into the station, I stood at the window looking for you, but my children were nowhere to be seen! The train moved on, the platform was empty, and I waited and waited. I stood there all alone with my luggage and you didn't come. So I finally took my suitcases and set out on the long walk all by myself."

There was no use trying to explain to her that we had expected her with the next train, and had just left the house to come pick her up. We should have been there for the earlier train, she insisted. Her disappointment that we hadn't been on the platform to meet her after such an arduous journey was too great.

We had never been late before, and were never late again. Even so, this once was inexcusable.

When we found out that Omi would be eligible to receive her pension in the west, we tried to persuade her to apply for her move to West Germany. We would have liked to have her with us, but she wouldn't hear of it, although she would have been financially independent. Too many factors spoke against it. She loved Dresden too much, and in the suburb where she lived, close to the Loschwitz Bridge, there was little damage from the bombings. She was satisfied with her large corner room and the lovely gardens in the neighborhood with various bushes and flowers blooming according to the seasons from early spring to late fall. She loved the splendid old red beech trees, the graceful larch trees and giant tulip trees that turned this part of town into a park. And how was she supposed to live without her beloved husband's grave, which she'd been taking care of for twenty years by this time? Besides, she had her women friends with whom she walked along the banks of the Elbe river and through the Große Garten after work, and on weekends they would sit in the Café of the Carola Schlößchen and have a slice of cake with whipped cream on top and a cup of coffee. During the winter they would go to the cinema. She also visited the zoological garden frequently and dreamed of days gone by, about her husband who had worked there, about Dresden's baroque silhouette that was beginning to slowly rise back up again out of the ruins, and of her son Rolf. However, what spoke even more against a move was the never-ending tension between her and her son-in-law, that also caused problems between her and her daughter, and we children felt it even during the three weeks of her annual summer visits. She always wept when she had to leave us, her children, and in the days before her departure her eyes were red and full of tears. Nothing helped, no promises that we would write her and send coffee along with the reminder that she would come back the following summer. Eleven months were a long time, the distance was vast, and the political situation always precarious. Those politicians, what did they know about the people? She had no illusions and no patience with the men who were in power in East Germany.

Every year, as the day of her departure approached, we would beg, "Omi, don't go back yet. Please stay another week or two!"

"Are you out of your mind?" was her answer, "if I do that, they won't let me come to you next year!"

"The doctor will write a medical certificate stating that you are sick and unable to travel, and we'll send a telegram to your place of work."

"They receive many certificates, they would never, ever believe me! I am never sick. I've never missed even one day of work."

Martha Richter, Dresden 1959

"But Omi, everyone gets sick some time. Stay at least this once for one more week, please!" I thought of how often I had deliberately missed a day of school.

"No," she said firmly, "I don't want to talk about it! Don't spoil our last days together. I'll come back next summer."

"They really don't deserve such a sense of duty," I grumbled, but I knew that she would not relent in this matter.

In 1960 my father was transferred to Worms. In July 1961, a few weeks before the building of the Berlin Wall, Omi came to visit us one last time, only we didn't realize it at the time.

On the evening of her arrival, she listened to the church bells and asked me to go to the cathedral with her the following morning. She admired the huge Roman cathedral, whose thick walls kept the interior cool even on the hottest summer days. Entering from the bright sunlight, it took a moment until my eyes adjusted to the twilight inside. When I looked around I saw Omi standing in front of one of the side altars. She was lighting a candle, then she knelt before

Mary and the child and said her rosary. In the meantime I walked from the east choir with the Baroque high altar by Balthasar Neumann along the left nave through the transept to the west choir, with the four round windows that had been built for the emperors, and back again. Since Omi was still praying, I sat down in one of the pews where she would be able to see me easily, and waited for her. We did not talk about what she had asked of Maria. It was the last time I was in a church with her.

On the second evening of her visit we were all sitting on the large balcony eating supper. We could see across the Rhein river all the way to the mountain range of the lovely Bergstraße, when Omi said unexpectedly, "This is a beautiful large apartment. You would have a room for me here. I think I would like to live here with you." Her words surprised me. Was she suddenly afraid of being alone in Dresden? When she was long asleep, her husband said to her, "If your mother moves in with us, then my mother will come, too."

"What did your mother ever do for us that she should come to live with us? Could you perhaps explain that to me? My mother has given us everything throughout her entire life. Besides, her pension would be more than enough for her to live on. She could even contribute to the rent."

"I cannot live in the same apartment with her," he said.

"But you could always take from her. Even the money for our airplane tickets from Berlin to Frankfurt."

He got up and was about to leave the living room, when he stopped and repeated, "Your mother is not coming!"

"Then you tell her that she is not welcome in spite of her tireless help!"

"She is your mother, so you tell her, and if she should come anyway, then ..." he yelled and slammed the door.

Three weeks later we accompanied Omi to the railroad station. She had not received an invitation to come live with us. As we said good-bye she cried her heart out, and embraced us over and over again. Did she have premonitions about the imminent political upheavals? Did she suddenly fear she would never see us again? And was there perhaps also a fear of loneliness and illness? We, on the other hand, hoped for the next summer, and consoled her with the prospect.

On the 13th of August 1961, a few days after her departure, the East German authorities began building the wall in Berlin. In the summer of 1962 she wrote to us that in the political aftermath she would not get permission to come to us. It was the first summer after our flight to the west without a visit from her. One year later, in 1963, she could have come again, but at that time she was already too sick, and had no more energy for such a long and uncomfortable trip. She died of colon cancer not quite a year later. We had not been able to visit her during her many months in the hospital. By the time her very last letter arrived in Worms, she had already died.

I had come home from grocery shopping, and got the mail out of the mailbox just inside the main front door. I recognized Omi's handwriting immediately on one of the envelopes. Because of her illness it was a little larger, looked scraggly and shaky, and the lines were going steeply up from left to right. My heart skipped a beat. Hope surged within me. Maybe she is still alive? Maybe she is feeling better again? I jumped up the stairs to the fifth floor as fast as I could. I dropped the bags with the groceries in the hall, ran into the living room, and tore open the envelope. The letter began like all her letters to us with the words "My beloved children." It was shorter than the others, the handwriting was nervous and jittery, but I could read every single word. As I was reading, I realized that it had taken a long time to get to us, and that the telegram from the hospital had reached us faster. Only then did I look at the date on the postmark, and through a veil of tears I realized a second time that she was dead. This letter was her last greeting to us from beyond death. She had died alone; no one had held her hand.

As I think back while writing about her, it seems that the distance of time to the past no longer exists. Everything seems to be in the present again, and it feels as if Omi had been with us only yesterday. I would not be surprised if a letter from her arrived momentarily announcing her next visit. My heart would jump for joy. I would run to the railroad station, leap up the stairs to the platform taking two steps at a time, and as always I would look at the second hand of the large station clock. My eyes would travel with it around its huge face, and I would watch and wait to see it jump to the number twelve. Time and time again I would look at the posted arrival schedule to make sure that I was on the correct platform. Then I would walk all the way to the end of the platform and wait impatiently for the train to appear. At first I would just see the huge white cloud of steam and smoke, then the huge, black locomotive below it, growing larger fast, racing toward me with a thundering noise.

The locomotive is almost at the station. I feel a strange dizzying sensation as this roaring iron monster passes, and take two steps back. The brakes squeal, steel on steel, a piercing, deafening sound that goes through me in a wild shudder when the express train, still at high speed, enters the station. I run alongside of it looking for Omi. The passengers are already opening the doors and jump off before the train comes to a halt. People wave and call out to each other. Then I see her standing in the frame of the open door. I wave at her like crazy, forget everything around me, and run to her to help her with the old brown suitcases with the reinforced corners. My grandmother is standing next to me, safe and happy, when the "All aboard!" announcement comes over the loudspeaker, *"Einsteigen bitte, Türen schließen! Vorsicht bei der*

Abfahrt des Zuges!" while the man with the signal disk runs along the length of the train, throwing closed the last open doors. The train picks up speed fast, and a moment later it disappears into the Kaiser Wilhelm Tunnel, and the hubbub is over.

During the long walk home, sweat streams down the beloved woman's face, but after the long train ride and the fear of the border guards, she is glad to be walking in the fresh air. She had been lucky once again, nothing was taken from her, although as always she had packed more than was allowed. I carry the heavy suitcases with her, and I can guess what's in them and feel rich for a moment.

I kept that last letter from Omi with Ulbricht on the stamp and the postmark from Dresden Altstadt. When I held it in my hands again the other day and saw the torn envelope, I remembered the mortal fear I had suffered because of her. I felt the despair and loneliness again, and tears were streaming down my face. Once again I became aware of how much I still miss this woman. And even today it seems we had been cheated out of those weeks in the summer of 1962 when our family had been kept apart because of the Cold War. The death of this woman was the hardest blow dealt to us during the division of Germany. It was as if someone owed us part of our lives, but I cannot file a claim, because I don't know where to turn. And one day I understood that I have so many letters from her because we lived so far apart for so many years. I must show my children these letters. They have never seen them. I have to teach them to read the old German handwriting, the date, the address, and pretty soon one word will follow the next. But will it be worth the effort? No one has time, we all work so much. Of what importance can letters in a strange handwriting possibly be, letters from an old woman who died long ago in a foreign country, before my own children had even been born?

32. An Elegant Woman

Whenever my mother went to town she always dressed very carefully in a well-tailored suit she had sewn herself or a lovely dress in the summer, white or dark blue gloves, matching shoes, hat and handbag, or an elegant coat and leather gloves in the winter. She was charming and full of joy, and conscious of the effect she had on others.

Toward the end of the fifties and into the early sixties, during the years of the so-called German economic miracle, factories and businesses were looking for workers everywhere. Banks, department stores and government agencies needed more employees. Because of her confident manner and well-groomed appearance, my mother was offered positions without ever asking for them.

"Frau Bergner, could you not at least work for us part-time? We have such a shortage of personnel, and are looking for someone like you for our ladies' department," the female department manager at the Kaufhof, one of the first German department store chains, said to her as she was inspecting new merchandise. She was surprised and somewhat confused by this unexpected offer as she told us about it at the supper table while looking provocatively at my sisters and me. We were excited for her and encouraged her as we could feel that she was most pleased and wanted to know all the details.

"Well, the manager said that I should come by her office tomorrow morning, and that she would take me through the building to show everything to me. She also promised they would train me on the job, that they were willing to discuss the work hours with me, and that I could even work full-time if I wanted to."

"And what else?" we wanted to know.

"Well, that's it. I thanked her for her confidence in me and left," my mother answered looking down at her plate. "I did tell her that I couldn't make up my mind just like that, that I would have to think about it and discuss it with my husband."

"But Mutti, that's wonderful! Things couldn't be any better!" we all said as if with one voice. What a sensation!

"Don't hide behind your husband, you don't have to ask him," I said to her when I noticed that she felt unsure. "This is your decision and no one else's. You must go, let them show you things and make you an offer. Don't say no before you've heard more."

At first she brushed it aside, but then she wanted to know more after all, and went back to the Kaufhof the next morning.

The department manager approached my mother the moment she saw her and asked her to accompany her to the executive manager. She explained that she had already spoken with him, and that he had an offer ready for her.

When my mother heard that, she evaded the meeting by saying, "I can't today, I am in a hurry, I am late as it is."

The department manager regretted this very much, but encouraged my mother saying, "Frau Bergner, please do come by my office whenever it suits you. We would love to have you work with us."

On her way to the exit, my mother walked by the jewelry counter Frau Schmitz was in charge of, who addressed her directly, "Frau Bergner, why don't you take a look at what came in this morning!"

My mother felt magically drawn to the display cases. Frau Schmitz produced a piece from under the counter and showed it to her. "Frau Bergner, just hold this bracelet, do you feel how heavy it is? It's very distinctive looking and strikingly beautiful, don't you agree? You won't get a piece like that anywhere else for this price. Can you see how wonderfully smooth and well finished the double security catch is? You won't get caught on anything with it, and you'll never lose it. Would you like me to put it on your wrist?"

My mother held her arm out, and Frau Schmitz admired the golden band on her wrist, and slowly leaned toward her as she whispered, "This is a unique piece. I put it aside for special customers like you. If I had displayed it, it would have sold already. If you like it, I could hold it for you until tonight."

My mother took off the bracelet, weighed it in her right hand and asked Frau Schmitz to hold it for her. Now she had to figure out how to convince her husband to buy it for her. She picked him up at work at 5 p.m. saying, "I want to show you something, but we must hurry, you are a few minutes later tonight than usual."

"And what do you want to show me that cannot wait until tomorrow?" He asked.

"Frau Schmitz put a bracelet on hold for me. I have always wanted a beautiful piece like that!"

"And what about the bracelet I gave you for your birthday?"

"Well, that's very nice, too. I wear it all the time, everyone knows it already. But the one I want to show you is an exceptionally beautiful piece with a double security catch. If I don't buy the bracelet today, it'll be gone."

Over time, jewelry became her passion, and she always found a reason why he should give her yet another piece.

At first my mother was pleased about the fact that the department store needed her and wanted to employ her. She felt stimulated, and calculated in her mind what she could buy with the money, until she realized that it would mean that she'd have to be at a specific place every day and would have to leave the house at a certain time.

"I wouldn't dream of going out to work," she said to me a few days later.

"But why not, Mutti?"

"Selling things, that's not for me!" was her curt reply.

"It would only be for a few hours per day, three or four times a week. You would have your own money, and could buy yourself peace and freedom with it – and jewelry if you like. Besides, there are other jobs, too. They would train you, remember?"

"But then my time is no longer completely at my disposal. And jewelry he can buy for me, after all, he owes me that much, and clothes and nice underwear, too."

"But, Mutti, don't you see that you have a whole new life ahead of you, now that we are grown up? You can't just sit around at home!" I flattered her and tried to change her mind, but she wouldn't hear of it.

"Just leave me alone! What do you know?" She said. "I don't ever want to talk about it again!"

"All right," I said.

She understood the irony and had to laugh, but she adhered to her decision. At the time she was only forty.

Starting in the sixties, she and her husband began to travel. At first they went to places close by, then to the Black Forest, soon all the way to Bavaria and Austria, and finally out into the whole world. Their marriage did not improve, however. By then she was only happy on rare occasions, but the trips were a welcome diversion. Soon the months between trips seemed longer and longer, and she became sick more often. Frequent visits to doctors and long stays in sanatoriums made the time pass faster.

In 1966 he was transferred to Koblenz, and I moved to Los Angeles a few years later. In Koblenz they applied for their first telephone, and her husband bought *his* first car. Since he had had a driver's license in the military – which had been taken away from him by the Americans when he became a prisoner of war – he only needed a few driving lessons for his new one. After the initial euphoria about the car settled down, my mother said that she would like to get her driver's license, too. He ignored her. When she repeated her desire, and finally insisted on it, he said, "Later," which meant "never". She began to urge him, and declared that she at least wanted to be able to drive in case of an emergency.

To this he answered, "I'll always drive you wherever you want to go, and in case of emergency we'll call the ADAC (General German Automobile Club)."

"Sure, and I sit there feeling stupid just because I don't know how to drive. I'm embarrassed to admit it when people ask me, now that we have a car!"

"Driving is not nearly as much fun as you might think," he insisted.

"I like to drive," I interjected, "and so do you. And Mutti would like it, too. Why of all people is she not supposed to drive a car?"

"Her nerves are not good enough. Just think how easily an accident could happen in heavy traffic."

"That's incredible. How can you say that? You make her feel insecure. Of course she can drive! Besides, look at all the people who drive."

"That's just my point."

"You cannot simply forbid her to learn to drive!"

"I am not forbidding her to drive, but you've seen how easily she scares and how often she screams, even when you are driving. I am sure she would confuse the gas pedal with the brakes in dangerous situations. I cannot be responsible for that."

I was indignant. "It's her responsibility, besides, how can you assume that? Driving a car is part of everyday life. And by the way, if I couldn't drive, I would feel insecure, too. Especially in the back seat."

"I can't understand that," he said. "I am not afraid in someone else's car."

"That's because you know how to drive. I can't imagine what it'd be like if I'd never driven a car."

"Well, it's not quite like that!" He said proudly all of a sudden. "When we have a long stretch of straight road ahead of us on our trips, and there is little traffic, I let her drive sometimes so she'll know what it's like. She's often said afterward that she'd never be able to drive such long distances all by herself, and that she'd never be able to drive so many hours at a time."

"Oh, this gets better all the time. Do you even know what you're saying? How disgusting! She doesn't need to drive to Paris, just to the store!" I said, and walked away.

When I noticed that she didn't get out of the apartment often enough because he rarely drove her so wherever she wanted to go, I encouraged her again. "Why don't you finally learn to drive? What are you waiting for anyway?"

"He won't let me," she almost stuttered, letting her arms hang as though a heavy load were pulling them down.

"What do you mean by 'he won't let you?' Why do you think you must ask for his permission if you want to get your driver's license?"

"Because he doesn't want me to learn."

I was furious with her. "Why do you say things like that? Why do you think that way? Of course he wants to prevent you from learning to drive. That's a simple question of power and control. He isn't the only man who thinks like that. But if you want to drive, he can't do anything about it!" I laughed and embraced her.

"He always wants to know what I am doing and where I am going. How am I supposed to go to a driving school without him noticing it?" she whined.

"He cannot forbid it, so he can find out about it. Are you aware of what you are saying?"

She was silent for a moment, then she said, "If I just go like you suggest, we would quarrel every day. And how am I supposed to get to the driving school?"

You quarrel every day anyway, I was about to say, but I suppressed it and simply said, "If he doesn't drive you, take the bus or call a taxi."

"And who will pay for the taxi?"

"Well, you of course! You have money. Try the bus first. Start living a little! Don't keep looking for excuses."

She said nothing.

"Don't you feel capable of it, Mutti?"

"Of course I do, but he's making it so difficult for me." She wiped away her tears secretly.

I knew her tears only too well. I felt sorry for her, and was angry at the same time. After all, she was gown up, but tears where usually her only weapon. I hugged her and whispered into her ear, "Mutti, no one can keep you from doing something you really want to do."

She freed herself from my embrace and sobbed, "You really have no idea!"

"That's what you always say, every conversation between us ends this way. Tell me, do you want to drive or don't you?"

"You really know nothing at all, I've tried everything already."

"I do have an idea. I've witnessed quite a lot. Get your driver's license to become more independent."

"You are different, you are strong. You can do anything."

Her "you are strong" sounded like a reproach. I was something she was not, and would never be, and therefore I could not expect it of her.

"You are just as strong. Where do you think I got my strength? From you! Just look at your life and everything you've reached!" I encouraged her.

"Even if I had a license, he still wouldn't let me have the car."

"But the car belongs to both of you! You have to talk about it and come up with a plan. You've accomplished so much. Few women could have done what you did, especially under those difficult circumstances, so don't give in today."

She was leaning against the sink and said, "That was back then. I was young, and still had lots of energy. I was full of hope, in spite of the circumstances. I was completely convinced that we would make it, that Kurt and I would do well if we just planned our lives together. But it didn't work out that way, and now I can't anymore. He took everything away from me and interfered in everything I did. He broke me and demoralized me until I gave up." Her voice trembled. She turned her head away from me and looked out of the window.

I looked out, too. I loved this view from half way up the hill over the meadows and trees all the way to the Rhein river. I watched the excursion and cargo boats go up and down the river. On the opposite bank stood the high rise of the Königsbach brewery, and behind it my eyes traveled up the hills into the Hunsrück mountains.

"Take your life back!" I said. "Your life isn't over yet, not for a long time. You can't just sit around and stop living. You are still so young! How can you say you don't want to try new things? Think of Grandma Moses. Only yesterday you read about her again and showed me her picture. Do you remember how excited you were when you heard about her life and her paintings? You were so passionate about this woman, and the fact that she began painting so late in life impressed you. She was already seventy and still achieved fame with her paintings. You can do what Grandma Moses did! Besides, think of your name, Hildegard, it always reminds me of Hildegard von Bingen."

She shrugged it all off and seemed to collapse even more. I was moved. Her appearance touched me.

"I need you," I said, "I need a mother, don't you understand that?"

"Yes, I know." Her voice was hoarse, and the "yes" sounded bitter. "But that's all very easy for you to say."

"It's not easy, but do you have a choice? Why don't you begin with something that you know well, sewing for example? Talk with a tailor in Koblenz, and ask her who creates fashion in the area. Go to Köln or Düsseldorf and inform yourself about what's happening. You sew so well, you have a good eye for elegant fashion, and you have so much imagination. You can improvise, I know you succeed in everything you try, dresses, skirts, coats. All you need is some courage."

"Later perhaps," she said. "Go now, leave me alone."

My suggestions troubled her more than they encouraged her, and she stole away from these conversations, went to bed with a book or disappeared into the bathroom and drank several bottles of beer. Sooner or later she would open the door again. She polished her shoes, scrubbed the tiles or washed a woolen sweater by hand. She did all these things with great zeal, expending a lot more energy than necessary, and forced cleanliness to the point of physical exhaustion. As she was working, she would mumble to herself the entire time without paying attention to anyone around her. No one interrupted her, no one diverted her thoughts.

Now and then I listened to her for a while, and was surprised how misunderstood she felt. Time and again she spoke about family members and events that had taken place decades ago. Occasionally she fell silent for several minutes or continued in a barely audible whisper. She shook her head, sighed, wept and implored God. In deep despair she rested her arms on the edge of the sink as if she was about to vomit. Because she seemed so remote, I interrupted her to take her away from those heavy thoughts that drained all of her energy and depressed her. I asked as casually as possible, "Mutti, what are you talking about?"

She said curtly, "I've lost all joy in my life."

"Don't think about those things anymore. They happened so long ago, and you can't change the past, but you can look ahead," I begged her.

"But what happened then is not over for me. The old memories come to me all on their own. They torment me day and night."

"But they come only if you let them."

"And if they come all the same?"

"Get out of their way, ignore them. If they creep back anyway, think of something else immediately. You'll see they will come less and less frequently."

"I don't know," she said skeptically, and added, "you all live so far away."

Instead of seeing the good things around her and venturing out, she adapted to life in a frighteningly small world. Soon she had reduced her surroundings so drastically there was hardly any space left. It was as though she was giving up room after room in her apartment voluntarily before her illness finally forced her to retreat. The time came when she no longer wanted to walk through the neighborhood, or the forest became too arduous for her, nor did she want to go to the edge of the woods anymore to sit on a bench and enjoy the view. Even the balcony had lost its attraction, and she said, "It's too hot outside today, there's such a draft, it's more comfortable in my chair," or she just said, "later, tomorrow, not now." It took all my power of persuasion to get her to join me on a drive along the beautiful Mosel river, or to accept my invitation to have a cup of coffee and some cake in a Café on the Rhein promenade.

What remained in the end was her side of the marital bed next to the window, the books on the shelf behind the headboard and on her nightstand, the bathroom, her easy chair with remote control for the television, the passenger seat in their Audi 100, and the walks up the hill to the little shopping center, to the grocery store, the bakery, the post office, the pharmacy and the clothing store, where she could exchange a few words with the neighbors and sales women. She rarely entered the kitchen anymore. He made the sandwiches for her, sliced a tomato and a cucumber, added a few radishes and nuts, quartered an apple or peeled an orange, and she ate it all the way he prepared it in her chair in front of the television.

Even if she was seldom happy with his plans for an upcoming trip or with some purchase for the apartment, she said, "You go ahead and chose, you'll pick the right places. It'll be all right the way you do it." That sounded just like she had always told us her mother had talked, and that her father had to make all of the decisions. Her husband never understood that her disinterested attitude was the result of decades of training her according to his image.

The older she got, the more she stuffed her suitcases with increasingly impractical shoes and clothes that weren't suited for their long travels. When she visited us, she brought along her complete new wardrobe, and sat in my house looking very distinguished and adorned with expensive jewelry. For a time, she wore only very light colored clothes with white or light beige shoes. Even in the worst summer heat she put on nylon stockings. Just a few years earlier, she would have helped me in the garden or with the cooking, but in these delicate clothes, knitted of the finest wool, she couldn't do any work. She wore fingernail polish with matching lipstick, and her white wavy hair was carefully combed. She had her hands in her lap and her legs crossed, and watched me as I cooked dinner. Her movements became poised to the point of being stiff. Her lightness and suppleness never returned. Not a trace of her former sensuality was left. I kept looking at her while I was cleaning vegetables, and thought, is that really my mother? I don't know her that way.

She told me he was planning another one of those long trips through the western states of America, and that she didn't want to drive such endless, tiring distances in the car anymore. Besides, they had already been everywhere.

"Then tell him when you can't sit any longer, and take a break. Better yet, stay an extra day wherever it happens to be really beautiful. You don't have to do everything he's planned. Come up with some ideas of your own."

"A whole day in a motel is boring, too," she lamented.

"But there are other things to do." I felt for her, put my arms around her shoulders and smelled her slightly tangy lavender cologne, which didn't go at all with her soft light-colored clothes. "Mutti, please cheer up and be happy! Do you remember how you used to say carpe diem?"

"That was a long time ago. I simply cannot be happy with that man."

33. Cancer Treatment in a German Hospital

In January 1998 I had to travel to Europe on business. My first appointment wasn't until Monday, but I left for Frankfurt on Thursday so I could spend the weekend with my mother. I called her, and she said, "Yes, Anne, please do come. That gives me something to look forward to, because I have to go back to the hospital for a few days. The surgery will be over by the time you arrive, but I won't be back home yet."

"What surgery?" I asked suppressing my fear and only expressing concern.

"It's mere routine," she assured me.

"But why do you have to go again so soon? You were just in the hospital a few weeks ago."

"As a precaution," she answered.

There was something else. I could feel it.

Her husband, who was listening in on our conversation on the other phone, said, "It's nothing, really, they only have to remove a few more polyps. They couldn't get them all last time."

"All right, I'll be there on Friday, and I'll come visit you in the hospital right away, Mutti."

"Yes, do come, I need you now. I won't be so alone then."

When I entered the apartment in Koblenz a few days later, my father walked toward me from the living room. He tried to help me with the suitcases.

"Thank you, I can manage," I said. He looked changed. "What's the matter, are you not well?"

"Why don't you come in first," he said.

"Is something wrong with Mutti?"

"There were complications during surgery."

"What kind of complications?" I asked, and immediately thought of cancer. I felt everything tighten inside of me. Suddenly my hands were ice-cold and my mouth was dry.

"I need a sip of water," I said, and went into the kitchen.

He followed me and asked, "How was the flight?"

"Good, but long. I'll change quickly, then we can go to her."

I was wide-awake, and thought of her countless hospital stays during the past forty years. We always called her, sent flowers and cards, and wished her a speedy recovery. She enjoyed the attention. He came to visit her daily. If the clinic was far away he took a reasonably priced room close by. Later, at the recommendation of the doctor, he had himself admitted as well. He was enthusiastic about the liberal settlement of his health insurance. And thus the years passed.

Her first reports from the hospitals and sanatoriums were always positive. She sounded happy and relieved over the telephone. One time in particular, in the early eighties, she sounded almost liberated. Finally she had found the right doctor who understood her and took her lot as a woman seriously. In euphoric words she reported how well things were going, and that for the first time in her life all her pain was gone. She praised the excellent food and the friendly staff. The underwater massages were fun and did her a lot of good. Everyone was most understanding, and the doctors took the greatest care in treating her. In short, she felt well, and spoke disparagingly about how unprofessionally she had been treated before. She was in high spirits for four or five days. A few days later I could hear disappointment creep into her voice. Things weren't going so great after all. After a week the complaints set in. The doctors were no better and had no more time for her than those before. The food was not that good anymore either. The daily treatments were beginning to be too strenuous. Her pains were also back, and much stronger than anyone could imagine. One of the doctors had actually dared to suggest to her to speak to a psychiatrist, but under no circumstances would she seek psychological help.

"I can't stand being treated like a child," she said. "These stupid people are around me from early morning until late at night. It's exhausting, and no one can help me anyway. I feel miserable and want to go home. I want my own bed and my own bathroom!"

I didn't know what to say. Besides, she wouldn't have accepted my suggestions anyway. Why was I thinking of this now on the way to the hospital? It all happened so long ago.

I mentioned to him that I would like to speak to the surgeon before visiting her. He wanted to come along, and had written several questions on a piece of paper. He searched in his wallet and his coat pockets. When he found the list at last, he read the questions to me.

At the hospital, a young doctor we met in the hall on the ground floor looked at his wristwatch and told us that at this time of the day we could find the Dr. Weber in his office two floors up, but we encountered him just a few steps further down the hall. When he recognized my father, he looked at him rather strangely, then he looked at me, and I knew they had found more than just the polyps they hadn't removed last time.

"Please come with me," Dr. Weber said, and we followed him to the elevator. My father pushed the buttons as if he were the elevator operator. Inside, he positioned himself next to the panel, asked all the passengers where they wanted to go, and pushed the buttons. We let people get on and off, took along a patient in a wheel chair with an intravenous drip, and then got off on the second floor. I heard the heels of my shoes echo on the hospital floor. The surgeon opened the door to his office and let us step in first. Only faint daylight entered the room through a tall narrow window so I could hardly distinguish the furniture. Then I saw the large, dark brown desk and the two obligatory chairs in front of it.

I didn't move, even after his invitation to take a seat. My father sat down, collapsed and then spread out. He appeared devout, and at the same time plumed himself importantly. Again he searched for his list, and became impatient because he couldn't find it. I had the feeling that I could deal better with the situation if I remained standing. Besides, I didn't want to give the doctor the pleasure of playing along and making myself comfortable on the second chair. He had not quite reached his own chair on the other side of his desk, which would allow him to keep a certain distance, when he looked at me surprised. Most likely I irritated him as he noticed my resistance. Or did I just want to believe that because it reflected my emotional state? Either way, he didn't feel at ease in the situation. I was angry now that I saw him before me. Up to then I had only heard of him.

My mother had been in the same hospital only three months ago for a colonoscopy that supposedly revealed nothing out of the ordinary. Why did she have cancer now? Why hadn't they noticed that twelve weeks ago? Where had they had their eyes? Cancer cannot grow that fast!

"Please sit down," Dr. Weber said to me, pointing at the empty chair.

I gave in and sat on the edge of the chair. After that he took his seat behind his desk.

As though through a heavy fog I heard that the cancer was not only in her colon, but that metastases had spread into the liver, which could not be removed surgically because they were too diffuse.

For decades she had been under medical treatment. She had always tried everything that was suggested to her. She had submitted to new methods and taken new medications. I realized how the full impact of the news about her illness didn't register with me right away. As far as I was concerned, the surgeon could have been talking about some other woman.

I needed to focus on something. I didn't want to look at the surgeon, but there was nothing else in the office. With its bare walls it looked more like a storage room. There were no pictures, no plants, only artificial light. Even through the window I only saw the gray light outside and the gray exterior wall of the building next door, so that my glance was thrown back. Things have to turn out all right, I thought, so much is possible these days, while I began to worry what's going to happen now, how long does she have left?

I was cold. The cold came from within. I observed myself. My hands, I had never seen them that way. The man in the white coat was most likely familiar with the helpless faces of relatives, their eyes not knowing where to turn, and at the same time asking for understanding, comfort and an explanation. He knew that they were still under shock at this early stage, that they still needed some indulgence on his part, and that they wanted to hear some reassuring words before they would be ready to understand that they would have to adjust fast to the unavoidable. Only then would they be able to bear the full truth.

The doctor was a quiet man of average height. He looked at us as though he were trying to figure out what to say. I had to pull myself together, because all of a sudden I wanted to scream at him and reproach him for having failed my mother. I smelled the disgusting hospital odor. The disinfectants reminded me of decay and death, and made me feel sick, but I couldn't simply leave the building again after having just arrived. I had to go to her. I wanted to, and yet didn't want to. My anxiety grew, and my skin began to burn. I was itching all over. The pale fluorescent light flickered before my eyes. I wiped my hand across my eyes and dabbed with my fingertips below my left eye to stop the twitching. It stopped for a moment, then came back so strongly that anybody who looked at me would see it.

What could I possibly say to her? How should I behave in her presence?

"You must understand, Herr Bergner, it came very unexpected for us, too," I heard the surgeon say, "but we'll get it under control again."

Us and *we*, who were these people? Why does he ingratiate himself to us? The correct use of the language was suddenly important to me. It was about her, and no one else. Aloud I said, "How long?"

"Well, three to four years anyway, you can count on that."

It sounded as if he had said ten years.

Her husband breathed a sigh of relief. His chest bulged. I turned away. I simply couldn't look at him. At the same time I felt sorry for him. Then I thought again of my mother.

At least not so fast, I comforted myself. Three to four years, that was better than nothing, and gave us time to get used to the inevitable. But how calculable was her illness really? Three to four years – I can still hear these words today.

I looked at the doctor. Four years, maybe that was calculated too high. She would be eighty-two, not that old considering how long people lived these days. Micha, her oldest grandson, would be eleven then. I must take something back to him from her. I could hear the blood throb in my head. The next moment I thought, maybe everything about her illness is a lie, and noticed that I was no longer taking in the doctor's words. His office was so cold and uncomfortable, I felt completely out of place. I looked at him and asked, "Could you please explain to me again what you just said?" I wondered whether he noticed my absentmindedness.

He calmly repeated the treatment he suggested in my mother's case. I nodded and stared at him, but still didn't grasp anything. Everything around me became blurred. I felt so tired. I gave myself a push because I realized that I couldn't concentrate anymore, and got up mechanically. As I left the room I said I would call if I had any further questions.

The surgeon also got up and took a few steps toward the door. Did he want to hold me back or let me out? I was closer to the door, and reached it before him. Was what I did impolite? I hadn't expected cancer, no, not cancer. Up to now she had always become well again, and I had gotten used to that.

I said to her husband, "Come on, let's go," and quickly walked into the hall. On my way out I thought, I'm sure it's not the first time that someone simply runs away under such circumstances. Maybe the doctor was even glad to be rid of us. Yes, for sure, he was relieved, because now he could concentrate on other things again. It takes energy to comfort someone.

We walked down the hall. Since he knew his way around, he passed me to be the first at the elevator. I interpreted the way he moved and talked as him wanting to be part of hospital life. We went up to the next floor. I fixed my eyes on the faces of two male nurses who were taking a man in his fifties to another floor, and regained my bearing. The elevator stopped, and we got off.

"Her room is down to the left, right behind the nurses' station," I heard him say.

How would I greet her, what would I tell her, how should I behave? During the few seconds it took to get to her room all kinds of words went through my brain, but I discarded them all again immediately. Nothing suitable came to mind. I had never felt more helpless. She must not see my nervousness.

I stepped through the wide open door ahead of him into the room, because I wanted to catch her first glance before she saw him, in the hope that it would be for me alone. She was in the bed closest to the window, and I walked over to her. She greeted me with a happy expression. I tried to smile at her lovingly while I said, "How are you, Mutti. Of all the times for you to be in the hospital when I'm here."

She answered my question with a counter-question, "How do you think I am, Anne? I didn't choose to be back here again so soon."

I bent over her and looked at her face searchingly, hoping she wouldn't notice how uneasy I felt. At that moment he entered the room. My body stiffened. I couldn't show any emotions when he was present, not even when he was behind me. I did not want him to witness my feelings. The mere thought of his presence paralyzed me. I almost despaired, and told myself, don't be so stupid, what is he to you? After all, it's about her. Don't let him come between the two of you! If you want to show her your love, then show it. Nothing else matters.

I looked around the room. It was a spacious and light double room with large windows that had a beautiful view of the right bank of the Rhein. Lovely houses surrounded by gardens with tall trees and bushes stood half way up the hill.

She looked so needy and alone in her bed. She wants your love and your support now, I reminded myself, she must come first! I bent over her again and touched her. It was as though my heart were growing larger. A tear dropped on her cheek.

"Don't cry, Anne, I'll be all right."

"Yes," I said softly, and tried to smile. "We brought you the best yogurt and fruit. Would you like to try some?"

She didn't want to. "Later," she said.

At the next visit, I thought, for sure during the next visit I'll be really loving to her, I'll do much better than today. I looked around for a chair so I could sit down next to her, when he pushed one toward me.

"Why did this have to happen to me?" my mother asked in a low voice when he had left the room for a moment. She meant the cancer. She was afraid of this insidious illness that had crept undetected into her body. Of all the possible illnesses, it had to be cancer, the one she feared most since her mother had died of colon cancer at the age of sixty-nine.

I was sitting very close to her. Her face seemed tense, but all hardness had given way to uncertainty and skepticism. She seemed so forlorn and vulnerable, so wounded, and so in need of love.

"Did you talk with the doctor already?"

I had dreaded that question. "Yes," I said, giving her a kiss and putting my cheek on hers. I needed time to think of an answer.

"How do you feel?" I asked again.

"Not so well, but I don't want to stay here. I want to go home to my bed. It's terrible here. The food is bland, just the smell of it makes me sick already, and at night it's so noisy that I can't sleep. The sleeping pills don't help. They aren't strong enough; they ought to give me more. And someone constantly bothers me with something." The thought of her own bedroom revived her.

"The medication from the surgery is still active in you," I said, "that's why the food doesn't taste good. You must drink as much as possible to flush the drugs out of your body. You'll see your appetite will return then." I gave her a cup of yogurt. She only took a few spoons full, and handed it back to me.

"Would you like me to order tea for you?" I asked.

"Yes, tea is better," she replied, and I went to the nurses' station.

When I was back I pulled my chair even closer to her bed so we could speak more easily, and took her hand. She could hardly keep her eyes open. The surgery had weakened her greatly, also mentally. She seemed mortally wounded.

"I am right here with you, don't worry," I whispered.

"That's good, Anne. I need you now."

Her words touched me. I felt like crying for hours and hours to weep out all my grief and heartache.

Finally the tea came. I held the cup for her, and she took tiny sips. This way we both had something to do.

He was pacing back and forth in the room with his arms folded behind his back. After four or five rounds, the room became too small for him. With his eyes wide open he walked out into the hall and looked into the opposite room. He was full of unconcealed curiosity, and I asked myself whether he was aware of his odd behavior. I let myself be irritated by him. When I noticed it, I concentrated on my mother again. Back in the room he stopped in front of the other woman's bed, who had her eyes closed, and read her chart, which was hanging at the foot of every bed. He stood as if rooted to the floor in front of the rectangular chart until the woman opened her eyes and gave him a castigating look.

It was very noisy in the room. People came continuously to see how the other woman and my mother were doing. She barely answered the quick, friendly questions. Suddenly, a lanky female therapist entered with a wheelchair, steering toward my mother's bed.

"All right, Frau Bergner," she called out much too loudly, "we are going to sit in this chair now for a while to build up your stamina. We want to get well again really soon, don't we?" This was supposed to cheer up my mother, but it had the opposite effect on her. What a silly woman I thought.

"I don't want to sit in the chair," my mother said, "it's too hard for me right now." Her whole body went limp, and I felt all of the energy leave her hand.

"Come on, Frau Bergner, let's not pretend to be tired!" the therapist cried jubilantly.

How I hated such empty phrases.

"But I can't," my mother repeated, "I am too weak."

"It's on our schedule, Frau Bergner, it's your turn now. We must try to prevent pneumonia. Come on, things will look much better once you are sitting in the chair, you'll see."

"I'd rather not," she protested, "maybe tomorrow."

"I'll help you. Together we can do it. You cannot just stay in bed all day."

My mother offered no more resistance, but she didn't help either. The therapist was optimistic, but didn't understand my mother's situation. The wheelchair was a monster, much too big for such a small sick woman. Only hard cold steel and plastic, no blanket, and no pillow for support.

I watched horrified. First the woman tried to get my mother out of bed from the side toward the window, which proved unsuccessful. The scene reminded me of a Charlie Chaplin film in its comic element, only no one was laughing. My mother couldn't get up from the bed and into the chair. Without additional help she won't make it, I thought. Then the chair rolled away because the woman had not set the brakes. She caught my mother so that she wouldn't fall over and out of bed. The stand with the intravenous drip was on the other side of the bed and couldn't be rolled around, the tube was stuck somewhere. How much could this woman pull on it without hurting my mother or tearing it out of the back of her hand?

"You must set the brakes," I said.

The therapist looked at me strangely. She had noticed it, too, but she continued cheerfully, and would not be discouraged. She moved the chair between the two beds and secured the brakes to try it from the other side. It was easier now with the drip, but my mother couldn't get up from that side either. She left everything to the woman who pulled and pushed. Why didn't she give up and leave? What difference could a day possibly make? But it was Frau Bergner's turn in room number four. The woman just did her work.

I would have helped, but there was no room for me between the two beds. Why didn't I say, leave my mother alone, instead of watching spellbound?

Damn it, this sick woman doesn't want to get up! Can't the therapist understand that? All they seemingly cared about was that she was supposed to get well, to move around again, climb stairs, go to the toilet, and dance around once more before she would die anyway. Some kind of revival before the execution. Did they have any idea that my mother had been lying in her television chair day in and day out for the past two years, and had gotten up only when it was absolutely necessary? Or that she no longer lifted her feet high enough when walking, and that there were days when she could hardly stand up anymore? She needed someone who would talk with her and uplift her mentally and emotionally and heal her soul. Someone should sit next to her, listen to her and try to understand her instead of pulling and pushing her around and submitting her to such an ordeal.

Besides, my mother was not wearing anything except a thin hospital gown, which is open at the back and spread out because it was only tied together at the neck. She would not be allowed to put on her own nightgowns until the next day, we were told. Another one of those rules. My mother said nothing, her husband said nothing, and I said nothing while the therapist continued cheerfully. But she couldn't possibly sit completely naked on the cold vinyl!

That was unpleasant and unhygienic. How could that be in a modern German hospital? I was angry with that woman at whose mercy my mother was, and yet I still watched in silence. Why do they torment sick people on top of all their misery and inflict such degradation on them?

Suddenly my mother was heaved off of the bed like a heavy, limp sack of flour and thrown onto the chair, from which she promptly slid off. Her legs flapped around and got tangled up like one of those old dolls with movable limbs. Her hospital gown slipped all the way up over her breasts leaving her stark naked. Seconds later she was kneeling on the floor, and would have fallen over completely except the space between the two beds was too tight. I saw the stunned expression on her face. As quick as a flash the therapist squeezed between my mother and the bed and knelt before her, grabbed her under the arms while talking to her kindly. She lifted her up and let her flop onto the vinyl seat with her naked bottom so we could all hear it. Then she apologized to us that my mother had fallen down, and pulled her gown back down.

"All right, Frau Bergner, you'll sit nicely in your chair now for a while." She stuffed her pillow behind her back, folded down the footrests, lifted my mother's feet on to them, and put the hospital slippers on her feet.

"My mother needs two more pillows under her arms for support," I said at last. "The metal arm rests are too hard and cold and narrow."

The woman went over to the closet, got two more pillows and pushed them under my mother's arms. Then she disappeared.

Wouldn't it have been better to crank up the head end of her bed as high as possible and support her with pillows? Idiots! What the therapist had done was inexcusable. I fetched two of the thin hospital blankets and spread them over my mother because it was cool in the room. She looked pitiful. We hardly dared to look at each other. The people on Käthe Kollwitz' pictures came to mind. Was it that bad? Yes, it was that bad for my mother. I felt terrible. I had let her down. She was alone, naked and sick unto death.

"I don't want to sit here like this," she murmured.

"I'll get someone." I walked out into the hall to look for help, and when I couldn't find anyone, I left a message at the nurses' station.

When I reentered to the room, my mother had to use the toilet. It was urgent. We rang the bell. A nurse arrived just in time. After that she was allowed back into bed. They cranked up the head end until she sat almost upright and gave her more pillows for support all around her. Now she was comfortable again. Why, then, the torture at first? She was relieved, and said, "I never want to sit on that chair again."

I agreed, "Yes, it's much better like that. You won't have to sit in the chair again. They already made a note of that at the nurses' station. You must defend yourself if they want to do something to you that you don't want, do you understand? They cannot force you, so tell them that. We'll take you home as soon as possible, I promise. The apartment feels so empty and strange without you. I miss you everywhere."

A faint smile flitted across her face.

"I'll talk to Dr. Weber again before we leave."

"Yes, please do that, Anne, and come back to me again afterward."

She didn't keep me back. I was glad I could leave for the moment. I was lucky and found the doctor still in his office. We had a better conversation this time.

When I returned to her room she said, "I know that I have cancer." She looked at me with a soft thoughtful glance and showed no fear.

She is making it easy for me, I thought. I was surprised and thankful. "Did you talk with the doctor about it?" I asked her.

"Yes, yesterday. He said that I have to recover from surgery first. He wants to talk to me about possible treatments tomorrow." She looked unhappy as she spoke.

"I'll visit you every day," I promised.

"Yes, Anne," was all she said. She was exhausted and seemed satisfied for the moment.

My eyes kept closing from drowsiness due to the long flight and the hospital air. "I am very tired. I have to go now, but I'll come back tomorrow morning. I love you, Mutti."

Five minutes later he and I were back in my rental car. As I was driving across the Rhein and saw the wide, beautiful valley and the banks on either side I suddenly found myself back in reality. She needs a woman she can trust, I thought, an intelligent woman who will listen to her and understand her physical and mental state. She needs a very different kind of help from what she is getting at the hospital.

Because he said nothing, I broke the silence. "Didn't you always say that you have very good health insurance? Can't you arrange for someone to visit her and talk with her? You know your way around. Inform yourself, ask other people and inquire about their experiences. Talk to the family physician or Frau Hamm. And what about Dr. Wiener? It would make things easier for you, too."

"It's not as easy anymore these days," he said slowly. "The health insurance doesn't pay nearly as much nowadays, and I would have to give detailed reasons to justify any kind of additional help."

"But she is so sick, and needs help!"

"That's just it, because she is so sick. They are trying to save money wherever they can."

"But she needs someone who will talk with her. Please try to find someone."

I was not used to being alone with him. I had to learn to talk to him in the house, in the car, while shopping. It had never been necessary to address him before. I had always avoided direct contact with him because I could never forgive him for how he had treated her. Every communication went through her, but this time we were alone for the very first time. His wife's illness took a lot out of him. He tried repeatedly to strike up a conversation with me. Most likely he needed some comforting words after they had been together almost daily for sixty years.

We sat in the living room and talked very little. It was a relief for me that we could make plans for the following day. Then I took a bath and went to bed.

The next morning I made several business telephone calls. I canceled appointments and postponed others for the following week. For the present I would only go to Frankfurt and Düsseldorf. I could do this in the mornings and would be back in the afternoons to visit her. Wherever I called, the people had kind words for me and passed on greetings for my mother. Even so I felt very alone.

Three days later we brought her back home. She wanted to go to her bed right away. He had bought flowers for her, and had put them in a vase in front of the three-section mirror of her dressing table. I sat next to her as often as I could in the days that remained before I had to fly back to Los Angeles.

She had been sick often during her life, and had always gotten well again. This made it easier for us to believe she would recover this time, too, and perhaps that was why we had not made sure after the diagnosis of her last illness that she would begin cancer treatment as soon as she had recuperated enough. She rejected an aggressive treatment because she wanted to try other approaches first. Maybe she didn't want to accept the truth? As I see it today, we were all wrong. I didn't want to admit for a long time that she had become older and more vulnerable, and that she was dangerously ill. She did not actively take part in the search for the best therapy, but left it to her husband, the doctors and the medication. Perhaps she sensed she would not have the strength to put up a fight, and therefore postponed the chemotherapy treatment for months. And yet she wanted to live! That I know for certain, she wanted to live. She clung to life down to her last breath.

34. A Wedding in Los Angeles

During the summer of 1998 my parents went on their last big trip to America to attend the wedding of Bettine's son in California. The festivities were a welcome diversion for my mother to avoid thinking of her illness, dismiss her doctor's advice, and postpone treatment until after her return. While she looked forward to the wedding, it seemed as though she was living in a timeless state, during which the cancer couldn't harm her, and in fact she felt well. She didn't want to talk about her illness either. And what about the rest of us? We all lacked the practice of talking about sickness and death. But she was always on my mind, and I rehearsed what I wanted to tell her, and explained to her husband during our phone calls how important the chemotherapy was for her, and that they shouldn't wait until after their return from California.

He didn't push for a trip to America as he had on previous occasions, but if they should decide to go, then he wanted to make big plans once again. They included strenuous trips through several western states and National Parks.

"Why such long trips?" I asked when he told me about his plans, full of pride. "That will delay her first treatment unnecessarily. Besides, you've been to all these places already."

"I've thought about that, too," he said, "but she wants to go the wedding at any cost."

"Well then, come to the wedding and enjoy yourselves, but stay for two weeks at the most."

"The long flight isn't worth it for just two weeks, that's too expensive," he replied. "I am planning these extra trips to make it worthwhile."

"What kind of logic is that? The flights cost the same either way. You would save a lot of money on hotels and car rental if you only came for two weeks. She never wanted to go on these long, exhausting trips anyway, and now she doesn't has the strength for it anymore. Why don't you think of her for once?"

"All right, but if we are already over there ..."

"She wants to come to the wedding, just to the wedding! Don't you understand? She doesn't want to go on any more extended trips."

"Well, but if we come, I want to see as much as possible once again."

"But she is sick! Let her come to the wedding, and leave it at that for this time."

"Maybe it'll be the our last time. I would like to travel really far once more.

I am getting older, too." It was enough to drive me to despair. How utterly unkind to think this way! What egotism!

"And what about her treatments?"

"Mutti wants to go to the wedding."

"To the wedding, yes, but not for two months, and not at a time when the doctor would like to begin with her therapy."

"But as long as we are coming ..."

I could have screamed. Instead I asked quietly, "What does the doctor say?"

"He says she can wait with the chemotherapy until after we are back."

"That's news to me. Did he change his diagnosis and his method of treatment? Are there new findings? Is it not as bad after all?"

"Well, I ..." he was searching for words.

"What is it?"

"Well, Mutti spoke with the doctor."

"Does he know how long you want to stay away?"

"More or less."

"Does he know exactly how long? By the time you are back she could be starting her second treatment already."

"Dr. Weber believes it will work out. She spoke with him."

"Where you there?"

"No, she wanted to go alone."

"It seems strange to me. I can't imagine in the case of colon cancer that a doctor is willing to wait so long before beginning with therapy. Unless he doesn't give her much of a chance anymore."

The wedding came and went. They traveled through the western states before and after the festivities. She was completely exhausted when they returned from the last excursion, and feared the hardships of the return flight. He had ordered wheelchairs for her at the airports, and congratulated himself for his consideration and foresight, and was delighted because this meant they would be able to board the plane ahead of everybody else. She lay listlessly and disinterested on the couch, and I could tell how sick she was. I gave her a glass of fresh orange juice I had pressed from oranges from the tree in my garden.

She took a few sips.

"Tell me about the trip, Where all did you go? Did you see anything new?"

"It was so tiring," she sighed. "I don't even want to think about it anymore. Never again am I going on such a trip."

I gave myself a push and asked, "Do you have an appointment with the doctor when you get back?"

"No, I have to call his office."

"In that case, please do so right away. I am worried about you."

"Yes, Anne, but first I have to recover from the trip, there's no point in going to the doctor or begin any therapy the way I am feeling right now."

"Please go to the doctor right away anyway! I am sure he'll have some good medication for you, and some supplements to help you recover faster."

Twice she went to a sanitarium in the Black Forest. She didn't talk much about it. Her reports sounded tired. When she returned from the third stay in January 1999, I was with her for a long weekend. It was a dreary and cold day. She was not feeling well. The chemotherapy took too much out of her.

"You cannot imagine how terrible it is. The inside of my mouth is covered with tiny blisters, and the mucous membrane is inflamed. I can hardly eat anything, nothing tastes good, and I have no appetite," my mother complained.

She only wanted mild herbal teas, a little yogurt without fruit, and fresh sauerkraut from the barrel. I added up the calories she was taking in during a day and became worried.

"I'll never go back to the sanatorium," she said suddenly, "nothings is helping. This is no life."

He tried to persuade her to continue. She paid no attention to him.

I brought her tea without honey, because even the honey burned. After a few sips she put the cup down, and said, "Anne, sit down next to me. I want to talk with you about my funeral."

Her words shocked me.

"Come on, sit down, I want to explain everything to you. I've decided to be buried at the Johannisfriedhof in Dresden in our family grave. That's possible again now. I want to go home."

She was in high spirits, almost excited as she talked about her parents' grave, and that she wanted to be buried there as well. I didn't know what to say. She helped me by telling her husband, "Come on, Kurt, get the letters so Anne can read what I've decided on and how I would like to have it. Explain our plans to her."

"There's not much to explain, Effi," he said.

I was angered by the way he said that. Why didn't he go along with her? She was expecting it from him. It was as important to her as if she was talking about plans for a festive occasion. He fetched the correspondence with the cemetery administration in Dresden, the mortuary in Koblenz, and the plans for her grave stone from a drawer in his bookcase.

"Here, Anne, read this. It's all paid for already," she said proudly. "I saved 20,000 marks in a separate savings account for my funeral."

After all the arguments and bitter fights over money throughout their married life, she didn't want to cost him anything in her death. I took the forms and letters gingerly. Even before I began to read, she explained to me how she envisioned everything, and how she wanted her name on the gravestone. The names of her parents and Rolf were to be regilded. We discussed it as though it were the most normal thing in the world.

We didn't talk long enough about it all, I thought later. She wanted to say so much more. I told her how often I had been at the grave with Omi, and that we took the streetcar to the cemetery, and my mother named all of the other relatives who were buried there as well. Some of the graves were no longer there. Then we talked about Dresden. It was a lively conversation.

A few days after my return to Los Angeles, her husband told me over the telephone that she had decided to continue her treatment in Koblenz. She did not want to go back to the clinic in the Black Forest.

After her death he once confided in me that he had expected more of the treatment, and that the doctor at the sanatorium in Freiburg, after having studied the initial findings when they arrived there for the first time, had been upset about the fact that they had waited for so long before they came to him, because they had wasted much valuable time.

"That was your fault," I was about to say, but held back.

In Koblenz they would give her medication to take orally. It wouldn't be so hard on her body, he explained, as if everything was going to be better from then on, and that she would continue on her way to recuperation. He was still hopeful. We all continued to hope, but what about her?

The condition of her liver worsened. Some months later, the news came that she wanted to stop all therapy because she could no longer tolerate it. It made her feel too sick and very weak. What was going to happen now? I knew it already, but wanted to hear something comforting anyway. I wanted someone to tell me she would be all right without chemotherapy, and would live three more years, the way the doctor had promised us ten months ago. At the same time I knew that it wouldn't be that way. I had seen her weakness and despondence. She had lost her will to live.

When I was back in Europe in the middle of March, she was no longer able to do anything without help. Once again I arranged my work so I wouldn't be gone overnight except for my visit with the students in Paris.

"I am so glad you are here, Anne," she said. "How long will you stay?"

"As long as possible," I answered. "Alexander will come subsequently, and when he has to leave, I'll return, and Bettine, too. We are going to take turns."

She nodded, "That's good, I need you now."

She lay in bed completely exhausted with her eyes closed, but maybe she wasn't sleeping? Maybe she just had her eyes closed because it was too much trouble to keep them open and because she didn't want to see the ugly wallpaper in her bedroom anymore with the bright floral pattern, or maybe because she wanted to turn away from life and not be disturbed anymore? She moaned and moved slightly. How long had she been in this state already, dying a little with every passing day? I was shocked by my own question, because her dying hadn't just begun when the doctors diagnosed an incurable cancer. She had started to die long before that, perhaps as far back as her wedding. I never called her "Mama," but now I wanted to take her into my arms and softly say "Mama."

I sat down on the edge of her bed and watched her in her helplessness. She hadn't invited me to sit down. I thought of our common past and the life I had lived without her. And I thought of the future when she would no longer be with us. Frequently I noticed an expression of deep fear in her eyes. They became even larger then. They begged for help that no one could give her.

"Anne, pray for me," she said softly, and turned her face just barely away from me. I hardly noticed any movement, but she let me know in this way that her request was completely unaccustomed to her.

"I will," I said, and thought, oh my God, how do I pray for her? I wanted to pray that she wouldn't have to suffer so much or for so long, but that was not what she was asking for.

Her skin was light and thin and very smooth. There were hardly any wrinkles, not even around her eyes, and no age spots. Her face had lost its fullness due to her illness, and now appeared more expressive. The skin was stretched more tightly over her bones. I took no more photos of her. I would never see her that way again.

"I would never have believed that someday I wouldn't be able to read anymore," she said, after we had been silent for a while. "When others would say that they were too sick to read, that their headaches were too severe, I used to think, I'll always be able to read. Now I know what it's like. I cannot read anymore. I can't keep my eyes open, and the books are too heavy to hold. But the worst of it is that I cannot work through difficult ideas anymore, and I can no longer concentrate. I forget again what I've just read, or I fall asleep over it. Anne, being old is terrible."

While the trees turned greener outside with every passing day and nature awoke to new life, she remained untouched by it all. The larger the buds became on the trees outside of her window, the deeper she withdrew inside herself. This last spring passed her by. There was no promise of new life for her dying body. I tried to imagine what was going on inside her, how the cancer cells were going wild, how they were multiplying with unchecked speed and metastasized, and I understood that nothing in the world could stop this process. The cancer penetrated into all her organs, taking complete possession of her entire body. Her death seemed unnatural and violent, and yet it came about fiendishly slowly because she had a healthy heart that kept on beating strongly, prolonging her dying.

I had to get out of the house. I needed some exercise and fresh air. I wanted to jump up and rush off, but felt inhibited in my mother's presence. The thought of leaving her alone gave me a guilty conscience. I moved slowly so it wouldn't look like I was escaping, and said, "I am going for a walk. I'll bring you some flowers. Do you remember how many flowers I used to pick for you?"

"I remember, Anne," she said, "you always picked so many flowers."

I only needed to cross the street and walk past a few houses, and I was in the forest. I thought of times long past. After half an hour I started on my way back, put the wild flowers into a glass vase, and went immediately to her room. I began by telling her that I would never forget all the things she had done for us. I reminded her of the many cakes she baked, and enumerated them: the poppy seed and apple cakes, the *Bienenstich*, a cake with a honey and almond topping filled with butter creme, the *Eierschecke*, a recipe from Saxony, and above all the *Dresdner Christstollen* and the various Christmas cookies.

"No one could bake as well as you," I added, "I miss those cakes."

She let me list everything, but said nothing, and I continued to talk about the dresses she sewed for us and the sweaters she knitted. I talked and talked and felt a heavy burden lifting from me.

When I finally paused, she said softly, "I don't want to be alone, I feel so alone."

"I'll stay with you," I promised, "we are always with you."

And although I wanted to say more, I lapsed into silence because I was a coward. I wanted to tell her, "I will miss you very much. I cannot imagine life without you." But these words would presuppose her death, and therefore I simply was not able to say how much I shall miss her. I also hesitated because after she had decided to stop all treatment, her doctor had told her there was no cure for her, and that she'd have about three to four more months, to which she had answered, "Well, I hope it won't be that soon! I would like to live a little longer."

She closed her eyes and withdrew as though she didn't want to see me. Was she in pain? How did she experience her body and the cancer inside of her?

Did she reflect upon her life and what was about to come? Or could it be that she no longer thought about anything, that everything had become too much of a strain for her, to the point that she didn't want to take part in anything anymore, and only longed for sleep? I realized how little I knew about dying and death and the loneliness she was experiencing. Did she desire comfort from the church? Did she believe in life after death? In a resurrection? We never talked about it.

When I looked at her in her bed, which wasn't actually her bed, because she was now on that part of the marital bed where her husband used to sleep, close to the door, I became aware of the absurdity of their marriage. She had long resisted moving to this side until her illness had progressed so far that even with our help it had become more and more difficult with every day and took longer and longer to get to her side of the bed. She had wanted to stay in her part of the bedroom that only she accessed, where she retreated whenever she needed to get away from it all, and where no one came too close. Here she had a sense of well-being, and felt protected by two walls. Her half of the bed had been by the window for over thirty years. From there she could see the crowns of two birch trees, the sky, the sun, the clouds, the rain, and the moon and the stars at night. That part of the bedroom had been her space, with countless pillows of all shapes and sizes. There she had her books, her hand cream and her reading glasses. Finally, after much encouragement, she agreed to the move to the other side next to the door. The mattresses had to be moved, too, because she did not want to lie on his.

35. The Death of a Woman

At the end of May 1999, I visited her for the last time. I knew that Kurt had ordered a hospital bed for her, which was set up in the living room. Alexander and Bettine were with her. She would be the first person in our family to die at home. We knew little about what this meant, but we learned more as the need arose, and together we felt our way through the process of dying. Every day we experienced something new, watched her every move, listened to her every word, every moan, and came running when she whispered our names. She could not talk anymore, and I don't know whether she moaned because she was in pain or because she wanted to tell us something.

Even at this late stage of her illness her husband interpreted it as a ray of hope when she took a spoonful of pudding, but the food flowed out of the corners of her mouth again like with an infant being spoon-fed for the first time. For the third spoonful she would not open her mouth. She looked straight at her husband, and tried to shake her head. He didn't want to understand that she didn't want anything anymore. She no longer desired any food. From then on she only took a few sips of herbal tea, and that only when we brought it to her and encouraged her.

I was sitting next to her when he joined us and said, beaming with joy, "She slept well last night, she is more alert today. You see, it's good for her when she doesn't get too much morphine. I am right about it." I put my finger to my lips. He shouldn't talk so loudly. We must be careful what we say close to her. I read that the hearing stays intact longer than all the other senses, so we must assume that she can understand us.

His words make me feel uneasy. Why don't we help her in her need? Why don't we make her leaving easier? He does not understand, and insists that she be given only the lowest dose of analgesic drugs, so that she remains 'conscious', as he calls it, instead of allowing her to sink into a semiconscious state.

"Why is she supposed to experience her dying in full consciousness? She can no longer move, and no longer wants any kind of nourishment. Why do you want to prolong her life by refusing her more morphine? Is that for her sake or for yours?" I asked him later in the kitchen.

He evaded my questions, and bought flowers for her almost daily. Countless vases with large bunches of flowers were standing in the living room and dining room. She couldn't see them. She never got that many flowers when she could have enjoyed them. Her birthday was in the middle of June, and he ordered seventy-nine long-stemmed dark pink roses, one for each year, but there were eighty-three. I counted them. According to the doctor's initial diagnosis she should have lived to be eighty-three. He wanted her to be happy about the flowers, to say how much she enjoyed them, but she was hardly able to lift her head high enough to see them in the large vase on the low round table. He held them in front of her eyes. "For your birthday," he said.

I pulled up a chair and sat next to her. "Can you hear me?" I asked.

"Yes," she breathed. "What are you doing?"

"I came to be with you."

"Yes, Anne, please don't leave me alone."

"We never leave you alone. We are all here with you."

"Yes," she said as if to acknowledge it.

A warm feeling went through me, and my hands moved softly over her face, her cheeks, her hands and her arms. I sat in silence next to her for a long time. Suddenly she lifted her hand and stroked my forearm.

The few days that remained until my flight back to Los Angeles went by fast. I said good-bye to her the evening before. She did not react. Only a barely visible twitching in her face betrayed that she had heard me. I packed my suitcase, but I couldn't sleep. She was downstairs in the living room on her sickbed, which became her deathbed, and I knew that I would never see her again.

I prolonged my leaving the following morning. When I finally had to go, I bent down over her face and said, "Mutti, I love you, I've always loved you so very much."

"Yes, Anne, I know, I love you, too. You are my daughter."

"Yes," I said. I did not tell her again that I had to fly back to Los Angeles, I simply couldn't do it.

It was our last moment together, the last sign of affection we extended to one another. The slow farewell of my mother let me experience how our family was beginning to loose its center, and I knew that nothing would ever really be well again once she will have left us.

On the autobahn I could hardly see the lanes. Repeatedly I had to dab the tears from my eyes. My head was so empty. Why was I leaving? Why did I not turn around and go back? I left all the exits behind me, filled the tank at the last gas station at Medenbach, and drove on to the Frankfurt airport.

She died on the 3rd of August 1999. The news over the telephone hardly sank in. I was wept out. It was not until months later that I had tears for her again, after I had finally overcome the shock and had worked through the many events of her final year, and the pain demanded its rights at last. What had been burnt into her heart, what was written into her soul when she died?

I only understood very slowly that it was over, that this woman, who was my mother, was gone forever. The longer I thought about her, the more I wrote about her, and the clearer her image became again, the more difficult it was to accept this last irreversible certainty of her going away from us. How can I let her go, when even today, months after her death, there remained so much that we never talked about?

Perhaps I am exaggerating. Even so I am in deep despair over the fact that we never encountered each other as adult women. Our eyes remained blind, and our feelings empty. Of course we helped each other out here and there, but there was a lack of love demonstrated toward one another. We never made this deep inner connection. No, I must not say it like that, of course we loved each other deeply, but we did not show it often enough. Especially during the last decades of her life, when we should have known better, we had become estranged, and no longer made an effort to tear down the wall between us. And that was not only because we lived six thousand miles apart for over thirty years, after all, we visited each other regularly. We could have used the Berlin Wall as an example, which was torn down at a time when she was still well, but we didn't even talk about that.

Only after her death did I become aware of how deep the chasm had become between us. I roamed aimlessly through my house, I screamed in despair and tore at my hair because the two of us had failed to work things through. When I came back to my senses, I was surprised at my outburst, which no one had witnessed. I stood in front of a mirror and looked at my face, and wept. I walked through the wide-open terrace door into my garden. I looked at my roses, took one of the full blossoms into both hands and breathed in its scent, but the memories didn't fade away. On the contrary, they increased and became stronger. I cried, 'She is dead, she is dead, what will I do now?' How can I find my mother, the woman she really was long ago before she became the way I knew her in the end, but not how she was in the beginning? I want to know what made her suffocate and why she died the way I had witnessed it.

This should not have happened to us! Both of us had failed each other.

Soon it's May, and the first Mother's Day after her death. The first Christmas and the celebrations bringing in the year 2000 are months behind us. That's how fast time flies. Her birthday and their wedding anniversary, Christmas and Mother's Day were always very important to her. When we were still small, she planned for Mother's Day, and baked and cooked and prepared everything for a family celebration while we painted pictures for her with red flaming hearts and colorful flowers. In later years we wrote her letters.

What would I write her this time, if she were still alive? I could try it with a letter, and continue writing until it really came from the heart. Instead

I am writing this book. It's the long letter to her for Mother's Day. I am still searching for my mother. I've always searched for her. I was tense, my back was stiff, and my shoulders hurt. I walked into the kitchen to get a glass of water and two aspirin.

I did not want a mother who gave up. I didn't want it for her either. She was unable to come up with the strength to live her life, and for her a divorce would have meant running the gauntlet. And yet, in our Grundgesetz, the Basic Law, the constitution for the Federal Republic of Germany, which was ratified on 8 May 1949, it says in Article 3, Paragraphs 2 and 3, "Men and women have equal rights. No one may be discriminated against nor given preferential treatment because of their gender, descent, race, language, homeland or origin, faith or religious persuasion." Did these truths seep into her consciousness so very slowly that she, as a woman, continued to live the life of a disadvantaged citizen, because the fight for equality before the law and in daily life was not only too hard, but also because she could not even envision equality for herself? Even though she defended herself for a long time against her husband and his twisted understanding of how a man and a woman should live in a marriage, she did not know how to fight for her rights, and so she continued to allow him to wield power over her. Our society is still toxic for women.

Epilog
Return to Dresden with Kevin Michael

At the end of June 2002 I busily prepared for a trip to Germany with Micha, my first grandson, and my second son Andreas, Micha's father. It will be Micha's first visit to Germany. I was very happy I would finally be able to show him where we, the German branch of his family, came from. On the morning of our arrival in Dresden we began our exploration through the Altstadt. Coming from the Brühlsche Terrasse, I wanted to take a quick look into the Katholische Hofkirche, and after that show them the Sistine Madonna in the Gallery of Old Masters in the Zwinger.

In the soft twilight inside the large church I was surprised to see an exhibition of eyewitness reports about the fire-bombing of the city on the 13th and 14th of February 1945, and the days immediately afterward. At first I wanted to give in to the impulse to leave, but then I began to read. I started somewhere in the middle after a few unsure steps along the displays, and was captivated immediately. It seemed as though I knew every one of those stories. My mother used to talk just like that about the bombing and the days that followed. Here were people who spoke the same way she did. I was amazed by something that should have been obvious to me, because we had been there after all. Even so, the question remained, "Why am I here reading this, and why am I so overwhelmed by it all?"

The ground seemed to quake beneath my feet. Outside the sun was shining, and it was a warm, pleasantly day, but I was shivering in the church. My intellect told me, you can leave any time, you didn't come to Dresden with Andreas and Micha for this, you don't have to read this. And yet I stayed and read sentence after sentence, one report after the other, when all of a sudden I came across the testimony of a woman who had said almost word for word what my mother had always told us. This woman and her family had reached the Fürstenstraße with great difficulty as they tried to escape the Altstadt after the second attack, and they, too, had fled to the Große Garten instead of the Elbwiesen. My mother's story could have been hanging in the Hofkirche right next to those of these other survivors. I looked at the people who were reading the reports and wondered what they knew about it and whether they could really imagine what had taken place during that night. By then I was close to tears. Why was I so sensitive? What's wrong with my nerves? It's been like that for decades. Will it ever stop?

Many young people were among the visitors. Most were younger than I was, so they couldn't have been there, but there were also a few very old and infirm people who were walking with canes or held on to each other. From their faces I could tell that they knew more. They seemed to agree silently, and it appeared to me that even after a lifetime they still couldn't comprehend what had happened.

An old couple walked slowly step by step from one board to the next, as if they were carrying a heavy load on their shoulders. They stood silently and a little unsteadily facing the eyewitness reports. They moved closer, their eyes slowly followed the lines of text, and they murmured the words inaudible to me. For me, they became part of the exhibition. No one else seemed to experience it as vividly. The woman reached for her husband's hand, and with her left hand she wiped over her eyes and forehead before they walked on to the next text. She stayed long in front of a particular story, deeply lost in thought. "Come on, love," I heard him say tenderly. He pulled her away slowly. What kind of memories might these words in front of her have awakened in her, I wondered as I was reading the same lines shortly thereafter. Could it be that she had been sitting in that very cellar with her family and neighbors?

Here and there, small groups commented on the texts with restrained voices. Younger people walked past them briskly and didn't waste much time with reading. They came to the church as tourists, and not to research the city's history in its darkest hour. While I was still engrossed in reading, I noticed that the light in the church had changed because the sun was coming through the windows at a different angle.

I looked at my wristwatch and saw that more than an hour had gone by. I looked for Andreas and Micha, who had been investigating the church for themselves, and we went to a Café across from the Frauenkirche to watch the rebuilding, which began in 1994, and my mother had not lived to see finished. While sitting there I remembered the photo of Dresden taken from a bird's-eye view shortly after the bombing, showing the angel on the town hall balustrade, and below him the completely destroyed city. The angel's face had lost nothing of its calm beauty, only the fingers of the left hand have been knocked off except for the index finger. The angel bends slightly downward toward the city below him, seemingly expressing compassion. The injured hand points at the bombed-out houses below as though the angel were saying, "Look what you people have done!"

A little later we took the streetcar to the Johannisfriedhof. Micha knows the woman he once called Omi is dead, and that we also came to Dresden to visit her grave. It was not easy for me on that first anniversary of her death.

Kevin Michael in front of the new cross for the cupola of the rebuilt Frauenkirche, Dresden 2002

And when my little Goldschatz saw my wet eyes, he put his hand in mine and said, "It's o.k., Anne. Poor Omi, maybe she can see us."

"Poor Omi," he's heard me say that, and I squeezed his hand and thought, he is the same age I was when I went to the cemetery with my Omi, whom I had visited as often as I could to escape the drama at home.

When we boarded the streetcar later that day to go from the main station to Striesen, because I wanted to show them the house where Grandmother had lived after the war, I remembered the Friday afternoons when I traveled by train to Dresden to spend the weekend with her. The cars had wooden benches. I stroked the smooth wooden slats, looked at the black screws, slid back and forth and fidgeted as I looked out of the window to my right and to my left over the rolling landscape of the Oberlausitz. The closer we got to Dresden, the more crowded the train became. At Radeberg everything was still all right, but when we traveled through the Dresdner Heide, the vast area of brush and heather after the town of Langebrück, the locomotive slowed down suddenly. A jerk went through the train, and I got scared every single time, although I knew what was ahead. We crept forward, feeling our way along the track. Railway men walked alongside the train, calling commands out to each other. Slowly we approached a bridge that led across a gorge through which a brook gurgled. The locomotive was already on the bridge, and it groaned under the heavy load. I held my breath and waited with a tingling feeling in my stomach until my car had also reached the bridge, and I knew that we had only the tracks and a timber scaffolding underneath us. I shuddered when I looked into the abyss that opened up below me. Spellbound, I saw the tops of tall pine trees directly below me. Black sandstone formations rose out of the ravine. I held so tightly onto the windowsill that the blood went out of my fingers, and I could see the white of my knuckles. It took an eternity until the entire train arrived safely on the other side, and with a jerk the locomotive pulled hard and moved faster again. I took a deep breath, one last shudder went through me, and then I looked once again into the wide countryside.

When we got to Klotsche I became restless again. The low gray houses of the villages and small towns were gone and we rode past elegant suburban villas with tall windows surrounded by large gardens. Depending on the season, jasmine, lilacs or roses were in bloom, but there were seldom people in the gardens. I looked at the villas lost in thought. They reminded me of the house we had lived in, and I began to play the same game I always played, without quite understanding what I was doing. With eyes wide open, I lost myself in fantasies and daydreams. The game was very simple: as long as the houses outside were untouched by bombs, I tried to imagine what it would be like if no destroyed houses and ruins were coming. Seeing the streets with villas, churches and small squares with a monument or a fountain in their centers that had survived. I tried to imagine how it must have been, and I thought that the train was going too fast. I wanted to stop time or turn back the wheel of history, I wanted to rescue something for myself, but within minutes, the first ruin appeared amongst the suburban houses, and soon more and more came. I was thrown mercilessly back into the present.

The further we traveled, the greater the destruction became. I shuddered as the panorama changed with increasing speed, and would have liked to send the train on a detour around the town, away from the ruins. I couldn't turn my eyes away from the cityscape as it became ever more grotesque, and I felt like I could no longer follow along with what was happening outside. Moments later there was hardly an undamaged house left between the ruins, where only the cellars and parts of the first floor were habitable. Bright red geraniums were flowering in front of cellar windows, defying death in their colorful splendor. We sped past houses without roofs, where only the outer walls remained standing with parts of staircases that lead nowhere and tiny front gardens surrounded by green hedges. In many of them people had planted vegetables and potatoes. House fronts had been torn away by the bombs and allowed me a view into former living rooms and bedrooms, where often a bent iron bed frame was still standing and blackened wallpaper was hanging down in shreds, or into bathrooms with discolored tiles that once had been white or green, and where parts of stovepipes, bent water pipes and the metal casing of electrical lines were hanging down. I saw twisted iron girders, whose bizarre shapes reached into an empty sky, and half-burned attics and dangerously lopsided brick chimneys. Fascinated, I looked into the destruction. I wanted to turn away, but driven by an inner compulsion, I kept staring into the rooms that lay there exposed to our morbid glances, defenseless and dead. Where were the people who had lived there before that night?

In the evenings the worst was covered by darkness, and I could only guess at the ruins that appeared as dark shadows. Now and then a glimmer of light penetrated through curtains from a room were people lived. During a full moon the ruins were eerie, and it was almost worse than in bright daylight.

Completely surrounded by ruins, the train finally entered the huge hall of the main station, and I got off. Omi was not there yet, so I had to wait. Without flinching, I looked up at the roof of the station in the hope of finding at least one piece of glass that had survived the bombing, but I never found even one unbroken pane, and for many years it rained and snowed into the station, onto the platforms, benches and the little shacks of the stationmaster and his staff.

The main station intrigued me, and while I was standing there looking at the roof, Omi suddenly came running toward me calling my name from afar. She hugged and kissed me and rescued me from the nightmare. She took my bag, and we rushed down the stairs, through the lower hall and out to the streetcar station. For those first years we rode through an endless expanse of ruins. Not a single house was left standing. Everywhere I saw nothing but ruins until we reached the suburbs. From the streetcar stop we walked along some pretty streets until we came to her house in Striesen. During one of our rides through Dresden, Omi once pointed our old street out to me, saying, "This was the Fürstenstraße before they changed the name, and over there stood our house."

During the Christmas holidays, Alexander and I flew to Germany again. My father had asked me to sort and give away her clothing and shoes. My mother's things still smelled of Tosca and Mouson Lavendel. As I opened her wardrobe I breathed her scent, although it had become much weaker and was blending with the smell of unwashed clothes. Thus time took even this memory away from me. It would not do any good to spray lavender cologne on her clothes now and then, because her body had turned it into the scent I had known since my early childhood and missed so much. The scent connected us. I had always found it very comforting.

The time came when I realized that there wouldn't be any more telephone calls from her. I shall never again hear her excited clear voice and the way she asked "Anne?" in her timid intonation when I answered with the American "hello."

On a day in October of 2003 I awoke so disoriented from a dream that I didn't know where I was for a moment. I looked at the clock on my nightstand. It was twenty minutes after seven, I saw that very clearly, but even so it took me several seconds before I was fully awake, and I wondered where I had left my cell phone.

Suddenly I knew that I had had a dream in which I was sitting in my car in front of a shop in Koblenz, and that I wanted to call my mother, because I had lost her, and since I could not find her anywhere I was hoping that she had gone home. I had the feeling that it was very urgent to get in touch with her, that she was waiting for me, and so I reached for my cell phone in my bag. But it was not my phone. I continued to search for it and suddenly had a second one in my hand, which also didn't belong to me, and then a third one. I was confused, and decided to just use one of them. After all, I thought, it didn't matter which phone I used to call her, the important thing was to contact her. But no matter how often I tried, I got no connection, it simply did not ring at the other end. Instead, the display showed an Euro amount that was decreasing rapidly while I repeatedly tried unsuccessfully to dial her number, and I became upset about my clumsiness. Finally there was only 1 Euro and 20 cents left, and I realized there would not be enough time for us to talk even if she did answer. I panicked, turned off the phone and desperately continued to look for my own cell phone. Suddenly I had five telephones in different colors and sizes in my lap, but mine was not among them. I was unable to reach my mother with any of them.

Some hours later I walked with my friend Gabi along the beach of Marina del Rey. We had talked about our mothers often, and I told her about my dream.

"How strongly you still are connected with your mother," she said, and we embraced each other.

All is Vanity

You will see wherever you look only vanity on this earth.
What people build today, others tear down tomorrow;
Where now cities stand, meadows will be,
Upon which a shepherd's child will play with the herds.
What now blooms in all its splendor, will soon be tread asunder;
What today defiantly stands, tomorrow is ash and bone;
There is nothing that is eternal, neither ore nor marble.
Now fortune smiles upon us, but soon troubles will thunder.
The fame of great deeds must pass like a dream.
Why should the game of time, a mere human, persist?
Oh, what is all of this that we hold to be so delightful,
But wicked vanities, as shadow, dust and wind;
But a meadow flower, which we can find no more!
Yet not a single human will contemplate eternity!

Andreas Gryphius, 1643

Written during the 30-years' war 1618-1648, Gryphius seems to foreshadow the great destruction of World War II.

Translation of the poem *All is Vanity* from the German *Es ist alles Eitel* by Angela Thompson

About the book

One life, one century. Sixty-five years after the bombing of Dresden and twenty years after the reunification of Germany, Angela Thompson paints a vivid and passionate picture of her mother, Elfriede Richter (1920-1999), in her book *Blackout: A Woman's Struggle for Survival in Twentieth Century Germany*. She captures the reader from the very first page as the story of her family's fight for survival unfolds after Hitler's rise to power, followed by World War II, the catastrophic bombing of Dresden, the emergence of two German states and the family's eventual escape to West Germany before the building of the Berlin Wall. In her search for understanding and universal truths, Angela Thompson presents a hauntingly personal insight into the heroic struggles of a woman who not only fights for survival but strives for dignity in her married life and the slowly emerging new German society after World War II.